T0342450

Reinventing State Capitalism

Reinventing State Capitalism

Leviathan in Business, Brazil and Beyond

Aldo Musacchio and Sergio G. Lazzarini

||| Harvard University Press

Cambridge, Massachusetts
London, England
2014

Library of Congress Cataloging-in-Publication Data

Musacchio, Aldo.
    Reinventing state capitalism : Leviathan in business, Brazil and beyond /
Aldo Musacchio and Sergio G. Lazzarini.
        pages cm
    Includes bibliographical references and index.
    ISBN 978-0-674-72968-1 (alk. paper)
    1. Government ownership.   2. Government ownership—Brazil.
3. Capitalism.   I. Lazzarini, Sérgio G.   II. Title.
    HD3850.M86 2014
    338.6'2—dc23
    2013035204

To Ximena and Valentina

and

To Edite and Juliana

Contents

Reinventing State Capitalism

1

Introduction

New Varieties of State Capitalism

In May 2007, the relatively unknown Brazilian firm JBS acquired Colorado-based Swift & Company for $1.4 billion and suddenly became the largest beef processing company in the world. Two years later, in September 2009, JBS made another surprising move by acquiring Pilgrim's Pride, an iconic American meat processing firm, for $2.8 billion. Where had a rather unknown Brazilian firm gotten the funds to finance such acquisitions? The answer was simple. The Brazilian National Development Bank (known in Portuguese as BNDES) had singled out JBS as a "national champion" and provided funding to make it a dominant player in the global beef and poultry market. Thanks to its $4 billion investments in JBS, BNDES eventually controlled 30.4 percent of the firm's shares, becoming its largest minority shareholder and, in turn, a minority shareholder of both Swift and Pilgrim's Pride.[1] These transactions, like many others conducted by governments and development banks around the world, raised interesting questions. Should governments use development banks, such as BNDES, to support firms? Should governments support firms by becoming minority shareholders? What are the implications of such investments for firms and for countries as a whole?

In July 2010, while the JBS story was unfolding in Brazil, a consortium of investment banks on the other side of the world launched the initial public offering (IPO) of Agricultural Bank of China (ABC) on the Shanghai and Hong Kong stock exchanges. ABC had traditionally been a "policy bank"—that is, a bank that lent according to the interests of leaders of the Chinese Communist Party. As a result, by 2008, over 25 percent of its loans were non-performing. To fix ABC before the IPO, the government bailed out the bank, cleaned up its balance sheet, and revamped its processes and governance.

Investor interest was enormous. This was the largest IPO in the world at the time; it raised almost $22 billion for shares—15 percent of the firm's capital—and the bank's share value rose to almost 30 percent above the issuing price in a couple of months. Yet it was not clear if the investors who bought the shares knew what they were getting into. Were they misguided? Could the Chinese government be trusted as a majority investor?

In both cases, investors were faced with something that was clearly state capitalism, but was clearly not the state capitalism they were used to. In this book, we study the rise of these new forms of state capitalism in which the state works hand in hand with private investors in novel governance arrangements. We define state capitalism as *the widespread influence of the government in the economy, either by owning majority or minority equity positions in companies or by providing subsidized credit and/or other privileges to private companies.* The new varieties of state capitalism differ from the more traditional model in which governments own and manage state-owned enterprises (SOEs)[2] as extensions of the public bureaucracy. We refer to this traditional model as *Leviathan as an entrepreneur.*

We identify two new models of state capitalism that go beyond the Leviathan as an entrepreneur model. In the *Leviathan as a majority investor* model, as in the example of Agricultural Bank of China, the state is still the controlling shareholder, but SOEs have distinct governance traits that allow for the participation of private investors. In the *Leviathan as a minority investor* model, state capitalism adopts a more hybrid form in which the state relinquishes control of its enterprises to private investors but remains present through minority equity investments by pension funds, sovereign wealth funds, and the government itself. In the latter model, we also include the provision of loans to private firms by development banks and other state-owned financial institutions. In our view, then, the rise of national champions such as JBS, whose expansion was based on subsidized capital from its home government, is a manifestation of the Leviathan as a minority investor model.[3]

The examples of Agricultural Bank of China and JBS are by no means curious exceptions. By some calculations, firms under government control account for one-fifth of the world's total stock market capitalization.[4] In Italy, for example, SOEs listed on the stock exchange (both majority- and minority-owned by the government) account for over 20 percent of stock market capitalization. In Greece, this figure is 30 percent, while in the Netherlands and Sweden it is closer to 5 percent (OECD 2005, 35). In large markets, such as Russia and Brazil, companies controlled by the government or in which the government has a significant stake dominate trading, and they account for between 30 and 40 percent of market capitalization. In China, companies in which the government is a controlling shareholder account for over 60 percent of stock market capitalization.[5] Furthermore, in our analysis of SOEs in myriad emerging countries (see Chapter 2), the Leviathan as a minority investor model is prevalent and covers almost half the companies in which the government has equity (the rest being majority-owned SOEs).

Thus it is very likely, then, that global investors will have to at least consider SOEs as potential investment targets. In fact, nine of the fifteen largest IPOs in the world between 2005 and 2012 were sales of minority equity positions by SOEs, most of them from developing countries.[6] One of the reasons why investors do not mind buying these securities is that governments share rents with them, which has often led to high returns. For instance, according to a report from Morgan Stanley, the stock returns of publicly traded SOEs from Europe, the Middle East, Africa, and Latin America between 2001 and 2012 "generated superior returns vs. [the] benchmark [indices]."[7]

Moreover, the firms that we study are by no means small. SOEs are typically among the largest publicly traded firms in the stock markets of developing countries. In fact, some large SOEs have also become some of the most profitable firms in the world. The number of SOEs among the one hundred largest companies in the *Fortune* Global 500 list, which ranks companies by revenues, went from eleven in 2005 to twenty-five in 2010. In 2005, there were no SOEs among the top ten, but by 2010, there were four—Japan Post Holdings, Sinopec and China National Petroleum (two of China's national oil companies), and State Grid (a Chinese utility).[8]

Still, many observers view the rise of new forms of state capitalism with apprehension. Political analyst Ian Bremmer characterizes state capitalism as "a system in which the state functions as the leading economic actor and uses markets primarily for political gain" (Bremmer 2010, 5). A Harvard Business School summit of founders and CEOs of some of the world's top companies identified state capitalism and its support for national champions among the ten most important threats to market capitalism (Bower et al. 2011). Managers of private firms often complain when they find their competitors heavily supported or subsidized by local governments.

Although not all investors and policy makers feel such apprehension (Amatori et al. 2011), for many the concerns stem from the large theoretical and empirical literature showing that, *on average*, SOEs are less efficient than their private counterparts (see for a review Megginson and Netter 2001).[9] In this literature there are three broad explanations for the inefficiency of state ownership (Yeyati et al. 2004). According to the *agency view*, SOEs are inefficient because their managers lack high-powered incentives and proper monitoring, either from boards of directors or from the market, or simply because managers were poorly selected in the first place (La Porta and López-de-Silanes 1999; Boardman and Vining 1989; Vickers and Yarrow 1988; Dharwadkar et al. 2000). According to the *social view*, SOEs have social objectives that sometimes conflict with profitability. For example, they may be charged with maximizing employment or opening unprofitable plants in poor areas (Shirley and Nellis 1991; Bai and Xu 2005). According to the *political view*, the sources of inefficiency lie in the fact that politicians use SOEs for their personal benefit or to benefit politically connected capitalists. Additionally, managers of large SOEs commonly face low pressure to perform because they know the government will bail them out if they drive their firms to bankruptcy (Vickers and Yarrow 1988; Kornai 1979; Shleifer and Vishny 1998; Boycko et al. 1996). State participation would therefore entail a "grabbing hand" detrimental to economic efficiency.[10]

In contrast, defenders of the *industrial policy view* see state investment as a way to promote development beyond what is possible under free markets. In this view, governments should help firms develop new capabilities, either by reducing capital constraints (Yeyati et al. 2004; Cameron 1961; Gerschenkron 1962), by reducing the costs of research and development, or by coordinating resources and firms to pursue new projects with high spillovers (Rodrik 2007; Amsden 2001; Evans 1995). According to this view, the creation of new capabilities in the local economy requires the "helping hand" of the government to mitigate all sorts of market failure.

Our book is *not* about whether one view is right and the others wrong; nor is it a test of whether private firms are more efficient than SOEs. This book is about understanding (a) how the world ended up with new forms of state capitalism and (b) the circumstances in which these new forms over-come some of the problems highlighted by the literature and solve a host of market failures that thwart development. Although each chapter proposes and tests explicit hypotheses related to different views of the role of SOEs, the book as a whole is about the nuances of state intervention and the condi-tions that make such intervention either more or less effective.[11]

Furthermore, we are not trying to argue that privatization is not a desir-able policy. We think, nonetheless, that the pushback against full-fledged privatization in large developed and developing markets makes the study of the new forms of state capitalism relevant. That is, even if the new forms of state ownership we study are a second-best solution from the point of view of economic efficiency, they are a solution that is often politically acceptable. In emerging markets, governments have encountered strong political op-position to sweeping programs of privatization. Shirley (2005) shows that, in Latin America, the popular rejection of privatization increased between the 1990s and the early 2000s. In BRIC countries, privatization programs have almost stopped in Brazil and India and have been proceeding at a gradual pace in China and Russia, with those governments now preferring to privatize only a small share of equity in their large SOEs.

Finally, we also do not claim that the new varieties of state capitalism are *universally* better than the previous varieties. We explicitly warn that the new varieties also have limits when it comes to taming the government's temptation to intervene politically in a firm. In the model in which Levia-than is a majority investor, for instance, the government is still a controlling shareholder, and, absent checks and balances, it may be drawn to intervene in strategic sectors such as energy, mining, and utilities. In the model in which Leviathan is a minority shareholder, equity investments or loan dis-bursements may actually benefit politically connected capitalists rather than financially constrained firms.

The Reinvention of State Capitalism

How have the new forms of state capitalism evolved over the years? For some observers, the rise of state capitalism to the forefront of global markets is a consequence of the global financial crisis that started in 2008. Bremmer (2010), for instance, sees that crisis as a shock that led to an alarming reemergence of state capitalism. Part of the concern comes from the fact that, even in a liberal economy such as the United States, the crisis led the government to bail out firms such as General Motors and AIG, a large insurance group, becoming a minority shareholder of the former and a majority shareholder of the latter. As the examples of Agricultural Bank of China and JBS illustrate, however, state capitalism was alive and kicking—and even expanding—*before* the crisis (Amatori et al. 2011; Bortolotti and Faccio 2009). Firms owned and operated by the government were privatized en masse in the 1980s, 1990s, and early 2000s, but state ownership and influence in those firms continued.

State capitalism peaked in the middle of the 1970s when European governments nationalized firms in large numbers. Around the same time, governments in developing countries either nationalized firms or created (and then owned) tens or hundreds of new ones. As a consequence, by the end of the 1970s, SOE output to GDP reached 10 percent in mixed economies and close to 16 percent in developing countries.

Then, between the 1970s and the turn of the twenty-first century, governments transformed the way in which they owned and managed firms. In the 1980s, governments and multilateral agencies experimented with reforms in SOEs to try to reduce the financial hardship both SOEs and governments themselves were facing. Officials tried corporate governance reforms, performance contracts for firms and managers, and training programs for SOE executives (Shirley 1999; Gómez-Ibañez 2007).

Yet these attempts were futile, and the political cost of privatization started to look small compared to the losses afflicting SOEs. For instance, as a consequence of the oil shocks of the 1970s and the liquidity crunch of the early 1980s, SOEs from all around the world ran average losses equivalent to 2 percent of GDP, reaching 4 percent in developing countries (World Bank 1996). SOE losses were then translated into national budget deficits, and those deficits exploded once interest rates spiked in the United States in 1979 and once debt markets were closed for developing countries after Mexico's 1982 debt default (Frieden 1991). Ultimately, as a consequence of those macroeconomic shocks and the fall of the socialist bloc, governments ended up privatizing thousands of firms (Megginson 2005), opening up their economies to foreign trade, and gradually dismantling capital controls.

Still, because sweeping privatization was politically costly, some SOEs were only partially privatized. Around the world, governments ended up becoming controlling shareholders and minority investors in a large number and wide variety of corporations, as can be seen clearly in Bortolotti and Faccio's (2009) survey of SOEs in OECD countries and in the evidence we present in Chapter 2 for a broader sample of countries. While countries such as Australia, Austria, Belgium, Chile, Denmark, New Zealand, Slovenia, and the United Kingdom each had fewer than fifty SOEs controlled by the government circa 2005, others such as Canada, Finland, France, Greece, Italy, Israel, Norway, and Sweden had between fifty and one hundred. The Czech Republic, Germany, Korea, Mexico, Poland, and Spain each had more than one hundred such firms. A more recent OECD report (Christiansen 2011) found that SOEs had a total equity value of US$1.4 trillion, of which 61 percent of these SOEs are firms in which the government holds minority stakes. Emerging markets such as Russia and China had thousands of SOEs, and others such as Brazil, India, Poland, and South Africa each had over two hundred SOEs at the federal level and many more at the provincial level.

Thus, the organization of state capitalism that we observed at the turn of the twenty-first century is the outcome of a long process of transformation, of gradually adopting what has been learned from thirty years of research on corporate governance and agency theories (Jensen and Meckling 1976; Hansmann and Kraakman 2004; Khurana 2002) and decades of experimentation with SOE reforms and with full and partial privatizations.[12]

We are aware that, in the past, SOEs in the United States and Europe commonly had governments operating as minority shareholders (Bodenhorn 2003; Amatori 2012; Sylla et al. 1987). In the twenty-first century, however, ownership arrangements in many SOEs were accompanied by more stringent corporate governance rules and more stringent requirements to list firms on stock exchanges.

New Varieties of State Capitalism

Our conceptualization of the new forms of state capitalism, then, is full of nuances to avoid the dichotomous views that pervade some of the literature.[13] Bremmer (2010) treats state capitalism as a general model of capitalism, juxtaposed with an idealized form of liberal market economy in which the government does not intervene in the running of corporations or the allocation of credit. For us, there are more intermediate types in between. We

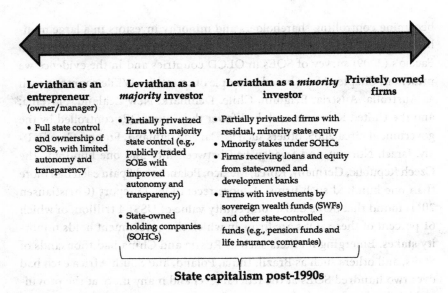

Figure 1.1. Varieties of state capitalism: alternative models of organization

therefore expand the spectrum of state intervention to include not only the model in which Leviathan is an entrepreneur—owning and managing SOEs (Ahroni 1986)—but also the models in which Leviathan is a majority investor or a minority investor (see Figure 1.1).[14]

In the *Leviathan as a majority investor* model, the government corporatizes or lists firms on stock exchanges. This is a form of partial privatization in which the state retains control while attracting minority private investors. Although there is wide variation in the corporate governance configuration of these firms, publicly traded SOEs tend, in general, to have relative financial autonomy, professional management, boards of directors with some independent members and with short tenures, and financials audited by professional accounting firms. In some cases, governments exercise their control as majority investors using so-called state-owned holding companies (SOHCs)—pyramidal structures of ownership in which the government is a majority owner in a company that then holds majority or minority equity positions in other companies.[15]

Governments can also influence the economy indirectly, acting as a minority shareholder and lender to private firms. This is the model we refer to as *Leviathan as a minority investor*. This more nuanced form of state capitalism is a hybrid form, in which private parties manage the companies that the government wants to support financially. Thus, we view this model of state capitalism as suffering less from the agency and social problems commonly found in SOEs that are wholly owned and controlled by the government. Furthermore, political intervention should also be low or minimal (although not absent) in this form of state ownership.[16]

Minority state participation in corporations is increasing worldwide. We argue that there are several channels through which states act as minority shareholders, such as directly holding residual shares in partially privatized firms and using state-owned holding companies to hold minority stakes in a variety of firms controlled by private investors. In this model, we also see governments using development banks, sovereign wealth funds (SWFs), and other state-controlled funds (such as pension funds and life insurance investments) to either lend to or invest in private companies. In India, for instance, the Life Insurance Corporation practically acts as a holding company for the government, with around $50 billion invested as of September 2011. In Brazil, as the JBS example shows, the national development bank (BNDES) has actively poured money into local corporations.

As a way to summarize the differences across the distinct models of state capitalism, Table 1.1 explains the main sources of inefficiency in SOEs according to the agency, the social, and the political views and how those inefficiencies might be addressed by the Leviathan as a majority and minority investor models.

We are nevertheless cautious because, even if these new models of state capitalism have improved incentives and monitoring inside the firm and have, in some cases, insulated SOEs from outright political interference, governments still can and often do intervene. These new models have their limits and can break down when the government's temptation to intervene is at its highest—for example, during a major economic crisis or in advance of a hotly contested election. As we discuss throughout the book, reducing political intervention in the model in which the government is a majority shareholder or reducing agency problems in the model in which the government is a minority shareholder will depend not only the private enforcement of investor rights (e.g., through the firm's own statutes and through the ability of stock markets and rating agencies to prevent the abuse of minority

Table 1.1. Theories of SOE efficiencies and inefficiencies

Theory of SOE inefficiency	Leviathan as an entrepreneur (i.e, owner and manager)	Leviathan as a majority investor	Leviathan as a minority investor
Social view	Double bottom line (e.g., social objectives such as low inflation or higher employment beyond profitability).	Maximization of shareholder value subject to political interference if the company is not insulated. Likely conflict if minority shareholders pursuing profitability clash with governments pursuing social or political goals.	Maximization of shareholder value. Minimizes government intervention to attain social goals (except in cases where governments have residual ability to intervene).
	Long-term horizon; government as patient investor tolerating losses.	Likely shorter-term horizon: markets are generally impatient with respect to losses; yet market pressure can help prevent short-term pressure due to political cycles.	Short-termism to please market analysts and investors.
Political view	Appointment of CEOs using criteria other than merit (e.g., political connections).	Professional management selected by the board of directors. Government has strong influence as majority shareholder.	Professional management selected by the board of directors. Government opinion matters only when government is an important shareholder or when it colludes with other shareholders.

	Government uses SOEs to smooth business cycles (e.g., hiring more or firing fewer workers than necessary).	Effect is reduced if the firm is isolated from political intervention.	Low political interference in management, except for industries in which the government has temptation to intervene (e.g., natural resource sectors) and when the government colludes with other minority shareholders.
	Soft-budget constraint (bailouts are likely).	Soft budget constraint still present (governments will likely bail them out).	Moderate budget constraint unless firm is singled out as a national champion. Then maybe bailout because firm is "too big or important to fail."
Agency view	Management has low-powered incentives.	Pay-for-performance contracts, bonuses, and stock options more likely (incentives may not be as high powered as in private firms).	High-powered incentives.
	Hard to measure performance (financial measures are not enough, not easy to measure social and political goals).	Stock prices and financial ratios as performance metrics. Customer satisfaction and feedback to measure quality of goods and/or services.	Stock prices and financial ratios as key performance metrics.

(continued)

Table 1.1. (continued)

Theory of SOE inefficiency	Leviathan as an entrepreneur (i.e., owner and manager)	Leviathan as a majority investor	Leviathan as a minority investor
	Poor monitoring: no board of directors (ministry regulates) or else politically appointed board (low level of checks and balances).	Board of directors with some independent members and some political appointees; depending on numbers, it can act as a balance to the government and the CEO. Yet government can co-opt board members.	Boards as principals of the CEO (monitoring/punishing).
	No clear punishment for managers who underperform.	Boards may fire managers who underperform.	Boards may fire managers who underperform.
	No transparency: incomplete financial information.	Improved transparency; accounting standards following GAAP or IFRS in several cases.	Improved transparency; accounting standards following GAAP or IFRS in most cases.

shareholders), but also on legal protections and regulatory provisions that tie the hands of governments and avoid discretionary interference.

In the last two chapters of the book, we look beyond government involvement as a majority or minority shareholder to examine instances in which governments use state-owned development banks to provide private firms with long-term, subsidized loans. Development banks are, in particular, an important and understudied vehicle of minority state participation. These banks are supposed to be relatively autonomous financial intermediaries specializing in providing long-term—usually subsidized—credit to promote industrialization or infrastructure projects (Armendáriz de Aghion 1999; Yeyati et al. 2004; Amsden 2001; George and Prabhu 2000). Yet the behavior and performance implications of development banks have been neglected in the literature, despite the fact that there are 286 development banks operating in 117 countries, some of them very large and financially healthy (such as Germany's KfW, the Korea Development Bank, and Brazil's BNDES). In contrast, there is a large literature showing how state-owned *commercial* banks perform poorly because they have social and political objectives that prevent them from becoming lucrative (Caprio et al. 2004; Beck et al. 2005).[17] We do not examine commercial banks in detail in this book because they are mainly focused on providing credit to households or working capital to firms. We are, instead, interested in looking at development banks, which provide long-term loans to promote industrialization or the construction of infrastructure and, thus, tend to be intimately linked to the process of economic development (Amsden 2001).

Brazil as a Case Study

Although we present a general discussion of the new forms of state capitalism, most of our detailed empirical studies of the implications of these new forms rely on firm-level data for Brazil. We think Brazil is a good setting in which to study the evolution of state capitalism for two reasons. First, state capitalism's rise in Brazil is similar to its rise in other parts of the Western world and in noncommunist East Asia where, partly by accident and partly by design, governments ended up owning and managing hundreds of firms between the 1960s and the 1980s (Trebat 1983; Baer et al. 1973). Therefore, we use the case of Brazil to show how external events led to transformations in the way the government intervened in the management and ownership of firms, ending with a major dismantling of the Leviathan as an entrepreneur model.

Second, Brazil had and still has all the different models of state capitalism we want to study, and we have decades of data on how those forms have worked. Through a variety of archival, public, and private sources, we have been able to compile detailed databases with a variety of financial variables to study the performance of the largest state-owned and private enterprises in Brazil between 1973 and 2009.

With such rich data on Brazilian firms, we test a series of specific hypotheses related to our study. For instance, we compare the behavior of private firms and SOEs before and after the shocks of 1979–1982 and show that SOEs adjusted their employment more slowly and thus faced greater losses throughout the 1980s. That is, we use the detailed case of Brazil to argue that the big crisis of the Leviathan as an entrepreneur model happened to a large extent because SOEs could not adjust to the drastic shocks of the 1970s and 1980s and therefore continuously bled the finances of the government.

Moreover, we use the Brazilian case to describe in detail the changes that were made in the corporate governance of SOEs, especially after 1990. Surveys such as Bortolotti and Faccio (2009) and OECD (2005) show how governments remained as either majority or minority shareholders after privatizing SOEs in the 1990s. Yet these studies do not look at corporate governance arrangements inside SOEs. We think it is important to examine how corporate governance arrangements have changed. In fact, we think that the policy prescriptions come from looking at the bylaws that have made some SOEs less prone to agency problems or political intervention. In Chapter 4 we show in detail the transformation of corporate governance in SOEs in which the Brazilian government is a majority shareholder, and in Chapter 7 we pursue even more-detailed studies of the corporate governance arrangements the Brazilian government adopted in the national oil company, Petrobras, compared to other national oil companies from around the world.

The Brazilian case also provides unique insights into the model in which Leviathan is the minority investor. BNDES's distinctive prevalence in the Brazilian economy provides a rich case to study development banks and their role as a conduit of state investments in the form of minority equity positions in private firms. Thus, using detailed data on minority equity investments held by BNDESPAR, the investment arm of the Brazilian National Development Bank, between 1995 and 2009, we conduct detailed empirical studies of the impact of these investments on firm behavior. Moreover, by examining how BNDES selects its target firms and the impact of its loans on firm-level performance and investment, we analyze in detail how Leviathan can act as a lender.

Our General Argument

Our book makes three broad arguments. First, we argue that governments have learned that they need more-sustainable ownership schemes and corporate governance regimes for SOEs. Our historical narrative maintains that as a consequence of the crisis of the late 1970s and early 1980s, the model of government ownership and management of SOEs became too inefficient and turned into a burden on the public finances. Governments restructured their portfolio of firms, privatizing those in which they had no policy reason to operate and changing the ownership structure of many in which they did want to keep an interest (for example, firms in industries with high rents from oil, mining, and utilities). Yet some states learned that in order to have more sustainable models for these firms, they needed to get the private sector involved in monitoring and funding SOEs as well as in sharing the losses of these enterprises. That meant the state had to share both the management and the rents.

Second, instead of debating whether state or private ownership is universally superior, we submit that there is much heterogeneity within each model of ownership. That is, part of our argument is that there is too much variation to generalize. Granted, we still find poorly managed SOEs subject to political interference, but we also find many SOEs that changed their governance practices and in which the government acts like an investor rather than a manager. Likewise, we find many instances of minority state ownership that actually help firms develop new, profitable projects, alongside instances of unjustified support to politically connected national champions. See for instance in Figure 1.2 the wide variation in performance in private firms and firms in which the government is a majority and minority shareholder. In sum, a generic attempt to answer whether state ownership is good or bad will necessarily miss the nuance and variation of organizational

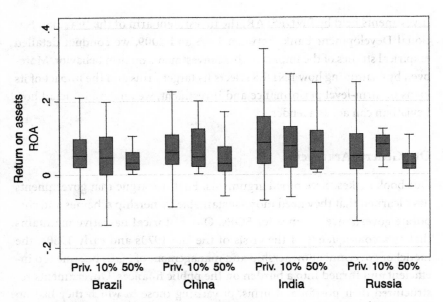

Figure 1.2. Dispersion in the performance of top private vs. state-owned companies with over 10 percent and 50 percent state ownership in BRIC countries using return on assets, 2007–2009

Source: Created by the authors from data in Capital IQ. This data summarizes the performance of SOEs and private companies among the 125 largest companies traded in the stock exchanges of Brazil, Russia, India, and China.

Note: The boxplot graph excludes outside values.

forms that emerged from the reinvention of state capitalism documented in this book. We essentially pursue an exercise of finding sources of firm-level heterogeneity across SOEs.

Third, we argue that the new models of state ownership, which we call Leviathan as a majority and minority investor, will more effectively work depending on a host of conditions that are detailed throughout the book and summarized in our conclusion chapter. For instance, if full privatization of an SOE is not an option, then a government can—and should—at least improve that SOE's governance protections in order to mitigate agency and political intervention problems. We argue that the new models of state ownership will be more effective when they have corporate governance arrangements that prevent abuses by the controlling shareholders—not only when the government is the majority investor, but also when the government is a minority investor and private parties are able to tunnel resources out of the SOE. Thus, when adopting the model in which Leviathan is a minority investor, we argue that governments should target private firms with good governance and with severe financial constraints. Over time, as local capital markets become more developed, the state should progressively exit and leave state participation for cases in which the financing of projects with high spillovers are too risky or hard to execute by private capitalists.

Put another way, the counterfactual of our argument for the Leviathan as a majority investor model is that, without checks and balances on the abuses of the government as a controlling shareholder, even listed SOEs, with minority private ownership, could end up becoming the inefficient SOEs of the past, with controlled prices, excessive debt, and endless needs for the treasury to cover their losses. That is, if the government tunnels out the rents and violates its partnership with the private sector, it may well scare away investors and go back to where it was in the 1980s.

Our counterfactual for the minority investor model is more complex. We argue that having the government investing in or lending to firms that have investment opportunities but that are not financially constrained will not compensate the opportunity cost of the government funds. Governments would therefore be better off using their investment arms to prop up financially constrained firms with latent capabilities, instead of large groups or national champions with ability to fund their own projects through internal capital markets. Furthermore, when financial markets are more developed, government investments in equity may be necessary only for firms that would hardly be financed by the private sector, for example small and medium-size enterprises with complex projects that are either too risky or too difficult to be financed by private financial intermediaries.

We have tried to keep the methodological and narrative approaches of the book as broad as possible to facilitate a conversation with a broad set of fields. Still, we have been as strict as possible in our empirical work to try to convince skeptics of our arguments. Notwithstanding such efforts, there will be readers who will not be convinced by our statistical work simply because governments do not choose to own firms or intervene in private companies at random; that is, there is no natural experiment in this book. For that reason, we are very conscious that our work may suffer from selection bias problems and that our results should be interpreted carefully, as we are not uncovering causality in the purest sense. In every chapter in which we deal with statistical work we have included a section explaining how selection bias may affect our results, and we have added a series of tests to minimize it or, when possible, guarantee that it is not driving our results. For instance, if we study the effect of government equity investments on the performance and capital expenditure of private firms, we make sure to examine what firm-level characteristics drive the selection of firms—to discard the possibility that governments are choosing high-performing firms *ex ante*. We also use matching techniques and other robustness checks to make sure our results are not purely driven by selection bias.

Overview of the Book

The first three chapters elaborate our argument in a general way, describing the global history of state capitalism and offering possible explanations for the origins and implications of the new models of state capitalism. Chapter 2 is a historical account of the rise, fall, and reinvention of state capitalism around the world in the twentieth century. We describe the efforts of governments in Europe and developing countries at various times to improve SOE performance and emphasize the evolution of state capitalism as a process of learning, of trial and error, and largely as a response to economic shocks. We end the story by explaining how the crisis of the Leviathan as an entrepreneur model led to the privatization policies of the 1990s.

Chapter 3 reviews the literature and the implications that each view of SOEs has for each of the ownership models we study. These views are building blocks for the testable hypotheses proposed in the subsequent chapters.

In Chapter 4, we begin using Brazil as a case study. We first describe in detail the macroeconomic story that led to the reinvention of state capitalism there in the 1980s and 1990s and explore some of the variation within Brazilian SOEs. We also describe the transformation of SOEs in Brazil after the privatization process.

In Chapter 5, we study CEOs as a source of variation in SOE performance. In the Leviathan as an entrepreneur model, governments had few levers to influence the performance of SOEs. Therefore, governments tended to re-place CEOs whenever they wanted to change the performance of these firms. Yet those efforts seem to have been futile, as we show that CEOs actually had very little influence over the performance of SOEs, except for top executives who attended elite universities. Those elite CEOs actually led firms to have better performance than the average state-owned firm.

In Chapter 6, we examine how the Leviathan as an entrepreneur model broke down in the 1980s. We show that SOEs facing economic shocks use policies significantly different from those of private companies. While private companies tend to fire workers to adjust their production capacity when faced with reductions in aggregate demand (that is, they fire workers to improve productivity while lowering output), SOEs fire significantly fewer workers or even hire new ones. The literature that compares SOEs with private firms usually assumes that the differences in performance between the two are always wide. We show how those differences in performance were, in fact, smaller before the 1980s and then widened in times of economic hardship.[18]

Chapter 7 examines the corporate governance arrangements that governments have adopted for their national oil companies (NOCs) after changes in the ownership structure to attract minority private investors. We study basic corporate governance traits in thirty NOCs, and show the extent to which some of these firms introduced important constraints on the controlling shareholder—the government. We then delve into a more detailed study of three national oil companies—Pemex, Petrobras, and Statoil—and examine the relationship between each government and its oil company. These cases highlight the importance of giving financial autonomy to managers while imposing checks and balances on the government's power.

Chapter 8 begins our examination of Leviathan as a minority shareholder. We start by studying the effects of having the government investing in minority positions in private corporations, using a detailed database of equity investments by Brazil's national development bank, BNDES, between 1995 and 2009. We find that these investments had positive effects between 1995 and 2002, but not after 2002. One of our explanations for the lack of positive impact after 2002 is that perhaps the rapid development of the local capital market after that year made government loans less important to reduce the financial constraints that Brazilian firms typically faced.

Chapter 9 is a case study of government relations with Vale, a Brazilian mining giant in which the Brazilian government is a minority investor. Here, we discuss the limits of the Leviathan as a minority investor model. We explain how, between 2009 and 2011, government pressure on Vale to invest in steel mills led to the dismissal of a very successful CEO. The chapter continues our study of the circumstances that can facilitate government intervention when the government is a minority shareholder. We argue that in industries with high rents, governments can use coalitions with quasi-state actors, such as pension funds of SOEs, to intervene in the management.

Chapter 10 introduces a discussion of the role of development banks and provides a historical narrative of the role played by BNDES for the industrialization of Brazil. Using data from 2002 to 2009, Chapter 11 shows that BNDES is lending to large firms that should be able to get capital elsewhere. We also shed light on the process through which the bank selects its target firms.

We conclude in Chapter 12 by compiling some of the lessons of our detailed studies. We focus on a discussion of the conditions that should make each of the models of state capitalism either work better or fail, and end the chapter with a practical section for politicians and managers in charge of running SOEs, development banks, and other state-owned organizations.

PART I

The Reinvention of State Capitalism around the World

2

The Rise and Fall of Leviathan as an Entrepreneur

One of the main arguments of this book is that there has been a significant transformation of the corporate governance of many SOEs since the 1970s. In order to understand the new varieties of state capitalism and their implications for economic efficiency, this chapter traces the rise and fall of state capitalism in the twentieth and early twenty-first centuries. The historical narrative of this chapter aims to show that the monitoring and management of SOEs changed as a process of trail and error. This process of learning went through different experiments and crises that led to the creation of large flagship state-owned firms, which are commonly publicly traded and in which governments act as majority and minority shareholders.

Therefore, in this chapter we argue that the privatization process that began in the 1980s in Europe and spread worldwide in the 1990s did not lead to a full disarticulation of the systems of state capitalism that were developed in the twentieth century, but to a transformation in the way governments manage and own their large SOEs. Under these new forms of ownership, SOEs are more professional, more transparent, and, in some countries, more isolated from the government.

Modern State Capitalism: A History

State capitalism had a gradual global expansion between the late nineteenth and early twentieth centuries. The rise of SOEs started in the nineteenth century on a wide scale when governments tried to solve basic market failures that led to natural monopolies. Then, governments stepped in to provide such public goods as mail, water, and sewage, and, later on, electricity, telephone, and railways. In most cases, providing such services started with government concessions granted to private companies. For instance, it was common in the late nineteenth century to find governments providing subsidies for railway construction or guaranteeing a minimum dividend for the shareholders of railway stocks. Eventually, because of service inefficiency or outright failure, governments ended up owning these services (Toninelli 2000; Millward 2005). For instance, after "widespread accusations of inefficiency, cartels, and corruption"(Wengenroth 2000, 106) in Germany in the 1870s, Bismarck attempted to create a unified national railway company. Although that initiative failed, the provincial governments of Bavaria, Saxony, and Prussia nationalized most of the private railways between 1879 and 1885, taking the share of state-owned railway miles from 56 percent to 82 percent of the total.

In this early stage of state capitalism, then, governments acted as insurers against failure. They made sure that companies providing important public goods were profitable and sometimes even explicitly guaranteed their success. But with the disruptions of World War I, the instability of the early 1920s, and the slowdown of the Great Depression, governments ended up having to take over the operation of many of these services.[1] The transfer of ownership was frequently a product of nationalizations, many of which should be understood as bailouts. In Latin America, governments created state-owned banks and railways, and then nationalizations and bailouts increased the number of state-owned firms in the first two decades of the twentieth century (Marichal 2011); in Europe, nationalizations happened more often in the 1920s; while in East Asia and Southeast Asia (for example, India), there were transfers of ownership either from colonial authorities to local authorities or from private owners to government agencies or holding companies (Bogart 2009; Bogart and Chaudhary 2012). In Africa, the advance of state ownership in the first half of the twentieth century was related to the important role of British authorities in the construction of railways. Figure 2.1 shows the gradual rise of state ownership of railways as a consequence of bailouts and nationalizations between 1860 and 1935.

The policy of bailing out ailing industries became more integral to government policy in Europe, Latin America, and Africa after the Great Depression. The prototypical example is the Italian Institute for Industrial Reconstruction (known as IRI). In 1933, the Italian government had to bail out the country's two largest universal banks, which in turn controlled a

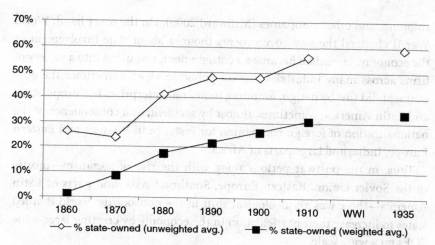

Figure 2.1. State ownership of railway miles around the world (% of total), 1860–1935

Source: Created by the authors from Bogart (2009) for data before 1935 and from Bureau of Railway Economics (1935) and Timpson (2006) for 1935.

Note: The top line shows the average, across forty-two countries, of the ratio of government-controlled miles to total miles. This panel is unbalanced. The bottom line shows state ownership of railway miles in a balanced sample of thirty-five countries we can track from 1860 to 1935 and represents the ratio of the total of all miles owned by the government in those countries to the total miles in all those countries.

variety of other companies. IRI had been created as a public entity to *temporarily* manage the banks' shareholdings and facilitate the restructuring of their problematic assets (Saraceno 1955). But "soon it appeared clear that the private sector was unable (and unwilling) to buy back all the assets . . . in the hands of the State" (Colli 2013, 5). In 1937, IRI became a permanent holding company of the Italian government. According to some calculations, IRI owned 20 percent of all Italian corporations on the eve of World War II (Colli 2013; Amatori and Colli 2000).[2]

The Rise of Leviathan as an Entrepreneur

The second stage of state capitalism goes from the 1930s to the 1980s. On the one hand, in continental Europe, the smooth increase in the state's presence in utilities before the Great Depression accelerated after World War II; governments owned and ran water, oil, gas, electricity, telecommunications, shipping, and other companies (Millward 2005). On the other hand, World War II changed the way governments thought about state involvement in the economy. Leviathan became an entrepreneur, venturing into a variety of firms across many industries beyond public services. Sometimes the government did this by design, founding industrial enterprises in Europe, Asia, and Latin America; sometimes almost by accident, as a consequence of the nationalization of foreign companies, for instance in Western and Eastern Europe, India, and large parts of Africa.

Thus, in the postwar period, along with the rise of socialism—mostly in the Soviet Union, Eastern Europe, Southeast Asia, and parts of Latin America—there was an ideological shift in the nonsocialist world that led states to increase their participation in the economy by creating large-scale SOEs on a wide scale.

Nationalizations in Europe

In Western Europe, governments began to nationalize important infrastructure enterprises in the 1920s and 1930s. In the United Kingdom, the government nationalized British Petroleum in 1914, mostly for strategic and security reasons (e.g., to supply the British navy); but this was unique in that management remained autonomous (Jones 1981). In 1926, however, the British government nationalized the British Broadcasting Corporation, and in 1927 it created the Central Electricity Board (Millward 2000). In France, the first major wave of nationalizations took place in 1936 and 1937, when the government nationalized aircraft and armament factories, amalgamated the largest private airlines into a new government-controlled company (Air France), and merged five railroads, putting them under the control of the new railway holding company, the Société Nationale des Chemins de Fer Français, or SNCF (Chadeau 2000).

In Italy, the government created the aforementioned Italian Institute for Industrial Reconstruction (IRI) in 1933 to take over the financial holdings of two of the country's largest banks, which had operated as universal banks, owning stock in large corporations as well as lending (Amatori and Colli 2000). Even after IRI sold some of those holdings to private parties, at the end of the 1930s it was still Italy's largest operator of electricity plants and of manufacturing facilities for steel, machinery, and shipbuilding (Brahm

1995). Francisco Franco, the Spanish dictator, copied the Italian system and created a similar holding company to bail out firms and manage national-ized firms (Carreras et al. 2000).

The initial wave of nationalizations intensified right after World War II (Lamoreaux 2009). Megginson (2005, 11) claims that the "economic and industrial mobilization that occurred during World War II dramatically increased the power (and prestige) of national governments as economic managers, and set the stage for the postwar surge in ideologically motivated state ownership."

During the war, Nazi invasions and expropriations significantly trans-formed the organization of economic activity. Since the late 1930s, the Nazi government had been integrating important German industries, such as steel, under the umbrella of a large holding company, the Reichswerke Her-mann Göring, created in 1937 and named after the number-two man in the National Socialist Party. The Reichswerke took over iron ore mining from private hands and created a new large steel mill. Another Nazi project was Volkswagenwerk, a state-owned car manufacturer born out of Adolf Hitler's desire to produce a "people's car" on a massive scale. "American engineers from the Ford Motor Company designed the Volkswagen plant close to the Hermann Göring Reichswerke" (Wengenroth 2000, 116).

With the Nazi occupation of new territories, particularly in Eastern Europe, the Reichswerke took charge of almost three hundred subsidiary firms, operating coal, iron, steel, weapons and munitions, and river and rail transport firms as core businesses and subsidiary firms in Germany, Czech-oslovakia, Poland, and Yugoslavia. It also had a division to control Soviet plants and Ukrainian mines captured during the war (Overy 1994, 162–163; Wengenroth 2000, 117).[3]

In France, right after the war, there was a fresh round of nationalizations. In 1945 and 1946, the government of Charles de Gaulle took full control of a series of banks (Banque de France, Société Générale, Crédit Lyonnais, Comptoir National d'Escompte, and Banque Nationale du Commerce et de l'Industrie); nationalized thirty-six insurance companies, coal firms, and two important manufacturing companies, Gnome et Rhône and automaker Renault; and increased its voting power in Air France. The government also increased its footprint in infrastructure by creating a holding company (Électricité et Gaz de France) to control Électricité de France and Gaz de

France, two of the largest utilities in the world (Chadeau 2000). Additionally, the French government introduced a comprehensive system of economic planning (Shonfield 1965).

In the United Kingdom, postwar government nationalization mostly targeted infrastructure companies and the coal industry. The most important nationalizations immediately after the war were those of the Bank of England and British European Airways in 1946; the coal industry in 1947; rail, buses, ports, and electricity in 1948; gas in 1949; and steel in 1951. These were large-scale nationalizations for which the government created a series of holding companies to operate the many small firms taken over from private hands.

The British government used two justifications to create large SOEs to control the nationalized industries. First, there was a problem of coordination, as private companies in some of those industries were not consolidating to reap economies of scale. For instance, by the 1920s, technical progress in electricity had made "large generating stations more economical, provided the transmission grids could be developed and electrical currents standardized" (Millward 2000, 164). Second, according to Millward (p. 165), "the failure of the interwar regulation of the infrastructure industries" was the other major reason why integration into state-owned conglomerates made more sense in those industries. The nationalization of the coal industry was the exception to that logic and was related to the volatility of income in the industry and the need for better labor standards. Still, this nationalization created what was perhaps the largest firm in Europe, the National Coal Board, which controlled eight hundred mines and had a workforce of almost 720,000 (Hannah 2004).

In Spain, the wave of nationalizations in the 1940s was part of the sweeping nationalist and fascist reforms of dictator Francisco Franco. Between 1941 and 1944, his government nationalized the railway companies, engine factories, shipbuilders, all telecommunications firms, and more (Carreras et al. 2000).

Partly as a way to recover control after the Nazi occupation and partly because of Soviet influence, postwar governments in Eastern Europe seized the assets that had been part of the German industrial apparatus as well as private companies. In 1945 and 1946, the Czechoslovak government nationalized mines, large industrial enterprises, power plants, gas and water works, ironworks and foundries, and a long list of other industrial enterprises. The Polish and Bulgarian governments did the same in 1946, followed by Yugoslavia, Hungary, and Romania (Sharp 1946; Einaudi 1950).

In 1946, the Austrian parliament, as part of a plan to expropriate German companies, "decided to nationalize seventy-one large business enterprises, 20 percent of the country's industry" (Stiefel 2000, 238), which ranged from chemical industries to machinery to mining. In 1947, the three leading banks in Austria were nationalized. Many of those companies, however, were reprivatized in the 1950s when the conservative party took power (Stiefel 2000).

After this initial wave of nationalizations, politicians and citizens in both Western and Eastern Europe saw SOEs as necessary solutions for coordination problems and market failures and as an important tool to overcome the difficulties of regulating certain natural monopolies. Moreover, European governments started using their resources to act as entrepreneurs in new sectors. In France, the government used holding companies to fund state-owned start-ups in sectors such as nuclear power, oil and lubricants, mining, and aerospace. In Germany, the state-owned holding companies left over from the 1930s continued to diversify their holdings into the 1960s. For instance, VEBA, originally an operator of coal mines, got rid of its coal operations and became an energy and petrochemical concern (Wengenroth 2000). In the 1950s, the Italian government developed three holding companies—Finmeccanica, Finelettrica, and Eni—to create, bail out, and invest in machinery manufacturing, electronic equipment, and oil and gas firms, respectively (Brahm 1995). The number of SOEs also exploded in Spain after 1945, with the holding company Industrial National Agency (INA) bailing out, nationalizing, and financing firms in electricity, oil, banking, chemicals, aluminum, telecommunications, engineering, and other sectors (Carreras et al. 2000).

A different wave of nationalizations took place in Western Europe in the 1970s and early 1980s, significantly expanding the influence of governments in economic activities. According to Toninelli (2000), "the main waves of nationalization occurred in France, Austria, Great Britain, and the Netherlands when [Labour, Socialist, and Social Democratic] parties were in power," as a way to achieve "'genuine' industrial democracy." In England, the government nationalized a series of underperforming water-distribution and manufacturing industries in the 1970s, among them Rolls-Royce and British

Leyland (Jaguar) in 1974 and British Aerospace and British Shipbuilders in 1977 (Millward 2000). In Germany, the government merged VEBA with the private firm Gelsenberg to create a national oil company. In Italy, the holding companies IRI, Eni, and EGAM, originally set up to control mining ventures, continued their expansion and diversification, even acquiring newspapers. Austria's equivalent of IRI, known as the OIAG, expanded its capacities into steel, nonferrous metals, chemicals, and more, partly by bailing out private firms (Monsen and Walters 1983).

The most sweeping programs of nationalization took place in France, Portugal, and Norway. In France, the government of François Mitterrand nationalized most of the banks and their industrial holdings. Through various holding companies, Mitterrand also increased government ownership of the Compagnie Générale d'Électricité, the electricity and nuclear power conglomerate; of CIT-Alcatel (telecommunications); and in aluminum, steel, chemical, and aircraft manufacturing companies (Monsen and Walters 1983). In Norway, the government used revenues from newfound oil to nationalize Norsk Hydro (the electricity conglomerate), create new state-owned banks, and venture into aluminum, oil refining, and other businesses. By 1978, this put the SOE output as a percentage of Norway's (non-oil) industrial GDP at around 30 percent (Monsen and Walters 1983).

Obviously, the biggest push toward state ownership of the industrial and services complex took place in the Soviet Union, which after World War II completed its transition to a planned economy. As Paul Gregory explained, "in a planned socialist economy the Communist Party assumes a leading role in directing economic activity." Yet the party used planning and SOEs to "control the output and input levels of only the most important industrial commodities . . . some commodities are not planned at all; in rare cases commodities are even allocated by the market" (Gregory 1990, 20–21). Still, as we show below, output coming from SOEs was close to 90 percent of the Soviet Union's GDP.

In fact, there is evidence showing that, before the 1980s, nationalized industries in Europe had rapid increases in total factor productivity, while also deploying capital rapidly. Millward (2005) shows that, between 1950 and 1973, total factor productivity (TFP) growth in nationalized industries in England—such as electricity, gas, coal mining, air transport, communications, and manufacturing (but not railways)—was higher than in similar industries in the United States, where these industries were privately run.

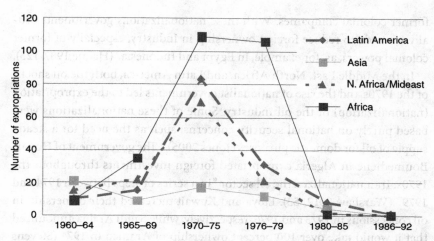

Figure 2.2. Number of nationalizations (expropriations) in developing countries, 1960–1992

Source: Created with data from Kobrin (1984) and Minor (1994).

Similarly, German and French firms in these industries had rapid TFP growth, faster than that of the United States, between 1950 and 1980. Part of this increase, he argues, was a process of catching up after the war. Moreover, his data also show British SOEs outperforming their American counterparts during the recessionary 1980s.[4]

Nationalizations in Developing Countries

The wave of nationalizations in developing countries, which had begun with railways at the turn of the twentieth century, accelerated after World War II, as nationalism drove the expansion of the state into activities formerly run by foreigners. Figure 2.2 displays the number of acts of expropriation of foreign direct investments in developing countries between 1960 and 1992 and shows that nationalizations reached a peak between 1970 and 1975, when 117 countries around the world carried out acts of expropriation. Nationalizations were more common in sub-Saharan Africa and Latin America, with North Africa and the Middle East close behind.

In Latin America, nationalizations were usually linked to bailouts, while in Asia and Africa, governments created SOEs after they nationalized former colonial companies. With these nationalizations governments usually wanted "to reduce foreign ownership in industry, especially of former colonial powers, as, for example, in Egypt and Indonesia" (Haque 1987, 123).

In the Middle East, North Africa, and Latin America, both the oil shocks of the 1970s and the rise of nationalist governments led to the expropriation (nationalization) of the oil industry. Some of these nationalizations were based purely on national security concerns, such as the need for a steady supply of oil for domestic purposes (Jones 2005).[5] The government of Houari Boumediene in Algeria expropriated foreign investments throughout the 1970s. Iran nationalized the oil sector "in a series of steps between 1974 and 1979" (Warshaw 2012, 53). Libya and Kuwait increased their ownership in oil concessions in 1973 and 1976, respectively, while Saudi Arabia announced that it would take over 100 percent ownership of Aramco in 1974 (Stevens 2012a and b). The Venezuelan government nationalized the oil industry in 1976 (Manzano and Monaldi 2008).

Beyond Nationalizations

Governments in developing countries also used SOEs as a way to industrialize. The objectives were to overcome coordination problems via investments in basic infrastructure (Baer 1969), to finance initial research and development in innovation industries (Evans 1995; Ramamurti 1987), to address perceived market failures and to forge alliances with foreign multinational corporations for the transfer of technology (Evans 1979, 1995), and to promote nationalistic import substitution industrialization programs (Guajardo Soto 2013, forthcoming).

The Chilean government, for example, used its development financial institution, CORFO, to create the electricity company ENDESA (1944), the steel firm Compañía de Acero del Pacífico (1946), and the national sugar industry as a whole (1952). In the 1970s, the government of Salvador Allende expropriated a series of firms and mines, and, by 1972, SOEs ended up contributing 40 percent to total GDP (Meller 1996, 58–60). In Mexico, the government bailed out or created almost one thousand SOEs between 1970 and 1990. In Brazil, the government initially used its development bank, BNDES, to finance the establishment of new electricity, steel, and telecommunication companies. The government then created holding companies to control these firms (see Chapter 4).

One significant difference between the large SOEs in, say, France and those in Latin America and Africa was that French state firms were organized as profit-making businesses, "operating often in a competitive environment, domestically or internationally"(Millward 2005, 184). This was the case in the aeronautics, airlines, and energy industries, among others (Millward 2005). In Latin America and Africa, however, governments usually protected SOEs because they were part of larger plans for import substitution or for the indigenization of industries that had formerly been in foreign hands. Even so, not all African and Latin American SOEs were isolated from competition. State-owned mining firms in Latin America, such as Codelco in Chile and Vale in Brazil, faced intense international competition from the start (Jones 2005).

The Zenith of Leviathan as an Entrepreneur

After the wave of nationalizations and the rise of an explicit effort to have Leviathan acting as an entrepreneur in manufacturing and services, the average output of SOEs to GDP in 1980 reached above 7 percent in developed economies and almost 12 percent in nonsocialist developing countries (see Table 2.1). Sheshinski and López-Calva (2003, 447) calculated that, in developing countries, the output of SOEs to GDP peaked in 1981 at around 16 percent. Nellis (2006, 6) estimated that, by the end of the 1970s, SOE output to GDP in Africa had reached over 17 percent.

In command or socialist countries, the figures were obviously higher, given that governments owned most firms and all banks. In Table 2.2, we show that, in 1989, most countries in Eastern Europe still had close to 90 percent of the output generated by SOEs, with the exception of Poland, which had a ratio of SOE output to GDP of only 70 percent. The ratio of SOE and government employment to total employment was also close to 90 percent, again with the exception of Poland, where private employment was already over 44 percent in 1989 (Aghion et al. 1994). Even in 1995, the World Survey of Economic Freedom calculated that most formerly socialist countries still had an SOE output to GDP of 60 percent or so (Messick 1996).

Furthermore, the share of SOE investment to total capital formation in all mixed economies reached 17 percent by 1980. This was partly a consequence of the prominence of SOEs in capital-intensive industries such as electricity, telecommunications, oil, and steel. For instance, while the output of SOEs in the United Kingdom was 11.3 percent of GDP circa 1975, public enterprises

Table 2.1. SOE output to GDP in mixed economies (mean), 1978–1985

	SOE output as a percent of GDP, 1975–1985
Developed countries	
Austria	6.5
Belgium	2.6
France	10.7
Germany	7.1
Greece	5.3
Italy	6.7
Portugal	22.2
Spain	4.0
United Kingdom	5.9
United States	1.3
Mean (developed countries)	7.2
Middle-income countries	
Algeria	69.9
Argentina	4.7
Botswana	5.7
Brazil	5.0
Chile	13.6
Colombia	6.9
Congo	10.4
Costa Rica	6.7
Dominica	3.3
Ecuador	8.6
Guatemala	1.1
Honduras	4.6
Korea, Rep. of	9.6
Mauritius	2.1
Mexico	12.0
Morocco	18.6
Nigeria	13.5
Panama	7.3
Paraguay	3.8
Peru	8.5
Singapore	15.0
South Africa	13.9
Taiwan	7.4
Tunisia	29.8
Turkey	6.3
Uruguay	4.0
Venezuela	23.1
Mean (middle-income countries)	11.7

Table 2.1. (continued)

	SOE output as a percent of GDP, 1975–1985
Low-income countries	
Bangladesh	2.5
Bolivia	13.0
Burundi	5.4
Cameroon	18.0
Central African Rep.	4.1
Comoros	5.6
Dem. Rep. of Congo	22.8
Dominican Republic	2.0
Egypt	37.1
El Salvador	2.4
Gambia	3.9
Ghana	5.8
Guinea	25.0
Guyana	37.0
India	10.8
Indonesia	15.4
Ivory Coast	10.5
Jamaica	21.0
Kenya	10.0
Madagascar	2.3
Malawi	7.0
Mali	13.6
Mauritania	25.0
Nepal	2.3
Niger	4.8
Pakistan	9.4
Philippines	1.5
Senegal	8.9
Sierra Leone	20.0
Sudan	48.2
Tanzania	10.8
Togo	11.8
Zambia	31.7
Mean (low income)	13.6

Source: Created from data in World Bank (1996), table A.1.

Table 2.2. Public-sector share of GDP in socialist/command economies in Eastern Europe and the Former Soviet Union, 1989

	Estimated SOE output to GDP, 1989		Estimated SOE output to GDP, 1989
Central and Eastern Europe		**Former Soviet Union**	
Bulgaria	93.8	Belarus	94.9
Croatia	91.5	Estonia	82.3
Czech Republic	95.9	Georgia	82.4
Hungary	87.0	Kazakhstan	85.0
Poland	71.4	Latvia	100.0
Romania	87.0	Lithuania	89.6
Slovak Republic	95.9	Russia	94.7
Slovenia	91.6	Ukraine	97.8
		Uzbekistan	90.2
Mean	89.3	Mean	90.8

Source: Calculated using the share of private output to GDP from Aghion et al. (1994), table 1. We assume all non-private GDP was produced by SOEs.

hired only 8.1 percent of the labor force. In Pakistan and Turkey, SOE output to GDP was 5.8 percent and 5 percent, respectively, while SOE employment relative to the size of the labor force was 2.1 percent and 3.9 percent, respectively.[6]

Efforts to Improve SOEs before 1990

Even as governments in developing and developed countries continued to nationalize or create new SOEs, the weaknesses of the Leviathan as an entrepreneur model became apparent. As put by Shirley and Nellis (1991, 1):

> Governments hoped that public enterprises would assist in development of "strategic" sectors, gain access to commercial credit that would be denied to small private businesses, fill "entrepreneurial gaps," empower numerically large but economically weak segments of the population, maintain employment levels, and raise the level of savings and investment. . . . [However] production quantity and quality frequently fell below projections, and the sector saddled governments with increasingly heavy fiscal and managerial burdens.

Moreover, CEOs in SOEs had to deal with a variety of social or political objectives, while trying to avoid losses or even generate profits. The multiplicity of objectives, the fact that politicians imposed noncommercial objectives on SOEs (such as maximizing employment during a recession), and the lack of performance incentives led SOEs to sustained losses.

According to Gómez-Ibañez (2007), postwar governments in Europe and developing countries took three approaches to reforming SOEs. First, from the 1950s to the 1970s, they focused on "injections of physical capital" and developing managerial capacity in SOEs through "technical assistance and training" (p. 4). For instance, in the 1950s, USAID, the United Nations, the OECD, the French government, and the Ford Foundation financed and supported the establishment of schools of public administration to train officials and managers of SOEs. With support from the Ford Foundation and USAID, American business schools advised and supported the development of schools—such as the Indian Institute of Management at Ahmedabad, the Asian Institute of Management in Manila, and the Central American Institute of Management Administration (INCAE), originally in Nicaragua but later moved to Costa Rica—that were "aimed at the needs of SOE managers." Yet no center was more important for training SOE managers than the International Center for Public Enterprise in Ljubljana, Yugoslavia, established in 1974. "At its peak it counted over forty countries as contributing members, published monographs and a journal, *Public Enterprise*, and trained hundreds of managers a year" (Gómez-Ibañez 2007, 8–9).[7]

Second, during the 1970s and 1980s, the focus of governments and multilateral organizations switched to improving "managerial incentives" in SOEs. The French government started to experiment with a new concept, the "contract plan" (CP), designed to "attack the problems of unclear or shifting objectives, insufficient autonomy of managers, and excessively constraining control systems," which were "perceived as major hindrances to public enterprise efficiency and productivity" (Nellis 1991, 279).

A CP set out the intentions, obligations, and responsibilities of the government and the CEO of the SOE:

A typical CP specifies enterprise objectives in terms of the desired overall socioeconomic impact, production goals, and/or quantities and quality of service to be provided. It defines policies and parameters with regard to such items as numbers employed, size and growth of the enterprise's wage bill, and social and noncommercial activities. Many CPs stipulate the physical and financial indicators that will measure enterprise performance . . . it also spells out the government's obligations and limitations. Many CPs establish the principle that the government will compensate the enterprise for costs incurred in fulfilling noncommercial objectives. . . . A typical CP lays out the enterprise's financing and investment program, noting the amount the enterprise must generate internally, the amount to come from government subsidy or equity injections, and the amount to be raised by credit, with or without a government guarantee. (Nellis 1991, 280)

In 1971, the French government signed its first CP agreement with large SOEs in which the SOEs proposed investment, employment, and financial programs and were required to turn to the market to finance them. In exchange, these firms were granted more autonomy from the government and were permitted to set their own rates and prices (Chadeau 2000; Gómez-Ibañez 2007). The government committed to compensate SOEs for "public service obligations imposed on firms . . . [such as asking] SNCF [to] operate unprofitable regional passenger trains" (Gómez-Ibañez 2007, 23). However, the government frequently reneged on such commitments because of unforeseen political and economic circumstances.

Governments in developing countries began adopting the contract plan system for SOEs in 1980, when Senegal adopted the French system of contracts. Such agreements then rapidly diffused to Francophone Africa, to Pakistan and the Republic of Korea in 1983, to China in 1986, to India in 1988, and, toward the end of the decade, to Anglophone Africa, Bangladesh, Argentina, Brazil, New Zealand, and Mexico. In fact, the World Bank asked governments to experiment with contract plans as part of the conditions of its structural adjustment loans (Shirley 1989; Shirley and Nellis 1991; Gómez-Ibañez 2007).

Contract plans ultimately failed in most countries, for various reasons. First, the performance targets were hard to measure, as they were usually a combination or weighted average of a variety of factors.[8]

Second, such contracts were complex and subject to a variety of macroeconomic and political circumstances; that is, they were incomplete or could not foresee every situation and thus had to be renegotiated frequently. For instance, in France, Électricité de France (EDF) and the national railways adopted the world's first contract plans in the 1970s, but when the oil shock of 1973 raised costs, EDF was forced to pursue out-of-plan investments in nuclear energy (Nellis 1991). The length of the contracts was later shortened, but even that did not fully solve the problem of incomplete contracts.

Third, SOE executives usually knew better than the government the firm's actual capacity to meet targets, so they tended to set soft targets for themselves. In some exceptional circumstances, the contracts included bonuses for executives who exceeded their targets. In addition, as we mentioned before, governments frequently reneged on the terms of the contract (Shirley 1996; Gómez-Ibañez 2007).

Mary Shirley, former public enterprise adviser at the World Bank, helped governments design some of those contracts in the 1980s. "I worked so long and hard trying to reform SOEs," she explained. "Yet, most of the cases of successful reform that we had included in the World Development Report of 1983 later actually turned into failures."[9] For instance, in a study of twelve contracts in Ghana, India, Korea, Mexico, the Philippines, and Senegal, in only in three companies did total factor productivity increase after the contract (Shirley 1996). A later study of 628 Chinese manufacturing firms found that productivity improved only if a significant portion of a manager's pay was linked to firm performance (Shirley and Xu 1998).

Governments also tried to solve the basic agency problems of SOEs by corporatizing these firms. That is, governments in the United Kingdom, Brazil, China, and elsewhere gave SOE boards and management financial and decision-making autonomy, thus reducing the need of having these firms achieve social and/or political objectives, therefore allowing them to improve efficiency. Yet such efforts did not produce the expected results, given the lack of strong regulatory agencies, sophisticated financial reporting, or external monitoring of CEOs through boards and other improved governance mechanisms (Gómez-Ibañez 2007; Nellis 2006).

The Fall of Leviathan as an Entrepreneur

The decline of the model in which the government acted as an entrepreneur, owning and managing firms, was brought on by two macroeconomic shocks.

First, with the oil shocks came inflation, price controls, and losses in SOEs. Second, in the United States, the Federal Reserve's reaction to the high inflation of the 1970s was a radical hike in interest rates that created a series of crises for developing countries.

The two oil shocks of the 1970s exposed some of the problems of political intervention in SOEs. As higher oil prices brought on higher inflation in both developed and developing countries, governments tried to control inflation by imposing price controls, particularly for the goods and services provided by public firms. Private-sector inflation and wages therefore increased more quickly than the controlled prices charged by SOEs, and by the late 1970s and early 1980s, price controls had eroded SOE profitability worldwide.

In the United Kingdom, for example, the oil shocks of the 1970s brought on the first systematic losses by SOEs since World War II, forcing the government to subsidize these firms. Millward (2000, 174) calculates that the profits of SOEs in the United Kingdom (once subsidies are subtracted) turned negative sometime after 1970 and reached a low in 1974. Monsen and Walters (1983) show that, between 1971 and 1981, the twenty-five largest SOEs in Western Europe suffered systematic losses and had lower profit margins and productivity growth than comparable private firms.

By 1980, SOEs, on average, ran losses of at least 1.75 percent of GDP in developed countries and almost 4 percent of GDP in developing countries. The first sweeping study of SOE finances by the International Monetary Fund found particularly large deficits in Asia, where the average aggregate losses by SOEs was 5 percent of GDP (mainly because of extremely large deficits in India, Taiwan, South Korea, and what is now Myanmar). The study warned about the macroeconomic instability that SOEs could generate, given that governments financed those deficits by borrowing or printing money. There were also vulnerabilities in the balance of payments because large SOEs tended to get loans from international banks and multilateral organizations such as the World Bank and therefore had large liabilities in foreign currency. Between 1976 and 1978, foreign borrowing by SOEs made up 23 percent of all borrowing on international capital markets tracked by the World Bank and 33 percent of foreign borrowing by developing countries (Short 1984).

In Latin America, the vulnerabilities of SOEs seemed to be less of a threat in 1980 because the overall deficit of SOEs was around 2.5 percent of GDP, and most of it could be covered with transfers from the government or by borrowing abroad. By 1982, however, those vulnerabilities had become a major problem, as high interest rates in the United States and Mexico's debt default and its subsequent contagion to the region complicated the refinancing of outstanding liabilities for the governments of developing countries (Frieden 1991). As capital markets closed for Latin American governments and SOEs, refinancing deficits became a problem, and some of the most aggressive capital investment programs came to a grinding halt.[10] In Chile, the crisis triggered a major program of privatization, while in most other countries, massive privatization came only in the 1990s. According to John Nellis, privatization adviser from the World Bank, Mexico's privatization program, which started in 1989, sent a signal that the traditional method of trying to reform SOEs had not been successful and demonstrated that massive privatization programs could increase revenues without much political backlash.[11]

Thus, as a consequence of the oil shocks of the 1970s and the global liquidity crisis of the early 1980s—especially in Europe, Africa, and Latin America—state capitalism was at a crossroads. Governments began to rethink the role of SOEs in the state apparatus and to consider not only major structural reforms to those organizations but also a major overhaul of systems of state capitalism.

We think there are at least five factors that led governments to dismantle some of the most problematic SOEs in the early 1990s. First, governments in developing countries and in Western and Eastern Europe included privatization in their packages of structural reforms. In Eastern Europe, privatization was part of the transition from a command economy into capitalism, and according to Perotti and Biais (2002) privatization itself increased political support for the new reformist governments. Reforms in Western Europe were also tied to policies to promote integration into the European Economic Community, which required governments to liberalize markets and reduce budget deficits.

Second, by 1983, voters in France and England, the trend-setters in Western state capitalism, started to reject SOEs and nationalizations and began to associate them "with economic crisis" (Kalyvas 1994, 335). This rejection partly explains the rise of conservative governments and the beginning of the massive privatization programs governments launched in Europe in the 1980s.

Third, politicians and government technocrats changed their beliefs about the importance of fiscal surpluses, and they realized that inefficient SOEs could weaken their own finances (Alston et al. 2013). That is, inefficient SOEs could, in turn, compromise the government efforts to stabilize their economies and their capacity to borrow in international markets. According to John Nellis, "governments reluctantly concluded that the financial burden that SOEs imposed on them was crippling their budgets. Then they were pursuing programs of structural reforms in which the IMF asked them to improve the financial performance of their SOEs, so they would come to the World Bank and ask us what to do." In the late 1980s, the IMF and World Bank started to include some privatization programs as part of the conditionality of their loans.[12]

The IMF, in sponsoring many of the structural reform programs, also imposed new reporting standards for governments. Among them were radical changes in the way governments monitored and reported SOE financials. In 1986, the IMF developed its first manual of statistics for governments and for the first time requested governments to systematically include the net balance of SOEs in their consolidated budgets (including net changes in assets and liabilities), along with SOE losses, debt issues, and subsidies. Complying countries would find it harder to use SOEs to hide subsidies or issues of external debt.[13]

Not only did governments realize SOEs had weakened their public finances in the early 1980s, but by the late part of the decade, developing countries had begun issuing sovereign bonds and needed to market themselves as fiscally responsible in order to borrow from international investors. By the early 1990s, seventeen developing countries had swapped the outstanding debt they had in arrears with international banks for so-called Brady bonds (low-interest bonds that were implicitly guaranteed by the United States).[14] A boom in sovereign debt issues from these "emerging markets" ensued, and government finances began to be tracked in real time by a large number of analysts and investors (Mauro et al. 2006).

Fourth, between 1986 and 1994, governments in over one hundred countries began opening up their economies as part of the Uruguay round of trade negotiations and therefore needed to make their economies more efficient in order to compete. That usually entailed dismantling price controls and the tariffs that protected many inefficient private and public firms.

Many countries also began lifting capital controls, thus facilitating global capital flows (Abdelal 2007; Edwards 2007).

Fifth, in the early 1990s, intellectual currents hostile to state intervention became the dominant voices in academic and policy circles. Theories of managerial inefficiency, bolstered by empirical evidence from many countries showing SOEs underperforming their private counterparts, led to a consensus that privatization should be an integral part of a country's development strategy (see for instance La Porta and López-de-Silanes 1999; Megginson and Netter 2001).

In sum, a combination of economic conditions, theory, and quantitative evidence led governments around the world to adopt privatization initiatives (Bortolotti et al. 2004). As globalization advanced, the fiscal pressures that governments experienced from sustaining inefficient SOEs increased and the opportunity cost of holding assets that were yielding negative returns became too high a price to pay. For governments with large debt burdens at high interest rates, the calculation was simple: Why pay 10–20 percent per year on liabilities while holding assets that yield near-zero or negative returns? In that context, privatizing was an obvious option—a financial no-brainer. In fact, in some privatizations, governments allowed investors to pay with government bonds, thus retiring debt while selling state assets (Anuatti-Neto et al. 2005).

Privatization

The system of SOEs that existed under the Leviathan as an entrepreneur model of state capitalism began to be torn down through massive privatization programs in the 1980s and 1990s. Margaret Thatcher in the United Kingdom and Jacques Chirac (then prime minister) in France began a wave of large-scale privatization programs; Chirac alone privatized twenty-two large firms in fifteen months between 1986 and 1988. Thatcher's privatization program is commonly identified as the beginning of this reform trend. For instance, the initial public offering of British Telecom in 1984 legitimized privatization programs worldwide. "The enormous share issue—by far the largest equity offering in history to that time—was met with strong demand by investors . . . in Britain and abroad . . . [and] showed that a global market for privatization share offerings existed" (Megginson and Netter 2001, 15).

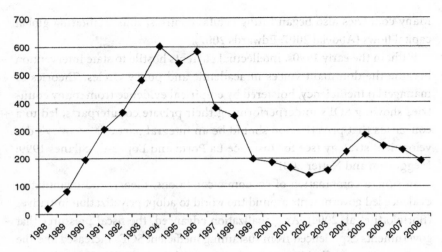

Figure 2.3. Number of privatization operations per year (generating revenues of at least US$1 million in 2005 dollars), 1988–2008

Sources: For Europe, we use the Privatization Barometer database, available at www.privatiza tionbarometer.net/. For other countries, we use the World Bank privatization databases (one from 1990 through 1999 and another from 2000 through 2008). We then add observations from the World Bank database for privatization transactions under $1 million for 2000–2008. All available at http://go.worldbank.org/W1ET8RG1Q0.

Note: Our data exclude Oceania because we did not have complete data for Australia and New Zealand. Also, information for the United States and Canada is missing.

In the mid-1980s, the privatization trend spread from the United Kingdom to Austria, Belgium, Canada, Chile, Denmark, France, Holland, Italy, Jamaica, Japan, Malaysia, Singapore, Spain, Sweden, and the United States (Megginson and Netter 2001).

In emerging markets, however, governments were slow to liquidate or privatize SOEs in the 1980s. Most of the privatizations then were of small companies or firms that had been bailed out in the past. Even in Chile, "the divested firms had virtually all been recently taken over [by the Allende regime]" (Berg and Shirley 1987, 5). Additionally, most privatizations in developing countries implied a full transfer of ownership.[15] For instance, out of 133 privatizations in Chile and 217 in Bangladesh before 1987, none were partial sales of equity.

Between 1988 and 2009, there were two privatization waves. In Figure 2.3 we plot the number of privatization operations between 1988 and 2008; it is clear that there was a major wave of privatizations in the 1990s, followed by a second wave after 2003. The first wave of privatizations was linked to structural reform programs, while the second is mostly explained by the partial privatization of firms in China (involving sales of minority stakes to private investors) and some former Soviet countries. Figure 2.3 shows clearly that, in terms of the number of operations, the 1990s were the golden years of privatization. After 1999, the number of transactions fell from a mean of around three to four hundred transactions per year to about two hundred per year.

Yet, while the number of privatizations slowed down after 2000, there was a significant change in the privatization strategy followed by governments in the first decade of the twenty-first century. In the 1990s, more than half of the privatizations included the transfer of control from government to the private sector. After 1999, privatizations included more concessions, leases, and sales of smaller blocks of shares, without necessarily transferring control to the private sector. Then, revenues collected from the issue of shares increased more rapidly after the successful IPO of a small portion of Rosneft in Russia in 2006, reaching record levels between 2006 and 2008 (see Figure 2.4). That is, partial privatizations became the norm after 2006, and governments in countries such as Russia, China, Brazil, and Turkey opted to privatize small percentages of ownership (that is, minority positions) in stock markets, rather than privatizing control.

The multibillion-dollar IPOs mentioned before had shown governments that they did not need to give up control to raise large amounts of money. Privatization gradually changed from a way to transfer ownership and control to a scheme to get revenue *without* transferring control. Even when governments did transfer control, it became common for them to keep minority stakes through various channels such as public investment or pension funds, state-owned banks, or state-owned holding companies.

New Varieties of State Capitalism across the World

Therefore, the outcomes of privatization were not necessarily a general stripping down of the state's productive assets. Privatizations faced intense political opposition, and in specific strategic sectors governments them-

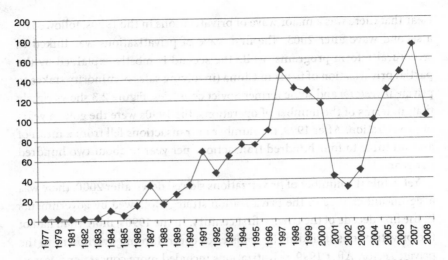

Figure 2.4. Privatization revenues worldwide (billions of 2005 US$), 1977–2008

Sources: See Figure 2.3.

Notes: Our data do not include privatization figures for Canada, the United States, Japan, Australia, New Zealand, or the Republic of Korea. The spike in revenues after 2005 is mostly driven by the following IPOs: Rosneft ($10.7 billion), Bank of China (almost $14 billion), and Industrial and Commercial Bank of China (almost $22 billion) in 2006; PetroChina ($9.15 billion), China Shenhua Energy ($9.1 billion), Sberbank ($8.8 billion), Vneshtorgbank ($8 billion), China Construction Bank Corporation ($7.95 billion), and China Pacific Insurance ($7.7 billion) in 2007. The dates of the sales in our database may not coincide with the actual date on which the IPO took place because the database is based on official announcements of privatizations.

selves decided that it was better to keep certain companies under state control. Bortolotti and Faccio's (2009) survey of SOEs in the rich OECD countries reveals that, between 1996 and 2000, despite previous strenuous efforts to privatize, the share of firms under government control did not go down, except in the capital goods, transportation, and utilities sectors.

For instance, in 2005, an OECD report showed the importance of SOEs in member countries (Table 2.3). We think there are two important trends to highlight. First, we see many companies in which the government is a controlling shareholder, sharing ownership with private investors (that is, the model of Leviathan as a majority investor). In France and Italy, the ratio of assets of SOEs to GDP was 25 percent, while in Finland this ratio reached 80 percent. In Korea and Turkey, it was around 20 percent of GDP. Guillén (2005) describes

Table 2.3. Number of state-owned enterprises with government minority positions in OECD countries, 2005

	Number of SOEs	Minority positions	% of minority-owned firms
Australia	12	0	0%
Austria	78	21	27%
Belgium	15	0	0%
Canada	100	15	15%
Czech Republic	>1,000	>120	12%
Denmark	27	10	37%
Finland	55	19	35%
France	100	33	33%
Germany	37	20	54%
Greece	50	14	28%
Italy	25	4	16%
Japan	77	n.a.	n.a.
Korea, Rep. of	30	4	13%
Netherlands	44	16	36%
New Zealand	34	3	9%
Norway	26	6	23%
Poland	1,189	691	58%
Slovak Republic	115	55	48%
Spain	40	15	38%
Sweden	58	7	12%
Turkey	39	n.a.	n.a.
United Kingdom	80	14	18%

Source: All figures are estimates by the authors using data from OECD (2005) and (for Poland) from Waclawik-Wejman (2005).

how Spanish SOEs were consolidated before 1996 and initially only partly privatized. Even after privatization, either the government or a government-owned bank kept a share in some of the largest Spanish companies.

Second, there is a significant number of companies (most often privatized firms) in which the government is not a controller but does actively participate as a minority shareholder (OECD 2005). That is, there has been an increasing role for Leviathan as a minority investor. OECD governments have minority positions in about 25 percent of the companies in which the government is a shareholder. In Germany, over 50 percent of the federal government's equity holdings in companies that are considered SOEs are minority positions (and that does not include companies with less than 25 percent of government ownership).[16] In Denmark, Finland, France, the Netherlands, Poland, the Slovak Republic, and Spain, over 30 percent of the companies that are identified as state-owned have the government holding a minority position.[17]

In Table 2.4, we see that governments in emerging markets still hold many state-owned firms and have minority positions in many other firms. In most of the countries for which we found data, the Leviathan as a minority investor model applies to almost half of the companies in which the government has equity (the rest being wholly owned or majority-controlled SOEs). This table also shows that, in emerging markets, SOEs still contribute a large portion of GDP and make up a good portion of total stock market capitalization (close to 30 percent on average).

More importantly, Table 2.4 shows the resilience of state capitalism in developing countries. Consider the following trends: while in former command economies SOE output to GDP decreased from 90 percent to less than 30 percent between 1989 and 2010, in other developing countries (such as Brazil, Indonesia, India, Turkey, Singapore, and Mexico), this ratio has barely moved, staying close to 15 percent.

An important part of the transformation of Leviathan from the entrepreneur model (owning and managing SOEs) to the majority investor model is the fact that governments transformed not only the ownership structure of SOEs, but also the corporate governance of the largest public companies. Governments started to list large SOEs on stock exchanges, professionalized the firms' managements, added boards of directors (often with independent members), and gave many of these large SOEs substantial budgetary autonomy. In Table 2.4, we can see that governments in emerging markets trade some of their SOEs in stock markets (usually the largest firms) and that those firms make up a large portion of the country's stock market capitalization. OECD governments have also taken this path; some of the largest energy and utility companies in those countries—such as Enel and Eni in Italy, GDF in France, and Japan Postal Bank—are among the world's largest firms by revenues and have been partly privatized, listed on at least one stock exchange, and have improved their financial transparency.

In Brazil, Russia, India, and China (BRIC)—the largest emerging markets—there are large numbers of firms in which the government holds majority and minority equity positions. In Figure 2.5, we show the distribution of ownership using a database of the 125 largest publicly traded companies (by

Table 2.4. Patterns of state ownership in emerging markets, c. 2010

	SOE output (revenues) to (non-financial) GDP	Listed SOEs[a]	SOEs as % of market capitalization[a]	Number of SOEs with majority control		Num. of firms in which the federal government has minority ownership
				Federal	State/local	
Brazil	30%	14	34%	247		
China	30%	942	70%	17,000	150,000	
Egypt				57[b]		59
India	14%	29	40%	217	837	404
Indonesia	18%	16	30%	142		21
Malaysia	36%	15	36%	52		28
Mexico	3%	0	0%	205		
Poland	28%			498		691
Russia	20%	12	40%	7,964	250	1,418
Singapore	12%	12	20%	20		
South Africa				270		
Thailand	26%	6	21%	60		
Turkey	14%			74	700	67
Vietnam	34%	461		1,805	1,559	1,740

Source: See Appendix 2.1. We include firms with government ownership of over 10 percent of equity as minority shareholdings and those with government ownership of over 50 percent as majority-controlled SOEs.

a. These estimates include companies under government control and those with minority ownership.

b. For Egypt, the number of SOEs given here is for 2005, but the number of minority-owned firms is for 2002.

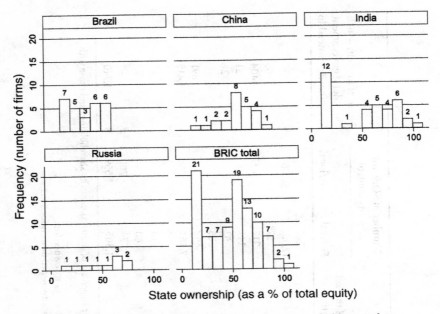

Figure 2.5. Distribution of the number of government equity holdings in large public traded companies in BRIC countries, 2009

Source: Created by the authors from Capital IQ and company web sites using a sample of the 125 largest publicly traded companies in the stock markets of BRIC countries.

market capitalization) between 2005 and 2009. We find Leviathan as a minority shareholder most often in Brazil and Russia, followed by India, where the government or one of its holding companies (for example, Life Insurance Corporation of India) hold minority positions in a variety of firms. In China, we see a greater bias toward large ownership stakes in publicly traded companies, but we still find some minority shareholdings. These minority stakes mostly occur through holding companies that are wholly controlled by the government and invest in a variety of firms.

Governments control both majority and minority positions in a large number of corporations using different financial arms of the government. In China, Malaysia, and Dubai, governments have state-owned holding companies (SOHCs) managing such equity positions. In Brazil, the investment arm of BNDES, called BNDESPAR, manages most of the bank's equity investments. That is, governments create business groups, sometimes focused on one sector but usually diversified into many sectors.

Therefore, governments use pyramidal ownership structures or state-owned holding companies to manage their ownership in a large number of firms, just like diversified business groups do in developing countries. These private business groups are usually a response to failures in capital, labor, and product markets (Khanna and Palepu 2000; Khanna and Yafeh 2007).[18] In the case of governments, groups or holding companies may not only solve some of those market failures, but also facilitate the monitoring and management of a large portfolio of firms.

In Russia, Gazprom is actually a pyramid with majority equity shares in Gazprom Neft (73.02 percent), JSC "TGC-1" (51.79 percent), and JSC Latvijas Gaze (53.56 percent), among others. In China, the State-Owned Assets Supervision and Administration Commission (SASAC) works as a holding company, overseeing over one hundred stand-alone companies and holding companies (Lin and Milhaupt 2011).

In India, Life Insurance Corporation (LIC) plays the role of large holding company for the government. LIC is the largest active stock market investor in India, with around $50 billion invested as of September 2011. The government controls LIC and selects its board and management teams. It often directs LIC to invest in the shares of SOEs, especially when demand for a firm's IPO is low. However, LIC and the government have sometimes disagreed publicly. Our computations indicate that, as of 2012, the government of India had invested in about four hundred companies through LIC, mostly in minority stakes, which make up about 4 percent of India's total stock market capitalization. The median investment of LIC was 4 percent of a company, and the mean was 7.4 percent. LIC is usually a passive investor. Yet when the government directs it to buy shares in partial privatizations, those investments significantly underperform the market.[19] Thus, LIC is an example of Leviathan as a minority investor.

In Brazil, SOE pension funds, the management of which is influenced by the government, have minority shareholding positions in several publicly traded firms and often behave as active investors, influencing a firm's strategy and even fostering mergers of firms in which they have stakes (Lazzarini 2011). By the end of 2012, Previ, the pension fund of the employees of the state-owned bank Banco do Brasil, was the largest pension fund in Brazil and the twenty-seventh largest in the world,[20] with total assets under management of around $83 billion, more than four times the market value of the holdings of Jorge Paulo Lemann, the richest Brazilian entrepreneur.

In the Middle East and Asia, many governments use state-owned and sovereign wealth funds (SWFs) to invest in local and foreign companies.[21] China Investment Corporation (CIC) buys shares (minority positions) in Chinese companies and banks. Mubadala, an SWF in Abu Dhabi, invests heavily in large domestic development projects in energy, telecommunications, health care, and other sectors.[22] Temasek, Singapore's state-owned fund, invests 32 percent of its portfolio locally, in companies such as Singapore Technologies Telemedia, Singapore Communications, Singapore Power, and Singapore Airlines.[23]

The fact that SOEs now figure prominently among the largest publicly traded European, Latin American, and Asian firms makes it almost impossible for investors to have a portfolio with good exposure to all sectors in those economies without including large SOEs.

Conclusion

This chapter describes the evolution of state capitalism around the world in the twentieth and early twenty-first centuries. There are two interrelated narratives. One story is about the continuous transformation of state capitalism, often due to unforeseen circumstances. The other story is about learning. Precisely because the rise of SOEs in the twentieth century was a product of crises more than of explicit design, governments had to experiment with corporate governance and managerial approaches, trying to figure out what worked and what did not. The shocks of the 1970s and 1980s showed some of the weaknesses of the SOE network in both developed and developing countries. Yet we emphasize that the history of SOEs is not one of punctuated shifts. Governments in the 1970s and 1980s experimented with various approaches to SOE reform before deciding to privatize them. The privatization itself was not as sweeping as the literature portrays it to be. Governments around the world kept large SOEs, either because they were in politically sensitive industries or simply because it was difficult to privatize them.

Both the failure of SOE reforms without privatization and the political complications of the privatization process led to the rise of Leviathan as a majority

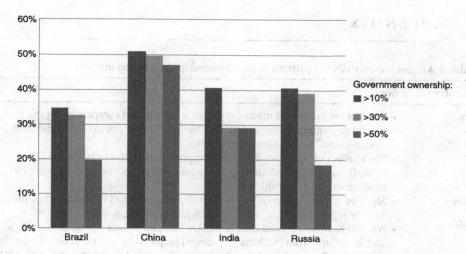

Figure 2.6. Market capitalization of state-owned enterprises relative to the size of the market in BRIC countries, 2009

Source: Estimated by the authors using data from Capital IQ. We include only the largest one hundred companies, which overestimates the size of government ownership for countries like India, but underestimates it for China. We only include in our analysis shareholders who hold over 10 percent of shares. Since some of the companies in our list are owned by other corporations, we had to trace the ultimate controllers of those firms using the respective stock exchange's site or the company's web page. For China we also used the page of SASAC, the state-owned holding company. Thus, our estimates show the value of firms controlled directly or indirectly by the government.

and minority investor. Governments around the world own majority and minority equity positions in many firms, as we have described in this chapter, but theories of the implications of these new corporate ownership and governance configurations are still incomplete. Moreover, the literature on SOEs does not say enough about the role of other actors, such as state-owned holding companies, sovereign wealth funds, and development banks. In the following chapter, we look—from a theoretical perspective—at the evolution of state capitalism after privatization. We examine why state capitalism emerged as it did and hypothesize about the implications of the Leviathan as a majority and minority investor models for firm performance and economic development.

APPENDIX

Table 2-A1. Sources to study the patterns of state ownership in emerging markets

Country	Source
Brazil	• Data on the number of majority- and minority-owned companies (for the federal government only) and on the share of SOE output to GDP come from "Estado Ltda." *Época,* November 6, 2011. • The number of SOEs listed and their importance relative to stock market capitalization are based on our calculations and consider only the largest 100 companies. All data from Capital IQ.
China	• Share of SOE output to GDP from OECD, "State-Owned Enterprises in China: Reviewing the Evidence," Paris: OECD, January 2009, p. 6. • Andrew Szamosszegi and Cole Kyle, "An Analysis of State-Owned Enterprises and State Capitalism in China," document prepared by Capital Trade Inc. for the U.S.-China Economic and Security Review Commission, Washington, DC, 2011. • The number of SOEs listed and their importance relative to stock market capitalization also come from the OECD study, p. 16, and are based on data from 2004.
Egypt	• The number of SOEs was calculated by subtracting the number of privatized, leased, and liquidated firms from the total number of companies under government control when the privatization program started in 1991. Mohammed Omran, "Ownership Structure: Trends and Changes Following Privatisation in Egypt," PowerPoint presented at the OECD Second Meeting of Working Group 5 on Corporate Governance, Rabat, Morocco, September 2005, available at http://www.oecd.org/document/50/0,3746,en_34645207_34645863_35395890_1_1_1_1,00.html. • The number of minority-owned companies (calculated using the ownership share of state-owned holding companies after privatization) comes from "Privatization in Egypt," *Quarterly Review,* April–June 2002. Mimeo, Carana Corp., 2002, at http://www1.aucegypt.edu/src/wsite1/Pdfs/Privatization%20in%20Egypt%20-Quarterly%20Review.pdf.
India	• Most data from OECD, "State Owned Enterprises in India: Reviewing the Evidence," Paris: OECD, January 29, 2009. • The number of SOEs listed and their importance relative to stock market capitalization are based on our calculations and consider only the largest 100 companies. Data for 2009. All data from Capital IQ. • Data on state-level public enterprises from India, Department of Public Enterprises, "National Survey on State Level Public Enterprises (2006–2007)," 2007, at http://dpe.nic.in/newgl/SLPErep0607.pdf. • Minority-owned companies correspond to the number of firms in which Life Insurance Corporation of India (LIC), a majority-owned SOE, holds minority positions. Data on LIC holdings from Bloomberg, www.bloomberg.com (accessed January 10, 2012).

Table 2-A1. (continued)

Country	Source
Indonesia	• The number of SOEs and minority-owned SOEs come from Andriati Fitriningrum, "Indonesia: Experiences in Managing the State Companies," PowerPoint presentation at the OECD-Asian Roundtable on Corporate Governance of State-Owned Enterprises, Singapore, May 2006, available at http://dpe.nic.in/newgl /SLPErep0607.pdf and http://www.oecd.org/dataoecd/61/22/37339611.pdf. • Listed SOEs and their importance relative to stock market capitalization from Rajasa and Hatta, "State of Indonesian State Owned Enterprises," Sovereign Wealth Fund Institute web site, August 2011, http://www.swfinstitute.org/swf -news/state-of-indonesian-state-owned-enterprises/.
Malaysia	• Data from Khazanah Nasional, "Seventh Khazanah Annual Review," January 18, 2011, PowerPoint available at http://www.khazanah.com.my/docs /30June2011_investment_structure.pdf (accessed February 10, 2012).
Mexico	• Data for Mexico come from Sunita Kikeri and Aishetu Fatima Kolo, "Privatization: Trends and Recent Developments" (November 2005), World Bank Policy Research Working Paper no. 3765, at SSRN: http://ssrn.com /abstract=849344.
Russia	• The number of SOEs, the number of SOEs listed, and the percentage of market capitalization come from Carsten Sprenger, "State-Owned Enterprises in Russia," PowerPoint presentation at the OECD Roundtable on Corporate Governance of SOEs, Moscow, October 2008. Traded companies exclude minority-owned firms. • The number of federal and municipal SOEs and minority-owned SOEs comes from Carsten Sprenger, "State Ownership in the Russian Economy: Its Magnitude, Structure and Governance Problems," Mimeo, Higher School of Economics, Moscow, February 2010, 5–8. The number of majority- and minority-owned firms is underestimated as it only accounts for direct ownership stakes; that is, it does not take into account ownership stakes held by companies that are, in turn, controlled by the Russian government. The number of state/local firms includes only municipal companies.
South Africa	• "An analysis of the financial performance of state owned enterprises," available at www.info.gov.za/view/DownloadFileAction?id=95671 (accessed March 12, 2012).
Thailand	• SOE output to GDP estimated using net income of Thai SOEs and GDP for 2004. SOE data from Pallapa Ruangrong, "ARGC Task Force on Corporate Governance of SOEs: The Case of Thailand," PowerPoint presentation, May 20, 2005, available at www.oecd.org/dataoecd/14/28/34972513.ppt.
Turkey	• Output to GDP represents net profits to GDP. Data comes from *2007 Public Enterprises Report,* p. 19; the number of local-level SOEs comes from p. 208. Our data on the number of federal SOEs and the distinction between minority- and majority-owned companies come from the lists on pp. 12, 189–190, 201, and 248–250. For our counts, we exclude financial firms such as banks or leasing and factoring companies owned by the Savings Deposit Insurance Fund

(continued)

Table 2-A1. (continued)

Country	Source
	(known as TMSF). The number of minority-owned firms refers to those controlled by the federal government, so out of 141 federal SOEs, 67 are minority-owned. All data from Republic of Turkey, Directorate General of State Owned Enterprises, *2007 Public Enterprises Report,* August 2008, available at http://www.treasury.gov.tr/.
Vietnam	• The number of minority-owned companies represents the "Joint stock Co. with capital of State" category from Vietnam, General Statistics Office, *Statistical Yearbook of Vietnam 2010,* p. 181, available at http://www.gso.gov.vn/default_en .aspx?tabid=515&idmid=5&ItemID=11974.
	• Data on the number of SOEs and their output to GDP from the General Statistics Office of Vietnam's web page, http://www.gso.gov.vn/ (accessed February 10, 2012); and Central Institute for Economic Management (CIEM), "Viet Nam Economy: State-Owned Enterprise (SOE) Reform and Market Structure," PowerPoint presentation at the Residential Training Workshop on Structural Reform of APEC, Singapore, August 2011, available at aimp.apec .org/Documents/2011/SOM/WKSP/11_som_wksp_006.pdf (accessed June 6, 2012).

3

Views on State Capitalism

Until now, we have provided both a snapshot of state capitalism at the turn of the twenty-first century and a historical account of the evolution of state capitalism worldwide in the twentieth century. The story leaves a set of questions in relation to Leviathan's actions in the market—questions we want to explore in the rest of the book, mostly using detailed evidence from Brazil. The questions that we want to examine, however, do not come out of thin air; there is a large body of literature that has studied both the origins of state capitalism and the implications of state involvement in the economy. Since we want to take the extant theories as building blocks for the hypotheses we test throughout the book, in this chapter we revise the existing views about state capitalism and state ownership of enterprises to then examine specific hypotheses in the following chapters.

Why Does State Capitalism Exist?

Several explanations have been advanced to account for the emergence of state capitalism.[1] Some arguments take the benign view that involvement in the economy helps the government solve a host of market failures, ranging from the need to promote coordinated investments (the *industrial policy* view) to the desire to pursue societal objectives beyond pure profit maximization (the *social* view). Other arguments adopt a more negative view by emphasizing governmental failure: state intervention is driven by the rent-seeking or political motivations of politicians, rather than by the need to solve a market failure (the *political* view). Still others emphasize that state capitalism was born not out of economic necessity, but out of an ideological preference for state intervention in the economy or a nationalistic policy to keep foreign investors out. This view emphasizes that the resilience of state capitalism has been a result of complex historical processes and inherited institutional conditions that are difficult to change (the *path-dependence* view). We next discuss each of these views in detail.

Industrial Policy View

The industrial policy view sees the provision of state capital as an important tool for solving market failures that lead to suboptimal productive investment. Three major sources of market failure are commonly identified. The first has to do with capital markets. In poorly developed financial markets, investment is severely constrained (Levine 2005), especially when firms need to undertake large-scale projects with long maturity. Governments can thus act as lenders or venture capitalists in circumstances in which private sources of capital are scarce. Indeed, a large literature on development banking proposes that state-owned banks can alleviate credit constraints in the private sector and promote projects with positive net present value that might otherwise not be undertaken (Bruck 1998; Yeyati et al. 2004). Moreover, in economies with significant capital constraints, governmental funding can alleviate capital scarcity and promote entrepreneurial action to boost new or existing industries (Armendáriz de Aghion 1999; Cameron 1961; Gerschenkron 1962).

The second source of market failure involves coordination problems. Governmental involvement may alter the nature and path of productive investments, especially when a given regional context is subject to externalities across industries and activities (Krugman 1993; Marshall 1920; Rodrik 2007). Hirschman (1958) famously proposed that backward and forward linkages in the production chain need to be created to spur local development. For investors to be interested in building a steel mill, they will need to have a stable source of iron ore and coke available, and they will need to see that there will be the logistic capability to get inputs in a timely fashion and sell outputs where they are needed. Following this logic, a "big push" by the government may be necessary to promote coordinated, complementary investments (Murphy et al. 1989; Rosenstein-Rodan 1943).

Such coordination problems will be magnified in a context of shallow capital markets. Were private capital abundant, governments could simply incentivize the emergence of new sectors through differential tax regimes or temporary protection. But under conditions of capital scarcity, direct or indirect provision of state capital may be beneficial to foster complementary investments. Trebat's (1983) in-depth analysis of Brazilian industrialization concludes that SOEs were instrumental to industry-level development in a context of scarce capital markets: "Public enterprise has been considered in Brazil as a shortcut to industrialization—an expediency forced upon policymakers by the absence of a well-financed domestic private sector and by Brazil's reluctance to allow transnational corporations into certain strategic sectors" (p. 116).

Third, Rodrik (2004) argues that there are externalities emanating from "discovery costs" that are high enough to prevent the development of new products or technologies. For instance, entrepreneurs need to experiment before finding out whether a product is feasible, a process that costs money and time whether it succeeds or fails. Yet if it succeeds, other entrepreneurs in that country can replicate the entrepreneur's success. Thus, Rodrik suggests, industrial policy should be focused on helping this discovery process in two ways. First, governments should provide as much information as possible on the costs of developing new products and new industries. Second, if necessary, governments should provide financial incentives, but these should not be excessively extended; rather, they should last just enough to help the discovery process. In addition, Rodrik argues, these subsidies should not go to an industry as a whole, but instead target new activities or products. Finally, these incentives have to be phased out if the process of discovery fails (Rodrik 2007, 105–106).

Perhaps the prototypical example of industrial policy in which a government absorbed the costs of discovery of what is now a major commercial product is the creation of the Internet. The Defense Advanced Research Projects Agency (DARPA) is the American government–sponsored lab credited with the development of the Internet. According to Mazzucato (2011), since the creation of DARPA in 1958, "it became the government's business to understand which technologies provided possible applications for military purposes as well as commercial use" (p. 77). Amsden (1989, chap. 11), explains how the government of South Korea played a role in coordinating and subsidizing discovery costs in many new industries such as automobiles and shipbuilding. The Brazilian government, through its SOEs and government programs, has subsidized the discovery cost for new products such as sugarcane ethanol (with the Pro-álcool program) and cellulosic ethanol made from biomass (currently under development in the research labs of the state-owned oil company Petrobras).[2]

Yet this discussion fails to account for the many and varied organizational forms of state capitalism. Governments may boost complementary investments by creating SOEs (with majority control) in multiple sectors. However, they may also relinquish control to private firms and provide equity through development banks or state funds. In still other cases, private firms themselves may create alliances to spur joint investment and access foreign capital and resources through global production chains (Pack and Saggi 2006; Coe et al. 2008). In other words, although the industrial policy view helps explain the role of state capitalism in addressing market failure, it does not explain why in some cases Leviathan is an entrepreneur or a majority investor, while in others Leviathan acts more indirectly through noncontrolling shares or targeted lending—that is, as a minority investor.

Social View

The social view asserts that state-influenced firms pursue a "double bottom line." That is, they will have "noncommercial" objectives that go beyond profitability or even contradict the simple principle of shareholder value maximization (Ahroni 1986; Shapiro and Willig 1990; Bai and Xu 2005; Shirley 1989). In the words of Shirley and Nellis (1991, 17), "noncommercial objectives include the use of public enterprises to promote regional development, job creation, and income redistribution; they often involve taking on or maintaining redundant workers, pricing goods and services below market (sometimes even below costs), locating plants in uneconomic areas, or keeping uneconomic facilities open." Governments may also determine the cost of inputs, set wage ceilings, subsidize interest rates, or give SOEs investment funds at preferential interest rates. Thus, according to the social view, corporations controlled by the state will emerge as a way to mitigate market failure by pursuing social objectives—such as high employment or low prices—beyond the logic of pure profit or shareholder value maximization.

Similarly, this departure from profit or shareholder value maximization means that state capitalism can pursue long-term goals that may be unpalatable to private investors seeking quicker returns (Kaldor 1980). While private investors may reduce their holdings in a firm or even exit it in case of unsatisfactory short-term performance, governments are usually more patient and are willing to cope with unprofitable firms in the short term. Moreover, some projects may deliver effective results only in the long term, and a more "patient" source of capital may be necessary to withstand periods of market turbulence. Governments can therefore act as "a financial partner" committed to supporting valuable projects with relatively long timelines (McDermott 2003, 22). Musacchio and Staykov (2011), for instance, argue that a key feature of sovereign wealth funds (SWFs) is their long-term, patient orientation. These funds, the authors argue, "are also more immune to 'animal spirits' and could more easily withstand market panic." In addition, "without any short-term pressure to return a significant portion of assets in cash to their governments, SWFs could afford to stay in their investments during market troughs" (p. 7).

Therefore, in the social view, state capitalism will *deliberately* attenuate the high-powered profit-based incentives of private capitalism. A reduced emphasis on profit maximization in the public sector is aligned with the analysis of Williamson (1999) of public-versus-private governance. He introduces the concept of *probity*: the need for "loyalty and rectitude" (p. 322) in various domains such as "foreign affairs, the military, foreign intelligence, managing the money supply, and, possibly, the judiciary" (p. 321). Williamson argues that low-powered incentives in the public sector guarantee probity by avoiding excessive "resource deployment from cost savings" (p. 325). In a similar vein, Hart et al. (1997) stress that public organization will be desirable when profit maximization causes an excessive emphasis on cost reduction at the expense of "quality" (for example, low-cost, for-profit private schools with little emphasis on whether students are getting a good education or not). Although Williamson (1999) and Hart et al. (1997) do not focus on the state ownership of corporations, their propositions are consistent with the social view. In this sense, state capitalism may emerge as a way to "tame" the profit-based, short-term motivations of markets.

Like the industrial policy view, however, the social view does not explicitly account for the varieties of state capitalism we find across countries. Arguably, governments will more easily prompt managers to pursue social goals if they have majority control—that is, if they can veto decisions that conflict with their desired objective to, say, avoid excessive unemployment or high prices. However, it is also possible that, through minority stakes, governments can have some degree of influence. One example is the long-term orientation of SWFs, discussed earlier. Governments may also try to induce other owners of partially privatized firms to follow social objectives; those owners may acquiesce to governmental interference as a way to preserve their interests in the firm or to receive future benefits, such as the continued provision of state capital. We will elaborate further on this issue in the following section.

Political View

While the industrial policy and social views see merit in certain types of governmental influence, the political view underscores the inefficiencies associated with *governmental failure* (Chong and López-de-Silanes 2005; La Porta and López-de-Silanes 1999; Shleifer 1998; Shleifer and Vishny 1994). Thus, Shleifer and Vishny (1998, 10) contend, "the key problem of state firms is government interference in their activities to direct them to pursue political rather than economic goals." Politicians and politically connected capitalists may extend their "grabbing hand" to divert public resources for their own benefit, with negative consequences for corporate performance. Political interference in SOEs can result in excessive employment or the selection of employees on the basis of political connections instead of merit or background; such employees will typically lack the high-powered incentive contracts commonly found in private corporations (such as bonuses or stock options). SOEs that suffer from too much political intervention may therefore make poor choices in product mix and location. They may fail to cut costs and streamline their operations in periods of crisis, and they may pursue inefficient, unprofitable investments in response to government pressure.

This problem is aggravated by the so-called *soft budget constraint* of state corporations (Kornai 1979; Lin and Tan 1999). With abundant and "patient" capital from the state, bureaucrats will be more likely to approve bad investments and use public funds to cover existing losses or rescue failed projects. Lacking the pressure of market investors demanding profitability, SOEs can be used as sources of cheap capital to meet the political objectives of governments and politicians. The political view diverges from the social view in regarding the low-powered market incentives of public governance as a critical downside. The resulting inefficiencies will be more acute depending on the extent to which political meddling distorts corporate decision making.

Although political interference is arguably more intense in SOEs with majority state control, the political view also explains certain types of interference that may occur when Leviathan is a minority investor. Public-private connections may be conduits of *cronyism*, a mechanism through which "those close to the political authorities who make and enforce policies receive favors that have large economic value" (Haber 2002, xii). In the political view, governments provide capital to firms not to channel funds to socially efficient uses, but rather to maximize their personal objectives or engage in crony deals with rent-seeking, politically connected industrialists (e.g., Faccio 2006; Krueger 1990; Kang 2002).

Recent literature has found empirical evidence consistent with the hypothesis that financing can be influenced by political factors such as election cycles and campaign donations (e.g., Claessens et al. 2008; Dinç 2005; Sapienza 2004). The implication is that governments provide capital to firms in return for political support—either through campaign donations to the government's political coalition or investment decisions that benefit politicians and their constituencies. Firms may request subsidized credit or cheap (minority) equity even in cases where projects could be funded and launched in a more normal fashion, using private sources of capital. The potential for cronyism also arises in the creation of "national champions" (Falck et al. 2011). That is, politicians and officials explicitly pick certain private firms to receive funds, either debt or equity, as a way to propel them to consolidate their sectors and grow. On the one hand, the creation of national champions is consistent with the more benign industrial policy view asserting that state capital can solve market failures thwarting industrial development. On the other hand, some argue, the criteria governments use to select particular firms over others are not clear and have sometimes been linked to political objectives (Ades and Di Tella 1997). National champions may therefore be another manifestation of governments' desire to influence the private sector to pay political dividends (Bremmer 2010).

Consistent with the political view and with our earlier discussion of partially privatized firms, several authors submit that some governmental influence remains even after firms are controlled by private investors. Bortolotti and Faccio (2009) find that, after 2000, governments of OECD countries kept some degree of control in 62.4 percent of their privatized companies.

Examining privatization events in transition economies, Pistor and Turke-witz (1996) observe that while private companies with state ownership ties benefit from "state-granted insurance" (p. 217), "the presence of the state as an owner has given it some leverage in influencing certain decisions, such as energy prices or the closure of factories in regions with high employment" (p. 231). Calomiris et al. (2010) find that when Chinese firms are privatized, those with close ties to the government perform better than their more isolated counterparts. Bennedsen (2000) offers a game-theoretic model in which one of the equilibria involves private capitalists acquiescing to state directives (for example, avoiding excessive layoffs) in return for subsidies. The implications of post-privatization business-government ties are also examined by Boycko et al. (1996) and Kaufmann and Siegelbaum (1996).

Therefore, while political interference may explain the desire to create SOEs, it also helps explain the emergence of hybrid (minority) state capitalism. Outright political influence through governmental fiat power is replaced by a more indirect and nuanced influence, often through crony ties. In the words of Shleifer and Vishny (1994, 998), "there is no magic line that separates firms from politicians once they are privatized."[3]

Path-Dependence View

The path-dependence view explains both the emergence of and variation in state capitalism as a result of idiosyncratic, country-level institutional features and historical processes. At a fundamental level, path-dependent processes occur because of complex interactions among political and economic actors who try to preserve their interests in the face of imminent change (North 1990). This view is based on three ideas. First, the rise of state capitalism in the twentieth century was linked to ideology and political institutions inherited from the past. Second, the defining event in the recent evolution of state capitalism was the privatization movement of the last few decades of the twentieth century (Megginson 2005; Bortolotti et al. 2004). Third, idiosyncratic, country-level institutional features determined how thorough the process of privatization was in each country (Stark 1994, 1996).

Stark's (1996, 1994) examination of market transition in East European countries offers an example of uneven and incomplete privatization. Compiling data from newly privatized firms in Hungary, Stark (1996) reveals that they remained partially owned by state actors (Hungary's State Property Agency and the State Holding Corporation) and that these actors also participated in numerous top Hungarian firms jointly with private and foreign owners. He notes that "ironically, the agencies responsible for privatization are acting as agents of *étatization*" (p. 1001). He refers to this process as a *recombination* of public and private resources, drawing on existing routines, practices, and social ties in the economy. Given that these "local" features tend to be country-specific, this view suggests not only that ownership relations will be heterogeneous across countries, but also that the importance of the state will vary greatly according to inherited conditions (e.g., Bebchuk and Roe 1999). "A new social order," writes Stark (1994, 65), "cannot be created by dictation—at least not where citizen themselves want a voice in determining the new institutions."

A related argument is that the feasibility of privatization will depend on local ideology and attitudes toward public or private ownership (Durant and Legge Jr. 2002; Hirschman 1982) and that governments will try to take those considerations into account when designing reform policies. Anticipating negative public reactions associated with privatization programs, governments may involve domestic owners and state agencies in the execution of those programs, while at the same time infusing state capital into the newly privatized companies as a way to signal to the public that the government remains present in the economy (Kuczynski 1999). Negative public reactions against privatization can be especially acute when SOEs are sold to large capitalists and foreign owners. For instance, in line with Stark's (1996) findings, the Brazilian Development Bank (BNDES) not only coordinated the whole privatization program, but also kept minority stakes in several companies (Lazzarini 2011; Inoue et al. 2013). De Paula et al. (2002, 482) argue that, in Brazil, mixed consortia involving foreign, private, and state actors helped to "dilute political criticisms that often accompany the transfer of privatized assets to foreign entities."

Bortolotti et al. (2004) also emphasize heterogeneity in the extent to which governments privatized SOEs, measured as total privatization revenues to GDP for 1977–1999. They find that privatization varied across countries according to three factors. First, the government's fiscal situation when the privatization program started determined the urgency to privatize SOEs. Second, the level of financial market development (measured as market capitalization to GDP and the stock market turnover ratio) also determined the feasibility of mass privatization programs as it facilitated share issue privatizations. Third, these authors find that authoritarian governments privatized less.[4] Thus, political

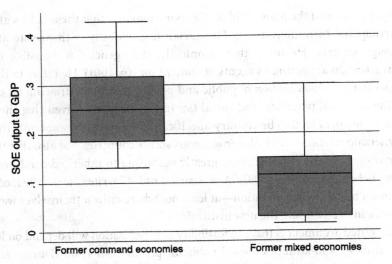

Figure 3.1. SOE output to GDP c. 2010 in former command and mixed economies

Source: Data from Table 2.1 (Chapter 2) matched with data from the appendix of World Bank (1996). Former command economies include China, Czech Republic, Finland, India, Poland, Russia, Slovak Republic, and Vietnam. Former mixed economies include Belgium, Brazil, Denmark, France, Germany, Greece, Indonesia, Italy, Mexico, the Netherlands, New Zealand, Singapore, Sweden, Thailand, and Turkey. We include Finland among command economies simply because of the large percentage of SOE output to GDP it had before 1989.

Note: The boxplot excludes outside values.

regimes—which tend to be very resilient—also seem to determine the extent of governmental ownership. In their study, however, it is not clear if governments in democratic countries actually prefer privatization or if they are driven to privatize because in such regimes there is more temptation to use SOEs for patronage purposes, for example, by appointing members of the ruling coalition to CEO or board positions in state-owned firms.

Figure 3.1 shows that state capitalism does have strong path-dependence, even after decades of privatization. In this figure, we plot the percentage of SOE output to GDP for a group of countries that were classified as mixed economies in 1980 (such as Germany, France, and Brazil) and economies that were considered command economies (such as China, the Czech Republic, and Russia). It is clear that in more recent years, SOEs are still more important in former command economies.

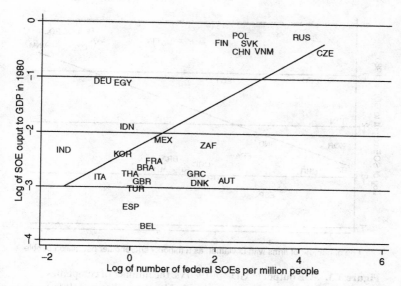

Figure 3.2. SOE output to GDP in 1980 vs. the number of federal SOEs per million people (c. 2010)

Source: Data from Table 2.1 (Chapter 2) matched with data from the appendix of World Bank (1996). Former command economies include China, Czech Republic, Finland, India, Poland, Russia, Slovak Republic, and Vietnam. Former mixed economies include Belgium, Brazil, Denmark, France, Germany, Greece, Indonesia, Italy, Mexico, the Netherlands, New Zealand, Singapore, Sweden, Thailand, and Turkey. We include Finland among command economies simply because of the large percentage of SOE output to GDP it had before 1989.

Furthermore, countries in which the state had a larger presence in the economy in 1980 tend to have governments with more SOEs in general and more minority investments in corporations in later years. Figures 3.2 and 3.3 depict these relationships in simple scatter plots. In Figure 3.2 we show a scatter plot of SOE output to GDP in 1980 and the number of SOEs controlled by the federal government circa 2010. It is clear that there is a positive relation showing strong path-dependence.

There is also strong path-dependence when it comes to the number of companies in which the government has minority ownership and the level of SOE output to GDP in 1980. Figure 3.3 shows that this correlation is high and that the countries in which Leviathan acts more as minority shareholder are also former command economies, such as Russia and a variety of Eastern European countries.

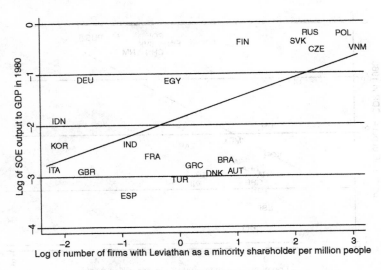

Figure 3.3. SOE output to GDP in 1980 vs. the number of companies with the government as a minority shareholder per million people (c. 2010)

Source: Data from Table 2.1 (Chapter 2) matched with data from the appendix of World Bank (1996). Former command economies include China, Czech Republic, Finland, India, Poland, Russia, Slovak Republic, and Vietnam. Former mixed economies include Belgium, Brazil, Denmark, France, Germany, Greece, Indonesia, Italy, Mexico, the Netherlands, New Zealand, Singapore, Sweden, Thailand, and Turkey. We include Finland among command economies simply because of the large percentage of SOE output to GDP it had before 1989.

In sum, the path-dependence view offers new insights on the prevalence of Leviathan as a majority investor and, perhaps more importantly, on the emergence of the hybrid model of state capitalism with Leviathan as a minority investor. In the path-dependence view, hybrid state capitalism will naturally result from existing rules, ties, and ideologies that existed before reform programs. Even with the transfer of assets to private owners, the state can maintain a presence in the economy as a way to preserve previous connections with the productive sector or to minimize public opposition toward reforms. Viewed from a different angle, a *lower* incidence of state capitalism may also be explained by political parties taking a favorable ideological position toward more liberal markets, as in Mexico and Chile (see, e.g., Bremmer 2010, 122).

In Table 3.1, we summarize these alternative explanations of why state capitalism exists in its current shape and form.

Table 3.1. Summary of the hypotheses that explain why state capitalism exists

Industrial policy view	Social view	Path-dependence view	Political view
a) Capital market failure: Government funds projects that otherwise would go unfunded	a) Mix of commercial and noncommercial objectives (e.g., need to keep the price of utilities low); cases where companies should not focus on cost reduction by lowering quality or coverage of services (e.g., potable water, roads / rail lines to small towns)	Idiosyncratic or historical country-specific factors that lead to pervasive state presence in the economy	a) Soft-budget constraint: political need to bail out underperforming firms
b) Coordination problems: externalities across industries cannot be realized because of a collective-action problem or lack of scale of small private producers (social rate of return is larger than individual company's rate of return on a project; e.g., infrastructure or vertically linked chains)	b) Long-term view for investments vs. private sector's short-term view		b) The "grabbing hand" hypothesis: officials create SOEs to use them for personal purposes
c) Discovery costs: private entrepreneurship is risky and yields downstream positive externalities	c) Williamson's *probity* (need for loyalty and rectitude in complex public services)		c) Political intervention: for political reasons, SOEs are led to make inefficient investment decisions
			d) Government desire to have national champions (SOEs or private companies with public support)
			e) Cronyism: an elite coalition supports the creation of state-owned firms for private gain (e.g., improved access to inputs or cheap funding)

Varieties of State Capitalism: Features and Performance Implications

We now consolidate the previous hypotheses into a comparative framework describing key attributes of each variety of state capitalism and its implications for firm performance and for social welfare. For the sake of comparison, we also consider features of private ownership in a hypothetical liberal market with minimum state intervention. As indicated in Table 3.2, we identify four general traits that should greatly differ across modes: the extent to which each model creates *agency problems* (i.e., managers whose goals are misaligned with firm-level objectives); the model's effect on the state's capacity to *coordinate and enforce societal objectives* in the economy; the observed level of *cronyism* defined by the extent to which political connections yield government favors to private companies; and the *rigidity of allocations* in the economy, indicated by the degree to which new entrepreneurial firms enter the system while old inefficient firms exit. We next describe these traits in more detail.

Agency Problems

Agency considerations have mainly been used to explain the empirical finding that SOEs with majority state control usually underperform private companies. In a nutshell, this view states that CEOs of SOEs are not motivated to exert effort and improve performance and/or are not monitored well by the board of directors, the regulatory agency of the industry, or the ministry in charge of overseeing the specific firm (e.g., Boardman and Vining 1989; Chong and López-de-Silanes 2005; Kikeri et al. 1992; La Porta and López-de-Silanes 1999; Yiu et al. 2005; Megginson and Netter 2001; Dharwadkar et al. 2000). The problem of delegating decisions to agents whose objectives may not be aligned with those of the principals has long been discussed by agency theorists (Jensen and Meckling 1976). The remedies for principal-agent misalignment normally involve performance-contingent incentive contracts for managers, direct monitoring by principals, or a combination of both. Those remedies, according to this view, are far more difficult to implement in SOEs than in privately owned firms.[5] Thus, incentive contracts usually work best when there are objective, readily observable

Table 3.2. The models of state capitalism in comparative perspective

	Leviathan as an entrepreneur (owner/manager)	Leviathan as a majority investor	Leviathan as a minority investor	Private ownership / minimum state intervention
Agency problems within firms	HIGH	MODERATE to HIGH[a]	MODERATE[a]	MODERATE to LOW[a]
State capacity to coordinate the economy and attain social goals	HIGH	MODERATE to HIGH	MODERATE	LOW
Potential for (public-private) cronyism	LOW	MODERATE	HIGH	LOW
Use of SOEs for patronage	HIGH	MODERATE to LOW	LOW	LOW
Ease of entry and exit	LOW	LOW to MODERATE	MODERATE	HIGH

a. The extent to which agency problems will be avoided will depend not only on the corporate governance design for firms, but on the level of public enforcement (laws, regulatory agencies, etc.) and private enforcement (stock exchanges, underwriters, etc.) of protections for minority investors (La Porta et al. 2006). See Chapters 7 and 9 performance metrics such as profits or share price (Holmstrom and Milgrom 1991). Furthermore, as noted earlier, Williamson (1999) submits that low-powered incentives for managers are a *defining* feature of state organization, a feature that will guarantee probity; that is to say, managers should not be incentivized to increase profits at the expense of more general social objectives.

Monitoring in public bureaucracies is also challenging (Alchian 1965; De Alessi 1980). Many activities in the public sector involve multiple principals dispersed across various domains (Dixit 2002; Moe 1984). By the same token, SOE managers themselves may not know who the relevant principal is or whom they should be accountable to. Is it the government, a ministry, a state-owned holding company, the population in general? Employees of SOEs often feel that they themselves are the principal.[6]

Related to this point, as suggested by the social view, governments often include social objectives in the assessment of SOEs, which can create a confusing set of goals for managers (Bai and Xu 2005). Should managers maximize profits, minimize salaries, or maximize employment? For instance, if the objective of an SOE is to maximize social welfare, it may not be clear for CEOs who the relevant stakeholder is, as it may be society as a whole, the citizens of a town in which the company operates, or the company's own workers. As we discussed in Chapter 2, regulators and the World Bank during the 1980s created scorecards to evaluate the performance of SOEs on a variety of social and financial goals, but their measurement was complicated, and, without a good system of incentives and monitoring, these scorecards stopped being used (Shirley and Nellis 1991; Gómez-Ibañez 2007).

State organizations, in the most stylized view of SOEs, also lack a well-defined group of monitors, such as shareholders actively participating in corporate boards. In fact, governments may appoint politicians or politically connected actors to "monitor" SOEs, thereby leading to the fundamental question of "who monitors the monitors" or "who guards the guardians" (Cabral and Lazzarini 2010; Hurwicz 2008). Unlike shareholders of private firms, those appointed board members do not have their own wealth at stake when executing their monitoring duties. In addition, managers in SOEs do not face the threat of a hostile takeover when they underperform relative to their peers and do not face the risk of bankruptcy, because they know the government will recapitalize or bail out the company if it becomes insolvent (Shleifer 1998; Vickers and Yarrow 1988).

What then can be said about the hybrid model in which Leviathan is a *minority* investor in private firms? In that hybrid model, the state does not directly control the firms, so we should generally expect that the aforementioned agency problems will be less intense than they are in SOEs. Even so, we argue that there can be room for *residual interference* in companies in which the government is apparently only a minority shareholder, because governments can participate in coalitions with other non-state actors in order to appoint politically connected managers and to influence decisions based on considerations other than efficiency. We discuss this issue in depth in Chapter 9.

Overall, agency problems in the hybrid, minority Leviathan model should be somewhere between the polar models of full state control and private ownership. Some studies of privatization and partially privatized firms confirm that, in some performance dimensions, they fare better than state-controlled firms, but not necessarily better than private companies (Boardman and Vining 1989; Majumdar 1998; Gupta 2005). In Chapter 8, however, we discuss some circumstances in which the minority Leviathan model may outperform private ownership if minority state capital helps revamp firm-level investment and if residual governmental interference is curtailed.

State Capacity to Coordinate the Economy and Attain Social Goals

The industrial policy and social views emphasize that state ownership can help solve market failure and attain social objectives beyond pure profit maximization. According to these views, the overall desire to *coordinate* economic development will therefore mandate some form of "entrepreneurial" governmental action. Arguably, SOEs with full state control can be vehicles to foster long-term fixed investments and establish myriad industrial "linkages" *by fiat*. Indeed, as we noted before, many authors argue that the late industrialization of countries in Latin America and South Asia involved some form of direct governmental action through SOEs (Di John 2009; Trebat 1983; R. Wade 1990; Jones and Sakong 1980).

Yet the political view argues that political intervention (or the fact that SOEs have a double bottom line) and soft budget constraints misalign the incentives of managers of SOEs or of protected national champions. In this book, we examine two aspects of the government's desire to coordinate the actions of firms—both state-owned and privatized—to achieve specific social goals. First, we look at how, in the Leviathan as an entrepreneur model, governments react to external shocks using SOEs to reduce unemployment. Second, we investigate whether there are conditions under which Leviathan can tie its hands and not succumb to the temptation to influence companies (state-controlled or privatized) in order to attain social or political goals even at the expense of other private shareholders.

As for the hybrid model of Leviathan as a minority investor, the government's capacity to implement such coordination will depend on residual interference in firms in which the state has minority stakes. When governments invest in or lend to multiple private firms without any concerted action with majority shareholders, their ability to influence decisions will not be much greater than it would be in the context of privately owned autonomous firms focused on profit maximization. However, as noted before, governments may form coalitions with other owners and therefore influence decision making indirectly. The case of Vale, the largest mining company in Brazil and the third-largest in the world, is illustrative (see Chapter 9). Mining is an industry in which the temptation of political intervention is high, and we would not expect Vale, as a privatized company, to be the victim of any government intervention. Yet we show how states can use their minority equity positions to exert pressure and indirectly control such partially privatized firms.

This risk notwithstanding, because such coalitions are not always possible, the model of Leviathan as a minority shareholder should grant governments only a moderate to low ability to intervene, compared to the model in which SOEs are pervasive. For instance, in Chapter 7 we look at corporate governance in large national oil companies, a domain in which the temptation of political intervention is high and in which governments usually have control of the company. Yet in some cases governments sell minority equity stakes to private investors and adhere to superior governance standards through public listing. We investigate whether, in those cases, corporate governance reforms successfully tie the hands of the sovereign.

Level of (Public-Private) Cronyism

We define cronyism as a mechanism by which politically connected private actors receive favors from the state. In the stereotypical model of Leviathan as an entrepreneur, the pervasiveness of state-controlled SOEs implies that there will be fewer private actors who can directly benefit from state initiatives. Although state bureaucrats and their cronies can establish mutual ties for their own benefit, most allocations will be influenced by and within the state through state bureaus and state-controlled corporations. China is an example, with several state-owned firms whose managers are closely tied to the government and to the Communist Party (Lin and Milhaupt 2011).

In contrast, in the models of Leviathan as a majority and minority investor there will be more opportunities for private firms to benefit from government favors. In the Leviathan as a majority investor model, private firms can benefit from procurement policies that benefit certain kinds of national firms. This favoritism can be disguised as industrial policy because it can indeed promote the development of a network of local firms; yet it is not clear if, in the long run, this policy alone leads to competitive global players (Porter 1990, 673). As Amsden (1989) and Rodrik (2007) exemplify, domestic procurement policies worked in South Korea only because they were temporary and usually included clear performance targets for the beneficiary suppliers.

Finally, in the Leviathan as a minority investor model, the presence of several private controlling owners whose firms largely draw from state capital magnifies the opportunities for cronyism. Consider, for instance, the case of equity investments or subsidized loans by development banks. When banks provide massive amounts of capital to industry, and subsidized interest rates are much lower than market rates, the benefit firms get from investing in political connections to attract cheap capital increase substantially.

Therefore, the more extensive and permeable public-private interface that prevails when Leviathan is a majority and minority investor suggests that there will be more cronyism in these hybrid modes. In the polar model where the state is a full owner of a variety of industrial firms and banks, most allocations actually flow within the state apparatus. So, in this case, there is reduced private capture or cronyism (even though, as we discuss below, there might be patronage).

In the final part of this book, we examine a series of hypotheses related to cronyism in the allocation of subsidized credit through development banks. Based on the political view, we investigate whether the allocation of BNDES subsidized loans are associated with firm-level donations to the campaigns of winning political candidates. In contrast, the industrial policy view suggests that firms borrow because they want to deploy the capital in a profitable project. In line with previous research (Claessens et al. 2008; Carvalho 2010), we find little evidence of the latter, but strong evidence that campaign donations are correlated with the amount of loans firms get from the government.

Use of SOEs for Patronage

Another dimension in which we think there are significant differences across the varieties of state capitalism is the extent to which governments can use SOEs for patronage purposes. By patronage, we mean not only favoring voters or companies, but, more specifically, using the appointment of SOE employees to benefit members of the ruling coalition. We expect the highest use of public companies for patronage in the Leviathan as an entrepreneur model, in which governments are free to appoint SOE officials. In the Leviathan as a majority investor model, states have less opportunity to appoint not only executives, but also board members and employees. The capacity to make such appointments will clearly depend on the separation between government and company; the more corporate governance and institutions permit a separation between Leviathan and SOEs, the less the SOEs will be used for patronage. That is why in the Leviathan as a minority investor model and in the model of private enterprise with minimal government intervention we see little use of firms for patronage.

Flexibility of Allocations (Ease of Entry and Exit)

Private ownership with minimal state interference is often associated with an inherent ability to churn out new entrepreneurial firms while at the same time avoiding the persistence of unproductive incumbents (Baumol et al. 2007; Bremmer 2010; Ahroni 1986). A key aspect of this model, in its stereotypical form, is low entry and exit barriers, which facilitate flexible adjustment to changing conditions such as technological disruptions or the emergence of more competitive foreign players. For instance, Messick (1996) clearly shows that countries with lower state intervention (e.g., lower SOE output to GDP or lower government consumption to GDP) tend to have lower barriers to entry.

Flexible adjustments and easy entry are more difficult to maintain under state capitalism. Governments may want to shield domestic firms and SOEs from foreign competition or to build national champions with the use of subsidized credit, import tariffs, preferential procurement policies, and explicit barriers to entry. As suggested by the path-dependence view, such interventions are likely have persistent effects. These effects can be positive if the supported firms had no other way to finance projects or had projects with extremely high social impact that the market would not finance. However, they could also have negative effects if a government supports firms that do not need or deserve any support (or when the opportunity cost of the funds used to prop up firms is too high).

Furthermore, given that direct state involvement is more pervasive in the Leviathan as a majority investor model, flexible adjustments will be easier in the Leviathan as minority investor model, even though the existence of political connections will create entry and exit barriers higher than those in the pure private ownership model. For instance, cronyism has been offered as an explanation for the bailout of large private groups in East Asia after the 1997 crisis (Kang 2002).

Issues Examined in the Rest of the Book

The next two parts of the book use detailed empirical evidence to test some of the hypotheses derived from the various views outlined in this chapter using detailed data of the evolution of state capitalism in Brazil. We divide the rest of the book into those two sections to separate clearly the tests that are related to Leviathan as an entrepreneur and majority investor and those that relate to Leviathan as a minority investor.

Among the issues examined in the remainder of the book are the following. For the Leviathan as a majority investor model, most of the literature on SOEs has focused on showing how SOEs have underperformed private companies, and, in a way, the assumption is that the gap in performance has always been wide. Drawing from the social and political views, we study how the behavior of SOEs differs during times of crisis and during the Brazilian democratic transition by looking at the turnover of CEOs and employees in public and private firms in the 1980s.

Moreover, rather than focus on whether performance increases right after privatization, we examine the corporate governance arrangements in the new SOEs in which the government is only a majority investor. This point is important because some countries are reluctant to privatize SOEs in certain "strategic" sectors. In those conditions, the Leviathan as a majority investor model may be the only option governments have to improve governance in these firms, and the goal of our study is to learn how to make it work. Drawing from the social and political views, we examine how checks and balances can be created to avoid governmental interference to pursue social or political goals.

There is also a long list of issues concerning the Leviathan as a minority investor model. Contrasting the industrial policy and political views, we try to answer several questions. For instance, when do government investments in minority equity positions improve firm performance or allow firms to invest in projects they would not otherwise pursue? Are Leviathan's minority equity investments more effective when financial markets are more developed? Are they more effective when corporate governance regulation is stricter? Which of the many channels of minority investment is more appropriate (e.g., development banks, pension funds, sovereign wealth funds, and so on)? Which conditions can reduce the potential of minority allocations to promote cronyism? What is the best way to manage partially privatized firms?

PART II

Leviathan as an Entrepreneur and Majority Investor

4

The Evolution of State Capitalism in Brazil

We now begin our study of state capitalism using the case of Brazil by studying the rise of Leviathan as an entrepreneur in this country and its transformation after 1990. This chapter first describes the concerted effort of the Brazilian government to coordinate resources to develop industries such as steel, telecommunications, and utilities. Then it shows how the SOEs in Brazil acted without autonomy, but not too much oversight, and expanded into multiple industries. This expansion eventually led to a major financial crisis when it became clear that SOEs were also part of the problem.

The chapter then narrates the transformation of Brazil after 1990, when a major program of privatization began. We end the chapter describing in detail the kind of corporate governance changes experienced by the remaining SOEs in Brazil.

The Early History of State Capitalism in Brazil

From the second half of the nineteenth century to about 1930 we have a first, rudimentary stage of state capitalism in Brazil. In this stage we find "Leviathan as an insurer against failure," as the Brazilian government provided subsidies to support specific industries and sometimes acted as residual owner. It provided incentives to prop up companies and sometimes guaranteed that a company would survive even if it went bankrupt under its original management. In industries such as banking, utilities, shipping, ports, and railways, governments allowed the operation of private companies, but selected certain national and foreign firms to receive such government guarantees or protection against failure.

For example, between the 1880s (if not earlier) and 1930, the Brazilian government gave subsidies to private shipping companies that carried on coastal trade within Brazil. Some of these propped-up firms (early national champions) ended up under state ownership in the long run when, after they encountered financial difficulties, the government injected capital and eventually became the controlling shareholder. The case of Lloyd Brasileiro illustrates this pattern. In 1890, the government merged four shipping lines that were receiving subsidies into Lloyd Brasileiro and protected it from foreign competition by restricting the number of firms that could receive subsidies and carry on internal trade. Even so, the company had to be bailed out in 1913 and fell under government control. In 1917, it was enlarged when the government gave it German ships expropriated during World War I. By 1937, Lloyd became an *autarquia*—a self-regulated and self-managed government body—and in 1966 it became an SOE (SEST 1985–1994; Baer et al. 1973; Topik 1987).

Railways followed a similar pattern. The government began giving out concessions in the 1850s, offering a minimum dividend of 5 percent. Apparently, this was not enough to lure railway entrepreneurs to Brazil, so state governments added a 2 percent guaranteed dividend. One of the first railway lines, running from the coast of the state of Rio de Janeiro to the mountains, went bankrupt, and the government took it over. Over time, partly owing to government support, it became the second-largest railway in the country.

The increase in government ownership of railways in the first half of the twentieth century was rapid, but did not happen overnight. Figure 4.1 shows that the government controlled just over 20 percent of the kilometers of railway in operation in 1900, but ended up with almost 100 percent by 1953. Most of the transfers of lines from the private to the public sector were either direct sales or the result of nationalizations built into the concession contracts. These concession contracts usually gave residual rights to the government and guaranteed transfer of ownership if the concessionaire did not meet its contractual obligations (e.g., if the firm did not build the promised rail lines or if it went bankrupt). For example, in 1904, one of the largest railway companies in Brazil (the Companhia de Estradas de Ferro Sorocabana e Ituana) went bankrupt, and the federal government became its owner. In 1905, the federal government sold it to the government of the state of São Paulo, which then leased it to Percival Farquhar, an American entrepreneur who was developing a railway trust by borrowing abroad and

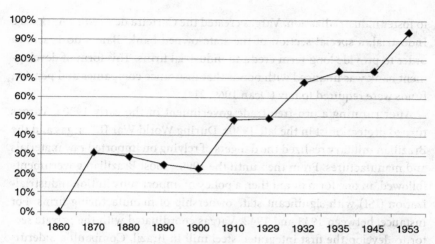

Figure 4.1. Percentage of railway miles under government ownership in Brazil, 1860–1953

Source: Created by the authors using data from Bogart (2009), Bureau of Railway Economics (1935), and Baer et al. (1973).

purchasing and leasing lines in Brazil. With the liquidity crunch of World War I, Farquhar's holding company (the Brazil Railway Company) went bankrupt, and the rail line returned to the state of São Paulo. Other lines operated by Farquhar went bankrupt and returned to federal control. After that, government ownership increased gradually, as lines all around the country went bankrupt and the state became a residual owner.[1]

In 1934, the government of Getúlio Vargas, a nationalist military president, passed the first Water Code, bestowing the ownership of waterways and waterfalls on the nation and allowing the government to regulate electricity rates. After that, the Brazilian government capped the maximum return on investment for private electricity generators and distributors at 10 percent. Some authors argue that this measure led private companies to eventually sell their assets to the government in the 1950s, 1960s, and 1970s (Centro de Memória da Eletricidade 2000; Baer et al. 1973).

In 1937, President Vargas's economic policy started to take a radical turn. First, he plotted a supposed coup against himself, in response to which he eliminated checks and balances by dismissing Congress and packing the Supreme Court with loyalist judges. In the same year, as an additional step to foster industrialization, Vargas created the Carteira de Crédito Agrícola e Industrial, a special section of the state-owned bank, Banco do Brasil, in order to provide long-term credit to industrial firms. This form of development bank was financed with bonds that insurance companies and pension funds were required to buy (Dean 1969, 214).

After running a pro-free-trade government in the early 1930s, Vargas turned protectionist in the late 1930s. During World War II, Vargas and the Brazilian military realized the dangers of relying on imported raw materials and manufactures. From then until the 1990s, most Brazilian governments followed, in one form or another, a policy of import substitution industrialization (ISI) with significant state ownership of manufacturing firms. For instance, between 1938 and 1942, Vargas coordinated with the private sector to develop the first integrated steel mill in Brazil, Companhia Siderúrgica Nacional (CSN), getting support and some funding from the United States. Because of scant private participation in the subscription of capital for the CSN, the Brazilian Treasury ended up with the bulk of voting shares, while pension funds bought the majority of the preferred (nonvoting) shares (Dean 1969; Musacchio 2009, 249; Wirth 1970).

Leviathan as an Entrepreneur in Brazil

Under President Vargas, the Brazilian state openly became an entrepreneur and ventured into a variety of sectors as a founder of major enterprises. The government had to step in partly because it wanted to promote ISI, but also because private stock and debt markets were in crisis and private investors were not willing to take the risks associated with the creation of new industrial companies in an environment of two-digit inflation (Musacchio 2009).

Among the new SOEs Vargas created were CSN, established in 1941; the mining company Companhia Vale do Rio Doce (CVRD), created in 1942; the Fábrica Nacional de Motores (FNM), founded in 1943; the soda ash producer Companhia Nacional de Álcalis, established in 1943; the electricity company Companhia Hidroelétrica do São Francisco (Chesf), projected in 1945 and opened in 1948; and the specialty steel products firms Companhia de Ferro e Aços de Vitória (Cofavi), established in 1942, and Companhia de Aços Especiais Itabira (Acesita), opened in 1944 (SEST 1981–1985). Many of these firms grew to be among the largest Brazilian industrial companies in the 1970s, when state capitalism peaked in Brazil.

In the 1950s, the Brazilian government had a second wave of creating important firms, in particular Petrobras, the flagship state-owned national oil company. The creation of Petrobras came after almost two decades of political debate about the model Brazil should follow for its oil industry. In the 1940s, the demand for oil and refined products increased rapidly, and the government realized it needed to have a plan for the industry. The question was both who would control the rights to exploit oil and who would control the rights to import, refine, and distribute oil and oil products. In the end, the government created Petrobras in 1953, granting it a monopoly on the exploration, extraction, refining, and transportation of crude oil and refined products (Law 2,004 of October 1953).[2]

Part of the financial support for the creation of new SOEs came from a new development bank created in 1952. In that year, a series of joint studies by the governments of Brazil and the United States concerned with the expansion of Brazil's infrastructure led to the creation of the Brazilian National Bank of Economic Development (BNDE in Portuguese, later changed to BNDES when "social development" was added to its mission in 1982). The objective of BNDE was to provide long-term credit for energy and transportation investments.

BNDE operated as a giant holding company for the nascent steel industry in the 1960s and 1970s, when it controlled some of the largest firms. The typical progression involved the financing of a minority portion of a company, and subsequently, through equity injections or through convertible debt, BNDE would become the majority shareholder. In 1956, BNDE and the government of the state of São Paulo financed the creation of a steel mill, Companhia Siderúrgica Paulista (Cosipa). Although BNDE began as a minority shareholder, subsequent capital injections made it the majority shareholder from 1968 until 1974, when the military government created Siderbras, a state-owned holding company, to play that role. A similar story took place with USIMINAS, another steel mill, partly financed by the government of Minas Gerais. This firm was controlled at first by a consortium of Japanese firms, but BNDE became the controlling shareholder through subsequent equity purchases in the late 1960s (BNDES 2002b; Schneider 1991; Baer 1969).

Over the following decade, BNDE assumed other roles, including financing machinery purchases in foreign currency, serving as guarantor in credit operations abroad, and lending directly to Brazilian companies. In the 1970s, BNDES began to invest directly in the equity of Brazilian companies. In 1982, it created BNDESPAR ("BNDES Participations") to manage those holdings (BNDES 2003).

In Chapter 10, we will study in detail the evolution of BNDES's programs and its changes in strategic focus since the 1950s. Most importantly, it changed from a bank focused on developing infrastructure to a bank aimed at aiding industrial companies, sometimes when they were in trouble. While the bank's initial strategy was focused on giving out loans at subsidized rates, after the 1980s it began investing in minority equity positions in private companies. Over time, the returns from such investments cross-subsidized the less profitable loan disbursements by the bank.

The Peak of State Capitalism and State Influence

The 1970s saw the zenith of state capitalism in Brazil. Contrary to the view of historians and sociologists who see the consolidation of state intervention under the government of Getúlio Vargas in the 1940s and early 1950s (Draibe 1985), the true reinforcement took place much later. It was under the military government (1964–1985)—in particular, the administration of Ernesto Geisel, a general who had been CEO of Petrobras—that Brazil had its largest expansion in the number of SOEs. In Figure 4.2, we show the number of SOEs created by year, and it is clear that the spurt takes place in the 1970s. (See Appendix 4.1 for a list of Brazilian SOEs according to their year of creation.)

The military government had an active industrial policy and created SOEs with the explicit purpose of developing new industries. According to Kohli (2004, 207), in the 1970s over 40 percent of total gross capital formation in Brazil came from SOEs. In Figure 4.3, we separate the new SOEs according to the main reason for which they were created. It is clear that most of the SOEs were created following clear industrial policy objectives and that only in the 1950–1980 period do we see some firms created for specific social objectives, such as food storage and distribution companies created to ensure enough

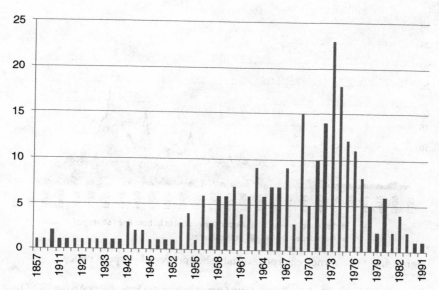

Figure 4.2. Number of new nonfinancial state-owned enterprises per year, 1857–1986

Source: Created with data from Brazil's State-Owned Enterprises Supervisory Agency (SEST) and the business magazine *Exame*, 1973–1977.

Notes: SOEs established before 1940 may be underestimated because of survival bias (i.e., because we built this graph using data on surviving companies in the 1970s and 1980s).

food supply as well as price stability. It is important to note that, during the 1970s, there was a spike in the creation not only of industrial firms (e.g., in aluminum, fertilizers, and oil), but also of utilities and public service companies, among the most important of which were water and sewage companies and the telecommunication complex (one company per state).

Trebat (1983) showed that during this peak of SOE creation, these firms ventured into multiple sectors and pursued what he called "empire building." SOEs were relatively autonomous during this period, but that autonomy depended on their being profitable. Profitable companies were less dependent on transfers from the Treasury and less subject to state intervention. Profitable firms, however, needed to find ways to invest their returns, which were not all taxed or captured by the government. Firms therefore built large conglomerates with a variety of affiliated firms in multiple sectors.

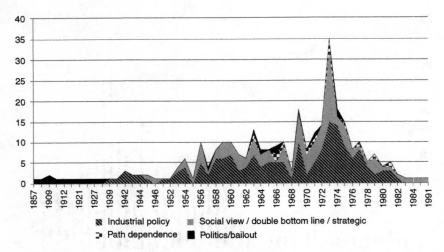

Figure 4.3. State-owned enterprises established per year, by type of policy, 1857–1991

Source: Created with data from Brazil's State-Owned Enterprises Supervisory Agency (SEST) and the business magazine *Exame*, 1973–1977. Coded by the authors.

Thus, Brazilian SOEs in the 1960s and 1970s were relatively anonymous. In 1967, the military government passed the Administrative Reform Law (Decree-Law 200, 1967), which granted SOEs the same treatment as private companies. Rather than forcing firms to follow any specific development plan, this law allowed firms to adjust to the general plans of the government while still allowing them to pursue their own activities (Wahrlich 1980). In fact, before 1979 the government of Brazil did not know what firms were doing because it did not monitor their cash flows.[3]

According to Trebat (1983), many SOEs were autonomous enough to run themselves almost as private firms. Some of the largest and more internationalized SOEs issued debt in foreign currency, opened subsidiaries in other countries, and acquired and developed firms at home that sometimes competed with the firms of other SOEs. Therefore, SOEs could venture into a variety of industries and why firms such as Petrobras and Vale ended up competing in various sectors (e.g., aluminum and fertilizers).

The expansion of large SOEs into sectors that were outside their core missions raised eyebrows among the technocratic elite in Brazil. In May 1976, Marcos P. Vianna, president of BNDE, the national development bank, sent a confidential memorandum to the minister of planning, João Paulo dos Reis Velloso, suggesting the privatization of sectors such as aluminum and fertilizers. It was precisely into those sectors that SOEs such as Petrobras, Siderbras (the steel holding company), and Companhia Vale do Rio Doce had ventured in the early 1970s. In his memo, Vianna worried that "there were few private firms among the top 100 companies of the country . . . which are dominated by state-owned and foreign companies." He also noted that the widespread participation of SOEs in numerous sectors "created a problematic picture whereby national private entrepreneurs are inhibited, leaving the impression of a deliberate policy of statization, which is definitely not the desire of the government" (Vianna 1976).[4]

Interestingly, Vianna's proposed privatization scheme did not involve competitive bidding by private owners. Instead, he envisioned a process by which BNDE itself would assign certain sectors to particular industrial groups in Brazil. He suggested that BNDE should "be authorized to act like an operational agent." As an "operational agent," BNDE would not only appoint private groups to take over state-led projects but would also provide those groups with state capital in such a way that "the debt should be repaid in proportion of the net profits effectively generated" and the period of amortization "would not be pre-specified." Loans would therefore act as preferred equity. This plan was not executed, but in the privatization program of the 1990s, BNDES did indeed act as an operational agent and participated in the equity of several privatized firms. Thus, Vianna's report anticipated the subsequent model of Leviathan as a minority investor.

The "statization" of the Brazilian economy was then partly accidental and partly a consequence of the empire building of SOE managers. It was puzzling, though, that the government did not really know how many SOEs existed and what SOE managers were doing with the cash surpluses they had. In 1973, Fundação Getúlio Vargas, an economics think tank, published the list of SOEs according to a census it conducted in 1969; the census stated that the federal and state governments controlled 251 firms (Centro de Estudos Fiscais 1973). Even in the 1970s the Ministry of Planning estimated that there were 175 federal SOEs. Yet in 1976 the magazine *Visão* published its own census, which showed the federal government controlled 200 SOEs, while state governments controlled 339, and municipalities, 32 firms (*Visão* 1976).

Still, the government did not start collecting SOE data in a centralized way until 1979 and did not start exercising full control of such firms until after 1983. In 1979, the government created the State-Owned Enterprises Supervisory Agency (known as SEST in Portuguese) and began to collect data on the companies in which it had a significant share of equity. This was partly because, as a result of the 1979 oil shock, the government ran into difficulties refinancing its debt as Paul Volcker, the chairman of the Federal Reserve Board in the United States, started to raise interest rates rapidly. Some Brazilian SOEs with strong cash flows in dollars were still allowed to borrow abroad, and the government saw the possibility of using some of them as a source of foreign exchange to help pay for oil imports. However, the government needed to collect information to figure out what companies were doing, why some required financial support from the Treasury, and—in particular—which ones could get foreign exchange.

Yet the interest rate hikes in the United States in 1981 complicated the refinancing of lines of credit for the SOEs as well. A year later, things got even more complicated for the managers of SOEs and for the Brazilian government when the government of Mexico suspended payments on its foreign debt, instigating fear among American banks and other foreign banks. These banks, partly out of fear and partly because they were ordered to do so by the U.S. Treasury, closed their lines of credit to emerging markets, including their lines of credit to the Brazilian government and its SOEs. This generated a balance-of-payments crisis that led the Brazilian government to seek help from the International Monetary Fund (IMF). Among the IMF's conditions for a stabilization package was that the Brazilian government control both the expenses and the debt issues of SOEs—especially debt issues in foreign currency—as a way to reduce the government's budget deficit. Therefore, after 1983, Brazilian SOEs were under tight scrutiny by SEST and by various ministries (Werneck 1987). Moreover, after 1985, the government controlled some prices, salaries, and hiring in state-owned companies and forced them to reduce payroll expenses nominally.[5]

The financial crisis of the 1980s and the government's failed attempts to control expenditures also led to rampant inflation, which by the late 1980s reached hyperinflation levels (more than 50 percent inflation per month). With such rapid price increases and with price controls in some industries, it was hard for SOEs to remain profitable and to keep up with debt payments.[6]

The 1979–1983 Crisis

The economic crisis that hit Brazil between 1979 and 1983 was the worst recession in this country's modern history. Brazil had its fair share of balance-of-payments and financial crises in the twentieth century, but no other recession was of such magnitude. For instance, Brazil was relatively unscathed by the Great Depression, thanks to its coffee export sector (Furtado, 1959), but the so-called Second Oil Shock in 1979 (the first being the 1973 spike in oil prices) hit Brazil hard. Brazil being an oil importer, the spike increased the pressures on both the balance of trade and the current account. One way to obtain foreign exchange to pay for imports was to borrow abroad. Up until then, the government had had relatively easy access to lines of credit from international banks, both directly and through its SOEs, especially those, such as Vale, that exported commodities. As Delfim Netto, minister of planning during the crisis, described it: "Petrodollars were a delicious thing. Arab countries would sell us oil and would deposit their profits in an American bank, which would then lend us the money."[7] By 1979, however, things started to change. According to Netto, "the oil price had gone from around $2 in 1974 to $12 per barrel in 1979. There was no way to increase our exports to cover such an increase in the price of imports."[8] In fact, the terms of trade for Brazil declined continuously between 1979 and 1982.

To make matters worse, the supply of credit dried up for Brazil rapidly between 1981 and 1982 for at least two reasons. First, as a way to fight inflation in the United States, the Federal Reserve Board under Paul Volcker had increased the benchmark interest rate in the United States rapidly (for instance, they notched up the rate from below 10 percent at the beginning of 1980 to almost 20 percent at the end of that year). Second, in 1982, even after interest rates had begun to fall in the United States, the government of Mexico declared a moratorium on payments of its foreign currency debt, spreading a contagion to all of the region that increased the borrowing costs for the Brazilian government and its SOEs and for private Brazilian firms (Cardoso 1989; Frieden 1991).

Overall, the picture for Brazil was bleak. On the one hand, interest rates on foreign loans increased (and bankers refused to extend lines of credit), while the prices of its exports collapsed. On the other hand, banks and the IMF rationed credit to countries according to a plan agreed on by the U.S.

Treasury, the IMF, the Federal Reserve, and a group of international bankers. This rationing affected private firms as well. The final blow was the rapid depreciation of the currency in 1982, making it even harder for governments and companies to repay their debts and increasing inflation in Brazil (Díaz-Alejandro 1984).

The 1980s are known today in Brazil and Latin America as "the lost decade." This is in part because of the recession that followed 1982. The government debt payments increased throughout the decade both because of the depreciation of the exchange rate, which made the service of foreign debt even higher, and as a result of the higher interest rates. Moreover, with the recession, tax revenues suffered, and the Brazilian government faced severe fiscal deficits. Since SOEs had financed the bulk of gross capital formation in the 1970s, in the 1980s total investment had a decline, contributing even more to the long recession. Finally, on top of the high interest rates the government had to pay on its debt after 1982, interest rates in government bonds were also indexed to inflation, so as soon as the government began using expansionary monetary policy in the later part of the decade, debt payments also spiraled up (Hermann 2005).

The 1980s as a "Not-So-Lost Decade"

Not everything was lost in the "lost decade." Two important transitions took place in Brazil in the second half of the 1980s. The first one was the transition to democracy in 1985. Brazil had a military government with indirect elections for president and a controlled electoral system with direct elections for Congress. Yet, after almost twenty years of authoritarianism with no direct elections for president (the president was elected by an electoral college stacked in favor of the military party, PDS), in 1982 the opposition parties won the majority in the lower house and took some gubernatorial elections away from the ruling military party. In 1983, right wing and leftist parties joined forces and started a campaign and later a law proposal to reform the constitution and allow direct elections for president. This campaign fueled a civil society mobilization called the *diretas já* campaign, which included massive rallies. Even though Congress voted down this constitutional amendment, the opposition candidate, Trancredo Neves, won the presidential race of 1985. Yet, in a dramatic turn of events, the night before

Neves was to be sworn in as president, he was admitted to the hospital and eventually passed away. His passing without being sworn in left the presidential seat to José Sarney, his vice president and a former member of the military regime's party (Skidmore 1988).

The second major political transition took place between 1986 and 1988, when the new constitution was drafted and passed. The Congress elected in November 1986 actually served as the Constitutional Congress. As Fishlow (2011) explains, the effort was quite inclusive, with "extensive participation by the public, as well as by nongovernmental organizations . . . [and] lobbies representing economic interests" (p. 6). For instance, the economic crisis of the 1980s and the transition to democracy gave worker parties and unions a new voice, and they demanded rights, using massive strikes and other ways to pressure the government (Skidmore 1988). Thus, the constitution of 1988 ended up including entitlements for a variety of groups that added to the fiscal pressures on the Brazilian government, which at that point was facing steep interest payments. Moreover, the constitution of 1988 forced the federal government to transfer a large share of its revenues to state and municipal governments, making its fiscal position even worse (Baer 2008).[9]

The Brazilian Privatization Program

The crisis of the early 1980s, the process of democratization in 1985, and the 1988 Constitution changed everything for SOEs in Brazil. The crisis forced the government to bail out SOEs continuously and increased the need to control expenditures in such firms. Moreover, with the fiscal pressures faced after the crisis—and exacerbated with the new entitlements included in the 1988 constitution—the Brazilian government lost control of the economy. The government relied excessively on monetary policy as a way to finance its debt (and to reduce the debt's value); thus, inflation got out of control.

A sweeping program of privatization became a necessity as the stabilization programs of the late 1980s and early 1990s progressively failed and led to interest rate hikes and price increases that made the government's fiscal position even worse. There were at least five failed stabilization plans that aimed to stop inflation and reduce the budget deficit: the Cruzado Plan (1986–1987), the Bresser Plan (1987), the Summer Plan (early 1989), the Collor Plan (1990), the Collor II Plan (1991–1992), and finally, the Real Plan, which did bring down inflation in 1995 and managed to keep government budget deficits and inflation under control (Fishlow 2011).[10]

Amid such an economic crisis, and facing steep interest payments and large expenditures stemming from the new constitution, the government looked more seriously at the possibility of shrinking the state's expenses and liabilities by privatizing firms. Having gotten off to a slow start in the 1980s, privatization had become a necessity for the newly elected President Fernando Collor de Mello in 1990 (Fishlow 2011; Pinheiro 2002). As Albert Fishlow explains:

> During the presidential campaign in 1989, privatization emerged as one of the issues emphasized by then governor Collor. This marked a new phase. Until that time, the issue had not gotten abundant press coverage. An overwhelming majority within Brazil believed that economic development and the state were inseparably linked. Privatization and foreign presence were both viewed with hesitancy. Congress reacted . . . [by] requiring the government to ensure that privatization of Petrobras was out of the question. (p. 52)

There were at least three motivations behind Brazil's privatization program. First, there was the need to control government expenditures in order to increase savings at the national level. Initially, the government tried to control expenses and salaries in SOEs, but because the government also tried to control prices by introducing price freezes, SOEs faced serious losses that required transfers from the Treasury to recapitalize these firms. That is, SOEs started to continuously siphon away some of the scarce resources from the government budget. Those transfers increased the budget deficit and contributed to the increase in total debt. As we show in Chapter 6, over 30 percent of SOEs were losing money and required aid from the Treasury or the development bank. In fact, most Brazilian SOEs were technically bankrupt. Thus, the government started to see some of the privatizations as a necessity to reduce expenses and not just as a way to attract cash to pay the extant debt.

Second, in the early 1990s—in the midst of financial instability, hyperinflation, and high budget deficits—the Brazilian government began to reconsider its investment in SOEs for purely financial reasons. With inflation skyrocketing, the government had to pay high interest rates on its debt, which increased the opportunity cost of holding equity in SOEs. For instance, the dividends paid by the mining firm Vale do Rio Doce, one of the most profitable SOEs, ranged between 0.5 percent and 5.2 percent during the 1980s and early 1990s. The average dividend for all federal SOEs was close to 0.4 percent from 1988 to 1994. Such returns were low compared to the high opportunity cost of the government equity. The Brazilian government had to make debt payments that could range from 20 percent per year, on average for all debts, to close to 1,000 percent for short-term debt in the early 1990s (Pinheiro and Giambiagi 1994).

Third, part of the government's adjustment program, beginning in 1990, was trade liberalization. Privatization was seen as a means for improving efficiency in the economy, not only by increasing the productivity of privatized SOEs, but also by liberalizing the prices of most industrial inputs in the country, which for the most part had been controlled in the 1980s and early 1990s.

Stages of the Privatization Program of Brazil

Brazil's privatization program can be divided broadly into three stages. In the first stage, from 1981 to 1989, privatization was part of the fiscal readjustment program of the government of President João Figueiredo, the last military government. That administration privatized twenty firms that were easy targets, either because they were small or because they had only recently become SOEs through bailouts of private firms. The government collected about $190 million from those sales. Between 1985 and 1989, the first two democratic governments sold another eighteen firms, raising the total privatization revenues for the decade to $723 million.[11]

The second stage of privatization goes broadly from 1990 to 1994. In 1990, President Collor (1990–1992) started a more sweeping National Privatization Program (Programa Nacional de Desestatização—PND) with BNDES, the national development bank, in charge of the divestiture process. BNDES selected, through a public tender, a consortium of two consulting firms to study and value each SOE that would be auctioned off. These firms would give recommendations on minimum auction prices that a privatization steering committee would have to approve (Baer 2008).

The PND focused on the privatization of relatively productive SOEs in strategic sectors, such as steel, petrochemicals, and fertilizers. Thirty-three firms were privatized between 1990 and 1994, yielding $8.6 billion in revenues (plus an additional $3 billion in SOE debts transferred to the private sector). More than 60 percent of the proceeds came from the privatization of steel mills, such as Usiminas (the first mill to be privatized). President Collor was impeached in 1992, but the PND was continued by President Itamar Franco (1992–1994), who privatized two of Brazil's flagship SOEs, steel mill Companhia Siderúrgica Nacional (CSN), in 1993, and airplane manufacturer Embraer in 1994. Most of the sales occurred through auctions in which the government accepted payment not only in cash, but also in so-called "privatization currencies," which were other government bonds, debentures issued by the state-owned steel holding company (Siderbras), and other forms of government debt. Between 1990 and 1994, the government collected 19 percent of its privatization profits in cash and 81 percent in these other "currencies."[12]

The final stage of the privatization process took place during the two presidential terms of Fernando Henrique Cardoso (1994–2002). Then, the government sold or transferred control of public services—such as electricity, telecommunications, and some financial firms—in order to improve service quality. The government also transferred the operation of ports, transportation and sanitation companies, and some highways to the private sector through a program of concessions. During this stage, the government collected $78 billion, mostly in cash.[13] Among the most important privatizations and partial privatizations of this period involved Light (in 1996), a utilities company operating in Rio de Janeiro; mining giant Vale do Rio Doce, privatized in stages between 1997 and 2002; and the Eletrobras and Telebras state-owned holdings of utilities and telecommunication companies (Baer 2008; BNDES 2002b).

The Rise of Leviathan as a Minority Investor in Brazil

Besides transforming some SOEs into majority-owned firms, the Brazilian government made the national development bank operate as a holding company for the government. Therefore, BNDES aided in the transformation of the state into a minority investor as well. BNDES played three roles in the privatization process of 1990 to 2003. First, echoing Marcos Vianna's prophetic report, it served as an operational agent of privatization transactions involving the sale of controlling blocks of SOEs. Second, it provided financing for the buyers in some of the privatization transactions. Third, it purchased minority stakes in privatized firms (and a variety of publicly traded firms) through its equity-holding arm, BNDESPAR.

BNDES was involved in the privatization process not only to deflect criticism that the state was losing its grip on the economy, but also by making available substantial capital in order to attract private players to the auctions. Approximately 86 percent of the revenues collected from privatization auctions came from block sales, with acquirers typically forming consortia that included domestic groups, foreign investors, and public entities such as BNDESPAR and the pension funds of state-owned companies (Anuatti-Neto et al. 2005; De Paula et al. 2002; Lazzarini 2011).

The privatization process in Brazil was thus accompanied by the rise of a new form of minority state ownership of corporations via equity purchases by BNDES through BNDESPAR. The size of these allocations—US$53 billion by 2009—triggered criticism that equity purchases favored large local business groups that, in fact, had the financial clout to execute their projects *without* help from the development bank (e.g., Almeida 2009). In Chapter 8 we test some of the implications of this model of state capitalism.

Table 4.1 also shows how BNDES's holdings (through BNDESPAR) increased for our sample of listed firms between 1995 and 2009. Such holdings can be *direct* or *indirect*. The former involves cases where BNDES participates as a direct shareholder of the target firm. On average, BNDES's direct equity stakes are 16 percent of a listed firm's total equity. Most of its purchases are part of an explicit investment strategy devised by BNDESPAR's management both to optimize BNDES's portfolio and to meet its development targets. For instance, some of the direct stakes are the product of direct bailouts or of conversions of debt for equity.

Indirect stakes, in turn, occur when BNDES owns an intermediate firm that in turn owns the target firm. Because pyramidal structures are complex and often involve non-listed companies, the size of BNDES's indirect holdings is not always publicly available. As an illustration of indirect stakes, consider Vale, for which the government privatized the control block of Valepar, a holding company owned by BNDESPAR, Bradesco (a bank), and other investors

Table 4.1. Equity stakes by BNDESPAR in a sample of listed firms (1995–2009)

Year	Number of BNDESPAR's equity stakes (direct or indirect)*	Number of BNDESPAR's direct equity stakes	Average direct holding as a percentage of total equity in target firms
1995	23	11	17%
1996	18	11	19%
1997	27	15	15%
1998	26	14	14%
1999	29	13	19%
2000	29	14	19%
2001	28	16	16%
2002	23	14	17%
2003	24	14	19%
2004	22	13	15%
2005	25	17	15%
2006	37	21	13%
2007	44	26	12%
2008	48	28	13%
2009	47	32	13%

Source: Created using the ownership data from the databases Economática, Interinvest, and Valor Grandes Grupos, as well as the reports companies have to file with the Brazilian Securities and Exchange Commission (Comissão de Valores Mobiliários, CVM).

*Indirect stakes occur when BNDESPAR buys a company that is part of a pyramidal ownership structure—that is, when it owns a company that in turn is a shareholder in another corporation (e.g., BNDES owns Valepar, which in turn owns Vale).

including pension funds of SOEs such as Previ (from Banco do Brasil) and Petros (from Petrobras). Thus, the state is an indirect holder of shares in Vale through state-related owners BNDES and pension funds, which in turn are shareholders of Valepar. As we discuss in Chapter 9, which presents a detailed case study of Vale, collusion among these state-related owners allowed the government to influence particular decisions in the company.

The Resilience of Leviathan as an Entrepreneur and Majority Investor in Brazil

In Brazil, the privatization process changed the face of state capitalism. Even as some of the SOEs that remained profitable in the late 1980s became targets for privatization between 1990 and 2002 (e.g., the steel mill CSN or the mining company Vale), the government kept other flagship firms under its control. Table 4.2 shows a list of remaining SOEs and state-owned holding companies (SOHCs) with majority government control by 2009. We identify 47 firms under the direct control of the federal government with assets worth $625 billion. Five of those are SOHCs that controlled 68 subsidiaries. Thus, including the subsidiaries, the Brazilian government controlled 115 firms with assets worth approximately $756.8 billion.

State governments also suffered a similar transformation. State-level SOEs, in turn, controlled forty-nine firms with total assets of $66 billion (see Table 4.3). That means that the federal government in Brazil had almost two times the assets under management (AUM) of the Government Pension Fund of Norway, the world's largest sovereign wealth fund, with AUM close to $500 million in 2009.

Not surprisingly, such remaining SOEs are present in sectors considered by the government as "strategic." Such is the case of Petrobras, in oil and distribution; Eletrobras, in electricity generation; Correios in postal services; Infraero in airports; Sabesp in water and sewage services (the water company of the state of São Paulo); Banco do Brasil and Caixa Econômica Federal in banking. The latter, in particular, were deemed as instrumental in providing credit lines for market segments not covered by private banks such as agricultural or housing credit.

We can also see that there is still wide variation in ownership among SOEs. The vast majority of SOEs are not listed. Out of the total federal SOEs only 5 percent of the firms are listed on the local stock exchange. In contrast, state-level governments in Brazil have listed a third of their SOEs.

It is hard to assert whether there was a major improvement in corporate governance and the quality of management in non-listed SOEs under the control of the federal government (or state governments) from 1990 to 2009. Most of these non-listed firms have audited financials, but do not have strong internal or external checks and balances. There were two major differences between these non-listed firms in 2009 and SOEs before 1980. First, in 2009 all of the federal SOEs reported their financials to the Department of SOEs (known as DEST) and were closely monitored by different ministries. They often had boards of directors in which ministers sat and tried to control and monitor the financial situation of the company. Second, since the 1990s, when President Cardoso put the public finances of Brazil in order, losses in

Table 4.2. Majority-owned federal SOEs and holding companies (SOHCs) in Brazil, 2009

Company	Industry	Number of subsidiaries (if SOHC)	Share of voting equity held by gov't	Listed on Bovespa (BSP) and/or New York (ADRs)?	Assets in US$ millions (2009)
Banco do Brasil	Finance	17	68	BSP-"Novo Mercado"	216,949
Banco Nacional de Desenvolvimento Econômico e Social—BNDES	Finance	3	100	No	124,558
Petróleo Brasileiro SA	Oil and downstream	34	57	BSP & ADRs	103,555
Centrais Elétricas Brasileiras (Eletrobras)	Electricity	11	78	BSP-Level 1 & ADRs	35,440
Banco do Nordeste do Brasil	Finance		100	BSP	6,290
Banco da Amazônia	Finance		97	BSP	2,563
Eletrobrás Participações (Eletropar, subsidiary of Eletrobras)	Electricity		68	BSP	40
Caixa Econômica Federal	Finance		100	No	112,260
Empresa Gestora de Ativos—Emgea	Public admin. various		100	No	7,571
Brasil Resseguros	Finance		100	No	3,408
Correios e Telégrafos	Public admin. various		100	No	2,295
Cia Nacional de Abastecimento	Food distribution/ storage		100	No	1,624
Cia Brasileira de Trens Urbanos	Transportation		100	No	1,263
Financiadora de Estudos e Projetos	Finance		100	No	1,218

Empresa Brasileira de Infra-Estrutura Aeroportuária—Infraero	Airport operator	100	No	773
Valec—Engenharia, Construções e Ferrovias	Construction	100	No	753
Serviço Social de Precessamento de Dados—Serpro	Data processing	100	No	645
Cia Docas do Estado de São Paulo—Codesp	Ports	100	No	593
Caixa de Participações	Finance	100	No	489
Casa da Moeda Brasil—CMB	Mint	100	No	348
Cia das Docas do Rio de Janeiro—CDRJ	Ports	100	No	348
Indústrias Nucleares do Brasil	Mining	100	No	286
Empresa de Tecnologia e Informações da Previdência Social	Public admin. various	100	No	239
Empresa Brasileira de Pesquisa Agropecuária (Embrapa)	Agriculture research	100	No	226
Empresa de Trens Urbanos de Porto Alegre	Transportation	100	No	158
Telecomunicações Brasileiras SA	Telecommunications	100	No	142
Cia das Docas do Rio Grande do Norte—Codern	Ports	100	No	125

(continued)

Table 4.2. (continued)

Company	Industry	Number of subsidiaries (if SOHC)	Share of voting equity held by gov't	Listed on Bovespa (BSP) and/or New York (ADRs)?	Assets in US$ millions (2009)
Hospital de Clínicas de Porto Alegre	Health services		100	No	118
Cia de Desenv. dos Vales do SF e do Parnaíba	Public admin. various		100	No	111
Cia Docas do Pará—Cdp	Ports		100	No	99
Ceagesp—Cia de Entrepostos e Armazéns Gerais de São Paulo	Food distribution/ storage		100	No	86
Empresa Brasil de Comunicação	Telecommunications		100	No	82
Indústria de Material Bélico do Brasil—Imbel	Manufacturing		100	No	79
Cia Docas do Estado do Espírito Santo—Codesa	Ports		100	No	78
Cia de Pesquisa de Recursos Minerais—Cprm	Public admin. various		99	No	73
Cia das Docas do Estado da Bahia—Codeba	Ports		100	No	73
Hospital Nossa Senhora da Conceição SA	Health services	3	100	No	68

Company	Sector			
Empresa Gerencial de Projetos Navais	Construction	100	No	65
Nuclebrás Equipamentos Pesados SA—Nuclep	Manufacturing	100	No	63
Empresa Brasileira de Hemoderivados e Biotecnologia—Hemobrás	Health services	100	No	63
Centro de Pesquisa de Energia Elétrica—Cepel	Energy research	78	No	52
Cia das Docas do Ceará—Cdc	Ports	100	No	29
Cia Docas do Maranhão—Codomar	Ports	100	No	19
Cia. de Armazéns e Silos do Estado de Minas Gerais—Casemg	Food distribution/ storage	100	No	12
Centrais de Abastecimento de Minas Gerais—Ceasaminas	Food distribution/ storage	100	No	10
Empresa de Pesquisa Energética	Electricity	100	No	10
Centro Nacional de Tecnologia Eletrônica Avançada	Manufacturing	100	No	7

Source: Data obtained from the Securities and Exchange Commission of Brazil, and the Department of Coordination and Governance of State-Owned Enterprises (DEST), Ministry of Planning.
Note: SOHC stands for state-owned holding company.

Table 4.3. Majority-owned state-level SOEs and holding companies (SOHCs) in Brazil, 2009

Company	Industry	Share of voting equity held by gov't	Listed on Bovespa (BSP) and/or New York (ADRs)?	Assets in US$ millions (2009)
Cia Energética de São Paulo	Electricity	94	BSP-Level 1	13,838
Banco do Estado do Rio Grande do Sul	Finance	100	BSP-Level 1	7,127
Cia. de Saneamento Básico do Estado de São Paulo	Water/sewage	50.3	BSP–"Novo Mercado"	7,060
Cia. do Metropolitano de São Paulo	Transportation	n.a.	No	5,546
Cia. Estadual de Aguas e Esgotos	Water/sewage	100	No	4,531
Cia Energética de Minas Gerais	Electricity	52	BSP-Level 1	3,883
Cia Paranaense de Energia	Electricity	85	BSP-Level 1	3,322
Banco Regional de Desenvolvimento do Extremo Sul	Finance	n.a.	No	2,398
Cia. de Saneamento de Minas Gerais	Water/sewage	53	BSP–"Novo Mercado"	2,268
Companhia Energética de Goiás Participações—CELGPAR	Electricity	100	BSP	2,201
Empresa Baiana de Águas e Saneamento	Water/sewage	n.a.	No	1,808
Cia. de Saneamento do Paraná	Water/sewage	60	BSP	1,590
Desenvolvimento Rodoviário (Sp)	Transportation	100	No	1,567
Saneamento de Goiás 1	Water/sewage	69	No	968
Cia. Riograndense de Saneamento	Water/sewage	100	No	786
Banco do Estado de Sergipe	Finance	94	BSP	733
Cia. Pernambucana de Saneamento	Water/sewage	n.a.	No	705
Centrais Elétricas de Santa Catarina	Electricity	50.2	BSP-Level 2	669
Cia. de Água e Esgoto do Ceará	Water/sewage	100	No	592
Banco do Estado do Pará	Finance	100	BSP	581

Company	Sector	%		Number
Cia. de Saneamento Ambiental do Distrito Federal	Water/sewage	n.a.	No	568
Cia. Catarinense de Águas e Saneamento	Water/sewage	77	BSP	526
Cia. Espírito Santense de Saneamento	Water/sewage	100	No	508
Banco do Estado do Espírito Santo	Finance	92	BSP	466
Cia de Gás de Minas Gerais	Gas	n.a.	No	397
Empresa Metropolitana de Águas e Energia	Water/sewage	98	BSP	376
Sociedade de Abastecimento de Água e Saneamento	Water/sewage	100	No	246
Cia de Eletricidade do Amapá—Cea	Electricity	100	No	183
Cia. de Tecnologia de Saneamento Ambiental de Brasil	Water/sewage	n.a.	No	154
Cia de Eletricidade de Brasília	Electricity	89	BSP	142
Cia. de Gás da Bahia	Gas	n.a.	No	136
São Paulo Turismo	Tourism	97	No	94
Empresa Baiana de Alimentos—Cesta do Povo	Food distrib./storage	n.a.	No	56
Cia. de Engenharia e Tráfego	Public admin./various	n.a.	No	54
Banco de Brasília	Finance	97	BSP	41
Centrais de Abastecimento de Campinas SA	Food distrib./storage	n.a.	No	32
Centrais de Abastecimento do Pará SA	Food distrib./storage	n.a.	No	n.a.
Centrais de Abastecimento do Rio de Janeiro	Food distrib./storage	n.a.	No	n.a.
Centrais de Abastecimento do Rio Grande do Sul	Food distrib./storage	n.a.	No	n.a.

(continued)

Table 4.3. (continued)

Company	Industry	Share of voting equity held by gov't	Listed on Bovespa (BSP) and/or New York (ADRs)?	Assets in US$ millions (2009)
Centrais de Abastecimento de Alagoas SA	Food distrib./ storage	n.a.	No	n.a.
Centrais de Abastecimento de Sergipe SA	Food distrib./ storage	n.a.	No	n.a.
Centrais de Abastecimento do Ceará SA	Food distrib./ storage	n.a.	No	n.a.
Centrais de Abastecimento de Goiás SA	Food distrib./ storage	n.a.	No	n.a.
Centrais de Abastecimento do Paraná	Food distrib./ storage	n.a.	No	n.a.
Centrais de Abastecimento do Espírito Santo	Food distrib./ storage	n.a.	No	n.a.
Centrais de Abastecimento do Rio Grande do Norte	Food distrib./ storage	n.a.	No	n.a.
Cia. Municipal de Limpeza Urbana (Rio de Janeiro)	Public works (cleaning)	n.a.	No	n.a.
Centrais de Abastecimento do Est. Santa Catarina	Food distrib./ storage	n.a.	No	n.a.
Centrais de Abastecimento do Mato Grosso do Sul	Food distrib./ storage	n.a.	No	n.a.

Source: Data obtained from the Securities and Exchange Commission of Brazil and the Department of Coordination and Governance of State-Owned Enterprises (DEST), Ministry of Planning.

SOEs became less acceptable because they could affect the deficit target of the government (always close to a deficit before interests of 2 percent of GDP—a benchmark set by the IMF) and, ultimately, Brazil's credit rating. Therefore, in 2009, the Ministry of Finance and others had clear incentives to monitor the performance of such firms.

Yet anecdotal evidence on the management and governance of the remaining SOEs after the privatization period indicates that many SOEs were subject to patronage and corruption. In May 2005, an executive of the Brazil's Postal Service, Correios, was videotaped receiving bribes in exchange for public contracts. This event triggered a series of accusations of under-the-table transfers of money from SOEs to political parties—the so-called *mensalão* ("monthly allowance"). Several SOEs were implicated, including not only Correios but also Banco do Brasil, Petrobras, and Furnas (an affiliate of the Eletrobras group).

Still, there was no firm attempt to reform the governance and control of SOEs up until the inauguration of President Luiz Inácio Lula da Silva's successor, Dilma Rousseff, in 2011. President Rousseff tried to appoint top executives with "technical" backgrounds (e.g., engineers or economists) in some of the firms controlled by the federal government. Yet, as we explain in Chapter 7, the perception in Brazil was that political intervention in SOEs actually increased after 2011. That is, our story suggests that there is not always "progress" in the governance of SOEs; there can be setbacks, caused by changing political objectives (such as a government trying to control the prices of an SOE's goods or services), which can undermine some of the reforms carried out after the 1980s.

Corporate Governance in Publicly Traded SOEs in the Twenty-First Century

Brazilian SOEs that were listed on stock markets, in contrast, underwent a transformation in terms of governance and management. Federal and state governments had to improve corporate governance and financial transparency in the firms they listed on the São Paulo Stock Exchange (Bovespa) (see Table 4.2 and Table 4.3).

SOEs in Brazil—as opposed to those in, say, China or Vietnam—already had the corporate form and reported their annual audited financials to

DEST even before they were listed. Still, upon listing, they had to follow the rules and institute the legal protections for minority shareholders that were included in the Joint Stock Company Law of 2001 (Law 10,303). For instance, the law acknowledges that the state, as a controlling shareholder, may have interests opposed to those of other shareholders and must therefore make an effort to protect the interests of those shareholders. Moreover, after 2001, minority shareholders got the right to elect a member to the board of directors (using proportional representation), and some transactions also began to depend on the approval of a qualified majority (two-thirds) rather than a simple majority. On paper, therefore, the controlling shareholder of SOEs—the state—had less power over certain transactions such as approving joint ventures or spinning off a unit.[14]

Among the federal government companies that listed their shares in Bovespa and in New York was Petrobras. President Vargas had created Petrobras in 1953 and given it a monopoly on the production of oil and gas. Yet until the 1970s, Petrobras was mainly a trading company, importing both crude and refined products. Then it started to branch out into downstream activities through partnerships with the private sector, eventually absorbing private and partly private refineries into its refining subsidiary, Petroquisa. Oil discoveries and the expansion of Petrobras into other activities made the company one of the largest in the Americas.

As part of the privatization and liberalization policies of the 1990s, President Cardoso liberalized the oil industry in 1997. In that year, he enacted the "Petroleum Law," which ended Petrobras's oil monopoly and opened oil and gas markets in Brazil to foreign investment and foreign competition. Cardoso also eliminated the restrictions that prohibited foreigners from owning shares in Petrobras. Finally, in August 2000, the Cardoso administration listed the shares of Petrobras on the New York Stock Exchange, through the American Depository Receipts (ADR) program. This also allowed Brazilians to use their retirement accounts to purchase Petrobras shares. By listing shares in New York and later in Europe (2002), Petrobras was forced to improve its corporate governance and financial transparency practices. The company had to adhere to the generally accepted accounting principles (GAAP), had to comply with the Sarbanes-Oxley Act (which demanded further disclosure of related-party transactions and executive compensation), and began to be monitored closely by rating agencies and investors, such as mutual and pension funds from Brazil and other countries (Musacchio, Goldberg, et al. 2009). In Chapter 7, we closely analyze the changes in Petrobras's corporate governance and compare them with the governance standards of a sample of national oil companies.

Yet few other federal SOEs were transformed the way Petrobras had been. The exceptions were Banco do Brasil, the largest state-owned commercial bank, and Eletrobras, a large utilities firm. Both were listed on the Bovespa and on the New York Stock Exchange, and both traded in segments of Bovespa for higher corporate governance standards. Firms can comply with three higher levels of corporate governance within Bovespa: the "Novo Mercado" (New Market) and the "Level 1" and "Level 2" segments. In the Novo Mercado, among other restrictions, companies cannot have dual-class shares (that is, all shares must have voting power), they must have a minimum free float of 25 percent of the total shares, and the board of directors have a term limit of two years, and at least 20 percent of its members must be external members. Firms listed as Level 1 need to guarantee that at least 25 percent of the capital is traded in the stock market (free float). These firms also have to present more detailed financial reports quarterly. Finally, companies listed as Level 2 have to add term limits of two years for directors, and additional rights for holders of nonvoting shares when there are mergers (e.g., tag-along rights or the right to walk away and getting their shares bought back). Finally, Level 2 firms agree to solve disputes between controlling shareholders and minority shareholders in arbitration, if necessary (Perkins and Zajac 2012). Just one SOE at the federal level, Banco do Brasil, is listed on the New Market; Eletrobras is listed as a Level 1 company (see Table 4.2). Petrobras tried to join the Level 2 segment in 2002, but Bovespa did not allow it because the power that minority shareholders would have for decisions such as mergers and acquisitions would go against the statutes of the firm and possibly against the interests of the nation.[15]

SOEs controlled by state governments adopted higher levels of corporate governance within Bovespa more frequently (see Table 4.3). Among the firms that joined the Level 1 segment were Banco do Estado do Rio Grande do Sul (banking) and energy firms Companhia Energética de São Paulo, Companhia Energética de Minas Gerais (utilities), and Companhia Paranaense de Energia. In the Novo Mercado, there were water and sewage firms Companhia de Saneamento Basico do Estado de São Paulo, Sabesp, and Companhia de

Saneamento de Minas Gerais. Finally, in Level 2, there was Centrais Elétricas de Santa Catarina (energy).

Part of the motivation for SOEs to adopt such corporate governance standards was to commit the firms to better management and close monitoring by shareholders and to commit the governments to let these firms operate as close as possible to profitability. Additionally, SOEs joined the segments of Bovespa with better corporate governance because the shares of firms traded in those segments had more liquidity, thus increasing a company's valuation and reducing its cost of capital. Adhering to superior governance practices therefore allowed these companies to attract extra funding. Sabesp, the water company of the state of São Paulo, decided to join the Novo Mercado in April 2002 and simultaneously issued convertible bonds in local currency to lower its dependence on foreign debt. Furthermore, according to the secretary of planning of the state of São Paulo, André Franco Montoro Filho, adhering to the Novo Mercado was a way to improve the management of Sabesp without having to privatize state control.[16]

Conclusion

In this chapter we have analyzed the evolution of state capitalism in Brazil, which, as argued before, is similar to that in other countries. Moreover, Brazil is an interesting setting in which to test some of the empirical implications of the new forms of state capitalism we outlined in Chapter 3, because there have been interesting changes in the corporate governance and ownership of SOEs, and there is also wide variation in governance and performance among SOEs. In the following chapter, we examine a particular source of heterogeneity: the role of chief operating officers of those SOEs in explaining variation in firm-level performance.

In this chapter we have also explained how the macroeconomic shocks that Brazil and other countries experienced in the 1970s and 1980s led the governments to rethink the financial rationale for holding so many SOEs. In Chapter 6, we discuss why, in the 1980s, the behavior of SOEs differed so much from that of private firms. To further demonstrate the variety of corporate governance arrangements in SOEs in which the government has majority control, Chapter 7 compares the governance of Petrobras with that of other national oil companies.

In the third part of the book, we assess the effect of having the government as a minority shareholder. Chapter 8 looks at the implications of equity purchases by the government for the performance of private firms, while Chapter 9 offers a detailed look at the case of Vale to show both the implications of privatization with minority state ownership and the limits of this model of state capitalism. We finish our study of Brazil by examining the history of BNDES and the positive and some negative implications of having the government lending to firms.

APPENDIX

Table 4-A1. Brazilian state-owned enterprises by year of creation

Year	Company	Acronym	Industry
1941	Cia. Siderúrgica Nacional	CSN	Steel
1942	Cia Brasileira de Cobre	CBC	Mining
	Cia Ferro e Aço de Vitória	Cofavi	Steel
	Cia Vale do Rio Doce	CVRD	Mining
1943	Cia Nacional dos Álcalis	CNA	Chemicals
	Cia Brasileira de Zinco	CBZ	Mining
1944	Cia Aços Especiais Itabira	Acesita	Steel
	Mafersa Sociedade Anônima	Mafersa	Transportation equipment
1945	Cia Hidrelétrica do São Francisco	Chesf	Electricity
1946	Cia. Municipal de Transportes Coletivos	CMTC	Transportation services
1951	Telecomunicações do Espírito Santo	Telest	Telecommunications
1952	Cia Energética de Minas Gerais	Cemig	Electricity
1953	Cia Siderúrgica Paulista	Cosipa	Steel
	Petróleo Brasileiro	Petrobras	Oil and downstream
	Telecomunicações Minas Gerais SA	Telemig	Telecommunications
1954	Cia Paranaense de Energia	Copel	Electricity
	Cia Telefônica da Borda do Campo	CTBC	Telecommunications
	Espirito Santo Centrais Elétricas	Escelsa	Electricity
	Indústria Aeronáutica Neiva	Neiva	Transportation equipment
1955	Hospital Fêmina	HFSA	Health services
1956	Centrais Elétricas de Goiás	Celg	Electricity
	Centrais Elétricas de Santa Catarina	Celesc	Electricity
	Centrais Elétricas Matogrossense	Cemat	Electricity
	Cia de Eletrecidade do Amapá	CEA	Electricity
	Hospital Cristo Redentor	HCR	Health services
	Usinas Siderúrgicas de Minas Gerais	Usiminas	Steel
1957	Furnas Centrais Elétricas	Furnas	Electricity
	Rede Ferroviária Federal	RFFSA	Transportation
1958	Centrais Elétricas de Rondônia	Ceron	Electricity
	Cia Energética do Maranhão	Cemar	Electricity
	São José Armazéns Gerais Ltda	SJAR	Food distribution/ storage
	Telecomunicações da Bahia	Telebahia	Telecommunications
	Telecomunicações de Alagoas	Telasa	Telecommunications
	Telecomunicações de Pernambuco	Telpe	Telecommunications
1959	Centrais Elétricas do Piauí	Cepisa	Electricity
	Cia de Eletricidade da Bahia	Coelba	Electricity

Table 4-A1. (continued)

Year	Company	Acronym	Industry
	Cia de Eletricidade de Alagoas	Ceal	Electricity
	Sistemas de Processamento de Dados	Datamec	Public admin. various
	Empresa Distribuidora de Energia em Sergipe	Energipe	Electricity
	Rede Federal de Armazéns Gerais Ferroviários	AGEF	Food distribution/storage
1960	Aços Finos Piratini	AFP	Steel
	Centrais Elétricas do Pará	Celpa	Electricity
	Cia de Eletricidade de Pernambuco	Celpe	Electricity
	Cia Estadual de Energia Elétrica	CEEE-Piratini	Electricity
	Petróleo Minas Gerais	Petrominas	Oil and downstream
	Telecomunicações de Rondonia	Teleron	Telecommunications
	Telecomunicações do Piauí	Telepisa	Telecommunications
1961	Centrais de Abastecimento de Pernambuco	Ceasa/PE	Food distribution/storage
	Centrais Elétricas Brasileiras	Eletrobras	Electricity
	Cia de Serviços Elétricos do Rio Grande do Norte	Cosern	Electricity
	Cia Estadual de Energia Elétrica	CEEE	Electricity
1962	Cia Brasileira de Alimentos	Cobal	Food distribution/storage
	Cia Brasileira de Armazenamento	Cibrazem	Food distribution/storage
	Cia de Telefones do Rio de Janeiro	Cetel	Telecommunications
	Cia Riograndense de Telecomunicações	CRT	Telecommunications
	Empresa Brasileira de Telecomunicações	Embratel	Telecommunications
	Vale do Rio Doce Navegação	Docenave	Transportation
1963	Aço Minas Gerais	Açominas	Steel
	Centrais Elétricas Fluminenses	Celf	Electricity
	Cia das Docas do Ceará	CDC	Ports
	Cia de Projetos Industriais	Cobrapi	Construction
	Cia De Saneamento do Paraná	Sanepar	Water/sewage
	Cia Energética do Amazonas	Ceam	Electricity
	Telecomunicações do Paraná	Telepar	Telecommunications
	Telecomunicações do Rio Grande do Norte	Telern	Telecommunications
	Usina Siderúrghica da Bahia	Usiba	Steel
1964	Cia de Eletricidade de Brasília	Ceb	Electricity
	Cia Pontapogrossense de Telecomunicações	CPT	Telecommunications
	Cia Brasileira de Trens Urbanos	CBTU	Transportation
	Cia. de Eletrificação da Paraíba	Saelpa	Electricity

(continued)

Table 4-A1. (continued)

Year	Company	Acronym	Industry
	Serviço Social de Precessamento de Dados	SERPRO	Public admin. various
	Telecomunicações de Brasília	Telebrasília	Telecommunications
1965	Cia de Eletricidade do Acre	Eletroacre	Electricity
	Cia Riograndense de Saneamento	Corsan	Water/sewage
	Cia Pernambucana de Borracha	Coperbo	Manufacturing
	Hospital Nossa Senhora da Conceição	Hosp. NSC	Health services
	Nuclebras de Manazita e Associados	Nuclemon	Mining
	Telecomunicações do Amazonas	Teleamazon	Telecommunications
	Ultrafertil SA- Indústria e Comércio de Fertilizantes	Ultrafertil	Fertilizers
1966	Cia de Navegacção Lloyd Brasileiro	Lloydbras	Transportation
	Cia Eletromecânica	Celma	Transportation equipment
	Cia Energética de São Paulo	Cesp	Electricity
	Itabira Internacional Company Ltd.—Itaco	Itaco	Trading companies
	Petroquímica União	Petroquímica União	Oil and downstream
	Seamar Shipping Corporation	Seamar	Transportation
	Telecomunicações do Maranhão	Telma	Telecommunications
1967	Alumínio SA Extrusão Laminadas	Aluminio	Aluminum
	Brasileira de Dragagem	n.a.	Water/sewage
	Cia Docas do Pará	CDP	Ports
	Cia Siderúrgica de Mogi das Cruzes	Cosim	Steel
	Cia Espírito Santense de Saneamento	Cesan	Water/sewage
	Empresa de Navegação da Amazônia	Enasa	Transportation
	Florestas Rio Doce	FRDSA	Agribusiness
	Petrobras Química	Petroquisa	Oil and downstream
	Saneamento de Goiás	Saneago	Water/sewage
1968	Cia de Gás de São Paulo	Comgás	Gas
	Cia do Metropolitano de São Paulo	Metrô-SP	Transportation
	Telecomunicações de Goiás	Telegoiás	Telecommunications
1969	Caraíba Metais—Indústria e Comércio	Caraíba	Steel
	Centrais Elétricas de Roraima	CER	Electricity
	Centrais Elétricas do Sul do Brasil	Eletrosul	Electricity
	Centrais Telefônicas de Ribeirão Preto	Ceterp	Telecommunications
	Cia de Pesquisa de Recursos Minerais	CPRM	Public admin. various
	Cia de Saneamento Ambiental do Distrito Federal	Caesb	Water/sewage
	Correios e Telégrafos	Correios	Public admin. various
	Desenvolvimento Rodoviário (SP)	Dersa	Transportation

Table 4-A1. (continued)

Year	Company	Acronym	Industry
	Empresa Baina de Águas e Saneamento	Embasa	Water/sewage
	Empresa Brasileira de Aeronáutica	Embraer	Transportation equipment
	Indústria Carboquímica Catarinense	ICC	Chemicals
	Meridional Artes Gráficas	Mag	Public admin. various
	Meridional do Brasil Informática	Meridional	Public admin. various
	Telecomunicações Aeronáuticas	Tasa	Telecommunications
	Telecomunicações de Santa Catarina	Telesc	Telecommunications
1970	Centrais de Abastecimento do Pará	Ceasa/PA	Food distribution/ storage
	Centrais de Abastecimento do Rio de Janeiro	Ceasa / RJ	Food distribution/ storage
	Centrais de Abastecimento do Rio Grande do Sul	Ceasa/RS	Food distribution/ storage
	Cia das Docas do Rio Grande do Norte	Codern	Ports
	Poliolefinas	Poliolefinas	Chemicals
1971	Centrais de Abastecimento de Alagoas	Ceasa/AL	Food distribution/ storage
	Centrais de Abastecimento de Sergipe	Ceasa/SE	Food distribution/ storage
	Centrais de Abastecimento do Ceará	Ceasa/CE	Food distribution/ storage
	Cia de Eletricidade do Ceará	Coelce	Electricity
	Cia de Água e Esgoto do Ceará	Cagece	Water/sewage
	Ferrovia Paulista	Fepasa	Transportation
	Petrobras Distribuidora		Oil and downstream
	Rio Doce Geologia e Mineração	Docegeo	Mining
	Telecomunicações do Ceará	Teleceará	Telecommunications
	Usiminas Mecânica	Usimec	Construction
1972	Braspetro Algerie	Braspetro Alegerie	Oil and downstream
	Centrais de Abastecimento de Campinas	Ceasa Campinas	Food distribution/ storage
	Centrais de Abastecimento de Goiás	Ceasa/GO	Food distribution/ storage
	Centrais de Abastecimento do Maranhão	Ceasa/MA	Food distribution/ storage
	Centrais de Abastecimento do Paraná	Ceasa/PR	Food distribution/ storage

(continued)

Table 4-A1. (continued)

Year	Company	Acronym	Industry
	Cia de Entrepostos e Comércio	Cobec	Food distribution/ storage
	Cia Petroquímica do Nordeste	Copene	Oil and downstream
	Empresa de Infraestrutura Portuária	Infraero	Public admin. various
	Petrobras Internacional	Braspetro	Oil and downstream
	Telecomunicações Brasileiras	Telebras	Telecommunications
	Telecomunicações de Roraima	Telaima	Telecommunications
	Telecomunicações de Sergipe	Telergipe	Telecommunications
	Telecomunições do Pará	Telepara	Telecommunications
	Valec—Comércio e Serviços Ltda	Valec	Trading companies
1973	Casa da Moeda Brasil	CMB	Public admin. various
	Centrais de Abastecimento do Piauí	Ceasa/PI	Food distribution/ storage
	Celulose Nipo-Brasileira	Cenibra	Manufacturing
	Centrais de Abastecimento da Paraíba	Ceasa/PB	Food distribution/ storage
	Centrais de Abastecimento do Amazonas	Ceasa/AM	Food distribution/ storage
	Centrais de Abastecimento do Espírito Santo	Ceasa/ES	Food distribution/ storage
	Centrais de Abastecimento do Rio Grande do Norte	Ceasa/RN	Food distribution/ storage
	Centrais Elétricas do Norte do Brasil	Eletronorte	Electricity
	Cia Docas do Maranhão	Codomar	Ports
	Cia das Docas do Rio de Janeiro—	CDRJ	Ports
	Cia de Saneamento Básico do Est. de SP	Sabesp	Water/sewage
	Cia Docas da Guanabara	CDG	Ports
	Cia Catarinense de Águas e Saneamento	Casan	Water/sewage
	Cia de Tecnologia de Saneamento Ambiental de Brasil	Cetesb	Water/sewage
	Fertilizantes Nitrogenados do Nordeste	Nitrofertil	Fertilizers
	Itabrasco	Itabrasco	Mining
	Itaipu Binacional	Itaipu	Electricity
	Navegação Rio Doce	NRD	Transportation
	Siderurgia Brasiliera SA	Siderbras	Steel
	Telecomunicações de São Paulo	Telesp	Telecommunications
	Telecomunicações do Acre	Teleacre	Telecommunications
	Telecomunicações do Amapá	Teleamapa	Telecommunications
	Valenorte—Alumínio Ltda.	Valenorte	Aluminum

Table 4-A1. (continued)

Year	Company	Acronym	Industry
1974	Acesita Energética	Acesita Energetica	Electricity
	Álcalis do Rio Grande do Norte	Alcanorte	Chemicals
	Bantrade Cia Comércio Internacional	Bantrade	Trading companies
	Centro de Pesquisa de Energia Elétrica	Cepel	Public admin. various
	Cia de Saneamento de Minas Gerais	Copasa	Water/sewage
	Cia Paulista de Celulose	Copase	Manufacturing
	Cia Siderúrgica de Tubarão	CST	Steel
	Computadores e Sistemas Brasileiros	Cobra	Manufacturing
	Cia de Desenv. dos Vales do SF e do Parnaíba	Codevasf	Public admin. various
	Cia Pernambucana de Saneamento	Compesa	Water/sewage
	Empresa de Tecnologia e Informações da Previdência Social	Dataprev	Public admin. various
	Empresas Nucleares Brasileiras	Nuclebras	Electricity
	Forjas Acesita	Fasa	Manufacturing
	Hispanobras	Hispanobras	Mining
	Rio Doce Internacional	RDI	Trading companies
	Sociedade de Abastecimento de Água e Saneamento	Sanasa—Campinas	Water/sewage
	Telecomunicaçõe s do Mato Grosso	Telemat	Telecommunications
	Telecomunicações da Paraíba	Telpa	Telecommunications
1975	Cia Siderúrgica da Amazônia	Siderama	Steel
	Cia Municipal de Limpeza Urbana (RJ)	Comlurb	Public admin. various
	Cia Nipo Brasileira Pelotização	Nibrasco	Manufacturing
	Cia Estadual de Águas e Esgotos	Cedae	Water/sewage
	Empresa de Portos do Brasil	Portobras	Ports
	Fábrica de Estrutura Metálicas	FEM	Manufacturing
	Indústria de Material Bélico do Brasil	IMBEL	Manufacturing
	Nuclebras Auxiliar de Mineração	Nuclam	Mining
	Nuclebras Engenharia	Nuclen	Construction
	Nuclebras Enriquecimento Isotópico	Nuclei	Chemicals
	Nuclebras Equipamentos Pesados	Nuclep	Manufacturing
1976	Centrais de Abast. do Est. Santa Catarina	Ceasa/SC	Food distribution/ storage
	Cia de Engenharia e Tráfego	CET	Public admin. various
	Cia Nal. de Construções Escolares do Est. São Paulo	Conesp	Construction

(continued)

Table 4-A1. (continued)

Year	Company	Acronym	Industry
	Cia Petroquímica do Sul	Copesul	Oil and downstream
	Ferritas Magnéticas	Fermag	Manufacturing
	Interbras	Interbras	Trading companies
	Interbras Cayman Co.	InterbrasCayman	Trading companies
	Mineração Viçosa	Min. Vicosa	Mining
	Petrobras Fertilizantes	Petrofertil	Fertilizers
	Rio Doce Finance Ltd.	RDF	Trading companies
	Valesul—Alumínio	Valesul	Aluminum
1977	Braspetro Oil Services Co.	Brasoil	Trading companies
	Cia das Docas do Estado da Bahia	CODEBA	Ports
	Fertilizantes Fosfatados	Fosfertil	Fertilizers
	Petrobras Mineração	Petromisa	Mining
	Petroflex—Industria e Comércio	Petroflex	Oil and downstream
	Rio Doce America Inc.	RDA	Trading companies
	Rio Doce Ltd.	Rio Doce	Trading companies
	Seagull Trading Co.	Seagull	Trading companies
1978	Alumina do Norte do Brasil	Alunorte	Aluminum
	Alumínio Brasileiro	Albrás	Aluminum
	Cia Brasileira de Participação Agroindustrial	Brasagro	Agribusiness
	Goiás Fertilizantes	Goaisfertil	Fertilizers
	Internor Trade Inc.	Internor	Trading companies
1979	Centrais de Abastecimento do Mato Grosso do Sul	Ceasa/MS	Food distribution/storage
	Empresa de Energia Elétrica de Mato Grosso do Sul	Enersul	Electricity
	Light—Serviços de Eletricidade	Light	Electricity
1980	Cia Docas do Estado de São Paulo	Codesp	Ports
	Embraer Aircraft Corporation	EAC	Transportation equipment
	Empresa Baiana de Alimentos—Cesta do Povo	Ebal	Food distribution/storage
	Empresa de Trens Urbanos de Porto Alegre	Trensurb	Transportation
	Prologo—Produtos Eletrônicos	Prologo	Manufacturing
1981	Eletropaulo—Eletricidade de São Paulo	Eletropaulo	Electricity
	Embraer Aviation Internacional	EAI	Transportation equipment
1982	Cia Docas do Estado do Espírito Santo	Codesa	Ports
	Empresa Gerencial de Projetos Navais	Emgepron	Construction
	Interbras France	InterbrasFrance	Trading companies

Table 4-A1. (continued)

Year	Company	Acronym	Industry
1985	Vale do Rio Doce Alumínio SA	Aluvale	Aluminum
	Cia Brasileira de Infra-Estrutura Fazendária	Infaz	Public admin. various
	Turis-Sul Turismo Sul Brasileiro Ltda	Turis-Sul	Public admin. various
1986	Cia de Gás de Minas Gerais	Gasmig	Gas
1991	Cia de Gás da Bahia	Bahiagás	Gas

Source: Created with the annual reports of Brazil's State-Owned Enterprises Supervisory Agency (SEST), created in 1979 to regulate federal state-owned enterprises (SEST 1981–1985, 1985–1994). Some of the data was complemented with the annual reports of the largest firms in business magazines *Exame* and *Visão*.

5

Leviathan as a Manager

Do CEOs of SOEs Matter?

The firing of baseball managers (and we might add, other managers in and out of sports) is a form of scapegoating, which, of course requires a scapegoat. One of the manager's legitimate roles is to serve as this symbol.

PFEFFER AND SALANCIK 1978, 16

Before continuing with our story of transformation of state capitalism in Brazil, in this chapter we turn our attention to the role of the chief executive officer of a state-owned enterprise. Governments, as controlling shareholders of SOEs, have few tools at their disposal to influence the performance of these firms in the short run.[1] Thus, governments commonly substitute CEOs either as an effort to turn around SOEs or as a scapegoat—that is, as a way to blame CEOs for the poor performance of these firms.[2] Yet replacing CEOs as a policy to affect the performance of SOEs assumes that these managers actually have influence to change course and that the influence they have will be reflected in measurable performance metrics. However, as we discussed before, SOEs often pursue objectives other than pure profit maximization. Moreover, governments may be tempted to appoint politicians or politically connected executives as CEOs.

Studying the CEOs of SOEs and their impact on firm-level performance is therefore a way to assess agency and political effects that may plague state-owned firms. We take advantage of the rich financial data we have for SOEs between 1973 and 1993 to explore the role of CEOs in explaining some of the variation in performance in those firms. Given the large variation in SOE performance over time within countries, within industries, and even within companies themselves, in this chapter we examine how much of that variation can be attributed to the role of CEOs. This question is in fact interesting because we do not know if CEOs can explain some of the variation in performance of SOEs; and if they do, we do not know what CEO characteristics matter more to have better results.

CEOs and the Performance of SOEs

Even for private firms, there is no consensus in the academic literature about how much influence CEOs have on financial performance. There are models explaining why CEOs *should* matter, based on the fact that different CEOs have different management styles, implement new policies, or convey different visions of a change in the company's direction (e.g., Rotemberg and Saloner 1993, 2000). Then there are a series of empirical studies looking at whether CEOs matter for firm outcomes. Some of these studies find that these top managers do not matter that much (Lieberson and O'Connor 1972; Thomas 1988; Pfeffer and Salancik 1978), while others find evidence supporting a stronger role for corporate leaders (Weiner 1978; Weiner and Mahoney 1981; Wasserman et al. 2010; Beatty and Zajac 1987). There is no similar work for CEOs of SOEs, but Salancik and Pfeffer (1977) look at whether mayors have an effect on changing budget allocations in their jurisdictions and find that they explain little of the overall variance in the expenditure variables.

One can think of many reasons why CEOs of SOEs may or may not be influential. The first consideration is that CEOs in SOEs are even more constrained than top executives in private firms. As discussed in Chapter 3, SOEs usually have no control over pricing, have restrictions on firing (at least political restrictions), and tend to have employees who are part of the civil service and thus are both hard to remove and less motivated to take risks. In private firms, there is a clear link between a CEO's influence and his or her power to implement policies (Adams et al. 2005); we would therefore expect that organizational constraints on CEOs of SOEs might weaken the CEO's effect on performance.

Second, there is the problem of political intervention. When governments intervene in the management of SOEs, we usually see two things. According with the social view, governments impose a double bottom line. Furthermore, in line with the political view, political intervention takes the form of clientelism or patronage—that is, the appointment of company officers on the basis of party affiliation and loyalty to the politicians in power rather than on the basis of merit or capacity to manage a firm.

Moreover, SOEs have a soft-budget constraint, since governments tend to bail them out when they go bankrupt, and the effect of this on the CEO's influence is indeterminate. On the one hand, CEOs of SOEs should feel freer to take risks and be entrepreneurial, as they know the downside risk for them and the firm is limited. On the other hand, CEOs of traditional SOEs (owned and run by the government) have few incentives to take risks or be entrepreneurial. Other than career advancement within the government bureaucracy, it is not clear what a CEO would gain by taking risks and even by making the SOE more profitable. In Brazil, the careers of SOE managers were relatively stable and long, supporting the idea that these bureaucrats were not prone to taking major risks or undertaking new projects just to improve the performance of the firms they managed (Schneider 1991).

Beyond the constraints and incentives of CEOs at the firm level, SOE performance is closely linked to the resources a CEO can gather within the network of government firms. CEOs of SOEs can negotiate the hiring and firing of workers with the ministry that oversees them and can attract government entitlements, such as subsidized credit, tariff protections, and ministerial support for pet projects such as plant expansion and vertical and horizontal integration with other firms. More important, perhaps, is whether a CEO can get the inputs the firm needs from other firms and, especially, from other SOEs. Thus, the CEO networks we study are fundamental to a CEO's ability do his or her job and to undertake projects that are important for the firm and for the government. According to Schneider (1991, 67–68), in Brazil during the 1960s and 1970s, "complex projects require[d] coordination among competing officials and agencies with overlapping, competing, or contradictory policy jurisdictions. Coordination among these agencies [was] possible only through standard political practices such as logrolling and personal exchange." Thus, beyond the contribution of CEOs in general, it is important to investigate which CEO-specific traits—such as education, network, political activities, and military training—improve or undermine an SOE's performance.

In this chapter, therefore, we study two questions. First, do the CEOs of SOEs matter for performance? Second, what kinds of CEO background are linked with better SOE performance?

Our empirical analysis is divided into three parts. First, we study the contribution of CEOs to explaining SOE performance. In our second test of CEO effects, we follow the methodology of Bertrand and Schoar (2003), who examine the effects of executives (CEOs and CFOs) who switched firms. They use dummy variables to track those executives who switched firms and then examine how much of the variation in firm performance is explained by the executive. In that way, the effect they pick up is the average contribution of those executives to their firms. The authors find that the effect of those CEOs and CFOs who switch companies explains 5 percent of the variation in firm performance (measured as EBITDA over assets, a proxy for return on assets).

Our third empirical test examines the effects of CEO background on SOE performance. We do this by separating CEOs by training, using education data. We study the effect of having a technical education (for example, the CEO majored in engineering), a military background, and a political background (the CEO had a political post at some point in his career). Finally, as a way to measure how connected a CEO might be with the political elite, we use a variable that captures whether a CEO attended one of a group of elite universities in Brazil.

Variance Decomposition and CEO Effects

A series of studies in the management literature looks at the CEO effect on performance by decomposing the variance of a performance variable (such as return on assets) into components. First, Lieberson and O'Connor (1972) decompose the variation in performance, discounting the year, industry, and company effects, and find that CEOs account for 14.5 percent of the total variance in profit margins, while the industry effect has the biggest impact on profitability, explaining 28.5 percent of the variance. Weiner (1978) and Weiner and Mahoney (1981) find that CEOs explain between 8.7 percent and 12.8 percent of the variance in profitability, but Thomas (1988) finds that CEOs explain only 5.7 percent of it. Wasserman et al. (2010) find that the CEO effects explain about 14 percent of firm-level market valuation (measured as Tobin's q). There is no similar work for CEOs of SOEs. Perhaps the closest study is Salancik and Pfeffer (1977), who look at whether mayors have an effect on changing budget allocations in their jurisdictions and find that they explain little of the overall variance in the expenditure variables.

We follow the latest studies of that literature and decompose the variance of our performance variables for SOEs in Brazil using panel data regressions in which we examine how much of the total variation in performance variables is explained when we add, one by one, year dummies, industry characteristics that vary over time (industry-year dummies), company fixed effects (characteristics of firms that do not change over time), and CEO fixed effects (a dummy for the tenure of each CEO).

We run a simple OLS regression using the following specification:

$$y_{it} = Year_t + Industry_i \times Year_{it} + \beta X_{it} + \gamma_i + \lambda_{CEO} + e_{it}, \tag{5.1}$$

where y_{it} represents firm-level performance—either return on assets (ROA), return on equity (ROE), leverage, or labor productivity (defined as either revenues per worker or net earnings per worker). We then add each of the variables one at a time: year fixed effects *(Year_t)*, and industry-year effects *(Industry_i × Year_{it})*. We then add a set of company characteristics *(X_{it})*, which, depending on the specification, may include firm age, leverage, labor productivity, and capital intensity (fixed assets); company-level fixed effects (γ_i); and, finally, all the CEO dummies, one per CEO (λ_{CEO}). For each regression we look at the adjusted R-squared to see how much each variable contributes to explain the variation in the dependent variable. Following the literature, we call the marginal contribution to R-squared of these CEO dummies "the CEO effect."

We repeat this procedure with a specification that estimates total factor productivity (TFP)[3] by decomposing the residual of a simple production function according to the contribution of the same dummies described above. The specification is

$$\begin{aligned} Ln(Revenues)_{it} = \beta_1 Ln(Employees) + \beta_2 Ln(Fixed\ assets) \\ + Year_t + Industry_i \times Year_{it} \\ + \gamma_i + \lambda_{CEO} + e_{it}, \end{aligned} \tag{5.2}$$

where $Ln(Revenues)_{it}$ is the log of real revenues in 1994 U.S. dollars, $Ln(Employees)$ is the log of the number of employees, and $Ln(Fixed\ assets)$ is the ratio of fixed assets to total assets, used to control for capital intensity. Because TFP fluctuates with business cycles and fluctuates more in some industries than in others, we use the same controls as before.

Brazil between 1973 and 1993 offers an interesting case study in which to examine the variation in performance of SOEs for at least three reasons. First, there were a large number of companies for which financial data was reported frequently by independent business magazines, and there were also detailed annual reports that firms submitted to SEST, the State-Owned Enterprises Supervisory Agency, beginning in 1982. We were therefore able to compile systematic financial and employment data for around 250 SOEs for twenty-one years (1973–1993). Second, during this period, there were many public firms operating within the same industry (see Table 5.1). Third, we have significant variation in performance within industries and within firms over time. Table 5.1 shows the variation in performance by industry for Brazilian SOEs between 1973 and 1982. It should be clear that the variation within industries and within companies is large and deserves further examination.

Obviously, when dealing with SOEs, there is always the problem that efficiency or performance is hard to measure because governments charge SOEs with a double bottom line. SOEs are usually charged with maximizing a social variable (e.g., maximizing employment or maximizing the coverage of the power grid), and at the same time they need to watch the bottom line and be profitable (Ahroni 1986). A money-losing SOE may serve a social purpose in the short run, but in the longer term it can become an unsustainable financial burden for the government (Shirley and Nellis 1991; World Bank 1996).

For that reason, we find our comparisons of profitability or productivity across SOEs less convincing than our analysis of the performance of companies over time. Different companies may be focused on solving different problems—making it unfair to compare their performances—but as long as a particular company is always charged with a specific double bottom line, then changes in performance over time that are not attributable to macroeconomic or industry conditions will more likely be the product of changes in leadership.

Table 5.1. Descriptive statistics of SOEs by industry, Brazil, 1973–1994

	Dictatorship (1985–1993)			Democracy (1973–1985)		
	Avg. num. of firms	Mean ROA	Std. dev.	Avg. num. of firms	Mean ROA	Std. dev.
Agribusiness	2	−0.009	0.07	2	0.006	0.07
Aluminum	5	0.233	0.17	5	0.045	0.21
Chemicals	5	0.169	0.16	5	0.036	0.29
Construction	4	0.003	0.14	4	0.018	0.11
Electricity	47	0.040	0.08	50	−0.016	0.09
Fertilizers	6	0.060	0.14	7	−0.034	0.10
Food distrib. & storage	17	−0.004	0.08	18	0.010	0.10
Gas	2	0.020	0.12	2	0.145	0.17
Health services	4	0.004	0.14	4	−0.003	0.22
Manufacturing	10	0.027	0.18	11	−0.116	0.16
Mining	10	0.127	0.17	10	0.063	0.19
Oil and downstream	12	0.065	0.07	13	0.048	0.08
Ports	11	0.013	0.08	11	−0.027	0.09
Public admin. various	13	0.047	0.13	14	0.000	0.15
Steel	17	0.052	0.18	18	−0.092	0.12
Sugar mills	2	0.009	0.07	2	−0.161	0.10
Telecommunications	40	0.054	0.05	42	0.040	0.05
Trading companies	11	0.072	0.16	11	0.086	0.12
Logistics	13	0.028	0.11	13	−0.022	0.15
Transportation equipment	6	0.079	0.11	7	−0.069	0.16
Water/sewage	11	0.005	0.07	10	0.014	0.09

CEO Effects in SOEs, 1973–1994

In Table 5.2, we show the estimated effect of CEOs on the performance of SOEs using simple variance decomposition. The estimated CEO effect is 14 percent of the variation in return on assets, which is in the upper bound of the estimates found in the literature (which vary between 8 percent and 14 percent). CEO effects also explain 14 percent of the variation in leverage. Finally, we find—surprisingly—that CEO effects explain 41 percent of the variation in labor productivity, while they explain only 1.5 percent of the variation in total factor productivity. The former result is a very strong effect and may reflect the fact that CEOs of Brazilian SOEs did not have

Table 5.2. Measuring the effect of CEO tenure in SOEs in Brazil, 1973–1994 (dummies for each CEO's tenure)

	Return on assets	Leverage	Labor productivity (earnings per worker)	TFP
Year	0.047	0.021	−0.002	0.664
Industry	0.074	0.221	0.022	0.100
Industry × year	0.149	0.060	−0.084	0.000
Business group	0.017	0.145	0.019	0.014
Company effect	0.094	0.284	0.378	0.121
CEO effect	**0.135**	**0.137**	**0.412**	**0.015**
Overall adj. R^2	0.593	0.868	0.745	0.914

Note: Estimates come from an OLS regression with random effects, clustering errors at the company level. The regression for company effects and CEO effects may also include controls for company characteristics, such as leverage, size (log of assets), capital intensity (fixed assets to assets), and earnings per employee.

many levers with which to improve or deteriorate the ways of their firms, but adding more employees was one variable that, at least before 1983, was at their discretion and that most likely deteriorated the productivity of the firm.

Now, how can we tell if these results show that CEOs of SOEs explain much of the variation or not? Comparing our results to the estimates produced for the effect of CEOs in the largest firms in the United States can be deceiving for two reasons. First, using the variance decomposition approach, we have the risk of confounding CEO effects with macroeconomic shocks that are firm-specific. Thus, comparing CEO effects in different moments in time and in different countries can be problematic. Moreover, the constraints faced by Brazilian CEOs may be different from those faced by American CEOs.

A better comparison would be to see the CEO effects for SOEs compared to those of large, comparable Brazilian private firms during the same period. We present the results in Table 5.3. We find that CEOs explain 7.3 percent of the variation in return on assets in private companies and 13.1 percent of the variation in leverage. That means that our estimates of CEO effects for SOEs are larger, at least when we use ROA as a dependent variable, and suggest CEO effects in SOEs may be more important than in private enterprises. We cannot do the same comparison using productivity as a dependent variable because we were not able to find annual data on the number of employees of private firms.

Table 5.3. Measuring the effect of CEO tenure in private firms in Brazil, 1973–1994 (dummies for each CEO's tenure)

	Return on assets	Leverage
Time effect	0.108	0.081
Industry	0.033	0.277
Industry-year	0.125	−0.269
Company effect	0.099	0.543
CEO effect	**0.073**	**0.131**
Overall adj. R^2	0.438	0.763

Note: Estimates come from an OLS regression with random effects, clustering errors at the company level. Each regression also includes controls for company characteristics, such as leverage (except when leverage is the dependent variable) and size (log of assets).

Table 5.4. Descriptive statistics of private companies and SOEs, 1973–1994

		SOEs			Private companies	
Variable	N	Mean	Sd	N	Mean	Sd
Assets (billions US$ 2009)	3117	1.87	4.91	2772	0.42	0.44
ROA	3133	0.03	0.12	2780	0.07	0.09
ROE	3133	0.05	0.45	2780	0.13	0.27
Leverage	3133	0.50	0.28	2780	0.49	0.20
Years with losses	3133	0.31	0.46	2780	0.13	0.33
Bankrupt (liabilities>assets)	3133	0.04	0.19	2780	0.01	0.08
CEO turnover	2213	0.29	0.45	1473	0.10	0.30

Something that may explain the fact that we have big effects for CEO effects in SOEs is the difference in turnover rates between private and state-owned companies. As we show in Table 5.4, every year about one-third of SOEs had changes in CEOs, while in large private firms CEO turnover was less common. Most of the largest firms we include in the sample were controlled by a family that may have had someone close to the family running the company. Having more CEO turnover in SOEs also increases the probability that our CEO effects are also capturing other factors that are spuriously correlated to CEO tenure. For that reason in the next section we focus on measuring CEO effects for only those managers that switched firms.

Identifying the Effects of CEOs Who Switched Companies

We then proceed to examine CEO effects by exploiting only the variation that comes from CEOs who switched companies. Table 5.5 shows the descriptive statistics of our entire sample of companies in order to describe the subsample of SOEs we use for this part of our study. We can see that the firms with CEOs who ran two or more firms in their careers were larger and had higher turnover, profitability, productivity, and asset growth. Thus, our subsample is picking up some of the best firms, but not necessarily the most capital-intensive ones.[4]

In Table 5.6, we show the results of our regression analysis of the contribution of those CEOs who switch companies to variation in performance and leverage. We follow the methodology of Bertrand and Schoar (2003) and display only the adjusted R-squared of the regressions with and without

Table 5.5. Descriptive statistics of companies run by CEOs who switched , 1973–1993

Variable	No switching CEO			With switching CEO			Means test	
	N	Mean	Sd	N	Mean	Sd	*t*-statistic	
Assets (billions US$ 2009)	1872	1.7	4.4	672	3.2	7.1	−6.47	***
Turnover (EBITDA/ assets)	1880	53%	85%	675	99%	137%	−10.00	***
Leverage (tot. debt/ assets)	1880	49%	30%	675	54%	31%	−3.5	***
Return on assets	1880	2%	11%	675	5%	13%	−7.11	***
Return on equity	1880	3%	51%	675	11%	71%	−3.24	**
Revenue per worker (thousands US$)	1880	123.9	278.3	675	350.7	455.6	−15.11	***
Profits per worker (thousands US$)	1772	5.7	215.7	553	−69.2	1,284.8	2.35	**
% of years w/ losses	1880	34%	47%	675	25%	43%	4.08	***
% of years in bankruptcy	1880	3%	18%	675	5%	23%	−2.59	***
Fixed to total assets	1588	65%	26%	570	48%	33%	−0.97	
Growth in assets	1867	1%	67%	670	4%	83%	12.28	***
Workers per million US$ in assets	1805	25.1	209.9	599	14.0	43.9	1.28	

Note: ***, **, and * denote significance at the 1%, 5%, and 10% levels, respectively.

Table 5.6. CEO effects using only those CEOs who switched firms

Variable	Return on assets (1)	Return on equity (2)	Turnover (3)	Leverage (4)	Rev. per worker (5)	Total factor productivity (TFP) (6)	Years with losses (7)	Years bankrupt (8)
Full sample (1973–1993)								
Number of observations	766	766	766	766	841	764	766	766
Adj. R-squared (without CEO dummies)	0.354	0.41	0.358	0.496	0.086	0.355	0.471	0.577
Adj. R-squared (with CEO dummies)	0.375	0.428	0.442	0.544	0.266	0.456	0.506	0.626
F-statistic	17.36	14.86	35.93	22.14	34.74	26.79	25.22	28.19
F test p-value	<0.001	<0.001	<0.001	<0.001	<0.001	<0.001	<0.001	<0.001
CEO effect (chg. in adj. R^2)	0.021	0.018	0.084	0.048	0.18	0.101	0.035	0.049
Dictatorship (1973–1984)								
Number of observations	371	371	371	371	418	370	371	371
Adj. R-squared (without CEO dummies)	0.117	0.479	0.462	0.474	0.078	0.252	0.568	0.629

Adj. R-squared (with CEO dummies)	0.139	0.473	0.486	0.511	0.214	0.29	0.573	0.696
F-statistic	7.5	5.93	8.41	9.54	13.5	8.65	6.9	15.73
F test *p*-value	<0.001	<0.001	<0.001	<0.001	<0.001	<0.001	<0.001	<0.001
CEO effect (chg. in adj. R^2)	**0.022**	**−0.006**	**0.024**	**0.037**	**0.136**	**0.038**	**0.005**	**0.067**
Democracy (1985–1993)								
Number of observations	395	395	395	395	423	394	395	395
Adj. R-squared (without CEO dummies)	0.543	0.471	0.303	0.561	0.111	0.543	0.438	0.59
Adj. R-squared (with CEO dummies)	0.574	0.478	0.293	0.612	0.336	0.615	0.486	0.623
F-statistic	8.82	6.26	5.1	11.54	17.74	14	9.86	9.5
F test *p*-value	<0.001	<0.001	<0.001	<0.001	<0.001	<0.001	<0.001	<0.001
CEO effect (chg. in adj. R^2)	**0.031**	**0.007**	**−0.01**	**0.051**	**0.225**	**0.072**	**0.048**	**0.033**

Note: All regressions include controls for workers per asset, fixed assets to total assets, firm age, and the log of total assets. ROA and ROE regressions control for leverage, labor productivity profits per worker, workers per asset, fixed assets to total assets, firm age, and the log of total assets. We exclude the results of the regressions that had profits per worker as a dependent variable because we consistently get negative values for adjusted R-squared.

dummies for CEOs who switched companies, the F test to see if those CEO dummies are jointly significant, and, finally, the contribution of these CEOs to the adjusted R-squared. We conduct three tests: one for the full sample, one for the sample that covers the period during which Brazil was under a military dictatorship (1973–1984), and one for the sample that covers the period in which Brazil had a democratic government (1985–1993).

In the second column, we show the results for return on assets. According to our tests, adding controls for the CEOs who switch companies explains an additional 2 percent of the variation in returns. This is lower than our previous estimate of 14 percent (considering all CEOs), probably because those estimates capture not only the CEO effect, but may pick up temporal firm-specific shocks that are spuriously correlated with CEO changes. The effect of these CEOs on ROA is a bit higher during the democratic period. Our results for return on equity (ROE) are less consistent, but for the full sample, CEOs who switch companies explain close to 2 percent of the variation.

In column 5 of Table 5.6, we show that the CEOs who switched firms explain almost 5 percent of the variation in leverage. In columns 5 and 6, we show the results when our productivity variables (either revenue per worker or total factor productivity) are used as dependent variables. In column 5, CEOs explain about 18 percent of the variation when we use the full sample with labor productivity as dependent variable. CEOs explain 10 percent of the variation in TFP according to column 6. This is consistent with the finding in the previous section that CEO effects were higher for the labor productivity regressions.

Finally, in the last two columns of Table 5.6, we use as dependent variables the number of years in which the company suffered losses and the number of years in which it was bankrupt. The CEOs who switched companies explain between 3.5 percent and 5 percent of the variation.

Our results show CEO effects that are a bit lower than those found by Bertrand and Schoar (2003). For instance, using their proxy for ROA, they find that CEOs explain about 5 percent of the variation in performance, while we find that CEOs explain only 2 percent. The difference may be related to the fact that some of the SOEs in Brazil were relatively autonomous (especially before 1985), but not all of them. Some of the SOEs in our sample also had social objectives that may have diverted attention from profitability. For instance, some of the switching CEOs in our sample were engineers who worked for a variety of telecommunications companies. These CEOs switched companies because they were sent by the holding company to set up or revamp the operation of telephone companies in Brazil's frontier areas (the Amazon region, the state of Mato Grosso, and the small states in the northeast), places where profitability was perhaps a lower priority for the government.

Still, our results are surprising because we find consistently stronger CEO effects during the democratic period (1985–1993), when controls over the budgets, salaries, and hiring policies of SOEs were tighter. How can that be the case? We think that the constraints over SOEs are not equally binding for all companies. CEOs with connections or those who are part of the clientelistic network of the ruling coalition may have more leeway to get additional inputs at privileged prices, for example, or to get loans from the development banks at subsidized rates. In fact, the SOEs with CEOs who switched companies outperformed the average firm in the sample. Moreover, we think that part of the CEO effects we find may also be reflecting changes in the connectedness of CEOs. As we show below, there were many CEO changes in the 1980s that involved the appointment (or firing) or CEOs educated in the best universities in Brazil.

Does CEO Background Matter for Performance?

In this section, we study how much a CEO's background explains company performance. The literature looking at the background of SOE managers usually concludes that CEOs and executives with technical backgrounds drive better company performance than other executives do (see Chapter 3). For Weber (1968), "the decisive reason for the advance of the bureaucratic organization has always been its purely technical superiority over any other form of organization" (p. 973). Amsden (1989) defends the idea that engineers and other technical employees recruited from the top ranks of local universities were fundamental for the development of large heavy industries in the Republic of Korea. Schneider (1991), Martins (1974), and Escobar (1982) defended the thesis that the best-performing companies in Brazil were run by executives with technical backgrounds (mostly engineers). For instance, according to Escobar, technical managers at Companhia Vale do Rio Doce, the largest state-owned mining company in Brazil, "do not view themselves as social workers" because "the engineer is assumed to choose strategies prompted by the same basic motivations as his colleague in private enterprise" (p. 107).

A second hypothesis is that military CEOs are different. Malmendier et al. (2010) look at the effect of CEOs' life experiences on company financial policies in the United States and find that military managers with combat experience tend to take more risks and to choose higher leverage. Benmelech and Frydman (2010) study military CEOs and find that they perform better during downturns than nonmilitary CEOs do and tend to engage less frequently in corporate fraud.

There were two types of military CEOs: those with general army, navy, or air force training and those with engineering degrees. Because we feel the latter had technical skills that were perhaps more relevant for the management of SOEs, we separate them for our tests into two different groups.

Now, we would expect that the leadership and technical skills that military CEOs acquired during their officer training may matter to improve performance in SOEs for the following reasons. First, military CEOs in Brazil had a management style and background different from those of technical CEOs or politicians. The career track of these servicemen was quite distinctive. "Officer cadets often come from military families and attend military high schools before entering the officer academy" (Schneider 1991). After the officer academy, colonels and junior generals were likely to spend a year at the military think tank, the Higher War College (Escola Superior de Guerra). Some officers chose to leave the armed forces and pursue careers as managers of SOEs. Just as Becker (1962) defends the idea that military officers have training in "a wide variety of skills and many—such as piloting and machine repair—are very useful in the civil sector" (p. 16), we, too, think that military CEOs have skills, particularly leadership skills, that are useful when they run SOEs (Groysberg et al. 2010).[5] A report by the firm Korn/Ferry International found that American firms led by CEOs with military backgrounds outperformed the S&P 500 index. The military leadership skills cited in the report as useful for CEOs were (a) learning to work as a part of a team, (b) organizational skills such as planning and effective use of resources, (c) good communication skills, (d) defining a goal and motivating others to follow it, (e) a highly developed sense of ethics, and (f) the ability to remain calm under pressure (Griesedieck 2006). It is likely that these skills are learned by Brazilian officers as well. Second, military CEOs may also have a set of connections they make during their training and rotations. Since Brazil was under a military dictatorship from 1964 to 1985, we may think that the network of military CEOs might have allowed them to connect to key people in the government, to secure resources and inputs and support for their projects in general.

A third hypothesis is related to a CEO's connections to the political elite and to other CEOs, rather than the kind of training he or she had. That is, perhaps what matters is not whether CEOs are politicians or have a technical background, but whether they attended an elite school. We separate training from elite membership by including a variable that separates CEOs according to whether they attended an elite university in Brazil.[6] We define elite universities as the federal universities plus the University of São Paulo and the Technological Institute of Aeronautics (known as ITA). The federal universities were and still are the best universities in the country. There is no tuition, and the admissions tests are extremely competitive; usually their graduates are the most talented college graduates in Brazil. Beyond federal universities, at USP and ITA the admission exams were extremely hard, and the training was among the best, especially for engineers. Thus, our dummy variable for whether the CEO attended elite universities may also be capturing the analytical capacity of the managers and other intellectual attributes.

We coded CEOs according to their undergraduate training. Brazilian universities, unlike those in the United States, do not offer liberal arts training. Students enroll in a specific field, such as civil engineering, and all of their courses from day one are focused on that field. In general terms, we divided our CEOs into five categories. First, we coded as technical all CEOs who had chosen a technical undergraduate major (e.g., engineering, economics, accounting, and business) or whose backgrounds were somewhat technical and relevant for the company (e.g., a geologist in a mining firm). Second, we coded as military all the CEOs who came from either the army, the navy, or the air force. Third, we coded as politicians any CEOs who held a political post between 1973 and 1993. Fourth, we coded as technical-military all the CEOs who had a military background *and* a degree in a technical subject. Finally, we also coded as technical-politicians all CEOs who, at some point, held a top political position and also had a technical degree. (For more details see Appendix 5.1.)

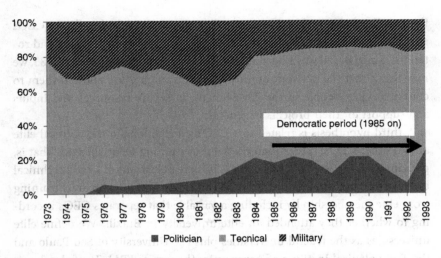

Figure 5.1. Distribution of backgrounds of CEOs of state-owned enterprises in Brazil, 1973–1993

For any given year, we have basic biographical information for between 100 and 250 CEOs of SOEs. Figure 5.1 shows the distribution of CEO backgrounds throughout our period. There are three patterns that should be noted. First, the number of politicians running SOEs rises after the democratic transition in 1985, increasing to over 10 percent of the sample. We consider this a logical outcome because we think that democracy increased the need to give out pork—including jobs in SOEs—to constituencies and party members. Second, the proportion of technical CEOs running SOEs remained relatively high (around 60 percent) throughout our period (or about sixty to one hundred technical CEOs per year). Third, the proportion of military CEOs is close to 30 percent before 1985, but even after that, it remains at around 20 percent, partly because we include companies that were closely tied to military aims. This proportion is not that high compared to the number of military CEOs in SOEs in Chile or Peru during the same period, where over 50 percent of the CEOs had military backgrounds.[7]

CEO Backgrounds and SOE Performance

To study if background and ability matter, we use our panel of SOEs and their CEOs to run regressions using Equations 1 and 2. We include fixed effects to try to control for company-level unobservables. Therefore, our results should be interpreted as changes in the performance within firms as a product of changes in CEO background. This setup allows us to disentangle the company effect from the CEO background effect (the most common problem in the literature on CEO background in Brazil) and helps us to minimize the endogeneity of a CEO's background according to the type of firm he or she works for (e.g., telecommunication companies usually hire engineers). This means that companies that always had a technical CEO, such as Companhia Vale do Rio Doce, cannot help us to identify the effect of CEO background on performance.

In Table 5.7, we examine the effect on performance of (a) CEO background and (b) our elite school dummy, with performance measured either as return on assets or return on equity. In our specifications, we include all the CEO background types simultaneously, and we experiment with leaving out the nontechnical civilian CEOs and the technical CEOs as excluding categories. Surprisingly, the coefficients for a technical CEO and for a politician CEO are not significant.

We find some weak evidence that military CEOs ran firms with higher return on assets when they took over from a nontechnical civilian manager (see columns 3 and 4 of Table 5.7). Yet military CEOs with technical backgrounds consistently improved the performance of the companies they ran. So we cannot discard the hypotheses that military training may provide managers with leadership skills that are helpful to make SOEs more profitable. Still, it seems that military managers with some technical knowledge helpful for the industry did consistently better. Our results indicate that switching either from a civilian or a nonmilitary technical to a technical-military CEO led to an increase in ROA of over 4 percent. This effect is not trivial given that the mean for ROA is 2.8 percent.

In all of the regressions in Table 5.7, we include the control for whether the CEO attended an elite university. This variable measures the effect of a change from having a CEO who did not attend one of these elite universities in Brazil to having a CEO who did. The results are significant, large, and consistent across specifications and work for both ROA and ROE. The effect of getting a CEO who attended an elite university could be an increase in return on assets ranging between 1.5 percent and 2.3 percent or an increase in return on equity ranging between 4 percent and 7.6 percent (the mean for ROE is 6.8 percent).

Table 5.7. Regressions: CEO background and SOE performance, Brazil, 1973–1993

Variables:	1 ROA Full sample	2 ROA Full sample	3 ROA Dictatorship	4 ROA Democracy	5 ROE Full sample	6 ROE Full sample	7 ROE Dictatorship	8 ROE Democracy
CEO tenure (years)	0.000 (0.001)	0.000 (0.001)	−0.001 (0.001)	0.004 (0.003)	−0.004 (0.005)	−0.004 (0.005)	0.001 (0.006)	−0.013 (0.020)
Elite university	0.023*** (0.008)	0.023*** (0.008)	0.019*** (0.008)	0.028** (0.015)	0.076** (0.035)	0.076** (0.035)	0.038 (0.027)	0.189*** (0.066)
CEO types:								
Technical	−0.007 (0.021)		0.020 (0.022)	−0.023 (0.040)	0.064 (0.087)		0.062 (0.084)	−0.191 (0.191)
Military	0.003 (0.042)	0.010 (0.032)	0.183*** (0.046)	0.112** (0.064)	0.040 (0.128)	−0.024 (0.090)	−1.135*** (0.398)	−0.021 (0.194)
Politician	0.002 (0.023)	0.010 (0.014)	0.050** (0.024)	−0.030 (0.043)	0.109 (0.091)	0.045 (0.052)	−0.056 (0.155)	−0.112 (0.169)
Technical-military	0.042* (0.021)	0.049*** (0.015)	0.087*** (0.028)	0.030 (0.033)	0.218** (0.095)	0.154** (0.063)	0.157 (0.120)	0.132 (0.118)
Technical-politician	0.006 (0.021)	0.013 (0.009)	0.020 (0.023)	0.004 (0.034)	0.114 (0.080)	0.050 (0.038)	0.008 (0.092)	−0.043 (0.137)
Nontech, civilian		0.007 (0.021)				−0.064 (0.087)		
Excluded background category:	Civilian	Technical	Civilian	Civilian	Civilian	Technical	Civilian	Civilian
Observations	537	537	275	262	537	537	275	262
Number of companies	84	84	60	63	84	84	60	63
Adjusted R-squared	0.5510	0.5510	0.5260	0.5590	0.4310	0.4310	0.7140	0.2880
R-squared within	0.7000	0.7000	0.6820	0.7100	0.6200	0.6200	0.8080	0.5310

Notes: All regressions include controls for firm characteristics (age, leverage, earnings per worker, workers per asset, and fixed assets to assets—as a proxy for capital intensity). Also, all specifications include year, industry-year, and company dummies. Robust standard errors in parentheses. Coefficients marked as ***, **, and * denote statistical significance at the 1%, 5%, and 10% levels, respectively.

This strong effect of the elite university variable suggests that the CEO characteristic that is most important for SOE performance is not necessarily being a politician or technical specialist, but rather belonging to an elite network within the government. That is, belonging to the Brazilian educated elite (and being smart enough to actually get into one of the elite schools) or the military elite provided managers with certain advantages. Therefore, our findings confirm previous claims that public-sector management is improved with either the screening of top talent (Amsden 1989; J. Wade 1995) or that it is fundamental for SOEs to be connected to the network of resources through formal and informal ties (Pfeffer and Salancik 1978).

That is, CEOs who wanted to undertake major projects needed to mobilize resources from different parts of the government and therefore needed a good network of connections and support among top bureaucrats. Moreover, it could be the case that in Brazil, as is the France (Bertrand, Kramarz, et al. 2007), some of the most important networks were created either in college, graduate school, or while attending the Higher War College, an extension school focused on courses on national security and strategic studies for elites. During our period college was more important than graduate school, and the Higher War College was also a central place within the network of political elites (Schneider 1991).

Now, trying to disentangle more what it means to belong to a network of people who attended an elite university, we conducted a further test. There is the possibility that what matters for CEO performance is not belonging to a broad elite network of people who attended top universities, or their intellectual abilities, but perhaps the CEO's connection to a direct superior, either the government minister regulating his or her company, or even the president. Thus, we devised three tests in which we check if (a) the CEO attended the same university as the president and the minister in charge of overseeing him or her; or (b) whether the CEO and these high-level politicians overlapped in college using a window of four years around their graduation dates; and, (c) whether the CEO and the respective minister or the president of Brazil attended the Higher War College simultaneously or overlapped while studying there (using graduation dates plus/minus two years because the programs were shorter). None of these variables, however, exhibit significant coefficients, and they do not weaken the coefficient for elite universities. Hence it seems that the broad network and the intellectual ability of CEOs who attended elite universities are what mattered, rather than their immediate connections to the minister or the president.

Conclusion

In this chapter, we have examined a factor that we think explains part of the variation in SOE performance over time. Because most of the research on SOEs has focused on comparing them with private companies, few studies have looked at how important it is for SOEs to have able CEOs. In fact, we argue that the competitive exams used by public universities in Brazil are perhaps better filters for top managerial talent (or at least *future* top managerial talent) than the exams *(concursos públicos)* used to select workers in SOEs. Then, after college, what mattered was the network that those CEOs who attended elite schools created.

Today, one of the major handicaps of the largest SOEs in Brazil is that they have to compete with private firms without having a competitive market for talent. SOEs in Brazil and in many other countries (e.g., India) are staffed through civil service procedures. That means that all managers have to be trained in-house and that the initial selection of managers has a path-dependent effect on a firm's performance. If the initial selection is flawed, or if the promise of lifetime employment generates moral hazard, then some SOEs are doomed to underperform.

The lesson, then, is that it is important to give SOEs the flexibility to select talented managers, including "outsiders" such as smart managers with technical backgrounds. Consistent with our discussion in Chapter 3, governments looking to improve performance of SOEs consider the importance of ability and backgrounds when selecting CEOs. Yet SOE employees usually push back against such selection criteria because they believe that outsiders do not understand the culture of the firm or the way in which SOEs work. Yet in our sample, the firms that were run by CEOs who switched companies (who were outsiders to at least one firm) outperformed the SOEs in the sample. Thus, inertia or corporate culture may not have prevented change in the large state-owned firms we study.

APPENDIX

Database of State-Owned Enterprise Performance, 1973–1993

Company Data

In order to examine the performance of SOEs in Brazil and the role of their CEOs, we collected a detailed database of around 250 SOEs between 1973 and 1993. Our data came mostly from SEST reports (Brazil, 1981–1985; Brazil, 1986–1993). We also added data for a set of companies controlled by Brazilian states; we collected this data from the business magazines *Exame* and *Visão*, which published financials and the number of employees of a large number of firms annually. We used these same sources to compile the database of federal SOEs from 1973 to 1979. We omitted from our sample firms with fewer than one hundred employees (e.g., small trading companies).

It is important to note that one of the reasons why economists and economic historians have not delved into quantitative studies of SOEs in Brazil in the 1970s and 1980s is the difficulty of dealing with different currency units and inflation when using financial data. The financial crisis of the early 1980s and the government's failed measures to control expenditures led to rampant inflation, which by the late 1980s had reached hyperinflation levels (more than 50 percent inflation per month). When prices increase that rapidly, it is hard for companies to keep their financials corrected for inflation. Moreover, in a period of such inflation, it is common to see the number of digits used for financial transactions increasing, which generates accounting confusion. For those reasons, the Brazilian government between 1970 and 1994 changed the currency five times, wiping out three zeros of the currency at least three times in less than twenty years.

Furthermore, since 1976, the Brazilian government had made it mandatory for companies to "correct" the value of their fixed assets according to the official inflation used to calculate the interest rates of the Obrigações Reajustáveis do Tesouro Nacional (ORTNs), a type of inflation-indexed bond the Brazilian government issued between 1964 and 1986.[8] ORTNs, however, usually underestimated inflation. Yet inflation increased so rapidly between reporting periods (from January 1 to December 31) that companies also had to adjust their sales and revenue (usually compiled monthly) to compile a figure for the December report in both their balance sheets and profit-and-loss statements. And even so, such adjustments did not render the figures comparable from year to year.

In order to deal with the different currencies and rapid inflation rate, we decided to convert all of our data into Brazilian real of 1994, when the Central Bank of Brazil fixed the exchange rate of the real to the U.S. dollar at 1-to-2. We converted our data in two steps. First, we converted all figures into reais (the plural of real), and then we deflated our series using the so-called IGP-DI price deflator.[9]

Moreover, because of the operational difficulties CEOs faced in the 1980s—with high inflation, price controls by industry, and obstacles to hiring new employees—improving their firms' financial performance was a daunting task. Return on assets of SOEs in the 1980s was usually negative, and many of the firms in our sample operated with negative equity (i.e., they were technically bankrupt) until the government recapitalized them. Given all these complications, we do not put too much trust in simple analysis of the figures, even if deflated. We put greater trust in comparisons of a company's performance over time, using econometric techniques that allow us to control for macroeconomic conditions that affected all firms or all the firms in one industry.

Data on CEOs and Their Backgrounds

We were able to obtain the name and tenure of 868 CEOs of state-owned (federal and state) enterprises in Brazil between 1973 and 1993. Given the nature of the data, our research for biographical information was unconventional and eclectic. We used the government biographical archives known as CPDOC, biographical dictionaries, biographies published by the companies, biographies available on the Internet, e-mails to the CEOs and former CEOs themselves, phone calls, and university records (including records from the Higher War College and other army schools).

Out of the 868 CEOs we identified (for close to 250 firms), we have complete biographical information for only 467 of them. This information includes date of birth, schools attended, BA major and graduate degree, membership in the armed forces, and some career data, such as years in the firm, whether the CEO had had experience in the private sector, and whether he or she had had experience in the firm's industry before becoming its CEO. We also know which CEOs in our database attended the Higher War College.

Using the education information we gathered, we coded whether a CEO had attended a federal university, as discussed earlier in this chapter. In any given year we have basic biographical information for between 100 and 250 CEOs of SOEs.

6

The Fall of Leviathan as an Entrepreneur in Brazil

During the early 1980s, most countries in the world experienced severe recessions, while in the late 1980s, a large group of countries democratized or abandoned economic systems based on central planning. During that decade, the differences in performance between SOEs and private companies widened noticeably. Since then, hundreds of papers have compared the performance of SOEs and private companies, almost invariably finding that the former underperform the latter, except under some circumstances such as when SOEs face competition (Bartel and Harrison 2005) or when SOEs have been able to act as private companies, with professional management and boards of directors that monitor them closely (Kole and Mulherin 1997). Less academic effort has been put into explaining what causes SOEs to behave differently from private companies when facing similar circumstances. In particular, why did SOEs start behaving differently in the 1980s in emerging markets, and in particular in Brazil? By examining these issues, we also shed light on why the post–World War II system of state capitalism (what we call Leviathan as an entrepreneur) went broke in the 1980s.

This chapter provides a causal story that shows how the behavior of SOEs differs from that of private firms. Most of the papers that examine why SOEs are more inefficient than private companies use cross-sectional comparisons of firms, while most of the theoretical literature focusing on the differences between private companies and SOEs also focuses on the problem of the double bottom line—the fact that SOEs sometimes aim to maximize social goals—or on the problem of political interference (see Chapter 3). But, to our knowledge, no one has offered a causal story of the demise of the Leviathan as an entrepreneur model. We do so by identifying economic and political "shocks" in the late 1970s and early 1980s that led SOEs to behave less efficiently than private companies. As a result of those shocks, the balance sheets of SOEs deteriorated, which ultimately led governments to privatize in order to clean up their own balance sheets. Our causal story, therefore, explains why the wave of privatizations started in the late 1980s and not in the early 1980s or late 1970s.

Our argument is straightforward: compared to private firms, SOEs tend to be more subject to political influence, and their managers may be less incentivized to pursue efficiency-enhancing adjustments. Our analysis of how SOEs respond to external shocks can provide important lessons on their distinctive behavior. For instance, we should expect SOEs to be more affected by political change than private firms are, because the president of the republic or the ministers in charge of particular industries have a voice in the management of SOEs and may be inclined to appoint political allies as CEOs or, quite often, to fire CEOs as scapegoats if the firm is not doing well. Also, because SOEs typically have a double bottom line, they may be less inclined than private firms to downsize their labor forces during an economic crisis.

We specifically examine the behavior of SOEs with full state control in order to study how SOEs respond to economic and political shocks that may affect their decisions to restructure their labor forces. And, indeed, we find that, during a crisis, SOEs lay off fewer workers than private companies do. We also find that when there is political turnover, such as a presidential succession, SOEs are more likely to switch CEOs than private companies are.

Context and Data

For this chapter, we built a database that tracks the performance and employment of 136 Brazilian SOEs (owned at the federal level) between 1973 and 1993. Our data were obtained mostly from the reports issued by SEST, an agency the Brazilian government created in 1979 to regulate federal SOEs (Brazil, 1981–1985; Brazil, 1986–1993). We also used the business magazines *Exame, Visão,* and *Gazeta* to compile the database from 1973 to 1979. These magazines published the financials, the number of employees, and the names of CEOs of a large number of firms annually. Given the comparative nature of our research question—the behavior of SOEs vis-à-vis their private counterparts—we also include 156 private firms, essentially the top private firms in Brazil in terms of total revenues during our period, to serve as a control group. Data from private firms came from various sources, such as *Exame, Gazeta,* and the companies' own web sites.

There are obvious concerns with selection bias in our sample. The most concerning selection problem would be that we are comparing bad SOEs with extremely good private firms (or vice versa). We address some of those concerns when we build our sample. For instance, we eliminate small SOEs from the sample, because they tend to be more inefficient. We also eliminate firms that are purely in public services, like hospitals and food storage. Finally, we match some of the largest private firms in Brazil with the large SOEs in our sample so that we have many SOEs and private firms within each of our industry codes (two-digit SIC codes). Another concern is even by grouping firms by industry, it is the case that a handful of SOEs in Brazil were in industries with a state monopoly (such as electricity, oil, and telecom); in such cases, our SOEs had no private counterparts. However, as we explain below, we tried to overcome some of those limitations by controlling for firm-level time-varying observable and fixed unobservable variables through fixed-effect specifications. We also perform robustness analyses using matching techniques based on company-level "fundamentals" such as size and financial indicators.

We take advantage of the fact that during our sample period (1973–1993) there are both exogenous macroeconomic shocks and the relatively exogenous break associated with the transition to democracy in 1985. This feature of our data set provides a unique opportunity to see how SOEs respond to distinct political regimes.

Our temporal window, in particular, covers an important economic shock, the crisis of 1979–1983, the worst recession in modern Brazilian history. We think that such a shock led to different behavior in SOEs and in private companies, a difference we should be able to capture empirically. In fact, Figure 6.1 shows that both SOEs and private companies were severely hit by the crisis, as the percentage of firms declaring loses increases in both cases. Yet SOEs seem to be taking more of a hit during the crisis. We believe this is linked to the way they react to an external shock, given the political constraints under which they operate.

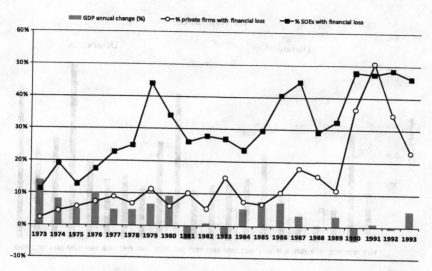

Figure 6.1. GDP growth and the losses of private and state-owned firms in Brazil, 1973–1993

Firm-Level Outcome Variables

Given the magnitude of the shock and the fact that it was an external shock, we would like to compare how SOEs and private companies reacted to this crisis in two dimensions: CEO turnover (the change in a company's CEO) and layoffs (variables that measure changes in the number of employees). We use *CEO Turnover*, a dummy variable coded as 1 if the company's CEO in a given year is different from the observed CEO in the previous year and coded 0 otherwise.[1]

Our variables measuring layoffs are of primary concern, because an economic crisis is when we think we should be able to find Leviathan tempted to use SOEs as a way to smooth things over either by hiring workers or by lowering the rate of layoffs below that which would keep production following demand without a decrease in labor productivity. In other words, SOEs may be forced to keep or even hire workers, just so the workers will not be unemployed—a social rather than a business priority. We estimate our primary variable of interest as the logarithmic value of the total yearly reported number of employees, $Ln(Employees_t)$. We then construct a measure of layoffs as $Ln(Employees_{t-1}) - Ln(Employees_t)$, which is positive if

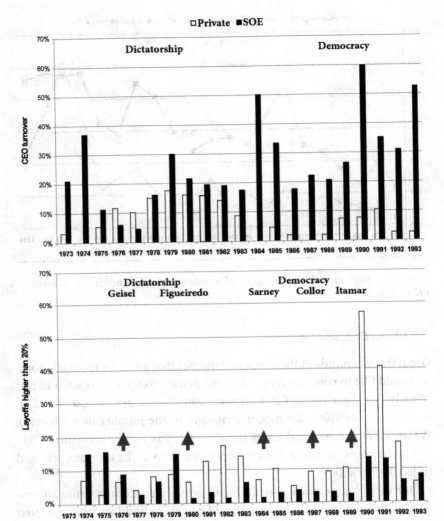

Figure 6.2. Percentage of SOEs and private firms changing their CEOs and layoffs, 1973–1993

Note: We define massive layoffs as reductions in the number of employees larger than 20 percent. The arrows denote change in the country's president.

there was a reduction in the number of employees between $t–1$ and t. As our final measures, we use two dummy variables: $\Delta Layoffs$, which is coded 1 if there is some reduction in the number of employees (i.e., when $Ln(Employees_{t-1}) - Ln(Employees_t) > 0$); and $\Delta Layoffs20\%$, coded 1 when that reduction is 20 percent or more in logarithmic terms (i.e., when $Ln(Employees_{t-1}) - Ln(Employees_t) \geq 0.20$).

Figure 6.2 depicts the percentage of SOEs and private firms that were observed with CEO turnover and large layoffs (i.e., $\Delta Layoff20\% = 1$). CEO turnover in SOEs is generally much higher than in private firms and tends to increase during the period of democracy (see the comparison tests in Table 6.1). Large layoffs, on the contrary, appear to be generally more frequent in private firms, especially during the economic crisis of 1981–1983 and in 1991, the year after the election of Fernando Collor de Mello. Collor implemented a controversial plan to curb inflation that drove the economy into recession. Although this event can also be considered an economic shock, causing a sharp increase in layoffs, we do not treat it as such in our analyses because it coincides with political change (election of a new president). The 1981–1983 crisis, in contrast, occurred during the term of a military president, João Baptista Figueiredo. Nevertheless, as we explain below, we always include in our regressions year dummies to control for temporal shocks in general.

Variables Capturing Political Shocks

We also want to study how SOEs react to political shocks. We tried to identify instances of political change that might affect turnover and layoffs. The dummy variable *Change in president* codes whether, in a given year, a new president of the republic was appointed (under the dictatorship) or elected (under democracy). Given that presidential change affects all firms equally in a given year, we also created a more fine-grained measure, the dummy variable *Change in minister,* indicating whether there was a change in the minister in charge of a firm's industry. For instance, during the dictatorship, the minister of mines and energy oversaw the mining, electricity, and oil industries.

In some specifications, both *Change in president* and *Change in minister* are also constructed separately for dictatorial and democratic regimes. For instance, *Change in president during democracy* is a dummy variable coded 1 if there is a change in the president of the republic in a given year between 1985 and 1993 and coded 0 otherwise.

Variable Capturing Economic Shocks

The dummy variable *Crisis* is coded 1 during 1981–1983, when there was the aforementioned shock causing a sharp reduction in GDP growth (see Figure 6.1). The specific impact on firm-level financial performance is captured by two variables: *ROA*, the yearly observed return on assets of each firm in the sample (i.e., net profits over total assets), and *Loss*, a dummy variable coded 1 if the firm reported negative net profit margin in a given year and coded 0 otherwise.

Additional Controls

We add several controls to our regressions. *Ln(Assets)* and *Ln(Employees)* serve as controls for firm size and measure the logarithmic value of the company's assets (in dollars) and number of employees, respectively. *Leverage* measures the company's ratio of debt to assets and is intended to capture variations in indebtedness that may influence a firm's decision to change the size of its labor force. As noted before, we also add year dummies to capture temporal factors affecting outcomes. In addition, as we explain below, given that we are essentially interested in interactions between political and economic variables and the type of the firm (SOE or private), in some specifications *ROA* and *Loss* (not interacted) are also added as controls. Finally, we always control for fixed (firm-specific) effects to avoid spurious inferences due to fixed unobservable factors influencing CEO turnover or layoffs. Appendix 6.1 presents the variables used in this study, with descriptive statistics.

Estimation Methods and Hypotheses

Our estimation strategy is based on two complementary methods: panel (fixed effect) estimation and differences-and-differences analysis.

Panel Estimation (Conditional Logit)

Using *CEO turnover*, *ΔLayoffs*, and *ΔLayoffs20%* as (binary) dependent variables for firm *i* at year *t*, we first run panel, conditional (fixed effects) Logit models specified where variables coding economic and political shocks are independent variables. The conditional Logit model estimates a likelihood function conditional on sufficient statistics for the fixed parameter associated with each firm (Chamberlain 1980). Thus, the model controls for firm-specific fixed unobservables, besides the observable controls described earlier.

In line with Kato and Long (2006), our strategy is to examine the sensitivity of SOEs to key variables—in our case, political and economic shocks—by interacting these variables with a dummy variable, SOE_i, coded 1 if the firm is an SOE and 0 if it is privately owned. Because our database does not have instances of change in state ownership, SOE_i is a fixed, firm-specific effect and hence is already controlled for in the conditional Logit model. Similarly, the main effects of presidential change or the economic crisis—events affecting both SOEs and private firms—are controlled for by the year dummies serving as control variables; our focal interest is in the interaction between those changes and state ownership. The main effect of ministerial change, however, varies by industry and therefore can be included as a control when the variable *Change in ministry* is used.

We additionally run split-sample, separate regressions for SOE and private firms. Some authors have noted that interaction terms in discrete choice models such as Probit and Logit can be problematic owing to the nonlinear nature of these models (e.g., Norton et al. 2004). We can therefore estimate the impact of political and economic variables separately for SOEs and private firms, and then examine how the coefficients of political and economic variables differ across those two groups.[2]

According to the political and social views, SOEs are more susceptible to political influence than private firms are. We therefore expect that the variables coding political shocks—*Change in president* and *Change in minister*—will more likely affect the turnover of CEOs in SOEs than in private firms. For instance, a newly elected president may appoint his friends or political allies as CEOs of state-owned firms.

We also expect the turnover of CEOs in SOEs to be higher during the democratic period. Because democratic regimes entail the formation of coalitions of parties and politicians, the appointment of CEOs of SOEs may be part of the process of allocating jobs among coalition members. That is, we view CEO turnover during presidential successions (and, to some extent, during ministerial changes) as a proxy for patronage; and we expect to find that there was more turnover under the democratic regime simply because, between 1985 and 1993, different ruling coalitions were coming in and out of power, while presidential successions under the military regime implied less turnover. We are not saying that the military regime did not have factions fighting for power at the top or that parties did not exist for congressional elections; military administrations greatly differed in terms of objectives and policy (Gaspari 2002a, 2002b, 2003a, 2003b). However, in general, we do expect to see a reduced turnover in the technocratic elite running SOEs during such administrations. This is partly because the military regime, taken as a whole, somewhat resembled a one-party rule or a government with a longer time horizon (McGuire and Olson Jr. 1996; Grier and Grier 2000). Furthermore, we know from Schneider (1991) that during this period bureaucrats and technocrats in SOEs had long and somewhat stable careers in the government.

In terms of layoffs, however, we expect to find that managers in SOEs are *less* responsive than private companies to economic shocks measured by the variables *Crisis, ROA,* and *Loss.* That is, we do not expect to see SOEs firing workers to the extent that private companies do when there is a downturn. This is because managers of SOEs tend to be less incentivized to pursue cost reductions in response to poor performance. Moreover, CEOs in SOEs usually anticipate that their companies will eventually be bailed out by the government. Therefore, they may prefer to avoid the unpleasant task of firing workers in the first place (Shleifer 1998; Vickers and Yarrow 1988; Bai and Xu 2005). The social view of SOEs (Ahroni 1986; Shapiro and Willig 1990; Toninelli 2000), discussed in Chapter 3, also suggests that governments may use SOEs as buffers against economic downturns in order to avoid rampant unemployment. In addition, in most countries there are legal restrictions to firing state employees. Although governments can, to some extent, reallocate personnel across state units, SOEs are much more constrained than private firms in performing such reallocations.

Differences-in-Differences Analysis

Using the democratic transition of 1985 and the economic crisis of 1981–1983 as cutoff periods, we implement a differences-in-differences technique adjusted for matching. We focus on two outcomes: change in the number of employees as a result of the shock (as in Card and Krueger 1994) and change in the turnover of CEOs. For the democratic transition, we compute firm-level averages of the variables for the periods 1977–1984 and 1986–1993, then assess their variation for SOEs and private firms. For the economic crisis, we measure pre-shock and post-shock outcomes as 1979–1981 and 1982–1984 averages, respectively. We then compare the estimates for private companies and for SOEs and check if the behavior of these two groups differed significantly from one period to another.

Again, we expect that change in employment as a result of the crisis should be less intense in SOEs than in private firms. The latter should adjust to the crisis by laying off employees, while the former should refrain from making such adjustments and may even *increase* hiring as a way to attenuate the impact of the crisis on the labor market. On the other hand, as we argued before, CEO turnover should increase after the democratic transition in the case of SOEs but not necessarily in the control group of private firms.

Simply computing pre-shock and post-shock averages of the outcome variables, however, can be misleading. We noted before that SOEs and private firms differ in terms of "fundamentals" such as size and financial indicators. Heckman et al. (1997) suggested a procedure to combine differences-in-differences estimation with propensity-score matching techniques to guarantee an improved comparison between distinct groups. Propensity-score matching allows for the creation of comparable control groups based on observable characteristics. A Logit regression with SOE_i as a dependent variable is estimated in the pre-shock period using, as covariates, the firm-level fundamentals—*Ln(Employees), Ln(Assets), Leverage, ROA,* and *Loss*—of both private firms and SOEs. Propensity scores are then created using kernel matching. This procedure identifies firms that are more likely to be SOEs, given their fundamentals, and weights those observations with the propensity scores, thus leading us to compare similar companies even if ownership is different (Nichols 2007). Private firms with larger propensity scores will therefore receive more weight in the estimation of outcome differences. In addition, we only consider matched SOE and private firms in regions of common support— that is, where SOEs and private firms are in a similar range based on their computed propensity scores (Heckman et al. 1997). These procedures make the SOE and private subgroups more similar in terms of their observable characteristics, thus reducing potential bias due to poor comparability.

Table 6.1. Comparative descriptive statistics: CEO turnover and layoffs

	By type of political regime			By type of firm		
	Dictatorship (1973–1984)	Democracy (1985–1993)	t (mean compar.)	Private firms	SOEs	t (mean compar.)
CEO turnover	0.172	0.243	−5.06***	0.098	0.281	−13.43***
	(0.008)	(0.012)		(0.008)	(0.010)	
Ln(Layoffs)	−0.044	0.023	−7.91***	−0.006	−0.025	2.178*
	(0.005)	(0.007)		(0.007)	(0.005)	
ΔLayoffs	0.338	0.519	−12.27***	0.389	0.447	−3.88***
	(0.010)	(0.011)		(0.010)	(0.011)	
ΔLayoffs20%	0.075	0.105	−3.50***	0.116	0.058	6.79***
	(0.005)	(0.007)		(0.007)	(0.005)	
Change in president	0.158	0.325	−14.55***	0.231	0.222	0.74
	(0.007)	(0.010)		(0.008)	(0.008)	
ROA	0.061	0.020	14.81***	0.069	0.015	20.58***
	(0.002)	(0.002)		(0.002)	(0.002)	
Loss	0.156	0.305	−12.95***	0.128	0.323	−17.32***
	(0.007)	(0.010)		(0.006)	(0.010)	
Ln(Assets)	19.369	19.409	−0.86	19.486	19.274	4.55***
	(0.029)	(0.039)		(0.016)	(0.045)	
Ln(Employees)	7.859	7.911	−1.43	8.290	7.413	25.73***
	(0.024)	(0.028)		(0.018)	(0.030)	
Leverage	0.513	0.449	9.48***	0.489	0.484	0.67
	(0.004)	(0.006)		(0.004)	(0.006)	

Note: †, *, **, and *** denote statistical significance at the 10%, 5%, 1%, and 0.1% levels, respectively.

Findings

Table 6.1 presents basic comparisons of the data by type of political regime and type of firm. It is easy to see the main patterns in the data. CEO turnover is higher during the democracy years than during the dictatorship. This may be related to the fact that presidential successions are more frequent during the democratic period. The number of times a minister was replaced also seems to have been higher during the democracy than during the dictatorship. Finally, layoffs are higher during the democracy, which corresponds with the post-crisis period. For instance, during the dictatorship, 33 percent of our firm-year observations were firms with losses, but that increased to over 50 percent during the democracy years. In sum, it seems as if the democracy years witnessed high turnover in political posts and high layoffs in SOEs and private companies.

The last two columns of Table 6.1 also show that SOEs have higher CEO turnover than private firms and that they tend to conduct massive layoffs less often than private companies. Yet the descriptive statistics also show the somewhat puzzling result that SOEs had layoffs (in general) more often than private companies, something we explore further in our empirical analysis below.

Results from the Panel Estimates (Conditional Logit)

In Table 6.2, we present the results of our analysis of the determinants of CEO turnover using panel data. First, let us analyze the effect of political shocks on turnover. Consistent with our expectation, CEO turnover in SOEs is significantly more responsive to political change than CEO turnover in private firms is, and the effect is more pronounced under democracy. Using the coefficients from columns 2 and 3 in Table 6.2, we can see that the coefficient of the interactions between *SOE* and the variables *Change in president* and *Change in ministry* are significantly positive and their coefficients are significantly larger when political change occurs in the democratic period than when it occurs during the dictatorship. In fact, changes in president or minister during the dictatorship do not seem to lead to significantly higher CEO turnover, or at least not to higher turnover for SOEs than for private companies.[3]

The effect of political change on layoffs is less consistent across specifications (see Tables 6.3 and 6.4). Change in the president of the republic under the dictatorship appears to increase layoffs; see, for example, the coefficient of *SOE × Change in president (dictatorship)* in specification 2 of Table 6.4. According to our interviews with ministers and with former CEOs of SOEs, CEOs appointed by new presidents tried to restructure their SOEs. In fact, SOEs followed the same legal regime as private companies, which allowed them to fire employees when necessary.

The effect of ministerial change on layoffs, however, apparently follows a different pattern. In Table 6.3, we can see that changes in minister were more likely to lead to layoffs during the democratic period than they were during the dictatorship This is consistent with the fact that, after 1986, Brazil was engaged in a series of radical structural adjustment programs that included downsizing (and sometimes privatizing) some SOEs. Yet this result is reversed when it comes to large layoffs (see specification 3 of Table 6.4).

Table 6.2. Determinants of CEO turnover

	All periods				
	(1)	(2)	(3)	(4)	(5)
SOE × Change in president	1.253***				
	(0.286)				
SOE × Change in president (dictatorship)		0.580			
		(0.366)			
SOE × Change in president (democracy)		2.199***			
		(0.504)			
SOE × Change in minister (dictatorship)			0.376		
			(0.349)		
SOE × Change in minister (democracy)			1.633**		
			(0.509)		
SOE × Crisis $(t-1)$				0.353	
				(0.301)	
SOE × ROA $(t-1)$					−1.590
					(1.905)
SOE × Loss $(t-1)$					0.356
					(0.496)
ROA $(t-1)$	0.447	0.436	0.169	0.411	1.651
	(0.818)	(0.820)	(0.850)	(0.813)	(1.695)
Loss $(t-1)$	0.044	0.023	−0.012	0.045	−0.289
	(0.177)	(0.178)	(0.184)	(0.177)	(0.458)
Additional controls					
Log of assets, employees, and leverage (all lagged; $t-1$)	Y	Y	Y	Y	Y
Year dummies	Y	Y	Y	Y	Y
Firm fixed effects	Y	Y	Y	Y	Y
N (total)	2,436	2,436	2,103	2,436	2,436
N (number of firms)	213	213	184	213	213
p (LR test)	<0.001	<0.001	<0.001	<0.001	<0.001

Notes: *, **, and *** denote statistical significance at the 5%, 1%, and 0.1% levels, respectively. Estimates of conditional (fixed effect) Logit models (standard errors in brackets). Dependent variable is *CEO turnover*, a dummy equal to 1 if there is a change in the CEO of the company in year *t*. In specification (3), the main (non-interacted) variable *Change in minister* is added in the regression. (*Change in president* already controlled for by the year dummies.)

Table 6.3. Determinants of layoffs, 1973–1993

	All periods				
	(1)	(2)	(3)	(4)	(5)
SOE × Change in president	0.290†				
	(0.170)				
SOE × Change in president (dictatorship)		0.261			
		(0.276)			
SOE × Change in president (democracy)		0.304			
		(0.201)			
SOE × Change in minister (dictatorship)			0.491*		
			(0.246)		
SOE × Change in minister (democracy)			0.798***		
			(0.209)		
SOE × Crisis (t–1)				−0.514**	
				(0.180)	
SOE × ROA (t–1)					−1.914
					(1.195)
SOE × Loss (t–1)					0.258
					(0.270)
ROA (t–1)	−1.538*	−1.541*	−1.746**	−1.372*	−0.505
	(0.604)	(0.604)	(0.677)	(0.606)	(0.879)
Loss (t–1)	0.023	0.023	0.034	0.033	−0.158
	(0.133)	(0.133)	(0.150)	(0.133)	(0.205)
Additional controls					
Log of assets, employees, and leverage (all lagged; t–1)	Y	Y	Y	Y	Y
Year dummies	Y	Y	Y	Y	Y
Firm fixed effects	Y	Y	Y	Y	Y
N (total)	4,251	4,251	3,335	4,251	4,251
N (number of firms)	292	292	239	292	292
p (LR test)	<0.001	<0.001	<0.001	<0.001	<0.001

Notes: †, *, **, and *** denote statistical significance at the 10%, 5%, 1%, and 0.1% levels, respectively. Estimates of conditional (fixed effect) Logit models (standard errors in brackets). Dependent variable is *ΔLayoffs*, a dummy equal to 1 if there is a reduction in the number of employees between t–1 and t. In specification (3), the main (non-interacted) variables *Change in minister* are added in the regression. (*Change in president* is already controlled for by the year dummies.)

Table 6.4. Determinants of large layoffs (20% of employees or more)

	All periods				
	(1)	(2)	(3)	(4)	(5)
SOE × Change in president	0.053				
	(0.281)				
SOE × Change in president (dictatorship)		1.495***			
		(0.434)			
SOE × Change in president (democracy)		−0.685*			
		(0.341)			
SOE × Change in minister (dictatorship)			0.541		
			(0.403)		
SOE × Change in minister (democracy)			−0.627†		
			(0.353)		
SOE × Crisis (t−1)				−0.877*	
				(0.402)	
SOE × ROA (t−1)					−2.492
					(2.038)
SOE × Loss (t−1)					−1.320**
					(0.495)
ROA (t−1)	−1.842†	−1.843†	−2.908*	−1.632	−1.013
	(1.012)	(1.021)	(1.149)	(1.018)	(1.344)
Loss (t−1)	0.056	0.077	−0.243	0.077	0.562†
	(0.240)	(0.241)	(0.279)	(0.240)	(0.300)
Additional controls					
Log of assets, employees, and leverage (all lagged; t−1)	Y	Y	Y	Y	Y
Year dummies	Y	Y	Y	Y	Y
Firm fixed effects	Y	Y	Y	Y	Y
N (total)	3,005	3,005	2,184	3,005	3,005
N (number of firms)	199	199	153	199	199
p (LR test)	<0.001	<0.001	<0.001	<0.001	<0.001

Notes: †, *, **, and *** denote statistical significance at the 10%, 5%, 1%, and 0.1% levels, respectively. Estimates of conditional (fixed effect) Logit models (standard errors in brackets). Dependent variable is $\Delta Layoffs20\%$, a dummy equal to 1 if $Ln(Employees_{t-1}) - Ln(Employees_t) \geq 0.20$. In specification (3), the main (non-interacted) variables *Change in minister* are added in the regression. (*Change in president* is already controlled for by the year dummies.)

There we can see a negative, moderately significant effect of *SOE × Change in minister* under democracy and a large positive coefficient for changes in minister during the dictatorship. These mean that large layoffs, which carry a high political cost, were more common during the dictatorship years than during the years of democracy (after 1985).

In Tables 6.3 and 6.4, we can also examine the effect of the 1979–1983 crisis on the behavior of SOEs in terms of layoffs. For instance, in specification 4 of these tables, we can see that SOEs are less likely to fire workers during an economic crisis than private companies are and still less likely to carry out large layoffs. We also learn from Table 6.4, specification 5, that SOEs are less likely than private firms to promote large layoffs as a consequence of a past economic loss, although there is no significant difference in terms of past profitability *(ROA)*.

Table 6.5 presents our results from the conditional Logit, split-sample regressions for SOEs and private firms. The first two specifications (1a and 1b) confirm that presidential change positively affects CEO turnover only in SOEs. Furthermore, the coefficient of *Change in president during democracy* is significantly larger than the coefficient of *Change in president during dictatorship*, according to a *Chi*-squared test of coefficient comparison. Presidential successions during the dictatorship were less likely to lead to layoffs than they were during the democratic years, yet there were some massive layoffs in SOEs after successions in the latter years. Interestingly, this exercise also shows, in contrast with previous results, that SOEs were less likely than private firms to conduct layoffs during the dictatorship, although the coefficients are not significantly different from each other.

Although the economic variables *ROA* and *Loss* do not significantly affect *CEO turnover*, a *Chi*-squared test of coefficient comparison using the estimates of specifications 3a and 3b confirms that unprofitable private firms *(Loss = 1)* are more likely to pursue massive layoffs than SOEs. Furthermore, an increase in *ROA* significantly reduces the likelihood of layoffs for SOEs but not for private firms. A possible explanation for this result is that an increase in profitability enhances an SOE's free cash flow, thereby reducing the incentives to restructure the labor force. In private firms, in contrast, increases in profitability can be more fully captured by private owners through dividends or reinvestment.

Table 6.5. Split-sample regressions comparing SOEs and private firms

	CEO turnover		ΔLayoffs		ΔLayoffs20%	
	SOEs (1a)	Private (1b)	SOEs (2a)	Private (2b)	SOEs (3a)	Private (3b)
Change in president during dictatorship	0.028 (0.361)	1.645 (1.131)	−2.083*** (0.368)	−1.332*** (0.357)	−0.001 (0.599)	−0.980† (0.549)
Change in president during democracy	0.898** (0.323)	−15.447 (1,836.570)	−0.941** (0.353)	0.011 (0.346)	0.105 (0.619)	−1.177* (0.592)
ROA (t−1)	0.152 (0.949)	0.968 (2.215)	−2.168* (0.869)	−1.044 (0.931)	−4.029* (1.612)	0.036 (1.508)
Loss (t−1)	0.056 (0.200)	−0.181 (0.531)	0.116 (0.187)	−0.032 (0.207)	−0.680† (0.391)	0.738* (0.321)
Ln(Assets) (t−1)	−0.078 (0.164)	−0.117 (0.331)	−0.393** (0.142)	−0.245† (0.147)	−0.548* (0.264)	−0.362 (0.225)
Ln(Workers) (t−1)	0.569* (0.261)	−0.192 (0.423)	1.894*** (0.254)	2.508*** (0.208)	2.357*** (0.430)	3.491*** (0.332)
Leverage (t−1)	0.015 (0.400)	−1.211 (1.172)	0.548 (0.360)	0.144 (0.475)	0.000 (0.648)	1.000 (0.815)
Year dummies	Y	Y	Y	Y	Y	Y
Firm fixed effects	Y	Y	Y	Y	Y	Y
N (total)	1,673	763	2,001	2,250	1,085	1,920
N (number of firms)	133	80	136	156	69	130
p (LR test)	< 0.001	< 0.001	< 0.001	< 0.001	< 0.001	< 0.001

Notes: †, *, **, and *** denote statistical significance at the 10%, 5%, 1%, and 0.1% levels, respectively. Estimates of conditional (fixed effect) Logit models (standard errors in brackets). Year dummies that are collinear with instances of presidential change are excluded.

Results from the Differences-in-Differences Analysis

Table 6.6 shows our final set of results, using a differences-in-differences estimation before and after the 1985 democratic transition (Panel A) and the exogenous shock of the 1981–1983 crisis (Panel B). Panels A and B show, for each event and outcome variable, the assessed outcomes for SOEs and private firms in the pre- and post-shock periods. The differences-in-differences estimator is an indicator of the change in outcomes for SOEs minus the change in outcomes for our control group of private firms. As we explained, these differences are adjusted for matching; that is, estimates are based on comparable groups of SOEs and private firms.

Panel A confirms again that political change leads to larger changes in SOEs than in private firms. After the democratic transition, the variation in

Table 6.6. Differences-in-differences estimation with propensity-score matching: SOEs vs. private companies Panel A. Pre- vs. post-democratic transition (1985). Pre-outcomes measured as 1977–1984 average; post-outcomes measured as 1986–1993 average.

Outcome variable	N	Pre-outcomes		Post-outcomes		Diff.-in-diff.	
		Private (P1)	SOEs (S1)	Private (P2)	SOEs (S2)	(S2-S1)-(P2-P1)	t
Ln(Employees)	489	8.390 (0.066)	7.614 (0.150)	8.440 (0.065)	7.783 (0.142)	0.118 (0.081)	1.45
CEO turnover	385	0.142 (0.016)	0.271 (0.022)	0.040 (0.015)	0.306 (0.022)	0.138 (0.040)	3.44***

Panel B. Pre- and post-economic crisis (1981–1983). Pre-outcomes measured as 1979–1981 average; post-outcomes measured as 1982–1984 average.

Outcome variable	N	Pre-outcomes		Post-outcomes		Diff.-in-diff.	
		Private (P1)	SOEs (S1)	Private (P2)	SOEs (S2)	(S2-S1)-(P2-P1)	t
Ln(Employees)	507	8.419 (0.072)	7.545 (0.142)	8.393 (0.073)	7.617 (0.137)	0.098 (0.047)	2.09*
CEO turnover	470	0.160 (0.002)	0.230 (0.030)	0.134 (0.030)	0.274 (0.024)	0.070 (0.051)	1.38

Notes: *, **, and *** denote statistical significance at the 5%, 1%, and 0.1% levels, respectively. Robust standard errors in brackets, clustered on each company. Propensity scores estimated with kernel matching, using *Ln(Employees), Ln(Assets), Leverage, ROA,* and *Loss* as covariates in a Logit regression for the pre-shock period. Differences-in-differences estimated in the region of common support.

the turnover of CEOs in SOEs was 13.8 percentage points larger than in our subsample of private firms. No significant effect is found in terms of employment, however.

In Panel B, we can see that the economic crisis has a significant effect on employment but not on CEO turnover. SOEs actually increased their number of employees after the crisis, while there was a slight reduction in employment in our sample of private firms. Overall, SOEs increased their labor force by 9.8 percentage points beyond the variation observed in the private sample. In fact, some of the data we collected at the firm level shows that SOEs hired new employees. Although we cannot ascertain the precise causes of the observed increase, this finding is consistent with the hypothesis that labor reallocations within SOEs are less sensitive to economic shocks and that governments may even use SOEs as vehicles to reduce the impact of economic crises on the domestic labor market.

Implications of our Findings

Our findings directly confirm some of the postulates of the political and social views described in Chapter 3. In the first place, it does seem that CEOs, during the democratic years, were appointed or replaced when there was a new president. This could be a good thing if presidential successions allowed new governments to weed out poor performers. Yet our empirical and qualitative evidence points in a different direction. For instance, according to Delfim Netto—former minister of finance (1969–1974), agriculture (1979), and planning (1979–1985)—throughout the military regime, ministers met with the president to discuss nominations and "chose the CEOs of state-owned enterprises after looking at eight or so curricula . . . even if someone said 'I have a friend who could run this,' we usually had someone better."[4] This process changed during the democracy, and CEO appointments were commonly tied to membership in the ruling coalition.

Our findings regarding CEO turnover have implications for the debate on the relative merits of democracies and dictatorships (Przeworski 1991; Acemoglu and Robinson 2006; Baer 2008). From this debate emerge two important hypotheses related to turnover in SOEs (even if the literature has not drawn the link to SOEs directly). The first hypothesis is that, economically, some autocracies may help isolate government from the pressures of interest groups with short-term objectives. According to Haggard, "authoritarian political arrangements give political elites autonomy from distributionist pressures" (Haggard 1990, 262). In that sense, this chapter shows that CEO turnover and employment policy in Brazilian SOEs were indeed more independent during the dictatorship than under the democracy. Although we do not claim that patronage was inexistent during dictatorship and our findings should not lead to the conclusion that authoritarian regimes are superior to democracy, it seems that under democracy CEO turnover depended more on the political cycle. Our results are also consistent with the findings of Iyer and Mani (forthcoming) for India, where "a change in the identity of a state's chief minister (the de facto executive head of the state government) results in a significant increase in the probability of bureaucrat reassignments in that state" (p. 724).

The second hypothesis is that systems with heavier state intervention in the management and ownership of firms withstand economic shocks better because governments can use SOEs to smooth the business cycle and use state-owned banks to increase credit. Our second finding partly confirms that view. We show that layoffs in SOEs are less sensitive to economic shocks than layoffs in private companies are. In particular, when facing a radical economic shock, SOEs are less likely to fire workers than private companies are. This finding is consistent with the social view of state capitalism. SOEs can be used to smooth the effects of a crisis and therefore can stray from the objective of maximizing returns. (Though in some cases that may never have been the main objective.)

We think these findings are important for our own argument in this book because they show the contingent nature of some of Leviathan's temptations. When facing shocks, especially harsh economic crises, there is a greater temptation to use SOEs as employment vehicles. On the one hand, that can make state capitalism more resilient to crises, especially domestic crises. On the other hand, when facing global crises with slow recoveries, SOEs can become a burden for the government. In Brazil (and in other Latin American countries), the liquidity crunch in global financial markets in the 1980s made it impossible for the government to continue to finance the losses of SOEs, so privatization became necessary. The first privatizations in Brazil took place in 1981, followed by the program of the early 1990s. Thus, the inefficiencies generated by the lack of adjustment during the crises had to be paid for later.

In sum, this chapter shows the state's temptation to intervene politically in SOEs and how that differs from what we observe in private companies. This chapter is based on data from the 1980s because it is in that decade when economic and democratization shocks in emerging markets and Europe affected the performance of SOEs, complicated the repayment of SOE debt in foreign currency, and, ultimately, widened the budget deficits of the central governments. These factors, we think, led multilateral organizations, such as the IMF, and governments to realize the inefficiencies associated with the Leviathan as an entrepreneur model. Those inefficiencies made governments rethink the role that SOEs should play in their economies and drove many countries to privatize these firms.

APPENDIX

Table 6-A1. Description of the variables used to study layoffs and CEO turnover

Variable	Description	N	Mean (std. dev.)	Min.	Max.
CEO turnover	Dummy equal to 1 if there is a change in the company's CEO in year t	3357	0.20 (0.40)	0	1
Ln(Layoffs)	Ln(Employees$_{t-1}$) − Ln(Employees$_t$)	4375	−0.01 (0.28)	−1.18	1.30
ΔLayoffs	Dummy equal to 1 if Ln(Layoffs) > 0	4375	0.42 (0.49)	0	1
ΔLayoffs20%	Dummy equal to 1 if Ln(Layoffs) ≥ 0.20	4375	0.09 (0.28)	0	1
Change in president	Dummy equal to 1 if there is a change in the country's president	5293	0.23 (0.41)	0	1
SOE	Dummy equal to 1 if the company is a state-owned enterprise	5293	0.28 (0.44)	0	1
Crisis	Dummy equal to 1 if the year of observation is 1981, 1982, or 1983	5293	0.16 (0.37)	0	1
ROA	Return on assets: net profit over total assets	5127	0.04 (0.09)	−0.32	0.34
Loss	Dummy equal to 1 if the company exhibits negative net profits	5134	0.21 (0.41)	0	1
Ln(Assets)	Logarithmic value of total assets (measured in dollars)	5277	19.39 (1.69)	7.32	24.84
Ln(Employees)	Logarithmic value of total employees	4909	7.88 (1.27)	4.61	11.64
Leverage	Total debt over total assets	5277	0.49 (0.24)	0.04	1.3

7

Taming Leviathan?

Corporate Governance in National Oil Companies

As we saw in Chapters 2 and 4, after the initial wave of privatizations of the 1990s, many former SOEs were fully privatized or closed. But others—especially the largest firms in "strategic" sectors such as natural resources—underwent two transformations. First, there was the transition from Leviathan as an entrepreneur to Leviathan as a minority investor, a theme we explore in the last chapters of this book. Second, many SOEs were either corporatized or partly privatized and listed on a stock exchange. That is, we observed the transformation from Leviathan as an entrepreneur to Leviathan as a majority investor.

In Chapter 4, we described this process of transformation in Brazil. The listing of Petrobras, and the corporate governance reforms which that entailed, make this company Brazil's most important example of Leviathan as a majority investor. By listing a large portion of the voting shares (nonvoting shares had been listed for decades), the government improved the company's governance by adhering to best practices such as transparency and monitoring through boards. Yet it is unclear whether or not political interference was curtailed. Kenyon (2006), referring to the listing of Petrobras, argues that "by issuing shares to private investors and adopting a commitment to transparency, politicians can raise the political costs of interference and avert policies that are damaging to [an SOE's] interests" (p. 2).[1] In this case, the government also allowed workers to use their forced-savings account, FGTS, to buy shares of Petrobras, thus, in theory, committing voters and the government to the new ownership scheme of the oil company. But is listing really enough to limit political intervention? What kinds of corporate governance contracts do governments design to minimize intervention in their controlled companies?

In this chapter, we examine the corporate governance of Petrobras in relation to the governance arrangements of thirty national oil companies (NOCs) across countries. With this analysis we hope to accomplish two things. First, we want to show the wide variation in corporate governance within the model in which Leviathan is a majority investor. Second, by discussing governance in NOCs and examining specific cases of state intervention, we outline the limits of the Leviathan as a majority investor model.

Our findings come from two sets of analyses. First, we analyze corporate governance in a sample of thirty NOCs. Second, we conduct a slightly more detailed analysis of governance and incentives in Pemex, Petrobras, and Statoil, the national oil companies of Mexico, Brazil, and Norway, respectively. We use these case studies because they show variation in both the level of corporate governance sophistication (e.g., to minimize agency problems) and the level of political intervention. In the end, we show how NOCs that are traded on stock exchanges have solved many of the agency problems we described in Chapter 3, but we also provide examples showing that listing is not enough to prevent political intervention in SOEs. We contend that listing should be accompanied by broader institutional reforms that reconcile the conflicting demands of governments and (minority) private shareholders.

Why Study National Oil Companies?

As we explained briefly in Chapter 2, NOCs are the product of a wave of nationalizations in the post–World War II era. Before 1950, only a few governments controlled a national oil company, but the wave of nationalizations we portrayed in Chapter 2 included the nationalization of many oil companies. These oil companies gave governments access to rents and became, in most countries, the largest SOEs.

In this chapter, we study corporate governance reforms in Petrobras and a sample of national oil companies for three important reasons. First, NOCs are perhaps the most important SOEs in the world. NOCs control around 90 percent of the world's oil reserves and 75 percent of oil and gas production. Analysts estimate that 60 percent of the world's undiscovered reserves are in countries in which NOCs are dominant players (Tordo et al. 2011).

Second, in NOCs we can see clearly the transformation of Leviathan from an entrepreneur (owner and manager) to new organizational configurations in which some of the problems of the "original" model of state capitalism have been addressed. Thus, the transformation of many NOCs into publicly traded corporations has commonly been equated with both a reduction of agency problems and a separation of the government from NOC management. The process of corporatizing an NOC or listing it on a stock market is usually accompanied by improvements in transparency, professionalization of the management, the introduction of performance or incentive contracts for top management and directors, and—arguably—an increase in competitiveness. Corporatization is the process through which a firm, in our case an SOE, "is restructured along the pattern of a modern corporation . . . [with] a governance structure that includes shareholders and a board of directors . . . [with] a chief executive officer and a chair of the board of directors" (Aivazian et al. 2005, 792) while retaining the state as the sole owner of the company. Listing involves many of the same changes, but adds the advantages of having other owners monitoring the managers and having stock prices reflecting the firm's performance. In short, the corporatization and especially the listing of NOCs have been identified as a way to alleviate some of the social, political, and agency problems of SOEs.

Yet the story is not that simple. There are limits to the Leviathan as a majority investor model, which we will explore in this chapter. NOCs mediate the stream of rents governments receive from the exploitation of oil and gas reserves. Therefore, it is in these firms that the government's temptation to intervene in SOE management is greatest. For instance, it is because of these rents that governments are so tempted to use NOCs to pursue social goals. Furthermore, when it comes to NOCs, governments usually want to be less transparent about how they manage their revenues (Ross 2012). Finally, NOCs are usually the most important or only actor in the politically sensitive commercialization of gasoline and gas, sectors that affect household income and business profitability directly and thus make governments more tempted to control their prices. Studying NOCs therefore allows us to examine when the supposed political autonomy afforded by the model of Leviathan as a majority investor breaks down.

Additionally, the very process of listing an NOC will complicate matters in this double bottom line setting because minority private investors, who would prefer the firm to pursue a strategy of maximizing shareholder value, may clash with governments pursuing social or political goals. In that setting, governments will find it hard to credibly commit to protecting minority shareholder rights (Pargendler 2012a). Still, as we explain toward the end of the chapter, the implicit contract to share rents in NOCs also includes sharing the losses from political interventions such as price controls or poor decisions of where to open refineries or whom to partner with in new projects. Even if the sharing of losses is implicit in the arrangements of NOCs and investors, the better the regulation and protection of investors in a country, the less NOCs will have to share losses that are the product of the whim of politicians.

From Leviathan as an Entrepreneur to Leviathan as a Majority Investor

Governments around the world viewed the listing of SOEs as a solution to most of the problems associated with the Leviathan as an entrepreneur model we discussed in Chapter 3. In the oil industry, too, there has been a trend toward the corporatization and listing of large national oil companies. In Table 7.1, we display how corporatization and listing should—in theory— address the main problems of SOEs in the Leviathan as an entrepreneur model.

In our view, corporatization and listing differ only slightly in terms of organizational configuration. Both include professional management, a board of directors that meets regularly and monitors managers' performance, and a certain level of transparency in the firm's financials. Yet, while having financials audited by a recognized private firm is always required for listed firms, it is usually—but not always—required for corporatized firms. Finally, the big difference between the two systems is that in listed firms there is improved monitoring of managers, either through market mechanisms (e.g., stock prices) or simply because other shareholders have incentives to monitor the firm's performance.

In Table 7.1, we present three basic differences—according to the social, political, and agency views—between listing an NOC and simply corporatizing it. First, in theory, corporatization does not bind NOCs to maximize shareholder value, as listing does, because the only shareholder is the government, which may want the NOC to have a double bottom line. On the other hand, corporatized NOCs have the advantage of not having to worry

Table 7.1. Taming Leviathan: Corporatization vs. listing of NOCs

Theory of SOE inefficiency	Features of the Leviathan as an entrepreneur model	How does listing change that feature?	Difference between listing and corporatization?
Social view	Double bottom line	Maximization of shareholder value subject to political interference if the company is not insulated. Likely conflict if minority shareholders pursuing profitability clash with governments following social or political goals	With corporatization, the government may pursue a double bottom line without negatively affecting minority shareholders pursuing profitability.
	Long-term horizon, government as patient investor tolerating losses	Likely shorter-term horizon, markets are generally impatient	No short-term pressure from market investors. Yet there could be government temptation to use SOE to smooth business cycles.
Political view	Appointment of CEOs using criteria other than merit (e.g., political connections)	Professional management selected by the board of directors	If isolated from politics, the board can choose managers. However, political appointment is more likely than in listed SOEs.

(continued)

Table 7.1. (continued)

Theory of SOE inefficiency	Features of the Leviathan as an entrepreneur model	How does listing change that feature?	Difference between listing and corporatization?
	Government uses SOEs to smooth business cycles (e.g., hiring more or firing fewer workers than necessary)	Effect is reduced if the firm is isolated from political intervention	Less government intervention than in corporatized SOEs; independent board members in listed firms may reduce, though not eliminate, outright intervention
	Soft budget constraint (bailouts are likely)	Soft budget constraint still present (governments will likely bail them out)	No clear risk of bankruptcy (governments will likely bail them out)
Agency view	Management has low-powered incentives	Pay-for-performance contracts, bonuses, and stock options more likely	Incentive contracts likely, except for stock options. However, double bottom line may attenuate incentives.
	Hard to measure performance because of the double bottom line	Stock prices as performance metrics	No market pressure. Governments have to set measurable targets.

No clear punishment for managers who underperform	Boards may fire managers who underperform	Managers may lose their jobs if they underperform; yet pressure should be less intense than in listed firms subject to external monitoring.
Ministries and agencies with weak incentives to monitor	Institutional investors, debt holders, rating agencies, and analysts monitoring performance	If NOC issues bonds, debt holders can monitor. If board has external members who care about their reputations, those members will also monitor.
No transparency: incomplete financial information	Improved transparency; accounting standards following GAAP or IFRS	Same as listed firms
Poor monitoring: no board of directors (ministry regulates) or politically appointed board (low level of checks and balances)	Board of directors with some independent members and some political appointees; depending on numbers, it can act as a balance to the government and the CEO. Yet government can co-opt board members.	Can have an independent board if it is isolated from the government and packed with professionals. However, political appointment is also more likely than in listed SOEs.

Source: This is an expanded version from a similar table presented in Pargendler et al. (2013).

about showing short-term results, as listing firms do, which allows corporatized NOCs to focus on making long-term investments and on depleting resources at a slower pace.

Second, when NOCs are listed, they are supposed to respond to the interests of a variety of shareholders, so their boards of directors should be more diverse and less influenced by the government. This does not necessarily happen with corporatization, because the government is the only shareholder picking board members (with rare exceptions such as Saudi Aramco, which is a corporatized NOC with governance arrangements similar to those of private companies and with a large number of external board members). Yet, even in listed firms, governments can co-opt board members and appoint public officials (e.g., ministers) who can influence the boards.

Finally, monitoring managers in listed firms should be more complex because, besides having the board to check and balance the power of the CEO, the firm might also be under pressure from markets. A company that, for example, tries to pursue a social objective that affects the interests of minority shareholders should be penalized by the market with a lower stock price. Yet corporatization could bring about a similar level of monitoring and make CEOs face similar market incentives if the company issues debt. Both issuing debt and selling equity offer "the added advantage of creating a group of private investors with a stake in the profitability of the company. The hope is that this group will make it harder for the government to pursue social goals" (Gómez-Ibañez 2007, 38). In that case, both credit-rating agencies and bondholders will operate as monitors, penalizing actions that may endanger the repayment of such bonds.

Despite the differences between corporatized and listed SOEs, these corporate forms have been widely adopted by governments to reform their SOEs and national oil companies. In a more recent OECD report, Christiansen (2011) estimates that 80 percent of SOEs in member countries operate as statutory corporations (i.e., they are corporatized). These firms account for 50 percent of total SOE employment in the OECD. This report also shows that the largest SOEs are usually listed, rather than just being corporatized. (One big exception is Pemex, the Mexican national oil company, which is not listed.)

The academic literature has found strong evidence to support listing over corporatization as a better way of running SOEs. For instance, a series of studies summarized in Megginson (2005, 106–107) finds overwhelming support for improvements in performance when SOEs are listed. Gupta (2005) finds that listed firms or SOEs that sold minority positions perform better than wholly owned SOEs in India. In contrast, Aivazian et al. (2005) also find that corporatization leads to improvements in performance in Chinese SOEs, especially because of corporate governance reforms that usually accompany the process of corporatization.

The pushback against corporatization is that without major changes in corporate governance, the reforms do not seem to be that efficient. Zhu (1999), for instance, argues against corporatization in China, because without a culture of autonomy and a system of corporate governance that monitors managers and keeps the government at bay, SOE reforms of this sort would not lead to major improvements in SOE performance. Studies of specific reforms, such as incentive contracts for managers, also fail to find improvements in SOE performance (Shirley and Xu 1998). Finally, Wang et al. (2004) show that Chinese SOEs that have privatized some of their capital and listed on stock exchanges rely less on debt finance and increase their capital expenditures, yet they do not seem to perform better than they did before listing.

Corporate Governance in National Oil Companies

In order to gauge the extent to which governments have corporatized and listed their national oil companies, in Table 7.2 we present a list of basic corporate governance characteristics in the largest national oil companies in the world. We define national oil companies as petroleum and gas firms in which the government is either the largest shareholder or the controlling investor.

Ownership

Out of the thirty NOCs we include in Table 7.2, fifteen are now listed on a stock exchange in their home country, New York, or both. Those fifteen companies have corporate governance regimes that, on paper, resemble those of

Table 7.2. Corporate governance in national oil companies

NOC	Country	Listed NOC	Total gov't share of voting stock	Size of BOD	External board members	BOD members appointed by gov't	Board members term (years)	Gov't officials on BOD	CEO and chair of BOD are not same person	Chairman is an external board member and non-gov't official	Budgetary autonomy	External auditors	Governance index#
Statoil	Norway	Y	70.8	10	7	0	2	N	Y	Y	Y	Y	7
Eni	Italy	Y	30.3	9	3	0	3	N	Y	Y	Y	Y	6
Ecopetrol	Colombia	Y	89.9	9	6	3	1	Y	N	Y	Y	Y	6
GDF Suez	France	Y	36.4	21	9	6	4	Y	N	N	Y	Y	5
Sinopec	China	Y	75.8	11	3	0	3	N	Y	N(**)	Y	Y	5
Rosneft	Russia	Y	83.0	9	3	0	7	Y	Y	Y	Y	Y	5
OGDCL	Pakistan	Y	85.2	11	8	n.a.	3	Y	Y	N	Y	Y	5
Saudi Aramco	Saudi Arabia	N	100	7	5	2	?	Y	Y	N(**)	Y	Y	5
Gazprom	Russia	Y	50.0	10	2	5	1	Y	Y	N	N	Y	4
CNOOC Ltd	China	Y	66.0	11	5	0	3	N	Y	N(**)	Y	Y	4
PTT	Thailand	Y	67.1	15	6+	0	3	Y	Y	N	Y	Y	4
ONGC	India	Y	84.2	17	8	17	2	Y	Y	N	Y	Y	4
Petro China	China	Y	86.7	14	5	0	3	N	Y	N(**)	N	Y	4
Petrobras	Brazil	Y	55.7	9	2	6	1	Y	Y	N(*)	N	Y	3
KazMunayGas	Kazakhstan	Y	62.0	8	3	5	3	Y	Y	N	Y	Y	3
Petronas	Malaysia	Y	100	16	7	9	?	Y	N	N	Y	Y	3
PDO	Oman	N	60.0	12	5	7	?	Y	Y	N	Y	N(?)	2

Company	Country													#
KPC	Kuwait	N	100	15	11	3	N	Y	?	N	Y(***)	N	N	2
PEMEX	Mexico	N	100	15	4	6	Y	Y	6	Y	N	N	N	2
Pertamina	Indonesia	N	100	7	2	5	Y	Y		N	N	N	N	2
QP	Qatar	N	100	7	0		Y	Y	Y	Y	N	N	N	2
Petro SA	South Africa	N	100	n.a.	0		N	N	Y	N	N	N	N	1
Sonatrach	Algeria	N	100	13	0	10	Y	Y	Y	N	N	N	N	1
Adnoc	UAE	N	100	10	0		N	N	n.a.	Y	N	N	N	0
EGPC	Egypt	N	100	n.a.			N	N	?	N	N	N	N	0
INOC	Iraq	N	100	n.a.			N	N		N	N	N	N	0
Libya NOC	Libya	N	100	5		5	Y	Y	?	N	N	N	N	0
NIOC	Iran	N	100	8	0	8	Y	Y	?	N	N	N	N	0
NNPC	Nigeria	N	100	9	0	9	N	Y	?	N	N	N	N	0
PDVSA	Venezuela	N	100	10	0	10	Y	N	2	N	N	N	N	0

Sources: Tordo et al. 2011, tables 4.6 and 4.7; Capital IQ: the relevant chapters in Hults et al. 2012); and corporate web sites.

Notes: Question marks denote uncertainty about the information, not because it does not exist, but because it is not reported. For instance, when board members are appointed by the government, their tenure is linked to electoral or political cycles. In other boards, the members' terms are not explicitly defined.

* According to Capital IQ, Timur A. Kulibayev, chairman of the board of directors of KazMunayGas, has close ties to the president of Kazakhstan. Thus it is questionable how independent he is as chairman.

** Chairmen in Chinese firms are usually portrayed as independent/external, but they are distinguished members of the Communist Party, so their independence is questionable.

*** Stevens (2012a) explains that the Kuwait government passed a series of reforms in 2004 that made KPC relatively autonomous from the government and the holding company.

\# Governance index: We calculate it as the sum of eight scores. First, we add 1 if some of the equity of the NOC has been privatized (0 otherwise). Second, we add 1 if the government is a minority shareholder because that signals less explicit desire to intervene politically. Third, we add 1 if there are independent board members. Fourth, we add 1 if the independent board members have a simple majority on the board of directors. Fifth, we add 1 if there are no government officials holding board seats. Sixth, we add 1 if the chairman is an external board member. Seventh, we add 1 if the firm has budgetary autonomy. Finally, we add 1 if the company's financials are audited by a private auditing firm. This give us an index that can range from 0 to 8.

private companies. For instance, listed NOCs have boards of directors with a good portion of external members (members who do not work directly at the firm but who have expertise in the industry), and they enjoy more financial autonomy from the government than non-listed firms.

There is significant variation in terms of the percentage of equity that remains in the government's hands after listing a company. In some firms, such as Eni (Italy) and GDF Suez (France), the government kept minority positions, while in the rest of the listed firms the government kept a majority of the voting shares.

The governments of some countries have chosen to corporatize their NOCs rather than list them. Therefore, in NOCs such as Aramco (Saudi Arabia), PDO (Oman), KPC (Kuwait), Pemex (Mexico), and Pertamina (Indonesia), corporate governance is somewhat similar to that of listed firms. For instance, they have boards of directors with external members who have technical expertise (and perhaps experience in the industry). Those firms also have audited financials (with the exception of Aramco, which is extremely secretive with its financials).

Board of Directors

According to our analysis of NOC boards of directors presented in Table 7.2, there is enormous variation across companies in terms of the size and composition of the board. Of particular interest to us is the variation in composition. Out of thirty firms, only Statoil, Ecopetrol, and Saudi Aramco have a majority of external board members. The rest of the listed firms have external or "independent" board members to the extent that these members are not employees, but they are for the most part government officials. The board chairmen of Gazprom (Russia), GDF Suez (France), OGDCL (Pakistan), ONGC (India), PTT (Thailand), Petrobras, and Petronas (Malaysia), for instance, are all by definition directly connected to their governments. In other, less transparent NOCs, the board includes no external or independent members. This is the case in NNPC (Nigeria), PDVSA (Venezuela), and NIOC (Iran).

In fact, in most of the listed NOCs, the chairman is the minister of oil and mines, minister of gas and mines, or minister of finance. In Sinopec, CNOOC, and Petro China, the chairman of the board is usually someone with a long career in the industry, but who has rotated among firms as part of the Chinese Communist Party's rotation of officers.

Financial Autonomy

Table 7.2 shows that listed NOCs, in general, have budgetary autonomy. That is, major investment decisions and the allocations of internally generated resources do not have to be approved by the government. This usually means that firms can pursue profitable projects more often and can spend more on exploration, R&D, and so on. (Exceptions are Petrobras and the three Chinese companies included—Sinopec, CNOOC, and Petro China. In these firms, some investments need government approval.)

Financial Transparency and External Monitoring of NOCs

Another important element to study is the level of transparency and external auditing in NOCs. According to the agency view, the difficulty of monitoring—or the lack of it altogether—is one of the biggest problems of SOEs. In Table 7.2, we can see that among corporatized, non-listed NOCs there is a lot of secrecy in the financial reporting. Many of these companies are not audited by external or reputable auditing firms. In contrast, listed NOCs have their financials audited by a private accounting firm, usually one with an international reputation. Here, the exception is Thailand's PTT, which is audited by the country's auditor general.

A Corporate Governance Index for National Oil Companies

To avoid portraying NOCs as having more separation from the state than they actually have, we included in the last column of Table 7.2 a corporate governance index that captures how independent NOCs are in practice rather than in theory. We calculate this index by adding eight scores that we assign to specific governance provisions. First, we assign a score of 1 if the company has privatized some equity (we code it as zero otherwise). Second, we assign a score of 1 if the government is a minority shareholder, zero otherwise. Third, we add 1 if the number of external board members is larger than zero. Fourth, we add 1 if external members have a majority of votes. This is an extremely important score because it is a sign that there are checks and balances to the CEO's power. Fifth, we add 1 if there are no government officials holding board seats. Sixth, we add 1 if the chairman of the board is an external board member (that is, not a government official or politician linked with the government's party or coalition or someone affiliated with the firm). Seventh, we add 1 if the firm has budgetary autonomy. Finally, we add 1 if the company's financials are audited by a private auditing firm. This sum give us an index that can range from 0 to 8. We sort the NOCs in Table 7.2 according to their corporate governance indexes, from those with stronger governance to those with greater government intervention.

Our corporate governance index provides three insights. First, many listed NOCs have corporate governance arrangements that are very similar to those of private firms. This is not to argue that private governance is a panacea, as large corporations still face corporate scandals and abuses by controlling shareholders and CEOs. Yet these new arrangements mitigate most of the agency problems that the literature in economics associates with NOCs. Also, some of these governance arrangements reduce political intervention by introducing checks and balances on the power of the controlling shareholder and the managers, mitigating some of the concerns of the political view.

Second, the variation in corporate governance is wide, and there are many listed NOCs that have little independence from the government, either because they do not have budgetary autonomy or because the board is packed with government officials or government-appointed members.

Finally, corporatized firms that are not listed do seem, in practice, to be less isolated from government influence than listed firms. Even if many of them have some independent board members, few have budgetary autonomy; governments still have to approve major investment decisions or directly decide the firm's budget each year.

Our sample of NOCs also includes more secretive companies—neither corporatized nor listed—with extremely low corporate governance indexes. Gathering the data for this table we realized how difficult some NOCs make it to find basic information about themselves, ranging from financial data to written statements about how the board works or who appoints its members. Many NOCs do not issue annual reports at all. Ross (2012) links the lack of transparency in some of the NOCs at the bottom of our governance

table to the desires of dictators or autocratic regimes to siphon funds to en-
rich members of the ruling coalition, to buy votes, or to benefit the party in
power. The IMF, in fact, has included transparency provisions for NOCs in
some of its financial aid packages for developing countries. Such has been
the case in Angola, where the IMF has been trying to get Sonangol, the national oil company, to improve its transparency and have its financials audited (Musacchio, Werker, et al. 2009).

Thus, in general, governments in many large economies have either corporatized their NOCs or listed them on stock markets in order to improve
the firm's efficiency. Why have these governments tried to make their NOCs
more efficient? The answer perhaps has to do with the aftermath of the crises
of the 1970s and 1980s and the financial difficulties some countries faced in
the 1990s (for example, in Eastern Europe after the fall of communism and
in Asia in the wake of the Asian financial crisis). The double bottom line
problem notwithstanding, governments have realized that underperforming SOEs make states weaker and can lead to fiscal difficulties. Alternatively,
profitable SOEs can make states stronger. Thus, gearing SOEs toward profitability and efficiency in the long run can be aligned with the government's
own financial objectives. For instance, profitable NOCs can generate dividend payments for the government, while simultaneously securing resources for the country. The question is whether those intentions can
prevail when governments face emergencies or extreme voter pressure (for
example, if there is a rapid increase in gasoline or gas prices before an
election).

In general, listed firms have more autonomy to make investment decisions
and have more control over their profits than corporatized firms do. Moreover, some listed NOCs—though not all of them—seem to be more isolated
from political intervention, not only with regard to profits, but also with regard to national strategy and objectives. This is partly because of the composition of their boards, but mostly because they have important shareholders
that have money at stake if the government decides to steer the company toward a goal that destroys value. The expectation of SOE reformers was that
governments would intervene less in listed NOCs because states care about
their reputations vis-à-vis minority shareholders or because some of these
shareholders are, in effect, their own voting public (for example, through
pension funds) (Perotti and Biais 2002). The idea is that if governments

intervene in listed NOCs, the pushback from shareholders such as large institutional shareholders, big banks, and private pension funds should be strong enough to tame the majority investor (the government) from trying to extract benefits from its control over the company. In sum, the commitment mechanism tying Leviathan's hands is linked to how much the government cares about minority shareholders, which is *not* to say that such a commitment will *always* occur in listed SOEs. As we shall see next, there is important variation in political intervention in those listed companies.

Does Governance Matter for Performance?

One obvious question when looking at corporate governance is whether it really matters for performance. In the case of SOEs or NOCs, we want to know two things. First, we want to see corporate governance aligning the incentives of owners (the government) and managers. Second, we want to know if corporate governance arrangements, by isolating management from social or political goals, are associated with superior performance by the NOCs. These questions are hard to answer and require sophisticated data that unfortunately are available only for a handful of oil companies (i.e., there are not enough observations to do serious econometric work). Thus, in this section, we provide only basic evidence to argue that, for NOCs, better governance, measured through our corporate governance index in Table 7.2, seems to be correlated with better performance.

In Figure 7.1, we can see that there is a high correlation between autonomy from the government and return on assets. A similar correlation is observed in Figure 7.2, which shows a scatter plot of the governance index versus the logarithm of labor productivity (net income per worker). There are at least two hypotheses that could explain this relationship. First, companies with a higher governance index allow managers to operate with profitability as the main objective rather than having to maximize social and political variables. Second, for most of the companies with a low governance index, such as Mexico's Pemex, the government taxes revenues heavily or directly controls the budget. Thus, in those companies CEOs can use less internally generated resources to invest in profitable opportunities. Alternatively, these graphs may be telling us that companies with better governance can attract

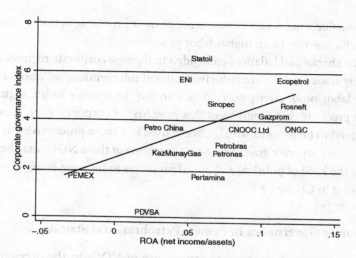

Figure 7.1. Corporate governance and return on assets in NOCs, 2011.

Source: Created by the authors with data from Table 7.2 and with financial and operational data from Capital IQ and PIW (2011).

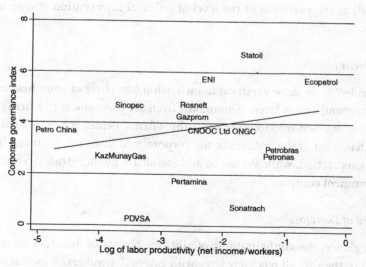

Figure 7.2. Corporate governance and labor productivity in NOCs, 2011.

Source: Created by the authors with data from Table 7.2 and with financial and operational data from Capital IQ and PIW (2011).

more outside capital and exploit more of their profitable opportunities in a more efficient way (with higher labor productivity).

If the checks and balances embedded in the new corporate regimes of the publicly traded NOCs are reducing political intervention, we would expect to see labor productivity correlated with our governance index. Figure 7.2 shows precisely this. Companies that have higher corporate governance indices tend to be firms in which labor is used in a more productive way. That is, the new corporate governance arrangements of these NOCs may be mitigating the kind of political and social pressures to increase employment we discussed in Chapter 3.

Corporate Governance in Pemex, Petrobras, and Statoil

After looking at the corporate governance of NOCs in the previous section, we now dig deeper in order to understand how Leviathan as a majority investor works in practice. For this purpose, based on Pargendler et al. (2013), we compare Petrobras with Statoil and Pemex. These comparisons allow us to study the main differences between corporatization and listing as well as the variation in the level of political intervention among listed firms.

Ownership

In Table 7.3, we show variation in ownership (the share of votes held by the government) and in levels of autonomy from the government (the firm's control over its own resources) in these three firms. Pemex is a non-listed firm that has most of the features of the corporatized firms we discussed in the previous section, while Petrobras and Statoil are publicly traded firms with government control.

Board of Directors

At a glance, the configurations of all three boards of directors seem very similar: they are all relatively large with external members. A look at who is on the board reveals that the boards of Petrobras and Pemex are packed with government officials and that external members are a minority. That is, despite the fact that Petrobras is listed, there is a high level of political

Table 7.3. Corporate governance in Petrobras, Statoil, and Pemex (July 2012)

	Petrobras	Statoil	Pemex
Corporate governance			
Is it chartered as a stand-alone company?	Yes (corporation)	Yes (public limited liability company)	No, part of government
Listed on a major stock exchange	Yes	Yes	No
Board of directors (BOD)			
Number of seats	9	10	15
Number of external directors	2	7	4
External directors are a majority?	No	Yes	No
Are government officials on BOD?	Yes	No	Yes
Shareholder rights and government power			
Dual-class shares (voting/nonvoting)	Yes	One class (one share, one vote)	Does not have shares
Share of votes held by government	50.2% (gov't) + 8.2% (BNDESPAR)	67%	100%
Gov't cash flow rights (% of total equity)	28.70%	67%	100%
Golden share or veto over major decisions	Veto rights because it owns majority of votes	Veto rights because it owns majority of votes	Veto rights over everything
Do minority shareholders have the right to elect a board member?	Yes, up to two	No	Not applicable
Relations with the government			
Taxes as % of revenues (2011)	25.2% net (34% minus deductions)	28% of revenues minus deductions for exploration and depreciation	56.2% of revenues
Additional payments to government	Dividends	Dividends according to ownership and taxes over all dividends of 3%	All additional profits minus deductions for exploration and depreciation

Source: Pargendler et al. (2013). Compiled from the companies' web sites and from questionnaires sent to Pemex.

intervention in the firm through the board of directors as well as through outright fiat power (for example, as we discuss later, the president of Brazil, directly or indirectly through government-connected board members, can request the CEO of Petrobras to pursue certain investments or actions).

In contrast, Norwegian law forbids government officials on Statoil's board of directors. In 1962, there was an accident in a state-owned mining company that had the minister of industry serving on the board. A political scandal ensued, blaming the accident on government negligence; the Labour government lost a confidence vote because of that. "Since then, no civil servant in Norway has been allowed to serve on the board of any state-owned company, protecting politicians and government officials when state-owned ventures go bad" (Thurber and Istad 2010, 20).

Financial Autonomy and the Government's Take

At the bottom of Table 7.3, we include a section that shows the extent to which the governments of Brazil, Norway, and Mexico tax their NOCs and how much the government takes in the form of dividends. The fiscal regimes of Petrobras and Statoil seem extremely similar. The government takes between 25 and 28 percent in taxes on revenues and then gets dividends according to the cash-flow rights of its shares (28.7 percent in Petrobras and 67 percent in Statoil). In Mexico, the government takes all of Pemex's profits—about 56 percent in taxes on revenues and the rest in dividends—then gives Pemex back some deductions for depreciation and to pay for exploration projects. In fact, between the government's cut and the payments Pemex has to make for pensions and interest payments to bondholders, the company often has negative profits.

Table 7.3 shows an interesting and puzzling pattern. Comparing the amount of taxes and dividends that the Brazilian and Norwegian governments take from Petrobras and Statoil, respectively, it would seem that the Brazilian government gives more financial autonomy to Petrobras than the Norwegian government gives to Statoil. Yet the government of Brazil needs to approve some of Petrobras's big investment projects, while Statoil seems to have more financial autonomy on paper.

In Table 7.4, we also compare basic indicators of financial transparency and budgetary autonomy. As we mentioned before, only the Norwegian government seems to give its national oil company complete budgetary autonomy. Petrobras needs government approval for certain investment projects, while Pemex needs approval for all investment projects and for its whole budget. In fact, Pemex has an internal control office and, additionally, needs to run major budget changes through the Ministry of Finance. Of the three, then, Pemex has the least flexibility when it comes to the use of the resources it generates.

Management Selection and Incentives

In Table 7.4, we also present a comparison of how these three firms choose a CEO. Petrobras's and Statoil's CEOs are selected by the boards, while Pemex's CEO is selected by the president of Mexico. In Petrobras, however, the board is packed with government officials and government-appointed members. Therefore, the appointment of a CEO is, in practice, a political process, and the president of Brazil has ultimate fiat power when it comes to who runs Petrobras. As a way to gauge political intervention in the appointment of top executives, in line with our discussion in Chapter 6, we comparatively assess the CEO turnover of the three NOCs. We see that, in Petrobras, the CEO has changed after three out of the last seven presidential elections. In Pemex, the appointment of CEOs is also highly correlated with presidential elections. In Statoil, however, the appointment of CEOs is relatively independent of the electoral cycles. That is perhaps why the CEOs of Pemex and Petrobras turn over approximately every three years, while Statoil's CEOs stay, on average, for seven years.

Our analysis also suggests that the backgrounds of CEOs are less political in listed firms, but it is hard to say because more than half of Pemex's CEOs, though politically connected, have strong technical backgrounds in the industry, and Statoil's CEOs, though generally technical, have also traditionally been politicians.

Finally, we also look at the variation in incentives and compensation for CEOs in these three NOCs. Although both Petrobras and Statoil adopt pay-for-performance contracts, Statoil is the only firm that gives stock options to its CEO. In both Petrobras and Statoil, the CEO actually owns shares of the company. Moreover, Petrobras and Statoil pay their CEOs salaries that are

Table 7.4. CEOs, incentives, and reporting in Petrobras, Statoil, and Pemex (July 2012)

CEOs/incentives	Petrobras	Statoil	Pemex
CEO selected by	BOD	BOD	President of Mexico
Current CEO	Maria das Graças Foster (technical CEO, though with close ties to President Dilma Rousseff)	Helge Lund (technical-politician)	Juan José Suárez Coppel (technical)
Profile of previous CEOs	9 technical, 1 technical-politician	2 technical-politicians, 2 technical, 2 politicians	4 technical, 2 technical-politicians, 3 politicians
Average CEO tenure in years	2.7	6.7	3.2
CEOs usually change after presidential elections	In 3 out of 7 elections	No	Yes
CEO compensation has pay-for-performance component	Yes	Yes	No
CEOs get stock options	No	Yes	No
CEOs have shares	Yes	Yes	No

Financials/transparency			
Autonomous budget	No, some investments need gov't approval	Yes	No, some investments need gov't approval
Audited financials (by a private firm)	Yes	Yes	Yes
Accounting standards	IFRS	IFRS	IFRS (since 2012)
Frequency of financial reporting	Quarterly	Quarterly	Quarterly
Main institutional investors	Local pension funds, Black Rock	Norwegian national insurance fund	Bondholders and Ex-Im Bank
S&P rating of long-term domestic currency bonds	BBB	AA-	A-
Regulation	National Oil Agency (ANP), linked to the Ministry of Mines and Energy	Norwegian Petroleum Directorate (NPD), reporting to the Ministry of Petroleum and Energy	National Carbohydrates Commission (CNH in Spanish), a decentralized agency linked to the Ministry of Energy (SENER)

Source: Pargendler et al. (2013). Compiled from the companies' web sites and from questionnaires sent to Pemex.
Note: IFRS stands for International Financial Reporting Standards, which are the standards set by the International Accounting Standards Board. IFRS usually requires companies to disclose more-detailed accounts than the generally accepted accounting principles (GAAP), which are the required accounting standards to list shares or trade bonds on the New York Stock Exchange.

somewhat compatible with the salaries of CEOs in private oil industry firms (for example, $2 million per year at Statoil), while Pemex pays its CEO much less, in line with high-ranking officers in the state bureaucracy (approximately $200,000 per year).

Financial Transparency and External Monitoring of NOCs

In terms of financial reporting and transparency, we can see that Petrobras, Statoil, and Pemex all comply with International Financial Reporting Standards (IFRS). The three firms report their financials quarterly, and they all have a credit-rating agency rating their bond issues. In part, the high levels of transparency in Pemex have to do with the fact that it issues bonds in various stock markets, which forces it to comply with international financial standards and to have a satisfactory credit rating.

Who monitors the CEO of these NOCs? In addition to the board of directors, the credit rating agencies, and bondholders, institutional investors play a part in monitoring the executives of Statoil and Petrobras. Local pension funds and American funds such as Black Rock are Petrobras's largest minority shareholders. Although Pemex, being unlisted, is not monitored by institutional investors, it does have creditors and rating agencies following the actions of its managers. Actions that destroy value for the company are penalized with lower ratings or higher interest rates.

Regulation of NOCs in Brazil, Norway, and Mexico

Another important factor in understanding NOCs, and SOEs in general, is regulation (Bortolotti et al. forthcoming). In all three cases, there are established regulatory agencies that report to governmental bodies (such as the Ministry of Energy) and which are, at least on paper, run by technical professionals. However, a deeper inspection of the roles of those agencies reveals profound differences. In Brazil, the National Oil Agency (ANP) is relatively weak and heavily influenced by the government. Furthermore, it has had a stained reputation, since ANP officials were caught requesting bribes from private companies.[2] As a consequence, the president of Brazil and the minister of mines and energy are the de facto "regulators" of Petrobras.

In Mexico, the government passed a law in 2008 creating the National Carbohydrates Commission (known as CNH). It was intended to be an autonomous agency run by commissioners with technical knowledge of the sector. In practice, however, not all the commissioners have been experts. Moreover, the de facto regulator of Pemex's actions is the Ministry of Finance, which controls the company's budget line by line, and whose minister is chairman of Pemex's board.

In contrast to the Mexican and Brazilian cases, the Norwegian Petroleum Directorate (NPD), while also subordinate to the ministry, is functionally autonomous and strong. As put by Thurber and Istad (2010, 28):

> Since the Norwegian Petroleum Directorate formally reported to the Ministry, it was initially felt necessary to have an independent board oversee the directorate to guarantee its independence from politics. In time, however, this board was judged to be superfluous, and in 1991 it was disbanded. . . . What ultimately protected the NPD from undue interference was the growing dependence of the Ministry on it for critical technical services and advice. (One early Ministry official said that the NPD tended to be viewed within the Ministry as its own technical department.) Any actions that would have severely disrupted this function would have been detrimental to both organizations.

The existence of an autonomous regulatory agency thus helped create institutional checks and balances that reduced the government's ability to directly intervene. And, in the case of NPD, such autonomy was apparently due to the presence of technical regulators with distinct industry-level knowledge.

The Risk of Political Intervention in the Leviathan as Majority Investor Model: The Case of Petrobras

In our analysis of NOCs above, we have shown that listing SOEs (including NOCs) mitigates or eliminates many of their common agency problems. Yet the model of Leviathan as a majority investor has its limits: even listed NOCs are not necessarily free from political intervention.

For instance, even at Statoil, which has many checks and balances on government intervention, there have been instances of political intervention. Although "direct intervention of the Ministry of Petroleum and Energy in

Statoil strategy has mostly disappeared, politicians continue to weigh in as though they were making policy for the company" (Thurber and Istad 2010, 9). Thurber and Istad mention that in October 2007 the government halted further developments of natural gas in the Troll field in Norway "on the grounds that such activity would likely harm the ultimate oil recovery from the field. . . . Statoil was highly displeased based on commercial considerations" (p. 33).

Yet these are relatively isolated instances compared to other examples we mention below. In this section, we examine how Petrobras has not managed to shield itself from political intervention, despite its listing in New York (through American Depository Receipts) and at the Bovespa, in São Paulo.

The Public Offer of Petrobras's Shares in 2010

On June 22, 2010, the board of directors of Petrobras approved an ambitious capital expenditure plan of $224 billion for 2011 to 2014, including expenditures to explore and develop the pre-salt oil fields off the coast of São Paulo. Foreseeing expenditures on the order of $45 billion per year for at least five years—more than Petrobras's cash flows could cover—the company decided to issue a mix of debt and equity. In fact, the company planned what might be the largest public offer in the world, with the sale of shares totaling $50 billion (Pargendler 2012b). The share issue, in and of itself, was a major accomplishment for any corporation, involving six investment banks acting as global coordinators and nine as joint managers (Dwyer 2011).[3]

Yet the government did not want Petrobras to sell voting shares to the public in a way that would dilute its own voting power. In fact, Brazilian law forced firms issuing new shares to give existing shareholders first priority to buy them. Simultaneously, the government of Brazil sold to Petrobras the rights to extract five billion barrels of oil or the equivalent at a price of $8.51 per barrel. Technically Petrobras would pay $42.5 billion to the government. Yet the government decided to use those proceeds to purchase new shares, thus increasing its voting power in the company.

Minority shareholders in Petrobras worried about this transaction. Of particular concern were the dilution of minority shareholder power, the fact that exploitation rights were negotiated without consultation with minority shareholders, and the fact that those rights were paid for before they were going to be used. Other minority shareholders complained that the price agreed to by Petrobras was too high.[4]

Implicit Gasoline Price Controls

The price of gasoline had been controlled in Brazil for years, but direct intervention in the management of the company mounted in early 2012. The appointment of Maria das Graças Foster, referred to as Graça Foster, as CEO of Petrobras in February 2012 was well received by market participants, because of her technical background; she had had a long career at the firm and was considered very knowledgeable about the sector. Graça Foster recognized that keeping gasoline prices low would undermine profitability and deteriorate the cash flow necessary to support future investments. At the time of her appointment, she gave an interview declaring, "If you ask me, is it necessary to adjust the price [of gasoline]? It is evident that it is necessary to adjust the price. . . . It is not sensible to imagine that someone who sells anything—anything at all, a cup, a notepad, gasoline, diesel—should not transfer to the market his or her advantages or disadvantages."[5]

Yet President Dilma Rousseff and her minister of energy publicly disavowed Graça Foster's statement and said that the price of gasoline would not be raised. They were both concerned that an increase in gasoline prices would accelerate inflation at a moment when the government was trying to force reductions in interest rates. In June 2012, the government allowed a minor adjustment—not enough to compensate for the large increases in the price of oil (at that moment trading close to $100 per barrel). These price controls directly affect the profitability of Petrobras's refining division. Therefore, investments in refining are less profitable for minority shareholders than investments in the profitable lines of business.

In May 2012, a group of foreign investors sent a letter to Graça Foster, criticizing the company's investment plan—approved by the board of directors—which would have invested heavily in refining despite there being no clear plan to lift price controls for gasoline. Echoing these investors' concerns, Petrobras announced a record loss of 1.34 billion reais (around US$662 million) in the second quarter of 2012, its first loss in thirteen years. Even if the loss was related to the write-off of a failed exploration attempt offshore, having the price of gasoline capped by the government certainly did not help profitability at Petrobras.

Investors also complained that the two board seats that the statutes of Petrobras guarantee for minority shareholders were not really representing minority shareholders (Rostás 2012). These complaints echoed the concerns of institutional investors Polo Capital and Black Rock; the candidates they had nominated for the board had been defeated. The winners, Jorge Gerdau Johannpeter and Josué Gomes da Silva, were seen by these institutional investors as too close to the government: the former was a steel industrialist regularly consulted by Presidents Lula and Rousseff, and the latter, also a businessman, was the son of Lula's vice president. They were elected by the pension funds of two SOEs—the banks Banco do Brasil and Caixa Econômica Federal—and by BNDESPAR, the investment arm of Brazil's national development bank. The Securities and Exchange Commission of Brazil supposedly investigated this board election, but without major consequences.

To be sure, political intervention in the oil business is commonplace across the world. However, it is not clear from the point of view of the Leviathan as a majority investor model why governments sometimes try to portray their NOCs as well-behaved listed firms, maximizing value for shareholders, if in the end the majority investor is willing to expropriate minority shareholders by tunneling or siphoning away profits to affiliated "businesses." The evidence presented above and below makes us conclude that the Leviathan as a majority investor model gave the government of Brazil a license to expropriate minority shareholders and use Petrobras for social and political purposes. Moreover, the absence of regulatory checks and balances, as in Norway, and the dominant position of Petrobras in the Brazilian oil sector allowed the government to intervene—that is, to "regulate" prices at will, even at the cost of reduced profitability.

Other Interventions in Petrobras

Petrobras has procurement policies that force its suppliers to have a high national content. Those policies are of interest to the government, the controlling shareholder; they help Brazilian industries develop and help Brazilian labor (and companies) acquire knowledge from abroad. But they are equivalent to an expropriation of minority shareholders, because national suppliers that are acquiring capabilities may be slower or more expensive to provide the parts, equipment, and services than comparable international suppliers.

Government interference can also occur when the NOC directly supports geopolitical moves by the government. In 2005, for example, Petrobras signed up for a joint venture with the Venezuelan oil company PDVSA to build a refinery in the Brazilian state of Pernambuco. This was a pet project of President Lula and President Hugo Chávez of Venezuela. Petrobras originally projected costs to be around $2.3 billion, but by 2012, the costs were expected to be $20 billion.[6]

Other Cases of State Intervention in Brazilian Listed SOEs

Brazilian government intervention is not limited to Petrobras. In 2012, for example, President Rousseff realized that her administration needed to take measures to tackle the recession that had hit Brazil that year. She began asking state-owned banks—in particular Banco do Brasil, the largest state-owned commercial bank in the Americas—to reduce interest rates somewhat artificially in order to push other Brazilian banks to follow suit (Romero 2012).

In September 2012, Rousseff announced extensions of private concessions to produce electricity that would otherwise be transferred to Eletrobras, an SOE listed on the São Paulo Stock Exchange. The government is Eletrobras's majority investor, but minority shareholders hold 35 percent of the equity. Preliminary calculations by Eletrobras estimated that the government's extension of concessions to private companies would generate losses of about $2.5 billion (R$5 billion), which could drive the company to report overall losses in 2013 (Polito et al. 2012).

Conclusion

In the Leviathan as a majority investor model, some governments have managed to separate ownership and management by following improved governance practices. These SOEs have more professional CEOs (selected on merit or talent), higher-powered incentive contracts, and more-transparent reporting systems. Transparency in the financial reporting of listed and corporatized firms makes it easier for both the government and private investors to monitor performance. In fact, governments can outsource the monitoring of these SOEs to the private investors who are minority shareholders, especially when these are large institutional investors. When compared to SOEs under the more traditional Leviathan as an entrepreneur model, those listed SOEs generally represent an improvement.

Yet governments have also used NOCs for social and political goals. The Brazilian government has found ways to tunnel resources out of SOEs to support objectives other than profitable investment. We saw in Chapters 4 and 6 that, in the 1980s, economic shocks led governments to control prices. Those price controls led to losses that went directly into the public finances of the government and which affected the government's capacity to pay its debt and to borrow in international markets. By the second decade of the twenty-first century, however, the Leviathan as a majority investor model seemed to be dealing with losses in a different way. Again, the objective of the Brazilian government was to use SOEs to control prices and inflation, but the effects on public finances were different from those we observed in the 1980s. First, price controls (for example, of gasoline) generated losses for SOEs in both the 1980s and the 2000s. Yet, in the latter period, the government, rather than face the losses itself, shared them with minority shareholders.

Second, in the 1980s, both price controls and political intervention to avoid layoffs led to many years of significant losses for SOEs. In the years that followed the privatization of Brazil's large SOEs, things changed. Although price controls could still lead to losses, many SOEs were run by professional managers and some operated in many ways like private companies. As a consequence, these firms could adjust to government price controls just as any private company would adjust to a lower market price: by adjusting investment plans, selling non-core assets, firing workers, or increasing its leverage. Thus, firms with majority state ownership have slightly more flexibility to adjust to shocks today than in the past.

PART III

Leviathan as a
Minority Investor

8

Leviathan as a Minority Shareholder

This chapter starts our analysis of the minority Leviathan model by studying the effects of government investments in minority equity positions in private firms. Although governments sometimes purchase such minority stakes as part of a bailout, as was the case when the United States government bought a minority position in General Motors in 2008, in many countries governments actively invest in equity using professional analysts and portfolio managers. Governments also become indirect minority shareholders by buying direct equity stakes in companies that own other companies. For example, the United States government became an indirect minority shareholder of PSA Peugeot when General Motors—of which the U.S. government was a minority shareholder at the time—bought a 7 percent stake in that company in March 2012.[1]

In this chapter, we ask a simple question: What are the firm-level performance implications when Leviathan becomes a minority shareholder? We use a database of equity investments by BNDES from 1995 to 2009 to study this question. We assess how equity purchases by BNDES affected the performance and investment of target firms.[2]

Hypotheses

According to the industrial policy view, discussed in Chapter 3, government purchases of equity can help firms by alleviating capital constraints. If a firm finds it hard to access long-term financing, government injections of new equity will help it to make investments in plant and equipment to achieve economies of scale, improve operations, acquire new technology, and so on—all of which should improve firm-level performance. This should be particularly true in the case of firms that have "latent" capabilities to invest in profitable projects but that are, at the same time, financially constrained because they do not have access to "patient" capital.

How can *equity stakes* by the state help in this context? Here we borrow from Williamson's discussion of the relative merits of debt and equity as a function of a firm's asset profile. Williamson (1988) argues that investments in non-redeployable assets (such as dedicated industrial plants and machinery) are best served by equity because of the higher flexibility of this financing mode. While debt requires a fixed return over the duration of the contract, equity can better adapt to changing circumstances that might negatively affect the value of such assets. Furthermore, shareholders have more discretion to meet and discuss strategies to reorganize the company and provide a longer-term time frame for the necessary changes.

Applying Williamson's logic to our context, we can predict state ownership of minority stakes will help improve firm performance by expanding firms' investment opportunities. This should be observed especially when firms have the possibility of investing in long-term fixed assets. Although not all fixed assets are non-redeployable (e.g., generic land), the extent to which the firm invests in fixed capital signals the degree to which the firm has projects with long-term maturity that are, therefore, riskier. This is precisely the kind of project that can benefit from the flexibility of equity as a financing mode. Furthermore, *state* capital will be particularly helpful when entrepreneurs do not have access to private-equity investors willing to accept riskier projects with a longer time horizon. In other words, the state itself will act as a private-equity investor. This would occur, for instance, in countries in the initial stages of industrial development (Mahmood and Rufin 2005; Cameron 1961).

In addition, minority ownership attenuates political intervention and thus helps governments solve some of the agency problems that state majority ownership usually entails. For instance, when the government is a minority shareholder, the majority owners and institutional investors (if they want to maximize profits) are likely to closely monitor executives or implement pay-for-performance compensation schemes to reduce agency problems. The risk of a bankruptcy or hostile takeover should also provide managers with powerful incentives to try to perform at least as well as or better than their peers (Ehrlich et al. 1994; Karpoff 2001; Alchian 1965).

Yet there are two alternative views of why governments end up with minority equity positions. One view, partly linked to the path-dependence view, is that such positions are the product of complex political processes whereby governments try to preserve their influence on the economy through embedded intertwined networks with local capitalists (Pistor and Turkewitz 1996; Stark 1996; McDermott 2003). The political view, on the other hand, would argue that governments may choose to allocate capital to specific firms in the form of equity investments for political reasons, perhaps because private owners have political connections and want access to cheap capital (Ades and Di Tella 1997).

Therefore, according to either of these two views, when the government buys a minority equity stake in a corporation, we should not necessarily find an improvement in performance or investment. The political view additionally suggests that the government may try to use equity as a bailout mechanism. For instance, convertible bonds purchased by the state may eventually turn into equity if the firm is in financial distress, and the government will in turn become a minority shareholder. This is precisely what happened to JBS, the meat processor singled out as a Brazilian national champion (see Chapter 1). There the government increased the size of its equity stake because the firm was in financial strain. If this phenomenon occurs systematically, then we should expect that equity investments by the state will primarily target firms with poor financial performance. In other words, instead of equity affecting performance, we should expect that past (negative) performance should influence whether a given firm will be observed with minority equity.[3]

The Contingent Effect of State Ownership of Minority Stakes

We propose that the effect of governments purchases of minority equity positions will depend on two major factors: the corporate governance of the target firm and the depth of existing financial markets (i.e., how bad the capital market failure is). We discuss these two contingent effects in turn.

Corporate Governance of the Target Firm

We expect the effect of equity investments by the government to be attenuated in firms that belong to *business groups*—collections of firms controlled by a holding company—for two reasons. First, business groups provide member firms that are credit-constrained with financing opportunities that flow through internal capital markets (Leff 1978). That is, groups can substitute for financial markets when external financing is scarce or costly (Khanna and Palepu 2000; Khanna and Yafeh 2007; Wan and Hoskisson 2003). In other words, group affiliates do not need government equity investments because they can use the internal capital market of the group to promote their new projects.

Second, minority shareholders of firms that belong to business groups are at the expense of controlling shareholders (the holding company of the group) and can be expropriated (Morck 2000). Most business groups are organized through complex pyramids involving firms that have stakes in other firms (Morck et al. 2005). Therefore, in countries with weaker protection for minority owners, equity investments by the state in a firm affiliated with a business group can be "tunneled" away through complex pyramids to support the controlling owners' private projects or to rescue struggling companies in other parts of the group (Bae et al. 2002; Bertrand, Djankov, et al. 2007). The government may thus add value for a business group's majority owners without necessarily improving the performance of the companies in which it invests. Consistent with this prediction, Giannetti and Laeven (2009) find that investments in minority equity positions by public pension funds in Sweden increase firm value, but the effect is reduced when firms are part of business groups.

Capital Market Development

For students of institutions, debt and equity markets in emerging and underdeveloped countries are frequently inhibited by poor legal protection and high transaction costs.[4] Moreover, in developing markets that suffer occasional or continuous inflation shocks or that suffer from external shocks (e.g., balance-of-payments shocks), financial markets tend to be underdeveloped, debt markets tend to be shallow, and debt instruments tend to have short maturities (Perotti and von Thadden 2006; Goldsmith 1986; Roe and Siegel 2006).

Part of our argument in this chapter is that minority equity purchases by the state can alleviate some of the constraints firms face in the capital markets of less-developed economies. That is, governments may sometimes substitute in part for markets. But once capital markets have developed, firms can raise equity capital by selling equity, issuing bonds, or obtaining loans (even long-term loans) from banks or financial institutions engaged in project finance. For instance, firms on the stock market can have a secondary issue of equity to raise more capital, and private firms can go public for the first time (by having an initial public offering or IPO). Moreover, if equity markets thrive and are liquid, it is easy for investors to sell their equity or exit investments after a certain period (Haber et al. 2008). There should therefore be less need for government investment, and the positive effect of governmental equity stakes should decline.

Shallow capital markets pose other problems besides the rationing of capital. The protections necessary to entice investors to buy equity or bonds are not present or are poorly enforced, and the information necessary to monitor managers is sometimes lacking (La Porta et al. 1998). Dyck and Zingales (2004) and Nenova (2005) assert that underdeveloped capital markets make takeovers less likely and magnify governance conflicts. In fact, both of these studies find that Brazil was the worst place to be a minority shareholder in the 1990s, because controlling shareholders could easily divert corporate resources away from the firm, either to themselves,[5] to pay for perquisites, or to support other firms they owned (Johnson et al. 2000).

Under those circumstances, we think that governments can perhaps replace markets as providers of capital and, more specifically, act as minority shareholders providing equity. The comparison of state-owned and private banks in India by Sarkar et al. (1998) indicates that, in the absence of well-functioning capital markets, private companies are not unambiguously superior to SOEs. However, as capital markets develop and offer more sophisticated mechanisms for capitalization and monitoring, new private investors will gradually replace governments as sources of equity capital.[6]

We think it makes sense to take financial development into consideration in our study, given that Brazil experienced a process of financial deepening during our period, with private actors and the government both pushing for significant changes in corporate governance. Between 1995 and 2009, Brazil's average stock market capitalization to GDP was 43.1 percent, compared to 98.7 percent in Chile and 129.7 percent in the United States. Thus, relative to other countries, Brazilian firms were more constrained in terms of equity financing. Yet, over the same period, stock market capitalization to GDP in Brazil jumped from 19 percent in 1995 to 73 percent in 2009 (Figure 8.1). Moreover, Brazil experienced a radical transformation of corporate governance

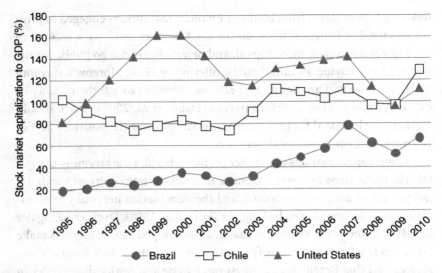

Figure 8.1. The evolution of capital markets in Brazil, compared to the United States and Chile (1995–2009)

Source: Created by the authors using the World Bank's Global Financial Development Database, available at http://data.worldbank.org/data-catalog/global-financial-development (accessed March 10, 2013).

practices, at least for a subset of firms. This was particularly true after 2001, when Congress passed a new Joint Stock Company Law that included more protections for minority shareholders and when the Brazilian Stock Exchange (Bovespa) launched the New Market (Novo Mercado). As we explained in Chapter 4, Bovespa segmented its listings according to corporate governance standards (Perkins and Zajac 2012).

Measuring the Effect of State Purchases of Minority Equity

In an ideal setting, in order to test the effect of government purchases of minority stakes we would like BNDES to buy shares of Brazilian companies randomly. But BNDES buys stakes in firms that it chooses or that choose the bank. Consequently, we pursue a second-best solution, which is to study what happens to firm performance when BNDES becomes a shareholder, using company fixed effects and time-varying industry-level effects (i.e., industry membership dummies interacted with year dummies) to control for unobservable factors that might affect ownership choice and performance (J. Wooldridge 2002). We thus essentially measure if performance and investment increase in firms that see increases in government ownership of minority positions. This is possible with our data set because our period of analysis is associated with intense corporate restructuring and changes in corporate control (e.g., privatizations).

In order to examine the effects of having the government as a minority shareholder, we created a database of ownership and financial variables for about 358 publicly traded corporations in Brazil between 1995 and 2009. Our database is not a balanced panel of firms; some firms come into the database as they join the stock market, and others leave the database as they are delisted, acquired, or go bankrupt.[7] See Appendix 8.1 for a definition of our variables and summary statistics.

A crucial aspect in the construction of our database was to track BNDES's minority equity stakes in Brazilian firms. We started by compiling the extent of BNDES's *direct* ownership—that is, cases where BNDES or BNDESPAR, the investment arm, appear as a direct owner of the target firm. We call this variable *BNDESDir*. But we also wanted to measure cases where BNDES is an *indirect* shareholder—that is, when BNDES owns shares in a given firm that in turn owns the target firm. If BNDES purchases the equity of the target firm either directly or through this cascading pattern of indirect ownership, we coded a dummy variable, called *BNDES*, as 1. Unfortunately, the extent of equity participation in pyramids is not readily available. Thus, cases where the *BNDES* dummy is equal to 1 indicate that BNDES is a direct or indirect owner of the target firm.

We also wanted to know if the target company was part of a business group—that is, a collection of firms with the same controlling shareholders. If so, we coded the set of affiliates in our database as members of a business group. This allowed us to study if equity investments by the government have a different impact on companies affiliated with business groups. To define group membership, we conducted a detailed analysis of shareholders' agreements available on the Securities Exchange Commission's web site. We identified owners that had distinctive control rights over a firm (i.e., those who had the largest number of seats on the board of directors). Multinationals with single subsidiaries in Brazil were not treated as groups, even though they usually control multiple units across the world, mostly because our goal was to find instances in which local controlling shareholders could use new allocations to transfer funds to other local units. About 46.7 percent of the observations in our database came from firms belonging to some group. To test our hypotheses that the effect of BNDES's equity depends on business group membership, we multiply the *BNDESDir* and *BNDES* variables by the dummy variable coding for group membership.

Effect of BNDES's Equity on Performance and Investment

Table 8.1 presents regressions examining how direct and indirect stakes by BNDES affect firm-level performance (measured as *ROA*, return on assets) and investment (measured as variations in the ratio of fixed assets to total assets, *ΔFixed*, and the ratio of yearly capital expenditures to total assets, *CapEx*). For simplicity, we report only the most important results. More detailed analyses and alternative specifications—including the use of propensity-score matching to guarantee a more comparable assessment of firms with and without BNDES—are presented in Inoue et al. (2013).

We see in specification 1 that companies in which BNDES entered as a minority shareholder (directly or indirectly) have a return on assets 7 percentage points higher than that of other firms. In specification 2, we find that the effect of an increase in the percentage of equity owned by BNDES has a significant and large effect on return on assets. The coefficient for our variable *BNDESDir,* a continuous variable capturing the fraction of the firm's equity owned by BNDES, implies that a 10-percentage-point increase in BNDES's direct equity (the average BNDES equity stake is over 10 percent) is associated with a 7.25-percentage-point increase in the firm's return on assets.

In specifications 1 and 2, we also test whether the impact of having the government as a minority shareholder changes when the target firm belongs to a business group. The interactions of *BNDES × Belongs to a group* and *BNDESDir × Belongs to a group* are negative and significant, implying that when BNDES buys equity in a company that belongs to a business group, the positive effect on performance is practically neutralized. This finding does not imply that belonging to a business group is detrimental to a firm's performance or access to resources. In fact, the *main* effect of our group membership variable indicates that belonging to such groups has a

Table 8.1. Regressions examining the effect of state minority ownership via BNDES, Brazil, 1995–2009

Variables	ROA (1)	ROA (2)	ΔFixed (3)	ΔFixed (4)	CapEx (5)	CapEx (6)
BNDES ownership						
BNDES (direct and indirect stakes—dummy)	0.070** (0.035)		0.043 (0.033)		0.020* (0.011)	
BNDESDir (direct stakes only—percentage)		0.725** (0.280)		0.582*** (0.212)		0.236** (0.105)
Group ownership						
Belongs to a group	0.108** (0.045)	0.104** (0.045)	0.033 (0.028)	0.026 (0.027)	0.024 (0.017)	0.023 (0.017)
Interactions with group ownership						
BNDES×Belongs to a group	−0.082** (0.039)		−0.076* (0.039)		−0.021 (0.015)	
BNDESDir×Belongs to a group		−0.963*** (0.319)		−0.846* (0.476)		−0.258* (0.150)
Controls						
ROA	N	N	Y	Y	Y	Y
Fixed	Y	Y	N	N	Y	Y
Observations	2,920	2,919	2,149	2,148	2,021	2,020
Number of firms	367	367	324	324	317	317
Adjusted R-squared	0.163	0.167	0.319	0.324	0.188	0.19

Source: Simplified results based on the approach employed by Inoue et al. (2013), which presents more detailed analyses and alternative specifications.

Note: All regressions include controls for leverage, the log of gross revenue, and whether the company is foreign, state-owned, or domestic (privately owned). We also include a constant and year, firm, and industry-year fixed effects. ***, **, and * denote significance at the 1%, 5%, and 10% levels, respectively. Robust standard errors in brackets.

positive effect on *ROA*. This finding is consistent with the literature that contends that business groups have ways to fill in institutional and capital market voids in emerging economies (Khanna and Palepu 2000; Khanna and Yafeh 2007; Wan and Hoskisson 2003). However, because group affiliates tend to be less financially constrained, the benefit of state equity should be lower than in the case of firms that do not belong to groups.

In specifications 3 and 4, we examine if increases in BNDES minority shareholdings lead firms to increase their fixed assets. We thus measure if having BNDES as a partner increases firm-level capital intensity, perhaps because firms undertake major capital-intensive projects they could not have undertaken without state equity. The results indicate that the effects are positive only when BNDES is a direct shareholder—that is, when BNDES injects capital directly into the firm. The effect is not positive for firms that belong to a business group; when BNDES buys an equity position in a firm that is part of a business group, the capital is apparently not used to increase investment in that firm. This finding could suggest two things. The first is that when firms that are members of a business group get equity investments, they are not doing so in order to undertake new capital investments. If this is correct, then our finding supports the idea that group affiliates are not as capital-constrained as stand-alone firms. Second, this finding could suggest tunneling: when BNDES comes in as a shareholder, the capital is used to benefit other firms inside the group (Bertrand et al. 2002).

Specifications 5 and 6 confirm these results. We use capital expenditures as the dependent variable and again find positive effects of BNDES ownership—both direct and indirect—of minority stakes. In specification 6, we again see that companies belonging to a business group experience a weaker positive effect from having BNDES as a minority shareholder.

Are Results Driven by Improved Access to Debt?

One concern we have with our analysis is that BNDES could increase *leverage* in a firm in which it has bought equity by opening lines of credit from its own banking arm or from other banks. We can test, however, whether BNDES's ownership has an effect on leverage in general. Using *Leverage* as a dependent variable (defined as total debt to total assets), and employing specifications similar to those in Table 8.1 we find that BNDES's equity allocations do not change leverage in a significant way. That is, companies are apparently not getting equity from BNDES and using this as a way to open a line of credit from BNDES or any other bank.

Still as an additional test, using data collected for the analyses presented in Chapter 11 and developed further in Lazzarini, Musacchio, et al. (2012), we tested if between 2002 and 2009 firms receiving BNDES's equity also received BNDES's loans—which are heavily subsidized and, unlike equity allocations, directly affect profitability. It turns out that the correlation is very small (-0.034) and not statistically significant at conventional levels. This small correlation is consistent with allegations that BNDESPAR, BNDES's equity arm, usually operates independently not only of the bank unit responsible for debt financing, but of other banks as well. This fact notwithstanding, in Chapter 11 we show that BNDES's equity reduces financial expenses, possibly because of an implicit guarantee of repayment given that the state is a shareholder and not because of a change in leverage.

The Effect of Capital Market Development

Part of our argument is based on the assumption that Leviathan's minority shareholder investments will have more impact when capital markets are shallow or when firms are more capital-constrained (Rajan and Zingales 1996). We thus tested if the effects of BNDES's equity investments on return on assets change as financial markets deepened. We interacted both variables of interest, *BNDES* and *BNDESDir*, with variables that measure financial development in Brazil as a whole. We use the following measures of financial development for this exercise: private credit to GDP, stock market capitalization to GDP, the number of IPOs per year, and the turnover rate of the stock market (value negotiated over stock market capitalization). Only when we interact the change in stock market capitalization (year on year) with *BNDESDir* do we find a strong and significant negative coefficient. That is, we find some support for the idea that when financial markets develop, government investments in minority equity have weaker effects.

In Inoue et al. (2013), we extended the research on the effects of government minority ownership by examining specifically how BNDES helps to promote capital expenditures of firms with *constrained opportunities*. We measured constrained opportunities by creating a composite variable with two key elements. First, following David et al. (2006), we measured investment opportunity as cases where Tobin's q was higher than 1.[8] Second, we gauged financial constraints by computing the ratio of net profits to the initial stock of fixed capital (Fazzari et al. 1988; Behr et al. 2012). The larger this ratio, the higher a given firm's ability to invest using profits from its own operations. We then considered that the firm had a constrained opportunity if its Tobin's q was higher than 1 and if *at the same time* it had a ratio of net profits to the stock of fixed capital that was *below* the sample median.

We found positive effects of BNDES purchases of minority equity positions on capital expenditures and ROA. Yet we found this effect was sharply reduced after 2002. In fact, the effect of BNDES's equity purchases becomes insignificant in the subsample of observations after 2002 (see Chapter 11). We then interacted the BNDES variables with the extent of stock market capitalization (as well as other institutional variables). Our results again confirmed that a reduction in the positive effect of state equity over time was likely induced by the evolution of local capital markets. Over time, the effect of BNDES's equity was reduced even in the case of firms with constrained opportunity (as defined before).

A problem with the previous analyses is that we lack cross-country heterogeneity in terms of institutional development. At the country level, if our hypothesis is right, we would expect to find that governments participate more as minority shareholders in economies in which financial markets are less developed. A simple way to check for such a correlation is to plot the number of firms that have the government as a minority shareholder (normalized by population), using the same database of government ownership we used in Chapters 2 and 3 of the book, against indicators of financial development. Figure 8.2 and Figure 8.3 show that there is a negative correlation between the number of firms in which the government has minority equity and two common measures of financial development—private credit to GDP and stock market capitalization to GDP.

We obviously do not want to claim causality: while it may be the case that government investment in equity positions in private firms is substituting for financial markets, it may also be the case that Leviathan is crowding out private financial markets—or has crowded them out in the past—which would also account for the depicted negative correlation.

Are Our Results Driven by Selection?

Since BNDES obviously does not make its investments randomly, we should further investigate if our results are driven by its selection process. For

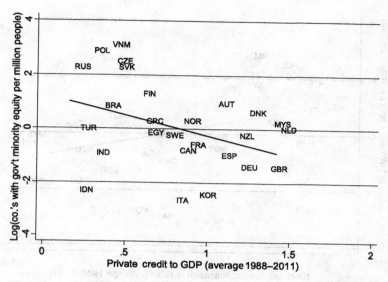

Figure 8.2. Number of firms with government minority ownership and ratio of private credit to GDP in twenty-eight countries
Source: Appendix 2.1 and World Bank, *World Development Indicators.*

instance, suppose that the government is selecting the best companies in which to invest, thereby increasing the probability of finding a positive correlation between government investments and firm performance. If, as critics of industrial policy contend, governments frequently "pick winners" that were already doing well (e.g., Pack and Saggi 2006; Almeida 2009), then the apparent positive effect of governmental stakes may be spurious—that is, past performance may be affecting governmental equity rather than the other way around.

However, a negative selection process is also plausible. As mentioned before, a hypothesis emanating from the political view is that the state may target poor performers that want to be bailed out (Haber 2002; Kang 2002). If this is the case, then we should expect a negative association between past performance and likelihood of BNDES's becoming a minority shareholder.

Another source of concern with our results is that our period of analysis covers the terms of two presidents—Fernando Henrique Cardoso (1995–2002) and Luiz Inácio Lula da Silva (2003–2010)—with quite distinct public

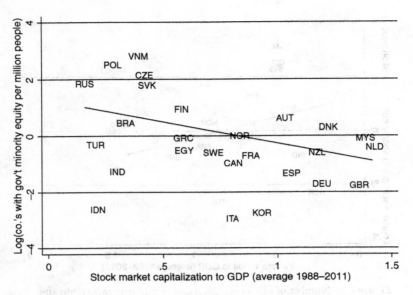

Figure 8.3. Number of firms with government minority ownership and ratio of stock market capitalization to GDP in twenty-eight countries
Source: Appendix 2.1 and World Bank, *World Development Indicators.*

policy orientations. While most of the privatizations in our period occurred during Cardoso's term, Lula's administration put a greater emphasis on using BNDES's capital to pursue an active industrial policy and to create large domestic national champions (Almeida 2009). When asked whether BNDES should promote national champions, Luciano Coutinho, president of the bank since 2007, strongly defended such policy: "I am well convinced by the relevance and need of this type of investment. By funding the creation of a giant . . . we would be promoting the emergence of a type of company with the capacity to compete globally and even become a leader in its sector in the international scenario. All the big developing economies have their big multinationals."[9]

Thus, our finding that the effect of BNDES has changed over the years may also be a result of changes in the government itself. Because no precise directional effect can be established *ex ante,* we leave this process of selection as an empirical question to be examined in a *post hoc* fashion.

Therefore, as an additional robustness test complementing our fixed-effect approach, we tried to shed light on the selection process by performing additional regressions using *BNDES* as a dependent variable. The results of our analysis—which, for the sake of simplicity, we do not display here[10]—show that BNDES did not systematically select companies based on past performance or other financial indicators. That is, we do not find any correlation between getting a loan or getting more loans and the lagged performance of the firms. These results hold for the entire period and also for the Cardoso and Lula periods considered separately. The only exception is that we find weak evidence that group membership positively affects the likelihood that the firm will receive direct or indirect BNDES equity; but this is not a major concern because we control for group membership in our regressions in Table 8.1. We thus conclude that there is no clear indication that our results are driven by BNDES's own selection process and that our detected effect of BNDES on firm performance and investment is not due to selection.[11]

Some Cases of Minority Equity Investments by BNDESPAR

We present below some short cases to illustrate the quantitative findings discussed above. These cases are not intended to test our hypotheses, but rather to shed additional light on the dynamics underlying our findings, especially with respect to how BNDES's allocations interact with the ownership profiles of target companies.

NET (Globo Group)

Globo is a powerful Brazilian media group. Founded by journalist Irineu Marinho in 1925 with the newspaper *O Globo* and thereafter controlled by the Marinho family, it was by the late 1990s active in television and radio broadcasting (TV Globo and Radio Globo, respectively) as well as in newspapers and a number of other activities under the holding company Globopar. Indirectly, through Globopar, the Marinho family held stakes in publishing and printing companies; cable, satellite, and Internet service providers; and other businesses.

By 1999, the Marinho family, through Globopar's pyramid, had acquired majority control of Globo Cabo—also known as NET—one of the firms under Globopar. Minority shareholders included Bradesco (a large financial conglomerate in Brazil), RBS (another Brazilian media group), and Microsoft, which had established an alliance with Globo to exploit broadband and Internet services. To support its ambitious plans to expand broadband infrastructure in Brazil, NET had borrowed in foreign markets; the debt was denominated in U.S. dollars. In 1999, BNDESPAR agreed to capitalize NET with the purchase of shares worth 160 million reais (around $89 million). The bank had earlier provided loans to support the group's expansion (Globo had aggressively invested not only in cable services through NET, but also in newspapers and satellite broadcasting through Globosat and Sky, the latter a local joint venture with Rupert Murdoch's group).

The Asian crisis affected Brazil severely, and in 1999 the government was forced to drop the peg it had had since 1995. Following the strong devaluation of the real in 1999, Grupo Globo's debt increased rapidly, putting financial strain on Globopar (the holding company) and a number of its units, including NET. When NET's market expansion proved unsuccessful, and demand (number of subscribers) fell short of expectations, the company posted successive losses. In March 2002, the situation became critical, and Globo announced a capitalization plan of 1 billion reais (around $430 million) involving the issue of debentures and a public offer of shares. BNDES agreed to make an injection of 284 million reais through BNDESPAR, with some of the funds going to buy equity and the rest going to buy debentures issued by Globo for this purpose.[12]

The bank's involvement was heavily criticized; some observers suggested that it was acquiescing to the pressure of a strong domestic group and rescuing a failing corporation. Even Eleazar de Carvalho, appointed president of BNDES in December 2001, expressed concern: "Where does this debt [of the group] come from? It comes from a financial strategy that was affected by currency devaluations . . . and also from inadequate market strategies. The restructuring initiatives of the company in the past were shown to be ineffective. So what would guarantee that this time things would be different?"[13]

BNDES made its capital injection conditional on a change in NET's governance practices, which, according to de Carvalho, were the "basic and primordial" cause of the problem. The company was to adhere to new standards of the São Paulo Stock Exchange that improved minority owners' voice and protection. But the financial stress persisted despite the new capitalization, and the group defaulted in late 2002. This case reflects our earlier observation that BNDES's minority stakes, although instrumental in supporting new investments, can come at the cost of potential shareholder conflicts when the controlling group's decisions fail to create value.

Eletrobras

In some cases BNDES also invests in the equity of state-controlled firms. Established in 1961 to boost investments in the energy sector, state-owned Eletrobras was consolidated during Brazil's military dictatorship into a pyramidal group with subsidiaries in electricity generation (Eletronorte, Chesf, Furnas, and Eletrosul), transmission (EPTE, Furnas, and Eletrosul), distribution (Light and Escelsa), and nuclear power generation (through Furnas and, later, Eletrobras Eletronuclear). Eletrobras also held investments through Lightpar, a holding company, and invested in firms such as Eletropaulo, an energy distribution firm in the state of São Paulo.

Although Eletrobras, with its subsidiaries, was instrumental in developing Brazil's electrical infrastructure, it was not a particularly efficient corporation, recording a loss of 139.7 million reais (about $145 million) in 1995 and incurring debt to the federal government on the order of 9 billion reais in 1996. In 1999, operational problems in Furnas's nuclear power plants sharply reduced generating capacity, requiring the purchase—at a high price—of energy from other firms to meet contractual obligations. Eletrobras also had to rescue Furnas, which owed about 578 million reais for electricity purchases. In fact, in 1997, an executive of Eletrobras expressed concern because of the likely underestimation of costs in Furnas's nuclear operations.[14]

Despite these problems, BNDESPAR had purchased equity in Eletrobras and some of its subsidiaries, increasing its stake in Eletrobras from 8 percent in 1995 to 19 percent in 1996. In 1999, Eletrobras managed to solve the debt problem of another subsidiary, Light, by transferring shares worth 203.8 billion reais to BNDESPAR.[15] This case illustrates our quantitative finding that BNDES's stakes, when they are entangled in business groups (even when the groups are controlled by the government itself), can be used to support inefficient internal allocations of capital and can result in no improvement in firm performance.

Aracruz

Aracruz had been a leading worldwide producer of cellulose pulp for three decades, its competitive edge derived from Brazil's abundant land and low production costs. Because pulp production is typically vertically integrated, Aracruz had investments in farms of eucalyptus (the tree from which pulp is extracted) and forest cultivation technology, as well as in processing plants. Its annual revenues circa 2003 were approximately $1 billion, and its assets were $3.5 billion (about 65.7 percent fixed).[16] With 98 percent of its production exported, Aracruz was considered a highly competitive producer with distinctive technology, especially at the farm level.

BNDES was instrumental in promoting Aracruz's initial development. With 38 percent of voting shares in 1975, BNDES helped fund approximately 55 percent of the industrial investments that enabled the firm to initiate pulp production in 1978.[17] BNDES later sold some of its shares to domestic business groups such as Safra and Lorentzen. However, Aracruz was in practice managed as a stand-alone firm. In 1992, managers at Aracruz executed a public offer of shares to support the firm's planned expansion, pioneering the use of NYSE American Depository Shares (ADS) in Brazil. Foreign listing required that Aracruz improve its transparency and control mechanisms to meet superior governance standards. Board members were given a voice in key decisions related to capacity expansion, acquisitions, and distribution of dividends. BNDESPAR, with approximately 11 percent of Aracruz's total equity, was active in the company's governance, having one representative on its board.[18]

In the 1990s, production efficiency was substantially improved through capital expenditures supported by the new capitalization program. Processing capacity jumped from 400,000 tons of cellulose per year in 1978 to 1.07 million tons in 1994 and 1.24 million tons in 1998. The ambitious expansion plan approved by the board in 2000 triggered some $800 million in new capital expenditures between 2001 and 2003, 75 percent of which was allocated to industrial processing plants and 20 percent to investments in land and forest technology. The case of Aracruz therefore illustrates how the equity of BNDES and other investors was used to boost productive fixed investments in a context in which improved governance practices helped mitigate expropriation of minority shareholders.

Conclusion

In this chapter, we have shown that having the government as a minority owner can have positive effects. Those effects may be weakened, however, when a firm either does not face strong capital constraints or is part of a business group that has its own internal capital market. We find evidence that having the government as a minority shareholder improves performance and increases capital expenditures, especially for firms that are not part of a business group. That is, there is some evidence that governments can use minority equity investments to solve some market failures. This provides some support for the industrial policy view described in Chapter 3. Also, it does not seem that having the government as a minority shareholder worsens performance because of political intervention or agency problems typical of state-controlled companies. On the contrary, we find evidence of improvements in performance that support the idea that having only a minority position allows governments to solve some market failures without worsening the management of corporations, as tends to happen in traditional state-controlled firms with poor governance.

Thus, this chapter advances our understanding of the relatively overlooked phenomenon of minority equity stakes by governments in emerging markets and, on a broader level, contributes to recent discussions about the advantages and disadvantages of state capitalism (Bremmer 2010). Our findings suggest a new programmatic agenda where scholars not only examine how firms react to limiting institutions (e.g., Khanna et al. 2005), but also how local policies can positively interact with private strategies to foster superior performance. That is, our study advances the literature on institutional voids by proposing ways in which local policies can overcome voids rather than create them.

Furthermore, our findings have clear policy implications. Some observers contend that government interference in the economy creates inefficiencies and crowds out private entrepreneurship. Our evidence suggests, however, that the government's purchase of equity stakes in publicly traded corporations may not be problematic, depending on a host of important contingencies. In particular, our results suggest that policy makers considering minority equity stakes as an industrial policy tool should avoid pyramidal groups with poor governance and target instead stand-alone firms; focus investments where there is a clear need to undertake productive capital expenditures by well-run firms; allocate equity capital directly in target firms instead of indirectly through layers of ownership; and progressively exit targeted firms as the local institutional context develops.

Admittedly, some of our results may be idiosyncratic to Brazil and its particular mechanisms of minority governmental participation. And while we have focused on Brazil's use of development banks, governments have also used public pension funds, life insurance companies, sovereign wealth funds, and state-owned holding companies to become minority investors (A. Wooldridge 2012). Thus, future work is needed to verify the generalizability of our results in other developing and emerging economies using other channels of state-owned equity. For instance, Vaidyanathan and Musacchio (2012) find that the government of India, using the Life Insurance Corporation as a holding company, has minority equity positions that account for over 5 percent of total market capitalization. Yet they do not look at the implications for firm-level profitability.

Finally, in this chapter we examined positive aspects of the investments of BNDES in equity. In the following chapter we assess the potential risk of such minority stakes. Namely, we study in detail the case of Vale, the Brazilian mining giant, as a way to examine some of the implications of minority investments by the government in politically sensitive sectors and when multiple minority state shareholders can collude to influence firm-level strategies.

APPENDIX

Table 8-A1. Variables used in the analysis of Leviathan as a minority shareholder

Variable	Description	Mean	Std. dev.
ROA	Net profit over total assets	−0.045	0.308
Gross revenue	Gross revenue of the firm (in billion dollars)	0.859	4.104
Leverage	Total debt over total assets	0.516	5.792
Fixed	Fixed assets over total assets	0.299	0.250
ΔFixed	Fixed$_t$ − Fixed$_{t-1}$	0.000	0.145
CapEx	Capital expenditures over total assets	0.070	0.096
BNDES	Dummy variable equal to 1 if BNDES is a direct or indirect owner	0.126	0.332
BNDESDir	Fraction of the firm's equity that is directly owned by BNDES (0 to 1)	0.011	0.048
Foreign	Dummy variable equal to 1 if the majority shareholder is foreign	0.184	0.388
State-owned	Dummy variable equal to 1 if the majority shareholder is the Brazilian state	0.070	0.256
Belongs to a group	Dummy variable equal to 1 if the firm belongs to a business group	0.450	0.498

9

Leviathan's Temptation

The Case of Vale

In the previous chapter, we argued that having Leviathan as a minority shareholder can alleviate some of the capital constraints firms face, while also apparently keeping the management of the beneficiary companies isolated from political pressures. In this chapter, we present a case in which we argue the temptation was too high for Leviathan to keep at bay. We present in detail one of the most controversial cases of state intervention in the management of a privatized company: Vale, the largest Brazilian mining company and one of the largest mining companies in the world.

We argue that Leviathan as a minority shareholder may be unable to resist the temptation to steer a company toward maximizing either social or political objectives. In Chapters 2 and 4, we described this form of *residual interference* as a feature of privatization programs where, perhaps paradoxically, the state was able to reinforce its presence through dispersed stakes in several privatized companies, using myriad vehicles of state ownership.

Residual interference should likely occur when two conditions are met. First, when there is collusion among *multiple* state-related actors such as national pension funds, pension funds of SOEs, development banks, sovereign wealth funds, jointly with residual control levers by the state (such as golden shares). Second, when state capital is in industries that have "quasi-rents"—that is, the rents obtained by owners excluding their past investments in fixed non-redeployable assets (Klein et al. 1978).

The latter condition is related to what Raymond Vernon called the "obsolescing bargain": once foreign companies in natural resource sectors have made the investment and transferred technology and managerial expertise to locals, there is the risk that the host government can expropriate the deployed assets (Vernon 1971). Vale is not a foreign company, but even domestic mining investors can face expropriation risk once they have paid the basic fixed non-redeployable costs of setting up the operation. Moreover, "once companies make these investments it becomes prohibitively expensive for them to withdraw, since they would have to leave these investments behind" (Ross 2012, 41).[1] In an extreme situation, governments will pursue outright expropriation of private assets. There are plenty of examples of renationalization in Russia under Vladimir Putin, and in Argentina, Repsol was renationalized in 2012. In our view, these are examples of the obsolescing bargain.

However, even if governments do not pursue outright expropriation, they may be tempted to capture part of the quasi-rents obtained by private owners. Many private concessions to exploit natural resources or provide utility services obtain substantial profits due to the rarity of the associated resources (e.g., mines and oil fields) or to favorable contractual terms (e.g., utility concessions allowing private operators to charge relatively high prices). Thus, firms will face the risk that governments will attempt to renegotiate contractual terms *ex post* or use part of the company's cash flow to support government pet projects.[2]

The Brazilian government's intervention in Vale was due to the company's large cash flow and past accumulated investments in a natural resource sector. Because natural wealth can generate large rents, and since, in most countries (except the United States), the subsoil belongs to the nation, privatized companies in natural resource industries are easy targets because politicians and voters identify the endowment that these firms exploit as clearly belonging to the society (Ross 2012).

In the following pages, we explain in detail the evolution of this case. We start by briefly describing the history of Vale, both as an SOE (1942–1997) and as a private company (since 1997). Next, we discuss the post-privatization ownership structure that allowed for Leviathan's residual interference even though the company was, at least on paper, not directly controlled by the government. We then provide details on the context that led the Brazilian government to intervene in Vale and oust its CEO.

Vale do Rio Doce: From Public to Private

Brazil is historically a mining country, and there has been a continuous struggle between the state and the private sector for control over mining resources. The Portuguese colonization of Brazil was based on the extraction of natural resources. First, the Portuguese exported wood, but in the seventeenth century, explorers discovered gold in the Sweet River Valley (Vale do Rio Doce) in the geologically rich Minas Gerais Province. Since then, subsoil rights in Brazil—as in most countries—have belonged to the nation, except for a fifty-year experiment when these rights were privatized between 1890 and 1942 (Triner 2011).

In 1919, an American railway entrepreneur, Percival Farquhar, partnered with the founder of a small foundry in Minas Gerais, the Itabira Iron Ore Company, and got government authorization to extend the railway that started in the iron ore region of Itabira to the port of Vitoria in the state of Espírito Santo.[3] It had taken ten years, however, to get this authorization, by which time the Great Depression had made it impossible to finance the project in the United States or Europe. After a few delays, President Getúlio Vargas suspended the concessions to export iron ore and the concession of the Itabira Iron Ore Company (Khanna et al. 2010). Despite Farquhar's efforts to get funding in the United States to integrate the foundry, a future steel plant, and the railway, Itabira Iron Ore went into receivership during World War II and ended up in the hands of the British government, which then ceded it to Brazil in 1940 when the latter declared war against Germany.

In 1942, through an agreement with the United States government, President Vargas created the Companhia Vale do Rio Doce (CVRD, or Vale), using the facilities of the Itabira Iron Ore Company, its railway network, and loans from the American Eximbank.[4] Simultaneously, Vargas created the Companhia Siderúrgica Nacional (CSN), the largest integrated steel mill in Latin America. Vale's initial public offering was for about $12 million, out of which the government bought all the voting shares, worth 55 percent of the value of the company. Pension funds and other government agencies bought 16.4 percent, and the private sector 28.6 percent, all in nonvoting or preferred shares (Triner 2011, 94).

From the beginning, Vale had a rapid ascent. By the late 1940s, it was already responsible for 80 percent of Brazilian iron ore exports. Between 1950 and 1970, Vale became the most important company in Brazil and a leader in the world iron ore market. According to Trebat (1983, 103), the financial performance and rapid expansion of SOEs such as Vale stemmed to a large extent from their autonomy from the federal government. Vale's top executives had long careers in the company rather than having been appointed by successive governments. They had pay-for-performance compensation schemes, and their salaries were high in comparison with those of executives of other Brazilian state-owned companies.

Vale's autonomy was also a product of its profitability, since it did not depend on subsidies from the Brazilian Treasury or loans from BNDES. Trebat (1983) estimated that Vale financed between 60 percent and 100 percent of its capital investment in the 1970s with its retained earnings. The remainder was financed by issuing long-term debt. In fact, some of Brazil's largest investment projects in the 1960s and 1970s were financed with loans from Japanese and German companies and agencies and with profits from iron ore exports.

Despite being a state-owned enterprise, Vale was always one of Brazil's most profitable firms, and rival exporters forced it to become a cutting-edge mining company early on. Vale's most important investment project was the development of the Carajás iron ore deposits in the state of Amazonas—estimated to be the world's largest iron ore reserves, with at least 18 billion tons of the mineral. By 1986, Vale was exporting all of the production from the Carajás mines.

This profitability also helped Vale to expand into other sectors. Under the leadership of Eliezer Batista and others,[5] the company used its retained earnings to buy companies in other sectors, both to diversify its investment portfolio and to create joint ventures. Throughout the early 1970s, Vale "sought broad diversification in the natural-resource sector and moved aggressively through subsidiaries and minority-owned affiliates into bauxite, alumina and aluminum, manganese, phosphates, fertilizers, pulp, paper . . . and titanium" (Trebat 1983, 52). Furthermore, by the 1970s, Vale's distribution network included railways, shipping lines, and a port. Thus, at the height of what Trebat called Vale's "empire building" period, the company owned twelve major subsidiaries and was an active partner in twelve joint ventures, primarily fueled with foreign capital.

Vale's expansion came to a grinding halt in the 1980s when the government's stabilization policies forced the company to reduce expenditures—especially capital expenditures. As we have explained in previous chapters, the government effectively imposed restrictions on imports, investment, remuneration, and—in general—on the size and autonomy of public enterprises (Werneck 1987). Even so, and notwithstanding the recession at home and abroad in the 1980s, Vale remained the most profitable SOE in Brazil and paid the highest dividends to the government.

Vale's (Partial) Privatization

By the late 1980s, the Brazilian government was facing a severe fiscal crisis, and holding equity in SOEs started to make less sense as a means to finance the government. The interest rates of Brazilian government bonds skyrocketed when inflation accelerated in 1990, and the dividends that Vale paid the government did not compensate for the opportunity cost of holding that stock. For instance, between 1988 and 1992, the government had to pay interest on its debt on the order of 20 percent per year, while the return on the equity it held in Vale was between 0.5 percent and 5.2 percent (Pinheiro and Giambiagi 1994, 95).

In 1995, the government accelerated the privatization process and put Vale on the list of SOEs to be sold. The privatization process was part of a larger strategy of structural reform of the Brazilian economy. The government wanted not only to use the cash from privatizations to amortize debt and reduce its debt burden (in fact, it accepted government bonds as payment in the privatization), but also wanted to make the economy more efficient and competitive. Privatization was a way to improve the management of Brazilian companies and to eliminate price controls and the subsidies (and bailouts) of inefficient companies.

Even though President Fernando Henrique Cardoso had polls showing that Brazilians approved of less government intervention in the economy, the announcement of the privatization of Vale immediately spurred public protests and political reactions. Vale and Petrobras were considered national symbols. At the time of privatization, Vale had already become the world's largest producer of iron ore and pellets, with a workforce of over fifty thousand employees. One senator expressed concern: "More than a mining company, Vale is a social development agency and does not operate in a monopolist sector."[6]

Another senator warned that "Vale's [mineral reserve] underground has not been sufficiently explored. If the company is sold, we will not know what we are negotiating." Luiz Inácio Lula da Silva, then a presidential candidate of the Workers' Party, also threatened that if he won the 1998 election, "We will audit the [privatized] companies to see if there was any wrongdoing, then we will decide what to do."[7] Cardoso was also criticized in open letters from the Brazilian bar (the Ordem dos Advogados do Brasil), the attorney general of Brazil, the largest national workers federation (the Central Única dos Trabalhadores), and the largest confederation of Catholic priests (Conferência Nacional dos Bispos do Brasil) (Cardoso and Setti 2006, 298).

However, President Cardoso dismissed such concerns and privatized Vale. He stated: "Strategically, what does Vale do? It gets rocks from, let's say, Carajás, puts them in the train, takes them to the port, and sends them abroad. . . . That's what iron ore production is all about. There's no important technology involved."[8] On May 6, 1997, the government sold control of Vale to Valepar, a holding entity representing a consortium or "control bloc" of key owners led by private entrepreneur Benjamin Steinbruch, who had already acquired control of other privatized companies such as steel producer CSN and electric power distributor Light. Steinbruch's stake in Valepar was indirect, through CSN. Valepar won the auction by offering 3.15 billion reais ($3.15 billion) for 41.73 percent of Vale's voting shares.

Alongside Steinbruch, there were other private owners such as domestic banks Opportunity and Bradesco, foreign owners such as Nations Bank, and a group of pension funds of SOEs, including Previ (from Banco do Brasil, Brazil's largest bank), Funcef (from Caixa Econômica Federal, another bank), and Petros (from Petrobras). With the privatization deal, the government also got golden shares giving it veto rights over certain decisions such as changing the company's name, the location of its headquarters, the voting rights of the company's shares, the control of the mines, and the company's mission and objectives.

In 2000, the company listed its shares in New York as American Depository Receipts (ADRs), and one year later, Steinbruch's CSN pulled out of Vale after an intricate negotiation that left Bradesco and the group of pension funds with a controlling stake in the company. In 2002, the very last step in Vale's complex, multiyear privatization finally took place when Brazil's National Treasury and BNDES (through BNDESPAR) sold their 31.5 percent stake. However, BNDESPAR kept some remaining stakes and even increased its participation in 2003 when Carlos Less, then president of BNDES, orchestrated a controversial 1.3 billion reais repurchase of Vale's shares to increase the "national" presence in the company.

Thus, even after privatization, Vale's financial relationship with the government was kept close and operated in at least two ways. First, the government received dividends from Vale through BNDESPAR's shares. Second, since 1979, the Brazilian government collected royalties on mineral extraction on the order of 1 percent to 3 percent of gross revenues (with rates varying depending on which mineral generated the revenues). In 2009, the company estimated that between 2001 and 2008, its average total contribution to Brazil (through taxes, dividends to the government, and payroll) had been on the order of $2.7 billion per year, while its total contribution between 1943 and 2000, when the government was the majority owner, had been only $283 million. Of the approximately $2.7 billion Vale contributed per year, $1.3 billion involved taxes.[9]

Vale's Strategy under Private Ownership

In 2001, Vale's board of directors approved the nomination of Roger Agnelli to lead the company as CEO. Agnelli, an economist with twenty years of experience with Bradesco, was the CEO of Bradespar, the bank's asset management company, which was one of Vale's controlling owners.

Between Agnelli's arrival and 2009, Vale went through a radical transformation. It went from being an iron ore mining company mostly serving the domestic market to being the second-largest metals and mining company in the world, based on market capitalization. Vale also became the world's largest producer of iron ore and iron ore pellets, the world's second-largest producer of nickel, and one of the world's largest producers of manganese ore, ferroalloys, and kaolin, and it had invested in developing and increasing its production capacity for bauxite, alumina, aluminum, copper, and coal. In addition, Vale was the only potassium producer in Brazil, with operations in Canada and Argentina. Potassium became an important input for Vale's fertilizer business.

Agnelli had a very clear plan of expansion for Vale that included aggressive geographic and product diversification through mergers and acquisitions as well as through greenfield and brownfield investments. His first step was to buy the Canadian nickel miner INCO in 2006 for $17.4 billion. In

2007, he made an offer to acquire Austrialia's AMCI Holdings, a coal miner. Simultaneously, he led Vale to diversify its sales to Europe and China, away from its traditional customers in Japan and the United States. His vision was consistent with the trends in the global economy that pointed to emerging markets as the main source of new global aggregate demand. Roberto Castello Branco, Vale's director of investor relations and chief economist, described the company's strategy as follows:

> We have a long-term view of this process. We believe that income levels in emerging markets are converging to those of developed countries. Moreover, countries like China and India are investing more on industrialization, urbanization, and housing than developed countries. For instance, the Chinese consumption of copper to GDP is close to the ratio the United States had at the turn of the century, when it was industrializing rapidly. (Quoted in Khanna et al. 2010, 5).

While many Brazilian companies found their country's lack of infrastructure a huge obstacle to growth, Vale developed its own infrastructure to overcome this obstacle. To support its mining operations, Vale became the leading provider of logistics services in Brazil and a leading world player in logistics for mining products. In Brazil, its integrated logistics infrastructure encompassed approximately ten thousand kilometers of railroad and five port terminals in four Brazilian states. In fact, Vale was responsible for 16 percent of all freight and 30 percent of port cargo handled in Brazil. "Up until 2001 we supposed logistics could become a core business responsible for almost 30 percent of our total revenues," said Eduardo Bartolomeo, an engineer who had been Vale's director of logistics, project management, and sustainability since 2006. "Nowadays, it represents merely four percent of our results but it is absolutely essential for us. It is our conveyor belt."

Given that the demand for Vale's products was thousands of miles away from Brazil, Agnelli focused on building a reliable logistics network to deliver iron ore from Brazil to China. It was important for Agnelli to focus the strategy of the company on gaining ground in the Chinese market for several reasons. First, although Brazilian iron ore was higher grade (i.e., had a higher iron content) than Australian ore, the latter was slightly cheaper in China because of lower transportation costs. Any reduction in shipping costs could therefore give Vale a big advantage in expanding its market share in China.

Second, the emergence of China as the most important consumer of iron ore in the world changed not only the logistics of the business, but also the pricing system. In 2008 alone, China consumed 52 percent of the world's iron ore production, 35 percent of the world's steel production, and 26 percent of the world's nickel production. While most metals are commodities sold in world markets at prices determined—by a variety of buyers—in stock exchanges (the so-called spot markets) or in futures markets, iron ore had traditionally been different. Since the 1970s, one of the Big Three—Brazil's Vale, Australia-based Rio Tinto, and BHP Billiton—would privately negotiate a price with a large steelmaker. Nippon Steel of Japan led pricing negotiations until 2005, when China became the world's largest ore importer. Then, the Chinese firm Baosteel and, eventually, the China Iron & Steel Association (Cisa) became the main negotiators of this benchmark price. However, gradually, smaller Chinese consumers of iron ore started to switch to spot markets rather than relying on the old benchmark system. By 2009, most of the iron ore purchased by China for that contract year was acquired via spot markets.

Vale needed not only to get closer to China, but it also had to adapt to the changing conditions in the iron ore market. For instance, small Chinese foundries and steel mills wanted the seller to take care of shipping and insurance, traditionally the buyer's responsibility. Vale needed to be able to serve those small Chinese consumers by including shipping and insurance in its price, while still beating the Australian iron ore prices. Investing billions of dollars in large ships was one solution. In fact, the estimated savings in transportation more than compensated for the investment and made Brazilian iron ore cheaper than that of its competitors.

However, because Agnelli's strategy for Vale essentially involved an emphasis on commodity exports to high-growth Asian markets supported by an integrated transport infrastructure, he increasingly became a target for critics from the Brazilian government claiming that Vale should instead promote new investment in the domestic market, especially in steel mills. The quasi-rents generated by a booming global market for natural resources were tempting from the point of view of the Brazilian government, which could use part of Vale's cash flow to support government-backed projects in the home country. And, as we describe below, a key vehicle of such interference was the intricate structure of minority stakes by government actors that remained after Vale's privatization.

Leviathan as a Minority Shareholder in Vale

Figure 9.1 depicts Vale's pyramidal ownership structure as of October 2009. Percentages refer to voting shares. Valepar, the holding firm that won Vale's privatization auction, owned more than 50 percent of Vale's shares and hence was the controlling entity. In the ownership structure of Valepar, no single owner held more than 50 percent of the shares. Litel, owned by the major pension funds of several state-owned companies, had the largest stake—49 percent. Private owners Bradespar (the investment arm of Bradesco bank), Japan's Mitsui, and Eletron (owned by Opportunity bank) together held 39.4 percent. BNDESPAR had a 11.5 percent stake in Valepar, besides its 6.9 percent direct minority stake in Vale. Although there was no clear majority owner, BNDESPAR and the pension funds (through Litel)

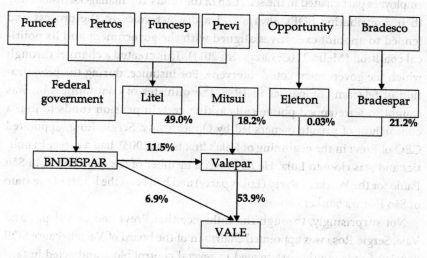

Figure 9.1. Vale's shareholding structure as of October 2009 (percentages refer to voting shares)

Sources: Vale's web site, http://www.vale.com/vale_us/media/ca1009i.pdf (accessed December 2, 2009); and Lazzarini (2011).

held, in the aggregate, 60.5 percent of Valepar. Hence, these state-related actors could collude and achieve a distinct voice in the governance of Vale.

We have discussed the behavior of BNDES in previous chapters. It will also be informative here to briefly describe the role of pension funds. In Brazil, there was a public pension system managed by the Ministry of Social Security, complemented by "closed" funds whereby pension benefits are restricted to the employees of particular companies, either private or state-owned. Previ, Petros, Funcef, and Funcesp—all shareholders of Vale—are examples of SOE pension funds. These closed funds receive contributions from the employees themselves as well as matching contributions from their companies. By 1997, pension funds in Brazil already had around $81 billion in total assets, of which 79 percent was owned by SOE pension funds. It was not uncommon for those funds to invest in the equity of other companies and even in their own companies. Thus, by 1997, SOE pension funds used to invest around 40 percent of their total assets in risky assets including equity. Between 1997 and 2008, the total value of funds' investment in risky assets jumped from 27.3 billion to 127.5 billion reais (around $71 billion).[10]

SOE pension funds were clearly influenced by the government. Although employees participated in the selection of the funds' top managers, historically their contributing SOEs always had a distinct voice in the process and tended to appoint executives aligned with the government and its political coalition (Mello 2003; Lazzarini 2011). This created a channel through which the government could intervene. For instance, during the privatization of telecom companies in 1998, the minister of communication was caught in wiretapped phone calls asking certain pension funds to join a consortium of private owners led by Opportunity. Sergio Rosa, appointed CEO of Previ in the beginning of Lula's first term (2003), had a career in politics and was close to Lula. He had been a member of the city council in São Paulo for the Workers' Party (Lula's party) and had been the leader of the state of São Paulo's bankers union.

Not surprisingly, through the influence that Previ had in Valepar and Vale, Sergio Rosa was appointed chairman of the board of Vale. Because SOE pension funds jointly participated in several control blocs and acted in tandem with BNDESPAR—not to mention the golden shares held by the government itself—Vale was subject to Leviathan's residual interference. Through these varied ownership mechanisms and a coordinated activism on the board, Leviathan as a minority shareholder became functionally a majority shareholder.

The Government versus Vale

In the fall of 2009, President Lula and some of his ministers launched a public attack on Vale's strategy, articulated both through the media and through Vale's board (Lazzarini 2011; Khanna et al. 2010). The offensive advanced on three fronts. First, for Lula, Vale "should not just open holes in the ground and export the mineral." In fact, Lula openly asked the company to invest in steel mills at home, even though analysts warned that the worldwide steel industry had idle capacity and that mining was much more profitable, on average, than steel production. Between 1996 and 2009, the average value added per worker in steel production (revenues minus cost of inputs divided by the total number of employees in the industry) was 395,000 reais versus 507,000 reais in iron mining.[11] Defenders of an active industrial policy, however, claimed that Brazil was suffering from an alleged "Dutch disease" whereby commodity exports strengthened the Brazilian currency and hence made industrialized products less competitive internationally (e.g., Bresser Pereira 2008).

Second, Lula was also concerned with Agnelli's announcement of layoffs as a response to the 2008 financial crisis. In December 2008, the company fired around 1,500 employees worldwide. Even though Agnelli justified this decision with the need to cut costs and stay competitive given the weakened demand, Lula publicly criticized the announced layoffs: "Vale has a lot of cash, earned a lot of money. Well, it is exactly in those moments of difficulty that executives also need to do their part. It is not only the government or the workers, it is everybody."[12]

Third, the government pressured Vale to buy ships made in Brazil, despite the fact that ships made in Brazil were twice as expensive as those made in Asia and the fact that there were no shipbuilders in Brazil capable of making the large-capacity iron ore carriers Vale wanted (the so-called Chinamax or Valemax ships capable of transporting four hundred thousand tons of ore per trip).

Agnelli had a two-pronged strategy to beat Australian companies in China. First, he wanted to create distribution centers—"virtual mines"—close to

Asia. Two were projected, one in Oman and the other in Malaysia. Second, Vale put forward an aggressive plan to boost its shipping capabilities, including the acquisition of at least twelve Valemax ships. In 2007, the company announced that it would buy those vessels from Chinese and Korean shipyards. This decision infuriated the government, which was trying to revamp the domestic naval industry. After years of having business-friendly policies, Lula was apparently tilting toward more heterodox measures such as preferential treatment for Brazilian suppliers and governmental intervention in sectors deemed as "strategic."

Complicating matters, there was a takeover attempt orchestrated by Eike Batista, a Brazilian entrepreneur named by *Forbes* as Brazil's wealthiest man in 2009. He was the son of Eliezer Batista, one of Vale's legendary presidents when the firm was an SOE. Eike Batista had made an offer to buy the shares of Vale that Bradesco owned in Valepar (see Figure 8.1). Batista also contributed to the public offensive by declaring that "Vale cannot export raw materials forever" and suggested that having him as the controlling shareholder would "help Brazil."[13] After Bradesco refused his offer, Batista suggested that Roger Agnelli could be replaced by Sergio Rosa, the head of Previ. Rosa backed Lula and Batista by declaring that Vale should invest in steel mills.

To placate these demands, Agnelli announced, in October 2009, an investment plan of 20 billion reais, including two steel mills in the north and northeast of Brazil. Batista's takeover attempt failed, but investors became increasingly worried by the escalating political interference in Vale. Famous billionaire George Soros, as well as other investors, sold part of their shares. This negative market reaction notwithstanding, the pressure on Vale and Agnelli escalated. Agnelli publicly declared in 2010 that Lula's Workers' Party had an interest in controlling Vale. Agnelli's position as a CEO became increasingly precarious, and he was eventually ousted in May 2011, despite announced profits 292 percent higher than in the first trimester of 2010. At the time of his departure, Agnelli declared: "The mission of the [private] company is to generate results to foster capacity and investments. The mission of the government is different. Completely different."[14]

He was replaced by Murilo Ferreira, a former Vale executive handpicked by the government. Ferreira had thirty years of experience at Vale and, in 2007, had been appointed president of Vale Inco in Canada. He had left the company in 2008 because of health problems, although there were rumors that he and Agnelli had also disagreed on some strategic matters. With his nomination backed by the newly elected president of Brazil, Dilma Rousseff (also from the Workers' Party), the expectation was that Ferreira would be more strategically aligned with the government.

Discussion

In previous chapters, we argued that an advantage of the model in which Leviathan is a minority shareholder is that it reduces the risk of outright political interference by the government in the management of private corporations, while at the same time preserving a channel through which state capital can alleviate market failure. However, reduced political interference is not guaranteed. Under certain conditions, the "minority" Leviathan may be not only tempted to intervene, but also equipped to do it. This is what we refer to as *residual interference*.

One condition is when private firms with minority state capital have substantial quasi-rents from the exploitation of country-level resources. This will be aggravated when the firm has already invested in fixed non-redeployable assets, so that is faces exit costs that put it in a disadvantageous bargaining position vis-à-vis the government (e.g., the "obsolescing bargain"). Such a condition is likely when private firms are operating in natural resource or utility sectors and have managed to obtain favorable concession contracts. In addition, interference will be more likely when Leviathan, despite being a minority investor, can collude with other shareholders and effectively attain a majority position. In the case of Vale, these other shareholders included BNDES and a group of SOE pension funds influenced by the government.

It will be instructive to describe a case in which residual interference did *not* occur because some of these factors were absent (at least until the completion of this book). Embraer, Brazil's "national champion" in the aircraft industry, was owned by BNDES, and by Previ, Bozano (a domestic group), and Europe's European Aeronautic Defense and Space Company (EADS). So here, too, Leviathan was a minority shareholder. After the 2008 financial crisis, Embraer also announced heavy layoffs, and the company purchased most of its aircraft parts from foreign suppliers instead of domestic firms. However, the government was not as eager to intervene in Embraer as it had been in Vale. Embraer's profitability depended on its ability to design new products and procure state-of-the-art parts (e.g., engines). Thus, forcing Embraer to develop domestic suppliers could substantially hurt its competitiveness in the short term. Furthermore, although BNDES and Previ were minority shareholders, they collectively held only 18.8 percent of the company's voting shares in 2009. Even if they colluded, they would not have a majority voice in relevant decisions.

Therefore, we do not think that the Leviathan as a minority shareholder model will always lead to intervention or even to the temptation to intervene. However, residual interference is a concrete possibility in capital-intensive sectors in which firms have a substantial cash flow to be exploited by colluding minority state actors attempting to implement government-backed initiatives.

10

Leviathan as a Lender

Development Banks and State Capitalism

Having analyzed Leviathan as an owner and manager of corporations and as a minority investor, we will now outline the theory of the government's role as a lender to corporations. We organize the tests of our hypotheses related to Leviathan as a lender into two chapters. In this chapter, we first outline a general theory of what development banks are supposed to do. We then describe the evolution BNDES's business model and discuss the intentions of some of its programs and their outcomes. In particular, we focus on the bank's revenue and funding models. In Chapter 11, we use systematic evidence of BNDES loans to publicly traded corporations and test empirically whether the bank is actually doing what development banks are supposed to do.

The implicit argument that comes out of the sixty-year-long history of BNDES is that in the early stages of development this bank made a big difference to promote industrialization and the development of key industries. Yet as Brazil got richer, the bank did not scale down and thus it lost its shininess. As we show, the bank is not like state-owned commercial banks, which traditionally depend more on the whim of politicians and tend to lose money all the time (Caprio et al. 2004). BNDES historically was run as a relatively efficient government bank, seeking to remain profitable even during hard times. Yet with its large size, and operating in a more developed economy, BNDES now has a hard time making the right selection of projects, and it is not clear if its current portfolio of loans and investments covers the opportunity cost of the funds it gets from taxpayers.

Development Banks around the World

According to Armendáriz de Aghion (1999, 83), "development banks are government-sponsored financial institutions concerned primarily with the provision of long-term capital to industry." This definition highlights two key aspects of development banks: their state-owned status and their emphasis on solving failures in credit markets, especially in the case of projects with long-term maturity.

Historical accounts show that development banks have existed at least since the nineteenth century, which saw the creation of Sociéte Général pour Favoriser l'Industrie National in Belgium (1822) and, later on, a group of institutions in France, including Crédit Foncier, Comptoir d'Escompte, and Crédit Mobilier, the latter playing an important role in European infrastructure investments such as railways in the nineteenth century (Armendáriz de Aghion 1999; Cameron 1961). The escalation of state-led intervention and the decline in private markets that followed the two world wars—a trend that Rajan and Zingales (2004) termed "the great reversal"—furthered the expansion of development banks and reinforced their importance. During the post–World War II reconstruction, the Marshall Plan required countries to channel international funds for reconstruction through domestic development banks, bringing about the creation of Germany's KfW (Kredintaltanlt für Weidarufban), the Japan Development Bank (JDB), and even Brazil's BNDES.

At the same time, new development theories started emphasizing structural problems inhibiting the industrialization of underdeveloped countries dependent on the production and export of basic commodities (Furtado 1959; Prebisch 1950; Hirschman 1958). In the view of these theories, state-induced savings and credit would be crucial to spur value-added, productive investments (Bruck 1998). Along these lines, Amsden (1989) also stresses the importance of development banks in late-industrializing economies. Financial institutions such as the Korea Development Bank, Amsden argues, were instrumental not only as a means to infuse long-term capital into industry, but also as a mechanism to screen private projects and establish well-defined performance targets.

Just as SOEs have survived the waves of privatization and structural change in OECD and developing countries, so did development banks. That is why they still play an important role in the current configuration of state capitalism around the world. In Table 10.1, we show that there are hundreds of development banks in the world as of 2011 and that almost half of these banks say they are focused on providing loans to diverse infrastructure

Table 10.1. Number of development banks around the world (2011)

	Development agencies (A)	General development banks (B)	Special-purpose development banks (C)	Commercial banks with development objectives (D)	Total, by region (E)
Africa	3	26	21	20	70
North America		1			1
South and East Asia	13	23	22	27	85
Central Asia		8	2	9	19
Europe		7	3	2	12
Latin America / Caribbean	4	29	17	1	51
Middle East		1	3	3	7
Oceania	1	5	5	4	15
Regional/global		20	5	3	28
Total, by type	21	119	79	69	288

Source: We counted and classified all banks associated with the World Federation of Development Financial Institutions and with European Development Finance Institutions, using the information on profiles and missions from their web sites: http://www.wfdfi.org.ph/members/list-of-members/ and http://www.edfi.be/members.html (accessed February 12, 2012).

Note on the classification scheme:

A. *Development agencies* includes investment authorities, training centers, and organizations that provide technical assistance to specific sectors, but that do not specialize in making loans.

B. *General development banks* are those focused on providing loans for or investing in the equity of industrial and/or infrastructure projects. It also includes banks that provide guarantees so that industrial or infrastructure projects can get private funding. General development banks can be regional, such as the Inter-American Development Bank, or domestic, such as the Korea Development Bank.

C. *Special-purpose development banks* are those financial institutions specialized in providing credit to agriculture, small and medium-size enterprises, and the construction industry. That is, we include banks that want to promote construction and housing developments for families that could not get mortgage loans from regular banks. This category can include agricultural banks, such as the Principal Bank for Development and Agricultural Credit (Egypt) and the Land Bank of the Philippines, and banks with more specific objectives, such as the National Housing Bank of India.

D. There are many banks that we classify as *commercial banks with development objectives* because these banks, public or private, operate as regular banks, but tend to have part of their portfolio focused on specific sectors that the government is targeting. Examples of this are Azerigazbank in Azerbaijan, the Banco de Desarrollo Productivo in Bolivia, and the Bhutan National Bank Ltd. in Bhutan.

and industrial projects. We identify 288 development banks throughout the world as of 2011, chiefly concentrated in South and East Asia (29.5 percent), Africa (24.3 percent), and Latin America and the Caribbean (17.7 percent).

Development banks gained new momentum after the 2008 global financial crisis. In 2009, the Argentine government announced its intention to create a national development bank. Even in the United States, there have been calls to revamp development banks. The 2011 U.S. federal budget included a $4 billion package to build a development bank supporting large infrastructure projects, although the project was not subsequently implemented.[1]

Yet there is little academic work examining if these banks accomplish what they say they do. A sizable literature uses qualitative case studies to highlight the importance of development banks in promoting industrial "catch-up" (e.g., Cameron 1961; Amsden 2001; Rodrik 2004; Aronovich and Fernandes 2006). For instance, in his study of state intervention in the banking system, Gerschenkron (1962) argues that without public participation, lack of trust among creditors and debtors would keep credit markets from deepening. In this perspective, private banks are reluctant to extend credit to long-term, risky investments, leaving value-enhancing projects unfunded (Bruck 1998).

Armendáriz de Aghion's (1999) model is perhaps the only formal theoretical effort to provide a framework with which to understand what development banks are supposed to do. She proposes that private banks typically underinvest in the expertise required to evaluate and promote new industries in the long run. Subsidized finance in the form of a development bank can therefore prompt new investment by filling that void of expertise.

What Are Development Banks Supposed to Do?

According to the *industrial policy* view, development banks specialize in the provision of long-term funding for projects that would go unfunded if they had to be financed by arm's-length financial markets (see Chapter 3). That is, development banks provide long-term subsidized funding for projects for which private funding would not be available, either because entrepreneurs face capital constraints or because they do not have full information about a project's profitability (Yeyati et al. 2004; Rodrik 2004; Armendáriz de Aghion 1999; Amsden 2001).

Under the industrial policy view, therefore, there are at least three inter-related spheres of action for development banks. First, they can alleviate capital scarcity and promote entrepreneurial action to boost new or existing industries, especially industries that need to finance capital-intensive projects (Cameron 1961; Gerschenkron 1962; Armendáriz de Aghion 1999). Second, development banks may finance projects that have long maturities or that have low financial returns but high social returns (Bruck 1998; Yeyati et al. 2004; George and Prabhu 2000). Finally, development banks have to engage in promotional activities in the event that "potential investment opportunities are not recognized and/or not acted upon by the private sector" (Kane 1975, 41). In other words, development banks have to either coordinate entrepreneurs to act or provide information about "discovery costs" (Rodrik 2007).

In contrast to this benign or positive view of development banks, the *political* view would stress two negative aspects. First, rent-seeking capitalists may request subsidized credit or cheap equity even for projects that could be funded and launched using private sources of capital. According to this view, politicians create and maintain state-owned banks or development banks less to channel funds to socially efficient uses than to maximize their personal objectives or to engage in crony deals with politically connected industrialists (La Porta et al. 2002; Ades and Di Tella 1997; Faccio 2006; Hainz and Hakenes 2008). The second objection, in the political view, is that development banks may bail out companies that would otherwise fail (this is the soft-budget constraint hypothesis, e.g., Kornai [1979]).

The debate concerning the mission and effects of development bank activity is nuanced even more when we take into account the government's desire to create "national champions." That is, politicians and officials explicitly target specific firms to receive funds—either debt or equity—as a way to propel them to consolidate their sectors and grow. Some argue, however, that the criteria governments use to select those firms are not clear and have sometimes been linked to political objectives (Ades and Di Tella 1997). A recent literature has found empirical evidence consistent with the hypothesis that financing can be influenced by political factors such as election cycles and campaign donations (e.g., Claessens et al. 2008; Dinç 2005; Sapienza 2004).

Under this less benign view, we would not expect development banks to be necessarily profitable because they could finance projects that do not have a positive net present value. They could also be making loans to lower the financial expenditures of firms, but without changing too much the financial performance of the firm in the long run. Moreover, under the political view, we would not expect to see the beneficiary firms using BNDES funds to increase capital expenditures.

Evaluating the actions of development banks, we think, requires two steps: in this chapter, we examine BNDES's general business model, using historical data from 1952 to 2009; and in Chapter 11, we conduct a more detailed econometric test of hypotheses derived from the industrial policy and the political views discussed before.

Why Look at BNDES?

Brazil is a good place to examine the role of development banks and the effects their loans have on companies because BNDES is one of the oldest and largest development banks in the world (Torres Filho 2009). Table 10.2 compares BNDES, the Inter-American Development Bank (IDB), the World Bank, the Korea Development Bank (KDB), and Germany's Kredintaltanlt für Weidarufban (KfW). In 2010, the value of loans disbursed by BNDES was more than three times the total amount provided by the World Bank. BNDES was also one of the most profitable banks in terms of return on assets, and one of the more profitable in terms of return on equity, except KfW. Finally, BNDES is one of the most efficient, with the highest profits per employee (of $2 million). In fact, profits per employee are almost ten times higher than those of the World Bank and almost two times higher than those of KfW.

In sum, BNDES is a large and apparently profitable development bank (compared to its peers), and if its lending policies are representative, then studying its behavior empirically may help us understand what other development banks do or should do. Given the prevalence of development banks across countries (see Table 10.1), understanding the effects of BNDES loans

Table 10.2. BNDES vs. other development banks, 2010

	Brazil's BNDES	Inter-American Dev. Bank (IDB)	World Bank	Korea Dev. Bank	Germany's KfW	China Dev. Bank
Financials and employment (US$ bn unless indicated)						
Total assets	330	87	428	123	596	752
Equity	40	21	166	17	21	59
Profit	6.0	0.3	1.7	1.3	3.5	5.5
New loans	101	10	26	n.a.	113	84
Outstanding loans	218	63	234	64	571	663
Staff	2,982	~2,000	~10,000	2,266	4,531	4,000
Performance ratios						
Return on equity (%)	15.0	1.6	1.0	7.8	16.7	9
Return on assets (%)	1.8	0.4	0.4	1.1	0.6	1
Profit/employee (US$ M)	2.0	0.2	0.2	0.6	0.8	1
Equity/assets (%)	12.0	24.0	38.7	14.0	3.5	8
Assets /employee (US$ M)	110.8	43.6	42.8	54.4	131.5	188

Source: Annual reports and Torres Filho (2009). For the World Bank, the financial year is from June 2009 to June 2010.

Note: Of all BNDES's new loans in 2010, $22 billion went to Petrobras.

may provide us with lessons for policy makers and development bank executives around the world.

BNDES's Business Model

The Brazilian National Bank of Economic Development (BNDE) was created in 1952 to provide long-term credit for energy and transportation investments, then expanded its scope by providing loans to a host of "basic industries" that the government wanted to develop, such as metals, oil, chemicals, and cement. In 1982, BNDE changed its name to BNDES when "social development" was added to its mission (Leff 1968b; Campos 1969).

There are three basic explanations for the creation of BNDE. The first explanation has to do with the role of the Joint Brazil–United States Development Commission, created in December 1949 and made up of engineers and technocrats from Brazil, the United States, and the World Bank. The Joint Commission decided to expand Brazil's infrastructure projects. To eliminate bottlenecks in transportation infrastructure and electricity, the commission recommended the creation of a mechanism to provide long-term credit for energy and transportation investments. The result was BNDE (Campos 1969).

Second, according to Simonsen (1969) and Musacchio (2009), the government of Brazil created BNDE to provide long-term credit after the retraction of bond and equity markets that began in the 1920s and 1930s and the rise of inflation after the Great Depression.[2] These authors argue that credit markets should have created inflation-indexed instruments to provide long-term credit, but various Brazilian laws prohibited indexation until the 1960s. Thus, a shortage of long-term financing followed the decline in bond markets of the 1930s, especially because banks focused on providing short-term loans. Short-term credit almost doubled between the 1920s, when inflation started, and 1950, when the stock of short-term loans reached almost 30 percent of GDP. Long-term loans, however, stayed below 2 percent throughout the 1950s and 1960s.

A third explanation for the creation of BNDES argues that the Brazilian government—particularly during Getúlio Vargas's second term (1950–1955)—created BNDE as an autonomous entity with a technical staff as a way to protect the bureaucracy and the national project from political clientelism. President Vargas did this while simultaneously building a political system based on strong corporatism, with newly created unions and business associations playing an important role (Schneider 1991; Nunes 1997).[3]

BNDE: From Public to Private Loans

During its first ten years of operation, BNDE focused on providing long-term funding for the renewal *(reaparelhamento)* of the railway system and the construction of new hydroelectric power plants. Most of the large projects BNDE financed were carried out by SOEs. For instance, Furnas, Cemig, and others SOEs built most of Brazil's largest hydroelectric plants and transmission lines with funding from BNDE and the World Bank (Tendler 1968).

In the late 1950s, the bank's focus began to switch to supporting the development of the still infant steel industry. As we explained in Chapter 4, in the 1960s BNDE served as a holding company for steel companies. In fact, in the 1960s BNDE financed about 70 to 80 percent of all capital investments in the steel industry (BNDES 2002a). During the 1950s and 1960s, most of the loans were long term, and the interest rate was, on average, 9.5 percent per year. For infrastructure loans, the rates were about 8 percent, and for industrial loans, the rates reached 11 percent. These rates were below inflation (Curralero 1998, 20).

Under the military government (1964–1985), BNDES changed its focus from lending to public projects to financing private companies. Figure 10.1 shows the change in focus of BNDE loan programs away from SOEs. Before 1964, almost 100 percent of the loans went to finance public projects, either directly by a government agency or indirectly by an SOE. But by 1970, the private sector received almost 70 percent of the loans, and by the late 1970s, public projects received less than 20 percent of the loans. Yet many of the private companies receiving loans in the 1970s (and later in the 1980s) were either following development plans laid out by the government or were "national champions," firms receiving special privileges and help from the government to either develop new industries, new technologies, or to gain market share abroad. BNDES, in fact, was not only lending to some of those private firms; it was also holding minority equity participation in some of them (Najberg 1989).

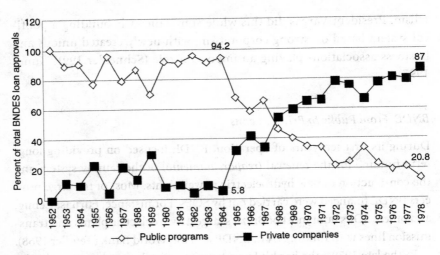

Figure 10.1. Distribution of BNDE loans among public and private projects, 1952–1978

Source: Created by the authors with data from Najberg (1989, 18).

In 1965, as part of the push to support the domestic machinery and equipment industry, the government created Finame, the first subsidiary of BNDES. Finame had the sole objective of providing medium- and long-term funding for the purchase of equipment in Brazil (BNDES 1987). The capital goods industry had been one of the fastest-growing industries before 1959, growing at approximately 27 percent per year according to Leff (1968a, 2), and the development of a domestic machinery industry was seen as a sine qua non for industrial development that was not dependent on foreign imports.

Over time, BNDE's revenue model changed from a heavy reliance on income from loans to income generated by majority and minority equity investments. Roughly between 1953 and 1974, BNDE obtained the largest portion of its profits from its loan business. We can see in Figure 10.2 that loan revenues started to pay off only after three years of operations and then grew rapidly (in real terms). Interestingly, the 1950s and 1960s is the period in which the bank was pursuing the kinds of activity the industrial policy supporters would want a development bank to do. In a market with severe credit rationing and with high discovery costs, BNDE was providing long-term financing and sometimes acting as an entrepreneur itself to finance the

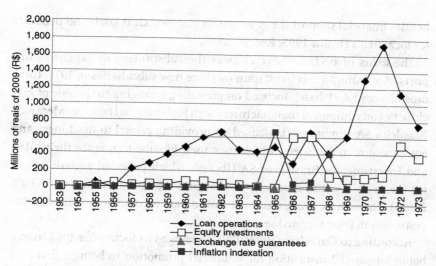

Figure 10.2. Profit/loss by business line, BNDE, 1953–1974
Source: Calculated by the authors from BNDES (1953–2010).

development of new industries such as steel, electricity, and chemicals. Returns in the equity business also started to pay off in the mid-1960s, when the industrialization push of BNDES was at its highest point, but the equity business did not provide a major share of revenues.

Between 1974 and 1982, BNDE's priorities were determined by the military government's second National Development Plan of 1974. According to this plan, BNDE aimed to change the energy matrix of Brazil (especially after the oil shock of 1979) in order to propel the development of a domestic basic raw materials industry (to depend less on imports), and to help consolidate the machinery and equipment industry (BNDES 1987).[4]

Moreover, after the oil shock of 1979, BNDES also used its funding to help reduce imports. One such effort was aimed at reducing the imports of capital goods. The government also charged the bank with supporting the emerging computer industry. Even if at the beginning it looked like a promising project (Ramamurti 1987), BNDES's continuous injections of cash into companies like Cobra (Computadores e Sistemas Brasileiros) did not yield a competitive microprocessor or computer industry in the long run. The failure of this program is more obvious when it is compared to the contemporaneous program to promote this industry in the Republic of Korea, where besides financial support the government imposed clear goals and penalties for local firms (Evans 1995; Rodrik 2007).

The focus of BNDE, above all, was the substitution of expensive imports. Accordingly, this bank spun off three new subsidiaries in 1974: Insumos Básicos SA (Fibase), focused on providing financing to the sale of machinery and equipment manufacturers with high national content; Mecânica Brasileira SA (Embramec), focused on providing capital to machinery and equipment manufacturers, which then used Finame to finance their sales; and Investimentos Brasileiros SA (Ibrasa), which provided growth capital for the private sector, especially in the consumer goods industry (BNDES 2002a). These three programs for the most part used equity to facilitate investments in their targeted sectors.

According to Curralero (1998), BNDE changed its focus after 1982 from a being a financial institution for industrial promotion to being a financial institution that aided the restructuring of state-owned and private companies. Those restructurings involved equity investments in amounts that ended up transferring control to BNDE.

The bank also changed its name in 1982 from BNDE to BNDES, as it adopted the objective of social development (hence the "S" at the end of the new acronym) and began using its subsidiaries to invest directly in minority (and sometimes majority) *equity* positions in Brazilian companies. In that same year, BNDES merged its Fibase, Embramec, and Ibrasa subsidiaries into a single investment arm: BNDES Participações (BNDESPAR).

The 1980s mark a turning point in BNDES's activities because about 45 percent of that decade's capital allocations went to equity purchases, up from 30 percent or less in the 1970s. The switch in focus may have been a consequence of the fact that bankrupt industries ended up coming under the control of BNDES or because equity became a better investment vehicle for BNDES in times of high inflation. This is because owing to Brazil's high inflation in the 1980s, BNDES began to lose large amounts of money on loans. Even if loans were supposedly indexed to inflation, they lost real value over time because between 1964 and 1986 they were adjusted for inflation using the so-called ORTN (Obrigações Reajustáveis do Tesouro Nacional—the official inflation rate used by the government for its inflation-indexed bonds), which usually underestimated the actual inflation rate.

BNDES and Inflation during the 1980s

The lending business of BNDES, then, suffered between the late 1970s and the 1980s as a consequence of inflation. Inflation spiked rapidly at the end of the 1970s, reaching levels between 40 and 80 percent per year, then increasing to over 100 percent per year in the early 1980s and jumping rapidly after 1986, until reaching levels over 1,000 percent per year between 1989 and 1994. Beginning in 1974, BNDES adjusted the interest of its loans by adding a pre-fixed correction of 20 percent per year (the average inflation between 1968 and 1973). If inflation was higher than that, then the bank refinanced the additional adjustments. Yet inflation went beyond 20 percent after 1974, and the fixed adjustment rate of 20 percent stopped serving its purpose. Eugenio Staub, CEO of Gradiente, an electronics manufacturing firm that received loans from BNDES, admitted in an interview that "pre-fixing interest rates at 20 percent was a mistake. Especially with an inflation rate that went from 20, to 30, to 45, to 80 and to 100 percent. Thus, today [1982], whoever pays 20 percent [of the pre-fixed adjustment] plus four, six, or nine percent [in interest] is truly a protégé [of the government], a privileged [borrower]" (Najberg 1989, 34).

Moreover, after 1979, the Brazilian government subsidized entrepreneurs borrowing from BNDES in at least three ways. First, the government imposed low interest rates on the loans (i.e., 4–9 percent). Second, the government allowed BNDES to start indexing its loans to 70 percent of the inflation rate, as measured by the ORTN, rather than using the whole inflation figure. As a result, BNDES experienced real losses on those loans, since ORTN usually could not track inflation correctly. The Treasury, however, paid BNDES for some of the difference between actual inflation and the ORTN rate. Najberg (1989) calculates that out of every dollar BNDES lent in the 1980s, borrowing companies effectively repaid 26 percent in real terms. Third, BNDES guaranteed some of the foreign-currency-denominated loans that Brazilian entrepreneurs acquired to import machinery and equipment. As a result, BNDES absorbed any losses (or profits) generated from currency depreciations (or appreciations).

Villela (1995) calculates that, despite the subsidies, most of BNDES's loans in the 1980s did not go to finance new capital formation, but instead went

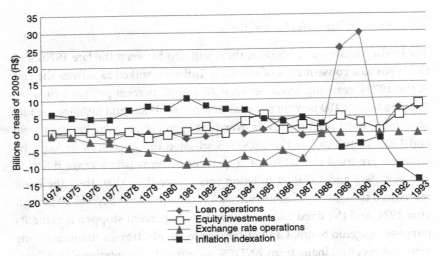

Figure 10.3. Profit/loss by business line, BNDES, 1974–1993
Source: Calculated by the authors from BNDES (1953–2010).

either to refinance previous loans or to subsidize exchange rate losses for entrepreneurs who borrowed abroad. He calculates that BNDES loans extended to finance new capital formation accounted for only between 4 percent and 6 percent of total gross capital formation in Brazil.

We identify the period 1974 to 1993 as a special period in terms of BNDES's revenue model (Figure 10.3). On the one hand, equity participations, rather than loans, became the most profitable line of business toward the end of the period. This change in the business model accompanies the process of reinvention of state ownership of companies that took place in the 1990s. In particular, the loan business of BNDES made the balance sheet of the government too dependent on government transfers. For instance, because of the fluctuations in prices and exchange rates, BNDES went from making money to losing money by indexing loans to inflation in 1989. Also, in the late 1970s and 1980s BNDES had to face losses related to guaranteeing loans in foreign currency (mostly for imports of machinery). It is during this period, as we described before, that BNDES's business model reached a crisis because loans ceased to be profitable and the government and Treasury made an explicit effort to use BNDES and incomplete inflation indexation to subsidize entrepreneurs.

BNDES after Privatization

BNDES survived and remained important even after the liberalization and privatization wave of the 1990s started under Fernando Collor de Mello (1990–1992) and continued under Fernando Henrique Cardoso (1995–2002). The bank was actually a key actor in those reforms in at least three capacities: planning and executing privatizations, providing acquirers with loans, and purchasing minority stakes in several former SOEs. Especially in the second administration of President Luiz Inácio Lula da Silva (2007–2010), BNDES was also involved in several large-scale operations and helped orchestrate mergers and acquisitions to build national champions in several industries (see Chapter 8).

BNDES's revenue model changed significantly after the national privatization program was in full swing (around 1994) and inflation had stabilized (1995). It is clear that, by then, most of the bank's revenues came from its equity investment business, which Figure 10.4 shows to be consistently profitable. The loan business, in contrast, did not become consistently profitable until after 2004. In Figure 10.4 we can compare the erratic behavior of loan profits after 1995 with the consistent profitability of the equity business.

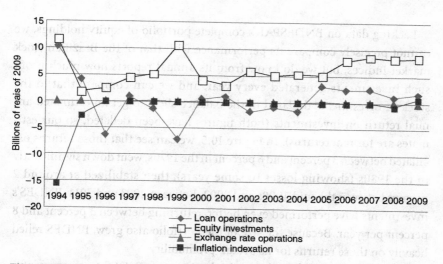

Figure 10.4. Profit/loss by business line, BNDES, 1994–2009
Source: Calculated by the authors from BNDES (1953–2010).

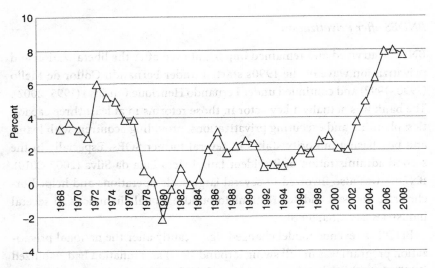

Figure 10.5. Returns of BNDES's investments in corporate securities, 1968–2009 (returns in R$, five-year moving average)

Source: Calculated by the authors with data from BNDES (1953–2010). Returns are calculated as profits from BNDES's investment portfolio *(carteira de participações)*—mostly through BNDESPAR—over the stock of such investments. All data were deflated using the IGP-DI index.

Lacking data on BNDESPAR's complete portfolio of equity holdings, we cannot precisely compare its performance with that of the Brazilian stock market indices, but we do know from its annual reports how much profit such investments generated every year, and we can compare that to the stock of investments declared in the balance sheet to get an estimated annual return on investments (both figures have been deflated, so our estimates are for real returns). In Figure 10.5, we can see that those returns oscillated between 3 percent and 6 percent in the 1970s, went down significantly in the 1980s (showing losses in some years), then stabilized at around 2 percent between the mid-1990s and 2002. Between 2003 and 2011, BNDES's investments have performed even better, returning between 3 percent and 8 percent per year. Because the size of the portfolio also grew, BNDES relied heavily on those returns for its overall profitability.

Although up until 2011 the equity business of BNDES was very profitable, the tide started turning against the bank in 2012. As discussed in

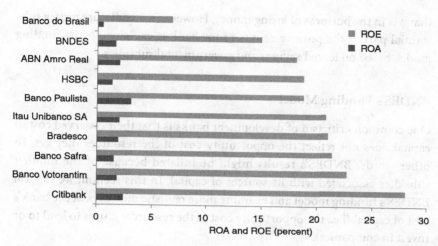

Figure 10.6. Average BNDES returns vs. Brazilian banks, 1996–2009
Source: Calculated by the authors using data from Bankscope.

Chapter 7, President Dilma Roussef started intervening in many industries, directly affecting firms that were in the portfolio of BNDESPAR—such as Petrobras and a host of energy companies. While the local stock market index Ibovespa gained 7.4 percent between 2011 and 2012, the value of the BNDESPAR equity portfolio shrank by 12.9 percent. Complicating matters, the national champions engendered during the second term of President Lula performed much worse than initially expected. A single firm in the portfolio, LBR Lácteos do Brasil (resulting from the merger of two milk processing companies), inflicted a loss of $330 million in the bank's total equity.[5]

Thus, BNDES is a strange animal. It is a development bank that for some time seemed to be good at making profits in its equity business, but it is not very profitable when it comes to its loan business. When we compare it with commercial banks in Brazil, which are some of the most profitable in the world, we can see that, in terms of return on assets (ROA) and return on equity (ROE), BNDES is the least profitable among the banks we include in Figure 10.6. Its high ROE might be a product of how BNDES structures its capital, keeping some perpetual funds as subordinated debt (see the discussion of BNDES's funding below for more details). Yet, although Figure 10.6 shows that BNDES is not in the business of making money, we cannot say that it is in the business of losing money. However, as we discuss next, a substantial part of the positive results of the bank is explained by its funding model, based on forced savings and governmental subsidies.

BNDES's Funding Model

One common criticism of development banks is that their observed cost of capital does not reflect the opportunity cost of the resources they get. In other words, BNDES's results might be inflated because of the implicit subsidies associated with its sources of capital. In this section, we explain BNDES's funding model and examine more realistic measures of the bank's cost of capital (i.e., the opportunity cost of the resources it uses to lend to or invest in companies).

BNDES's business model is easier to understand if we start by examining the bank's sources of funds. Figure 10.7 shows the types of funding source between 1952 and 2007. We can see that BNDES experimented with two basic funding models in its first sixty years. It started as a bank dependent on government transfers and deposits. In the 1960s, the largest sources of funds, within the government transfers and deposits, were the transfer of revenues from income taxes and from the government's deposit of the so-called "monetary reserves" (Prochnik 1995). Brazil did not have a proper central bank until 1985; before then, government agencies, the Treasury, and state-owned banks conducted monetary policy and managed the reserves.

BNDES's financing model changed dramatically in 1974 when the government introduced two new payroll taxes, the Programa de Integração Social (PIS) and the Programa de Formação do Patrimônio do Servidor Público (PASEP). These contributions were originally intended to finance an unemployment insurance program but became a permanent part of the bank's capital as subordinated debt. Initially, the government mandated that BNDES had to pay PIS/PASEP deposits a basic return of 3 percent (plus an inflation indexation using the ORTN index) or the net return of the investment of such funds (net of administrative costs).[6]

The amounts coming from payroll taxes transferred by the government changed in 1990 when the government consolidated worker unemployment insurance funds under the Fundo de Amparo ao Trabalhador (FAT).[7] FAT funds are transferred to BNDES in perpetuity and are therefore considered

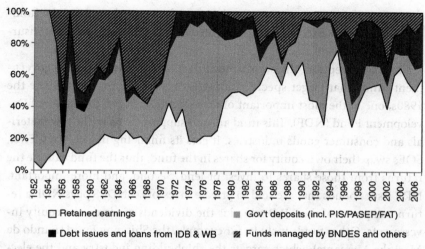

Figure 10.7. Sources of funds by type as a percentage of total funds, BNDES, 1952–2007

Source: Created by the authors using data from Prochnik (1995) and Prochnik and Machado (2008).

subordinated debt on BNDES's balance sheet.[8] Therefore, the idea behind the design of BNDES was that with FAT as a source of capital, the government would channel forced worker savings to the bank in order to promote new investment.

BNDES gets a pool of money from the FAT fund and it pays back an interest rate in return. The interest rate it pays varies according to how the FAT funds are used. Thus, BNDES pays back the so-called federal long-term interest rate (TJLP), for the tranche of funds it lends in local currency, and the London interbank rate—and any foreign exchange loss or gain—for loans made in foreign currency (Prochnik and Machado 2008).[9] After 2009, a disproportionate amount of the bank's funding came from long-term loans from the Treasury at low interest rates between TJLP and TJLP + 2.5 percent (Lamenza et al. 2011).

The most important change in BNDES's financing model in the 1980s, however, was the switch from payroll taxes to retained earnings. From the 1980s to 2008, BNDES saw retained earnings grow and began using them as its main source of funds. This was to a large extent a product of the returns on investments in securities using BNDESPAR. During this period, government deposits and government transfers became almost irrelevant for the funding of operations, except for the mandated transfer of unemployment insurance funds.

From its inception, the bank funded part of its operations with government funds that target specific industries or social programs. Since the 1980s, one of the most important of these funds has been the National Development Fund (NDF). This fund aims to support firms in the raw materials and consumer goods industries. It gets its financing in two ways. First, SOEs swap their own equity for shares in the fund; thus the fund can use the returns from those shares to invest or lend. Second, and more important, NDF issues bonds that are sold to private investors. BNDES pays NDF a return composed of the TJLP rate plus the dividends made on the equity investments. Other funds include, for example, the Shipping Fund (Fundo da Marinha Mercante), which targets the shipbuilding industry and the electricity sector.

BNDES Funding and Its Distortions

According to many observers, BNDES's current funding model creates important distortions in the Brazilian economy. First, the portion of BNDES funds that comes from workers unemployment insurance accounts (FAT and formerly PIS/PASEP) are part of the multiple payroll taxes Brazilian entrepreneurs need to comply with. According to the *Doing Business Indicators* for 2010, the total tax rate Brazilian entrepreneurs have to pay, as a percentage of profits, is 69.2 percent, compared to 64.75 percent in India, 25.3 percent in Chile, and 46.3 percent in the United States.[10]

Second, after 2008, the proportion of total BNDES funding coming directly from the government increased significantly. Those funds were financed with government debt, for which the government had to pay between 9 percent (in 2011) and 8 percent (in 2012) in interest. By paying such high rates for the borrowed funds, the government could be crowding out private investment.

Third, one criticism of the Brazilian government is that it is funding BNDES with debt, thus increasing gross debt. Yet BNDES officials argue that such funding does not increase net debt (that is, total gross debt minus total government assets). This is because the money the Brazilian Treasury channels to BNDES is used to purchase assets, such as equity or debentures, or to lend. The problem with this logic is that even if the net debt does not increase in terms of book values, there is a risk that the assets BNDES buys with such government funding may have market valuations lower than book value. Thus, if the assets of BNDES were fully marked to market, then net debt in Brazil would probably have increased in the post 2008–2009 crisis scenario, given that some of the equity investments of BNDES have lost value. Moreover, some of the loans BNDES grants are converted into equity and therefore are also exposed to fluctuations in market valuation. What this means is that the government is increasing its net debt position by borrowing to fund BNDES, and it is not properly accounting for it on its books.

Is BNDES Acting Like a Bank?

Banks are in the business of financial intermediation. They take deposits from savers and are supposed to lend those funds to entrepreneurs or governments to help them finance projects that are at least as profitable as the rate the banks charge for their loans. Thus, banks make money on the difference between their lending rates and the rates they pay to deposits, the so-called net interest margin (NIM). Brazilian commercial banks, for instance, have had some of the largest NIMs in the world and have been, up until now, very profitable.

Development banks are in the business of taking government funds and lending them to support specific industries or firms to carry out projects that have long-term maturation or that have high social impact and which commercial banks would not be willing to finance. Development banks fund their operations mostly by taking money from the government, such as monetary or foreign exchange reserves, special taxes designed to support specific industries, workers savings accounts, and direct Treasury transfers. Development banks usually also issue debt to finance their operations. In theory, they lend those funds in an attempt to solve market failure.

The net interest margin for a development bank should therefore be low, at least compared to that of commercial banks. In Figure 10.8, we compare BNDES's net interest margins with those of some of the largest banks in Brazil. We can see that BNDES charges the lowest NIMs among the banks in our sample, no matter what methodology we use to estimate NIMs. We include two estimates. First, we show a measure that uses all interests and

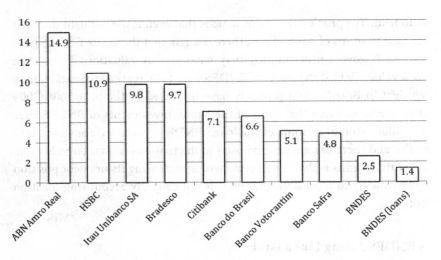

Figure 10.8. Net interest margins in large banks in Brazil (average, 1996–2009)
Source: All data from Bankscope and BNDES, *Annual Reports,* 1997–2010. Net interest margins calculated with Bankscope's data as net interest income over earning assets, except for BNDES (loans), which we estimated using data from the detailed P&Ls and balance sheet. The latter NIMs are estimated as interest earnings on loans over total loans minus interest payments and fees over funding (deposits, debt, and Treasury transfers).

fees generated from all income-earning assets over earning assets, which shows an intermediation margin of 2.4 percent. Second, we use a measure of NIMs just for BNDES's loan business, taking only interest and fee income from loans minus the interest costs over total loans. The results using the latter method are smaller, with a margin of 1.4 percent. That is, BNDES makes very small margins on its loan business, but it also makes loans with low risk. In 2010, the overall index of nonperforming loans was only 0.15 percent of total loans (BNDES 2010).

Yet we do not think that development banks can be judged like normal banks, not only because they do not charge market rates for their loans, but also because they do not pay market rates for the totality of their funds. In fact, they usually have a low cost of capital because they obtain funds from the government and from compulsory savings accounts. Thus, their cost of capital does not reflect the opportunity cost of the resources they get. Furthermore, it is not easy to figure out what the cost of capital is for a development bank. Below, we make an attempt to estimate BNDES's NIMs that takes into account the opportunity cost of funds and a more realistic measure of the cost of capital.

First we calculate BNDES's weighted average cost of capital (WACC) and compare it with the benchmark interest rate in Brazil as a way to get an idea of the cost of capital BNDES would have to pay to fund its operations at market rates. We calculate WACC for each year between 1995 and 2009, using the following formula:

$$\text{WACC}_{BNDES} = i_d * \frac{\text{deposits}}{\text{assets}} + i_{fc} * \frac{\text{debt} + \text{workers funds} + \text{treasury transfers}}{\text{assets}} + i_s * \frac{\text{equity}}{\text{assets}},$$

where i_d is the cost of deposits and i_{fc} is the financial cost BNDES pays for the debt it issues, for the funds it gets from the workers funds, and for the direct transfers it gets from the Brazilian Treasury. We calculate these two rates using BNDES's profit and loss (P&L) statement and its balance sheet. The cost of capital for BNDES's equity, i_e, is computed using a simple capital asset pricing formula—$i_{rf} + \beta_{equity} * [E(r_{market}) - i_{rf}]$—which is the sum of the risk-free interest rate and the beta of BNDES equity times the risk premium of the entire Brazilian stock market (i.e., the difference between the expected stock market index, Ibovespa, and the risk-free rate). Since BNDES's stock is not publicly traded, we make the assumption that its beta behaves like that of Banco do Brasil, the largest state-owned bank in Brazil.[11]

Table 10.3 shows our estimates of WACC, from 2002 to 2009, against the benchmark interest rate in Brazil. We can see that BNDES's WACC is significantly lower—on average, about 7.5 percent lower on average—than the benchmark rate. BNDES then lends some of those funds at a slightly higher rate (with a NIM of 1.4–2.5 percent) or invests them in bonds or equity.

Finally, we examine BNDES's net interest margin, taking into account not the actual cost of its funding, but the opportunity cost of its funding. For instance, the resources flowing into development banks could be used to reduce total government debt or for other purposes, perhaps earning a higher social rate of return or improving social welfare. We cannot perform a complete welfare analysis comparing the impact of BNDES loans with

Table 10.3. Estimated weighted average cost of capital of BNDES vs. benchmark rate, 1995–2009

	WACC BNDES	SELIC (benchmark rate)
1995	16.6	53.1
1996	16.3	27.4
1997	11.6	24.8
1998	8.4	28.8
1999	15.7	25.6
2000	1.4	17.4
2001	0.7	17.3
2002	11.8	19.2
2003	6.2	23.3
2004	5.5	16.2
2005	4.5	19.0
2006	5.3	15.1
2007	4.8	11.9
2008	4.7	12.5
2009	4.4	9.9

Source: Calculated by the authors using a weighted average of the cost of capital (by source of funding) and using the beta of the Banco do Brasil stock as a proxy for BNDES's cost of equity. We estimated this beta by running an OLS regression of Banco do Brasil against the Ibovespa index, using daily prices obtained at Bloomberg. The Central Bank's rate (SELIC) comes from the Central Bank's web page, http://www.bcb.gov.br/?INTEREST (accessed November 25, 2011).

the alternatives, because we would have to calculate the returns those funds would earn in other uses. What we can assume is that the resources BNDES gets from the government should, at the very least, generate something close to the government's cost of capital (SELIC). We can therefore perform a simple counterfactual examination of what BNDES's net interest margins would be if it had to pay the SELIC rate to fund its loan operations.

In Table 10.4, we can see that if BNDES had to fund its operations using a rate closer to the benchmark rate (SELIC), its net interest margins would be negative in most years. The difference between the interest rate BNDES charges and SELIC is very close to the difference between TJLP and SELIC. The main difference would be the amounts BNDES charges for loans in foreign currency. In sum, the implicit subsidy in BNDES loans leads it to "pay" approximately 7.5 cents per dollar loaned.

Table 10.4. BNDES intermediation margins using the opportunity cost of its funding, 1995–2009

	NIM1 (net int./loans – SELIC)	NIM2 (TJLP – SELIC)
1995	−36.6	−35.4
1996	−13.0	−16.4
1997	−14.1	−14.9
1998	−18.6	−10.7
1999	−6.6	−13.1
2000	−5.7	−7.7
2001	0.1	−7.3
2002	1.9	−9.2
2003	−20.0	−12.3
2004	−8.5	−6.5
2005	−12.8	−9.3
2006	−8.9	−8.2
2007	−7.4	−5.6
2008	−0.6	−6.2
2009	−8.2	−3.9

Source: Counterfactual estimates using the average interest rate charged on loans (interest income from loans over total loans) minus the benchmark SELIC rate. We also include the simple difference of the rate at which BNDES lends (TJLP) minus SELIC as another approximation of the bank's actual NIM. The differences between the two series are due to the fact that NIM1 includes for gains/losses in exchange-rate transactions and fees. Data from BNDES, *Annual Reports,* 1997–2010, and the Central Bank's web page, http://www.bcb.gov.br /?INTEREST (accessed November 25, 2011).

Conclusions and Implications

In this chapter, we explained BNDES's business model. The Brazilian government created BNDES to fund infrastructure and industrial projects that would not be funded through market mechanisms because of their long maturation or large capital needs. Between the 1950s and the 1970s, that motivation seems extremely relevant, given the state of financial markets in Brazil and the low level of international capital flows to the country (partly restricted by barriers to entry and capital controls). But the motivations that got Alexander Gerschenkron and Rondo Cameron excited about development banks in the 1960s and 1970s may not hold in the Brazilian context of the twenty-first century. As financial markets develop, the degree to which BNDES still solves market failures tends to be reduced (see Chapter 9).

Moreover, if that impact is no longer large, then attention has to be paid to the distortions generated by the bank's funding model.

We showed that BNDES is profitable and manages to get positive net interest margins, mostly because it has an extremely low cost of capital (compared to market rates) and because most of its profits come from its investments. However, its margins largely depend on subsidized capital provided by the government. If we try to compute the true cost of capital of the bank, the final picture is much less positive. Of course, the strategy of allowing negative to low margins in the loan business and covering them with returns from the investment arm makes sense for a development bank if the loans are used to fund projects that would otherwise go unfunded. To inform this debate, in the next chapter we study the lending behavior of BNDES and how the bank is affecting the performance and investment of its target firms.

11

Leviathan as a Lender
Industrial Policy versus Politics

In this chapter we present empirical evidence on the role of development banks according to the *industrial policy* and *political* views. We use part of the database we used in Chapter 8, which tracks firm characteristics and performance for publicly traded corporations in Brazil, together with an original database that tracks BNDES loans to firms traded on the São Paulo Stock Exchange. Because BNDES does not disclose firm-level loan data for confidentiality reasons, we focus on publicly traded companies, which are required to provide detailed information on the origins of their debt.

As the reader may recall, the industrial policy view assumes that development banks operate in environments with capital scarcity. By specializing in long-term finance neglected by the private sector, development banks facilitate the execution of valuable investments and projects that would otherwise not be carried out (e.g., Yeyati et al. 2004; Bruck 1998; Armendáriz de Aghion 1999). Development banks may also set high standards for firms and lend to them conditionally on meeting specific targets (Amsden 2001). Thus, according to this view, development banks should improve investment and performance. For instance, if firms are constrained in long-term financing, loans from development banks may allow them to undertake capital expenditures to capture economies of scale or acquire new technology. This, we think, should be expressed as improved firm-level profitability (return on assets [ROA] and operational performance as measured by EBT-IDA/assets) or market valuation using Tobin's q (market value of stocks plus debt divided by total assets). Of course, an observed increase in profitability may instead be due to subsidized funding (i.e., a reduction in financial expenditures to total debt). However, if development bank loans prompt investment in valuable projects, then the effect on performance should occur beyond a simple reduction in interest payments. Following the same logic, BNDES loans should also positively affect a firm's capital expenditures and its stock of fixed capital.

As for the determinants of loan allocations, on the one hand, the industrial policy view would argue that loans from development banks should go to firms that have valuable projects for which the market could not or would not provide sufficient capital or complementary investments (e.g., Rodrik 1995; Lin and Chang 2009; George and Prabhu 2000). If those advantages are "latent," development banks may not necessarily target firms with superior (actual or past) performance. Therefore, we would not expect to find that high-performing firms get the financing, unless they use it to finance capital-intensive projects with long maturities. On the other hand, development banks may pick firms with good performance, either to boost "champions" or to guarantee repayment (Amsden 2001).

The political view, in contrast, places more emphasis on the process of selection. Governments can use their development banks to bail out failing corporations (the *soft budget constraint* hypothesis) or benefit politically connected capitalists (what we call the *rent-seeking* hypothesis). For instance, well-connected firms may receive subsidized loans from development banks in exchange for favors to politicians, including campaign donations. Dinç (2005) finds that during election years in emerging markets, the lending activity of government-owned banks is greater than that of private banks. Sapienza (2004) shows that, in Italy, the performance of the ruling party in elections affects the lending behavior of state-owned banks. In Brazil, Claessens et al. (2008) show that a firm's campaign donations are correlated with access to preferential financing. Carvalho (2010) studies the criteria for the allocation of BNDES's loans and finds that firms in regions governed by politicians allied with the federal government receive more funding from the bank.

Therefore, well-connected actors may have superior ability to attract loans or equity from development banks, even for projects for which they would be able to get capital elsewhere (Haber 2002; Krueger 1990; Ades and Di Tella 1997). Because, according to this view, BNDES may give out loans for reasons other than efficiency, there is no clear prediction on the effect of loans on firm-level performance or investment. Even when development banks promote the creation of national champions through industrial consolidation, the final effect of allocations is not straightforward. Reduced competition should increase economic rents; but it may also create incentives for restricted output and investment. In the political view, the only clear positive effect we expect to find from loan allocations is that firms should have lower financial expenditures once they get subsidized credit. When BNDES loans are given out to companies that did not need them, or when firms get loans just to lower their cost of capital, then BNDES loans are simply a transfer from the state to private capitalists, without necessarily having any effect on economic activity or investment.

In this chapter, we test these predictions using two sets of regressions (Lazzarini et al. 2012). The first set examines the impact of BNDES loan allocations on firm-level performance and investment, while the second set assesses the determinants of allocations, using BNDES loans as dependent variables and firm-level performance and political factors as independent variables. In both cases, to control for unobservable factors, we use fixed-effects specifications, including time-invariant firm-level fixed effects and time-varying year and industry-year effects. Thus, we fundamentally measure how variations in BNDES's loans affect variations in firm-level performance and how firm characteristics affect the level of loans companies receive.

BNDES Loans: An Overview

Data

We use part of the database described in Chapter 8, but this time we track the amount of loans received by publicly traded corporations. We collected unique data from the annual reports of 286 firms publicly traded in BM&F Bovespa, the São Paulo Stock Exchange, between 2002 and 2009 (we did not have access to data from earlier years). We identify loans by BNDES in two ways: through a direct inspection of the declared source of the funding (BNDES or other banks) or, when this information was not available, through an examination of the reported interest rate paid. Because BNDES and its affiliates lend at a subsidized rate, TJLP (see Chapter 10), we assume that a firm has BNDES loans when it reports paying TJLP rates.

Besides some of the issues discussed in Chapter 8, it is important to discuss up front two limitations of our data. First, BNDES is not choosing firms at random. Therefore, there may be selection bias in our results. We address this toward the end of the chapter, making clear what these problems could be and using different estimation techniques to both study selection (among publicly traded corporations) and show why this is not an issue for our results.

Second, there is a different kind of selection problem with our data. Our database on loans from BNDES covers a little over 30 percent of the total loan portfolio (based on data for 2009). This is because there are loans to private (non-listed) firms that are not disclosed by BNDES. However, our data are ideal to study BNDES credit allocations to publicly traded corporations, and our results indicate that there are important lessons to be learned about how these large corporations behave when they get subsidized loans.

Now, one important caveat, before we continue, is to disentangle the relationship between BNDES's equity investments and loans. Even if 84.5 percent of firms with BNDES equity also have loans, almost 90 percent of the firms with BNDES loans (87.9 percent, to be precise) do not have equity investments by the bank. Therefore, we think we can separate the study of loans and equity. In fact, as reported in Chapter 8, the correlation between having loans from BNDES and having equity investments by BNDES is rather small, −0.034.

Cross-Sectional Evidence

Let us begin with a simple cross-sectional analysis answering the following question: How do firms with and without BNDES loans differ? We consider a host of firm-level characteristics related to the above predictions on the effects and determinants of BNDES lending activity (see Appendix 11.1). The first set of variables is related to firm-level performance and investment activity. Thus, the profitability of firms is measured by *ROA* (net return on assets) and *EBITDA/assets* (operational return on assets). The latter is particularly important because the subsidy associated with BNDES loans may distort an analysis of profitability through ROA, which is net of financial expenses. We also measure the performance of firms as assessed by the stock market, through a simplified proxy of *Tobin's q*. Because BNDES loans

Table 11.1. Characteristics of firms with and without BNDES loans

Variable	Firms that do not have BNDES loans			Firms that have BNDES loans		
	N	Mean	Std. dev.	N	Mean	Std. dev.
ROA	290	0.039	0.008	887	0.056*	0.003
EBITDA/assets	279	0.075	0.009	887	0.123***	0.004
Tobin's q	239	1.199	0.071	887	1.147	0.032
Finex/debt	129	0.328	0.020	689	0.265***	0.007
Capex/assets	273	0.069	0.008	852	0.078	0.003
Fixed assets / assets	290	0.157	0.013	887	0.266***	0.008
Ln(assets)	290	12.287	0.107	887	13.119***	0.053
Tobin's q	239	1.199	0.071	887	1.147	0.032

Source: Based on Lazzarini et al. (2012).

Note: Asterisks denote the statistical significance of a two-tailed mean comparison test, where *, **, and *** represent $p < 0.05$, $p < 0.01$, and $p < 0.001$, respectively.

may help reduce the cost of capital, we also add the variable *Finex/debt*, measuring the ratio of firm-level financial expenses (loan payments) to debt. The final two variables are related to investments: *Capex/assets* and *Fixed assets/assets* measure yearly capital expenditures and the total stock of fixed capital relative to the stock of all existing assets, respectively.

The first important pattern that comes out of our data is that the cross-sectional variation does show that firms that receive BNDES loans are larger and exhibit superior performance in terms of higher *ROA*, higher *EBITDA/assets*, and lower *Finex/debt* (see Table 11.1). Although the latter may have to do with loan subsidies, from a cross-sectional standpoint it seems that BNDES loans are associated with firms with superior operational performance (net of financial expenses). Firms receiving loans also appear to have a larger proportion of fixed assets—which, at first glance, seems to be consistent with the industrial policy view, as discussed before.

When we look at the distribution of loans in our database by industry or by company, we can see that BNDES was focused on lending to electricity and telecommunications companies in the past but had changed its focus to commodities by 2009. In Figure 11.1, we show the percentage of loans in our database by industry (2002–2009); the two dominant sectors are public

Table 11.2. Percentage of BNDES loans in our database by company

Company	Percentage of total loans in our database	
	In 2004	In 2009
Petrobras (oil)	14.5	39.4
Telemar Norte Leste (telecom)	10.4	7.7
Vale do Rio Doce (mining)	—	8.5
Suzano (paper & energy)	3.4	2.6
Brasil Telecom	—	3.2
Neoenergia (electricity)	3.2	2.5
CPFL Energia (electricity)	6.8	—
VBC Energia (electricity)	2.7	2.0
CSN (steel)	4.2	2.3
Klabin (paper)	1.3	2.1
Aracruz (cellulose)	2.4	—
Cesp (electricity)	11.2	—
Sadia (food and agribusiness)	3.2	—
CPFL Geração (electricity)	—	2.1
Embraer (airplanes)	—	1.4

Source: Our calculations, based on our database of publicly listed firms (Lazzarini, Musacchio, et al. 2012).

services—such as electricity, gas, and sanitary services—and oil and gas extraction. Table 11.2 shows the distribution of loans by firm. We see that, in 2004, the distribution of loans to the largest fifteen companies was more diffused, with electricity companies as the largest borrowers; but by 2009, Petrobras had become the largest borrower, taking almost 40 percent of that year's loans to publicly traded corporations.

According to the industrial policy view, we would expect BNDES to be lending to companies in industries in which there are tighter credit constraints, perhaps because projects take longer to mature and usually have cash flows in local currency. Industries that have cash flows in foreign currency and that can therefore borrow abroad at low cost should not be among BNDES's largest borrowers. Yet, in Figure 11.1 and Table 11.2, we can see that this is not how things have evolved in Brazil. There is a large concentration of loans to resource-intensive companies such as Petrobras (oil and gas extraction) and Vale (mining). Almeida (2009) observed that, during our

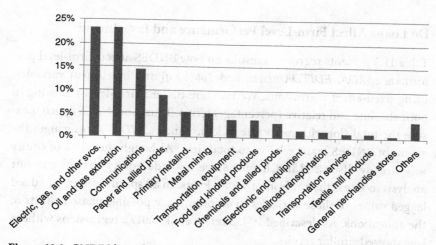

Figure 11.1. BNDES loans by industry as a percentage of total loans, 2002–2009

period of analysis, BNDES had focused on basic commodity sectors such as mining, oil, and agribusiness (see also Schapiro, 2013).

One of the justifications presented by BNDES executives is that those are sectors in which Brazilian companies have a comparative advantage, thereby creating a natural opportunity to develop national champions. Luciano Coutinho, president of BNDES, explained the logic of this type of industrial targeting: "We chose sectors in which Brazil had superior competitiveness, agribusiness and commodities. . . . Brazil was a great exporter, but it was not possible to prop up international companies in these sectors. For this reason, we defined that, whenever there was competitive capacity, such internationalization would be implemented" (interview, Dieguez 2010).

This pattern of choice may also explain our cross-sectional finding that BNDES tends to target large and profitable firms (Table 11.1), which are natural candidates to be singled out as champions. However, these results are merely descriptive and do not control for a host of factors influencing loans. Using more robust econometric methods, we next examine whether loans have really contributed to firm-level performance and investment. We also assess in more detail the factors that are driving BNDES's choice of its targeted firms.

Do Loans Affect Firm-Level Performance and Investment?

Table 11.3 presents regression results on how BNDES affects firm-level performance (*ROA, EDITDA/assets*, and *Tobin's q*) and investment variables, using fixed-effect regressions. We measure BNDES firm-level financing in both absolute and relative (percentage) terms. Thus, *Ln(BNDES loans)* measure the total (logarithmic) value of loans, and *%BNDES loans* gauges the extent of BNDES loans relative to total debt. Although the effect of equity was already discussed in Chapter 8, we also add equity variables in our analysis to assess their role jointly with loans. In all specifications, we added lagged values of those variables to accommodate possible phased effects of the allocations. As described in Lazzarini et al. (2012), regressions without lags showed similar results.

In virtually all model specifications (1 to 6), we find no significant effects for the BNDES variables on firm-level performance. Our data are thus inconsistent with our prediction, derived from the industrial policy view, that loans from development banks improve firm performance by allowing firms to invest in valuable projects that would otherwise be left unfunded. Once we control for particular industry- and firm-level traits, we find that BNDES loan allocations have no particular effect on profitability or market valuation.

No effect is also found in terms of equity. Although in Chapter 8 we showed a positive effect of BNDES equity on performance and investment, the significance disappears in more recent years. A possible explanation, discussed in that chapter, is that the development of the local capital market reduced severe financing constraints affecting Brazilian companies in the last century.

As expected, specifications 7 and 8 in Table 11.3 show that companies that borrow from BNDES pay less in interest payments overall. The subsidy included in BNDES loans reduces firms' cost of capital. Based on the estimated coefficients of specifications 7 and 8, Lazzarini et al. (2012) compute that BNDES loans reduce the cost of capital by a percentage differential somewhere between 4 and 12 percent, which is more or less consistent with the subsidy included in BNDES's interest rates (see Chapter 10).

Although we do not find significant effects of BNDES equity on performance, specification 8 unveils an interesting effect: an increase in 1 percentage point in BNDES equity reduces by 2.1 percentage points the firm's financial expenditures. Extra equity from BNDES apparently serves as an implicit guarantee of repayment. This result is consistent with the industrial policy view where state equity helps reduce failure in the credit market. However, it is also consistent with the political view if creditors perceive firms with BNDES equity to be bailed out in case of poor performance.

With respect to the effect of BNDES loans and equity on investment, results are not very consistent across alternative specifications. While there is a positive effect once we consider the logarithmic value of loans (specification 9), the effect becomes not significant if we take the ratio of BNDES loans to the firm's total debt (specification 10). Also, assessing the effect of BNDES loans on the ratio of the stock of fixed capital to assets, we find no significant result, except for a marginally significant negative effect of *%BNDES loans* in the last column.

All told, these results are inconsistent with the industrial policy view: subsidized loans appear to be simply a transfer of income from the state to large firms, without any consistent effect in terms of investment or profitability. The examination of the process through which BNDES selects its targeted firms, discussed below, sheds more light on this finding.

Is BNDES Targeting Good or Bad Firms?

The lack of consistent investment- or performance-enhancing effects of loans can be explained in two ways. First, as implied by the soft-budget constraint hypothesis (of the political view), BNDES may be giving loans to underperforming firms and may even have to bail out failing companies. Those underperformers may artificially survive even if they have no real competitive advantage. Alternatively, the bank may be simply picking firms that would not need subsidized credit in the first place. Thus, if BNDES is lending to well-performing firms rather than to underperformers, then we can make the argument that the bank is "picking winners."

There is nothing wrong with picking winners if the beneficiary firms are borrowing for reasons related to the industrial policy view—that is, out of need rather than opportunistically. However, BNDES may be picking winners capable of investing in profitable projects regardless of subsidized loans or that could be borrowing through other means (i.e., companies that are not facing capital constraints). If this is the case, increased loans

Table 11.3. Effects of BNDES financing on firm performance and investment, 2002–2009 (fixed-effect regressions)

	ROA		EBITDA/assets		Tobin's q		Finex/debt		Capex/assets		Fixed assets / assets	
	(1)	(2)	(3)	(4)	(5)	(6)	(7)	(8)	(9)	(10)	(11)	(12)
Loans												
Ln(BNDES loans)$_t$	−0.002		−0.003		−0.009		−0.013*		0.004*		−0.002	
	(0.002)		(0.003)		(0.008)		(0.005)		(0.002)		(0.005)	
Ln(BNDES loans)$_{t-1}$	0.001		0.002		−0.01		0.005		−0.001		0.000	
	(0.003)		(0.003)		(0.015)		(0.006)		(0.002)		(0.002)	
Ln(BNDES loans)$_{t-2}$	−0.001		−0.004		−0.03		−0.001		−0.004		−0.004	
	(0.003)		(0.004)		(0.021)		(0.006)		(0.002)		(0.003)	
%BNDES loans$_t$		0.018		0.025		0.085		0.101		0.000		−0.041†
		(0.026)		(0.031)		(0.173)		(0.065)		(0.021)		(0.024)
%BNDES loans$_{t-1}$		0.038		0.028		−0.078		−0.124**		−0.007		−0.018
		(0.029)		(0.036)		(0.127)		(0.047)		(0.024)		(0.031)
%BNDES loans$_{t-2}$		−0.011		−0.012		−0.074		0.093		−0.063		−0.020
		(0.027)		(0.029)		(0.173)		(0.069)		(0.061)		(0.045)
Equity												
Ln(BNDES equity)$_t$	−0.002		−0.004		0.000		0.001		−0.003		0.001	
	(0.002)		(0.003)		(0.006)		(0.006)		(0.003)		(0.002)	

	(1)	(2)	(3)	(4)	(5)	(6)	(7)	(8)	(9)	(10)	(11)	(12)
Ln(BNDES equity)$_{t-1}$	0.001 (0.004)		0.001 (0.004)							0.001 (0.002)	0.003 (0.002)	
Ln(BNDES equity)$_{t-2}$	0.004 (0.005)		0.003 (0.005)							−0.001 (0.002)	−0.001 (0.004)	
%BNDES equity$_t$		−0.092 (0.151)		−0.156 (0.186)	−0.024 (0.016)	0.692 (1.084)	−0.135 (0.284)	−0.014 (0.009)	0.277 (0.352)			0.182 (0.207)
%BNDES equity$_{t-1}$		−0.07 (0.272)		0.069 (0.258)	0.030 (0.019)	−1.529 (0.982)	−0.003 (0.120)	0.003 (0.007)	−2.100*** (0.496)			0.109 (0.133)
%BNDES equity$_{t-2}$		0.315 (0.367)		0.191 (0.383)		2.561 (1.955)	−0.135 (0.204)		−0.171 (1.704)			−0.048 (0.184)
N (total)	600	553	590	545	501	468	539	422	416	582	600	553
N (firms)	172	161	168	159	160	150	158	130	129	168	172	161
p (F test)	< 0.001	< 0.001	< 0.001	< 0.001	< 0.001	< 0.001	< 0.001	< 0.001	< 0.001	< 0.001	< 0.001	< 0.001

Note: All specifications include the following controls: fixed assets to total assets, whether the firm is foreign, whether it belongs to a business group, the log of total assets, and leverage. Specifications also include firm, year, and industry-year fixed effects. Two-tailed tests where †, *, **, and *** represent $p < 0.10$, $p < 0.05$, $p < 0.01$, and $p < 0.001$, respectively. Robust standard errors in brackets (errors are clustered at the firm level). More detailed results are in Lazzarini et al. (2012).

should not necessarily result in more investment or enhanced firm-level performance.

In Table 11.4, we examine the issue of whether BNDES is lending to good or bad performers. We present a set of regressions that look at the determinant of BNDES loans measured both as the logarithm of the amount of loans and the ratio of BNDES loans to total debt (as a percentage). Our objective was to find out if lagged firm-level performance variables (*ROA*, *EBITDA/assets*, and *Tobin's q*) are highly correlated with the amount of loans a firm receives from BNDES.

Specifications 7–9 of Table 11.4 reveal some positive effects of *ROA* and *EBITDA/assets* in some specifications, but the level of significance is marginal. We also fail to detect any significant effect of *Tobin's q*. Although we do not find strong, consistent effects of performance variables, our data at least allow us to reject the soft-budget constraint hypothesis that BNDES is systematically bailing out poor-performing firms.

Thus, if anything, allocations are not generally targeting bad projects. BNDES may actually be trying to select good candidates for national champions or guarantee repayment by avoiding systematic lending to bad firms. The reader may recall from the previous chapter that only after 2004 do we find BNDES having positive net income on loans. Yet our data show that the correlation between BNDES loans and performance seems to be significant only from performance to loans and not the other way around. Yet when those large firms get subsidized loans, they are not investing in capital-intensive projects or in projects that increase their profitability.

Every time we asked a BNDES official, government official, or entrepreneur who had gone through the process of borrowing from BNDES, we heard the same story.[1] The potential borrower has to present a project plan for how the money will be spent and the impact that the project will have. Those projects are then evaluated by a technical committee that makes loan recommendations. For big loans, there is also a loan committee with top executives from the bank that decides on technical and industrial policy criteria. Reflecting this process, the bank has generally reported low default rates. This helps explain our finding that, contrary to the soft budget hypothesis, BNDES is not generally targeting bad projects.

Is BNDES Lending to Politically Connected Firms?

If firms benefiting from subsidized BNDES loans are not increasing capital expenditures or improving performance after they get their loans but are enjoying lower financial expenditures, one has to wonder whether there is a political channel that may be determining which firms get loans. In particular, many studies have found that, in Brazil, political campaign financing is a crucial mechanism through which firms establish political connections. Large election districts and an open-list competition create incentives for politicians to trade "pork" for private money to support costly campaigns (Samuels 2002). Thus, we examine the connection between campaign donations by firms and the amount of subsidized loans those firms get from BNDES.

Brazilian corporations, unlike those in the United States, can make cash donations directly to candidates, rather than to parties, and so can foreign firms with local subsidiaries. The official limit for domestic firms is 2 percent of their gross revenues, but "under the table" donations are pervasive (Araújo 2004). Furthermore, while lobbying is a common practice in Brazil, it is not necessarily carried out by business associations. Owing either to the lack of business associations or to their weakness, firms have incentives to establish their own connections to politicians. According to Schneider (2004, 93–94): "On paper, Brazilian [business] associations organized nearly all of business, had massive resources that they spent on sophisticated research and coordinating departments, and appeared regularly in the press to air business's views on the issues of the day. Yet, most prominent businesspeople and top government officials readily admit that these impressive-looking associations were in fact weak and unrepresentative, and economic and political elites regularly circumvented them."

Such a political environment makes political connections at the firm level extremely important. Government favors, protection, and other forms of support may depend on the direct connections firms establish with politicians through campaign financing. In fact, studies have found strong associations in Brazil between campaign donations and firm-level profitability (Bandeira-de-Mello and Marcon 2005), preferential financing (Claessens et al. 2008), and access to government contracts (Boas et al. 2011).

In line with such studies, we consider reported campaign donations as a sign of the extent of a firm's political connections. Luckily for us, candidates

Table 11.4. Determinants of BNDES loans, 2002–2009 (fixed-effect regressions)

	Ln(BNDES loans)						%BNDES loans					
	(1)	(2)	(3)	(4)	(5)	(6)	(7)	(8)	(9)	(10)	(11)	(12)
Performance variables												
ROA_t	0.924 (1.459)						0.195† (0.114)					
ROA_{t-1}	2.868† (1.663)						0.141 (0.118)					
ROA_{t-2}	0.676 (1.535)						0.178† (0.107)					
EBITDA/ assets$_t$		1.430 (1.360)						0.204† (0.118)				
EBITDA/ assets$_{t-1}$		2.157 (1.625)						0.106 (0.124)				
EBITDA/ assets$_{t-2}$		1.744 (1.757)						0.215† (0.116)				
Tobin's q$_t$			0.134 (0.270)						0.036 (0.027)			
Tobin's q$_{t-1}$			0.244 (0.210)						0.046 (0.030)			
Tobin's q$_{t-2}$			0.321 (0.331)						−0.021 (0.027)			

Donations	(1)	(2)	(3)	(4)	(5)	(6)
Total number	0.000			0.000		
	(0.008)			(0.001)		
For winning candidates		0.170**			0.015**	
		(0.062)			(0.005)	
For losing candidates		−0.147**			−0.013**	
		(0.049)			(0.004)	
For winners minus losers			0.146**			0.013**
			(0.051)			(0.004)
N (total)	1,212	1,136	910	1,243	1,243	1,243
N (firms)	267	253	226	286	286	286
p (F test)	< 0.001	< 0.001	< 0.001	< 0.001	< 0.001	< 0.001

Note: All specifications include the following controls: fixed assets to total assets, whether the firm is foreign, whether it belongs to a business group, the log of total assets, and leverage. Specifications also include firm, year, and industry-year fixed effects. Two-tailed tests where †, *, **, and *** represent $p<0.10$, $p<0.05$, $p<0.01$, and $p<0.001$, respectively. Robust standard errors in brackets (errors are clustered at the firm level). More detailed results are in Lazzarini et al. (2012).

in Brazil are required to disclose all donors to the Superior Electoral Tribunal (TSE). The electoral authorities then release data on election finances for each candidate. We used this data to match individual firm contributions to politicians with election results. Thus, for each firm, we have the number of candidates (running for president, senator, or state or federal deputy) to whose campaigns the firm officially contributed in the previous election. Given that our data on firm performance and BNDES loans run from 2002 to 2009, we examine if the data on campaign donations for the elections in 2002 and 2006 help us understand which firms get subsequent loans from BNDES. Data from the 2002 campaign are used to see if there is a correlation with loans obtained between 2003 and 2006. We then use campaign donations for the 2006 elections to examine the correlation with loans given between 2007 and 2009.

There could obviously be self-selection in the data on campaign donations; that is, the most profitable firms may be approached by a larger number of candidates. Thus, we separate donations to candidates who won and donations to candidates who lost, considering that election results have an exogenous component due to random events affecting political competition (Claessens et al. 2008). In addition, we compute a variable we call *Donations for winners minus losers,* which tracks the number of donations that went to candidates who won minus the number of donations that went to candidates who lost. This variable thus measures the bets of firms in a more exogenous way, because firms clearly do not control which of the candidates they support will win or lose an election.

We use the selection regressions from the previous section and add our political variables. The results are also in Table 11.4. We find that donations *in general* do not affect loans (specifications 4 and 10). Clear effects appear, however, when we separate between donations to winners and to losers—either when we consider these variables separately or when we use the difference between the number of winners and the number of losers. Donations to winning candidates increase the amount of received loans, while the opposite effect is observed with donations for losing candidates (specifications 5–6 and 11–12).

Based on these estimates and the average size of BNDES loans in the database (US$166 million), Lazzarini et al. (2012) estimate that the gain for donor firms from each additional donation to a winner would bring net benefits ranging between US$1.1 million and $3.4 million. In contrast, the average donation per winning candidate for each firm in our database was US$22,820 in 2002 and $43,903 in 2006. Even if we consider that there may be substantial donations under the table—estimated by Araújo (2004) as two to ten times the official figures—the magnitude of the estimated effect is far from trivial. In addition, these political ties may help firms to receive benefits beyond loans.

Because the result of an election has an exogenous component caused by random factors influencing political competition (Claessens et al. 2008), our separate findings for winners and losers suggest that our results are not merely driven by self-selection. However, one might argue that firms with good cash flow (which tend to be targeted by the bank) have more money to distribute to politicians and even have superior ability to identify potential winners (Claessens et al. 2008). There is, however, no significant correlation between donations for winners and firm-level performance variables. And while there is significant correlation between donations for losers and the performance variables *ROA* and *EBITDA/assets,* the correlation coefficient is small and *positive* (0.06). In other words, well-performing firms are more associated with giving donations to *losers* than to winners. The effect of donations also remains significant when we add to the same regression financial performance variables such as *ROA* and *EBITDA/assets.*[2]

How should we interpret these findings? We do not think our results are evidence of an outright give-and-take relationship between BNDES and the companies making campaign donations. As noted before, the selection of loans tends to be highly technical. BNDES is well known for having a competent staff that scrutinizes a borrower's ability to repay a loan (Schneider 1991; Evans 1995). We think there is another channel explaining our results. There is evidence that firms that donate to winning candidates are more likely to be involved in governmental contracts (Boas et al. 2011; Lazzarini 2011). Therefore, winning a governmental contract increases the odds that the firm will receive substantial funding from the bank. Alternatively, certain donors are more likely selected by the government as national champions, and their sectors are more likely subject to industrial policy targeting. Because in the Brazilian economy there are several candidates of potential champions, donations can possibly increase the likelihood that a particular firm will be singled out and supported with massive loans.

Conclusion

Collectively, our results indicate that BNDES loans are apparently transferring subsidies to large firms without any substantial benefit in terms of improved firm-level performance or investment. In addition, in line with the rent-seeking hypothesis, we find that campaign donations appear to influence BNDES allocations, although apparently this effect does not cause bad firms to be systematically selected. Thus, it is not the case that BNDES is generally picking bad projects, with negative implications for its own financial health. A likely reason for our results is that the politically connected firms in our database are not underperformers in general. These firms want cheaper credit, but they are not bankrupt firms in need of a financial lifeline. Even good firms have incentives to be politically connected as a way to guarantee subsidized loans. Furthermore, good firms may use connections as a hedge against adverse political decisions.

Therefore, although our results are not aligned with the industrial policy literature, which sees development banks as mechanisms to unlock productive investments through state-led credit, they do not completely support the opposing perspective of development banks as tools to help and rescue failed industrialists. This is not to say, however, that bailouts never occur. For instance, in 1998, a group of firms, including Electricité de France (EDP) and AES Corporation, acquired control of Eletropaulo, a former state-owned company in the electricity sector. BNDES provided the acquirers with US$1.2 billion in loans. However, by 2003, the acquirers were on the brink of default, and BNDES decided to reconvert part of the loans into shares and convertible bonds. A similar sequence of events took place with the Brazilian meatpacker JBS, which, as discussed in Chapter 1, received loans (in the form of convertible bonds) to pursue its program of international expansion. The expansion, however, came at a cost of a substantial debt, and in 2011, JBS and BNDES agreed to reconvert part of BNDES's loans into shares. But while these cases are important, our findings indicate that they are not the norm, at least in the period covered by our database.

A caveat, however, is that we focus only on profitability and investment; we do not measure if allocations support social initiatives or if they yield externalities that are not measured in our database. For instance, a private project, even if individually unprofitable, may encourage complementary investments in related industries or contribute to aggregate employment. Thus, we are not in the position to completely reject the industry policy perspective. Moreover, our results apply only to large Brazilian firms, for which we could collect loan data at the firm level. This limitation notwithstanding, our results should by no means be interpreted as not telling us something about the impact that BNDES has in the economy as a whole. At least we should wonder why the bank is targeting large firms that apparently have other means of financing.[3]

In sum, the role of BNDES as a lender and minority shareholder provides nuance to the discussion of the role of the government in business. The findings of this chapter do not show BNDES doing what development banks are supposed to do, or at least we do not find strong results to support that view. Yet the results of Chapter 8 show that BNDES as an investor can help to solve some of the capital market failures that exist in emerging markets. Given that the database used in this chapter covers the period after 2002, a likely explanation of those diverging results is that Brazilian firms, more recently, became less constrained in their access to external financing. Large, listed firms, such as those in our database, may have become less dependent on state capital. They are apparently more attracted to the subsidies accompanying loans than the loans per se.

In the concluding chapter, we consolidate our findings with a set of theoretical and practical implications for the study of state capitalism.

APPENDIX

Table 11-A1. Database used to assess the effect of loans, 2002–2009

Variable	Description	Mean (std. dev.)	Min.	Max.
Performance, investment				
ROA	Net profit divided by total assets	0.025 (0.118)	−0.464	0.308
EBITDA/assets	Operational profit (net of taxes, depreciation, and interest) to total assets	0.088 (0.121)	−0.377	0.403
Tobin's q	Market value of stocks plus debt divided by total assets	0.880 (0.794)	0.062	4.831
Finex/debt	Financial expenses (loan payments) divided by total debt	0.303 (0.204)	0.000	0.994
Capex/assets	Capital expenditures divided by total assets	0.073 (0.092)	0.000	0.998
Fixed assets / assets	Fixed assets divided by total assets	0.293 (0.248)	0.000	0.995
BNDES financing				
Ln(BNDES loans)	Logarithmic value of BNDES loans reported in the balance sheet (1,000 US$)	7.479 (4.731)	0.000	16.781
Ln(BNDES equity)	Logarithmic value of BNDES equity (% participation times book value of equity, 1,000 US$)	0.835 (2.988)	0.000	16.205
%BNDES loans	BNDES loans divided by total loans	0.244 (0.271)	0.000	1.000
%BNDES equity	BNDES equity divided by total equity	0.011 (0.049)	0.000	0.450

Table 11-A1. (continued)

Variable	Description	Mean (std. dev.)	Min.	Max.
Political variables				
Donations	Number of candidates receiving donations by the firm in the last election	5.814 (17.972)	0	171
Donations for winners	Number of candidates who received donations and won the last election	3.320 (10.130)	0	89
Donations for losers	Number of candidates who received donations and lost the last election	2.488 (8.119)	0	82
Donations for winners – losers	Donations for winners minus donations for losers	0.832 (3.748)	−8	38
Controls				
Belongs to a group	Dummy variable coded 1 if the firm belongs to a business group	0.473 (0.499)	0	1
Ln(assets)	Logarithmic value of total assets (1,000 US$)	12.636 (1.686)	1.386	19.015
Leverage	Total debt divided by total assets	0.186 (0.174)	0.000	0.957
Foreign	Dummy variable coded 1 if the firm is foreign controlled	0.200 (0.400)	0	1

Source: Lazzarini et al. (2012).

12

Conclusions and Lessons

In this book, we document the reinvention of state capitalism that occurred around the world at the end of the twentieth century. The model of state capitalism in which the government was an owner and manager (the model we call *Leviathan as an entrepreneur*) came of age in the 1970s but reached a major crisis in the 1980s, when the global liquidity crunch put it to its ultimate test. Governments realized that with little control over what SOE managers did, and given their own temptation to use SOEs for political or social goals during the crisis (for example, to employ more workers than necessary or to have SOEs issue debt on behalf of the government), the model had become too costly to sustain. SOEs went from being a tool for development to being a drag on development and a burden on the government's balance sheet.

The economic shocks of the 1980s, we argue, not only created the need for reform, but also led multilateral organizations to induce countries with SOEs to improve their monitoring tools and their financial reporting. For instance, in 1986, the IMF published, for the first time, a guide to government financial statistics that clearly stated that an SOE's net profits or its net change in assets should be published as part of a government's financials. As governments in emerging markets restructured their debt to banks in the developed world and began the conversion of that debt into sovereign bonds tradable on the largest stock exchanges, they realized they had to shed the burden of a large number of money-losing SOEs. The privatization drive, therefore, helped these governments put their financials back in order and rid themselves of some of the most inefficient SOEs. And, as a way to attract minority private capital, many of the remaining state-controlled firms adopted new governance practices such as public listing and professional management. The mixture of minority private capital and publicly listed, state-controlled firms gave rise to a new model of state capitalism, *Leviathan as a majority investor.*

The 1990s wave of reform and privatization brought about yet another new model of state capitalism. Governments kept control of a large number of SOEs, but changed the way they ran their flagship firms, either corporatizing them or listing them on stock exchanges. The state retained minority equity positions in some of the privatized firms—sometimes with veto rights embedded in so-called golden shares—and began to make more use of sovereign wealth funds, holding companies, and development banks to acquire minority positions in private firms. In some cases, the state actively used minority investments to promote industrial consolidation or foster the expansion of domestic firms, leading to the emergence of new national champions. This transformation gave rise to the model of state capitalism that we call *Leviathan as a minority investor.*

The rise of Leviathan as a majority and minority investor changed the incentives inside SOEs. In some of the largest SOEs in emerging markets, the most common agency problems found in SOEs before the 1980s were reduced, although not eliminated. Partly as a result of these changes, SOEs in many countries have become profitable and voracious global players. Rankings of the world's largest corporations now include SOEs from the largest emerging markets. Many emerging multinationals combine private ownership with some form of minority state participation. The new picture of state capitalism is different from the pattern of state intervention in the pre-1980s command and mixed economies. State capitalism has evolved into a complex, multifaceted phenomenon characterized by an array of distinct models.

This is *not* to say, however, that these new models have always improved the performance of SOEs or that they make SOEs better than pure private ownership. Rather, we argue that we should stop seeing SOEs as monolithic entities full of agency problems and with weak governance. The book shows that it is possible to improve the governance arrangements of these firms and mitigate some of the most basic agency problems. Political intervention can also be tamed in countries in which there is a stronger rule of law, certain checks and balances to government action, and a somewhat autonomous, technical bureaucracy deciding when governments should invest in private firms. As we explained below, there are contingencies that might allow a government to choose each of those new models of state ownership to more effectively achieve its industrial policy or development objectives.

Conditions That Will Increase the Benefits of Each Model

We propose a contingent view of state capitalism. Instead of trying to prove that state investments in firms are universally superior or inferior to purely private investment, we see things in a different way. For us, SOEs should have their place in the economy if certain key contingencies are present. In many countries, the models of Leviathan as an entrepreneur, Leviathan as a majority investor, Leviathan as a minority investor, and pure private ownership are likely to coexist. Therefore, the agenda should be to examine the *conditions* that will make each model more prevalent and more conducive to firm-level efficiency and country-level development.

Obviously, the degree of state ownership in an economy is determined by political, ideological, and historical factors. For instance, countries with a political ideology leaning toward statism may rely more heavily on the Leviathan as an entrepreneur or majority investor models, while more liberal governments may prefer to minimize state ownership of firms. Even if we agree that ideological or political factors are crucially important to influence the choice of a given model, describing complex political interactions and how they change governmental objectives is beyond the scope of this book.

Therefore, taking these path-dependent effects as given, Table 12.1 explains three conditions that should influence the effectiveness of each model of state ownership. These conditions are (a) the extent of *externalities requiring economic coordination,* (b) the development of *local capital markets,* and (c) *additional institutional features* related to the quality of the bureaucracy, the rule of law, and the regulation of industries. Below we discuss each condition in detail.

Externalities Requiring Economic Coordination

When basic infrastructure is lacking, private entrepreneurs will find it extremely hard to do business. For instance, as we mentioned in Chapters 3 and 4, to develop a steel industry (whether private or public), there has to be infrastructure to supply the mill with coal and coke, and there have to be mines in operation, power sources, transportation infrastructure, and so on. As we explain in Chapters 4 and 10, in Brazil and in other countries the Leviathan as an entrepreneur model helped provide the first industrializing

Table 12.1. Conditions that make each model of state capitalism work more effectively to achieve industrial policy and development objectives

	Leviathan as an entrepreneur	Leviathan as a majority investor	Leviathan as a minority investor	Private ownership
Externalities requiring economic coordination	Pervasive market failure; difficult to coordinate	High to moderate	Moderate	Low
Development of local capital markets	Extremely shallow	Medium to high development with protections for minority shareholders	Moderately shallow, yet with the presence of firms with good governance practices that could become targets	Highly developed with strong investor protections
Additional institutional features	Technical bureaucracy running SOEs (restrained patronage)	Checks and balances against governmental interference in SOEs (effective regulation and some degree of within-sector competition)	Technical bureaucracy running bureaus responsible for industrial policy (restrained cronyism)	Effective government regulation

"big push" when private entrepreneurship and capital were either scarce or too afraid to invest.

When the need to coordinate different industries or actors is high to moderate, the model in which Leviathan is a majority investor may work well—for instance, when there are few or no private investors willing to take the risk of undertaking large projects with high spillovers. Then having the government take the majority of the downside risk may generate the push needed to get such projects started. Additionally, this model may work well if the government needs to forge alliances and share ownership of a company with foreign capital to, for example, develop a new industry or introduce foreign technology (Evans 1979; Cardoso and Faletto 2004).

In contrast, the Leviathan as a minority investor model will be more beneficial when the need of coordination is moderate—that is, when there are entrepreneurs willing to take the risk but they need the government to help finance the projects because private financial intermediaries see it as too risky or too hard to evaluate (see Chapter 8). The state may also become associated with private capital if there are opportunities to upgrade local capabilities or develop new sectors using an existing infrastructure. Over time, through learning externalities, private entrepreneurs may gradually step in and promote new firms and projects (Hausmann and Rodrik 2003). As the local economy becomes more and more diversified, with many interindustry linkages, the benefits of state capital to promote coordination will likely decrease, and hence private ownership should become more and more prevalent.

Development of Local Capital Markets

The industrial policy view posits that governmental action at the industrial level will be particularly useful when shallow underdeveloped capital markets preclude private entrepreneurial action (see Chapters 3 and 8). In our view, shallow capital markets not only make it difficult for private firms to access capital, but also make it harder for private investors to obtain company-level information to help them monitor and discipline managers. Moreover, stock markets with active investors and high liquidity reduce agency problems by making managers concerned about takeover threats. Less-developed capital markets make takeovers less likely and thus magnify governance conflicts (Dyck and Zingales 2004; Nenova 2005).

Thus, we think that Leviathan as an entrepreneur is more likely to be beneficial in countries in the very early stages of capital market development. The comparison of state-owned and private banks in India by Sarkar et al. (1998) lends some support to our claim. They conclude that, in the absence of well-functioning capital markets, private companies are not unambiguously superior to SOEs. Bortolotti et al. (2004) find that privatization tends to be positively associated with developed financial markets. That is, when capital markets are liquid and have strong investor protection, the benefits of private ownership tend to increase substantially.[1]

The model in which Leviathan is a minority shareholder, in contrast, will be more beneficial when capital markets are moderately shallow. We use the qualifier "moderately" because, without *some* degree of capital market development, governments may not have at their disposal a private sector with publicly traded securities that would allow for the channeling of resources and then the monitoring of those investments. As capital markets become more developed, the benefits of government investments in minority positions in private firms will likely diminish. Firms will have more and more access to external financing and alternative forms of capitalization such as IPOs, publicly traded debentures, and depository receipts. We therefore propose that the Leviathan as a minority investor model will be more appropriate in the intermediate stages of capital market development.

In Chapter 8, for instance, we found that the positive effect of BNDES's minority equity allocations on firm performance and investment was significant in the 1990s, but diminished thereafter. We argued that one likely explanation is that capital markets in Brazil grew rapidly after 2003. We also showed that the benefits of minority state equity largely depend on the governance of the target firm. In particular, our results suggest that governments should avoid investing in pyramidal business groups—which not only have internal capital markets at their disposal but also have the risk of minority shareholder expropriation (that is, state capital may be "tunneled" through the pyramid to support the controlling owners' private projects or to rescue other firms in the group). Therefore, the Leviathan as minority investor model should be more beneficial not only when capital markets are moderately shallow, but also when the state can find firms that have good governance but need extra capital to develop new projects.

As for the model in which Leviathan is a majority investor, we submit that it will work best when capital markets are fairly developed and minority shareholders are protected against expropriation. One may ask: If capital markets were developed, why would we need state majority investment in the first place? Recall, however, that the model in which Leviathan is a majority investor may emerge when the dominant political ideology is not in favor of full privatization and when the government still wants to keep a double bottom line for the SOEs it considers strategic. Thus, if full privatization is not an option, developed capital markets can help governments discipline SOE managers and attract extra capital.

Reforming SOE governance requires laws that protect shareholders. Public listing should improve SOE governance because it should reveal company-level information and allow more effective monitoring by external investors. Yet, as we document in Chapter 7, the problem is how to protect minority investors from the behavior of controlling shareholders, especially when the controlling party is the government itself. Therefore, both the majority investor and minority investor models will work better if there is less corporate abuse by controlling shareholders (Djankov et al. 2008). In fact, with better investor protections, governments will find it that much easier to attract investors to purchase minority positions in SOEs traded on stock exchanges.

Additional Institutional Features

We see the Leviathan as an entrepreneur model as problematic when it comes to accountability because governments may use SOEs to extract quasi-rents for political purposes and pet projects. For instance, the literature on the so-called "natural resource curse" emphasizes that abundant oil or mineral reserves can be used to fund and perpetuate authoritarian regimes (e.g., Sachs and Warner 2001; Ross 2012).

Thus, the performance of the Leviathan as an entrepreneur model should improve when governments prioritize the selection of professional, competent, and public-minded managers. Management of SOEs, in this view, should be delegated to public servants with a sense of duty and with inclinations toward rectitude and professionalism (Wilson 1989). Although, at first glance, such a reform might exacerbate the agency problem—that is, professional managers might feel less accountable to their governments—managerial autonomy may create its own incentives for the development of a skilled bureaucratic class with long careers in their own industries. Trebat (1983, 79) claims that "a competent staff can develop, over time, a reputation for professionalism that discourages interference by less-well-trained civil servants in the ministry."

In Chapter 5, for instance, we empirically tested how important CEO selection is to SOEs and found that managers educated at top local universities outperform other managers. If part of the variation in the performance of these firms is explained by the abilities and networks of their CEOs, then governments should realize they need to choose good CEOs to keep their SOEs from becoming a drag on the public finances in normal times and perhaps to reduce problems during a crisis. This, in turn, requires the development of cadres of capable managers from elite universities. Several governments in South Asia have excelled for decades at selecting and training their bureaucrats and SOE employees. By making entrance into public service competitive and by continuing to push employees to acquire skills, these governments have mitigated part of the management problems that plagued traditional SOEs.[2]

In the model in which Leviathan is a majority investor, having a strong rule of law (besides strong investor protections) will be fundamental so that private investors who are minority shareholders can both monitor the firm's managers and counterbalance the majority power of the government. That is, in order to attract private investors, the "grabbing hand" of the state needs to be restrained, both inside the corporation (through better corporate governance) and outside the corporation (through an independent judiciary and regulatory agencies). For instance, if the state abuses its power as a controlling shareholder and there are no courts to stop such actions, this model of state capitalism will be less efficient at generating managerial autonomy and a single bottom line for SOEs. As we discussed in Chapter 7, the national oil companies that are recognized as more efficient have more sophisticated corporate governance systems and tend to operate in countries with stronger rule of law and stronger checks and balances from independent regulatory bodies. Analyzing European utilities, Bortolotti et al. (forthcoming) also find that effective regulation increases the market value of SOEs.

A caveat—also discussed in Chapter 7—is that when an SOE pursues a double bottom line, there is always the risk for minority private investors that the governments will intervene for political gain. As long as the rules are relatively stable and there are checks and balances for governmental actions, private investors may accept that part of an SOE's strategy will be to meet certain social goals while at the same time guaranteeing satisfactory profitability. But when a government frequently changes the type and intensity of its intervention, private (minority) investors will become increasingly reluctant to provide SOEs with extra capital.

Good antitrust regulation may also ensure that SOEs constantly pursue efficiency gains. Several authors have stressed that SOE performance is affected by the competitive environment (Bartel and Harrison 2005; Boardman and Vining 1989; Caves and Christensen 1980; Lioukas et al. 1993; Vickers and Yarrow 1988). When SOEs have to compete for contracts or clients, there is less room for excessive governmental interference; in particular, there is less leeway to transfer resources from SOEs to the government, which would render the firms less able to invest and compete. Consistent with this hypothesis, Bartel and Harrison's (2005) empirical analysis of private and public firms in Indonesia reveals that "there may be an agency problem associated with public-sector ownership, but only when firms are given access to government financing or protected from import competition or foreign ownership" (p. 142). The authors point out that reforms that enhance the competitive pressure on SOEs can be useful and may be easier to implement in countries where there are strong objections to privatization.

The model in which the government is a minority shareholder is likely to work in countries where the policy makers who choose those investments have a well-established bureaucratic ethos of professionalism and public-mindedness (Evans 1995; Williamson 1999). This is because, as Ades and Di Tella (1997) show in their theoretical model, there is risk of corruption when bureaucrats are in charge of selecting national champions to receive government favors such as subsidized credit. In Chapter 11, we found that although BNDES is not systematically bailing out bad firms, some of its loans seem to be going to firms with superior political connections. That is why the literature on industrial policy emphasizes how important it is that decisions of where to invest government money be in the hands of a skilled technical staff with superior analytical capabilities and a sense of professionalism in their policy-making duties (Evans 1995; Schneider 1991). If government investments follow clear criteria by which to evaluate targets and include disciplining mechanisms to end capital injections when performance is poor, the negative effect of cronyism in this model of state ownership should be greatly reduced.

Finally, the benefits of private ownership will significantly increase when governments craft effective regulatory systems that promote investment but at the same time address potential distortions that might occur when firms neglect performance dimensions valued by the population (Bortolotti and Perotti 2007). Wallsten (2001), for instance, examines the privatization of telecom in Africa and Latin America and observes that while privatization in tandem with effective regulatory systems appeared to improve a host of service performance dimensions, privatization alone resulted in lower service penetration to the population.

Lessons

Lessons for Governments

This book has many lessons for policy makers. The main message, in light of our discussion above, is that governments should act *selectively,* aligning each model of state organization to particular conditions in order to increase its performance (see Table 12.1). For instance, the Leviathan as a minority investor model seems to work more effectively to solve capital constraints for private companies when financial markets are moderately shallow. State equity investment in firms that have access to domestic and foreign financing will be less effective at generating capital expenditures at home and at promoting latent, profitable projects. The Leviathan as a majority investor model, in contrast, seems to be more appropriate when there are checks and balances to outright political interference. Reforming SOEs by listing them in order to improve transparency and governance will not be enough if governments still have the temptation and the means to intervene in the management in ways that destroy value for minority shareholders. Governments should be aware of the reputational consequences of their interventions, especially if interventions can inflict financial harm on minority shareholders.

From Chapter 2, it should be obvious that while privatization may solve many of the problems associated with SOEs, many new problems can arise when regulation is poor and when there is residual temptation to intervene. Furthermore, governments find it hard, for political reasons, to privatize flagship SOEs, national oil companies, and other public utilities. Under such constraints, it may make sense to reform rather than replace SOEs, at the same time creating checks and balances against discretionary intervention.

Another important consideration is that the models of state capitalism we have discussed are not mutually exclusive. In many countries, various models coexist and even reinforce one another. For instance, private firms can create competitive pressure for SOEs and help improve their efficiency; and the state may pursue minority investments in private start-ups to promote entry and the creation of new capabilities. Although the public debate is rife with polarized discussions on the merits of governmental intervention versus free markets, in reality there are diverse forms of state capitalism that can address distinct types of market failure and even help promote economic development.

Lessons for Investors in SOEs

Investors, too, should recognize the benefits and risks of the various models of state capitalism. In the Leviathan as a majority investor model, investors should understand that SOEs typically pursue a double bottom line and that there will be times when Leviathan cannot resist the temptation to intervene and will abuse its power as controlling shareholder to tunnel away SOE profits for its own political purposes. However, this does not mean that SOEs should be avoided as investment targets. They can be extremely valuable because they usually benefit from natural resources and large public projects. One possibility is to target only SOEs with superior governance and a track record of minimal governmental intervention, but the irony is that such firms may be overpriced, and the lack of intervention may be temporary (see, for example, the case of Petrobras in Chapter 7). Therefore, investors should preferably target SOEs with the potential to yield valuable rents (i.e., with latent projects) and with signs of reduced political intervention that are not fully incorporated in the market valuation of those SOEs. Monitoring the ideology of the government in place and the political environment influencing the government's willingness to intervene seems to be critical.

In the Leviathan as a minority investor mode, investors should target stand-alone firms with growth potential—stand-alone in order to avoid the risk of tunneling—and evaluate the risk of residual interference. This should require a detailed examination of the shareholdings of different vehicles of state ownership (development banks, pension funds, and so on), as well as a careful analysis of the possibility of collusion among state and non-state actors. We saw in Chapter 9 that such collusion can greatly facilitate interference in firms with minority state capital. In addition, the risk of residual interference is higher in industries with high quasi-rents—precisely the preferred target of many investors. Thus, understanding how the various vehicles of minority state ownership work, especially with respect to their permeability to state interference, becomes particularly critical.

Lessons for Private Companies Competing or Transacting with SOEs

We argued that being a minority shareholder in an SOE, especially in a strategic sector such as oil or mining, is risky. However, governmental intervention can also affect other firms in the same or adjacent sectors. For example, as long as the government of Brazil controlled the price of gasoline, the profitability of companies producing ethanol, one form of which can be used as a substitute for gasoline, would be severely affected. Firms likely to be affected by SOEs in the market should therefore examine the objectives of those SOEs and the political conditions and trends influencing the likelihood of intervention.

Another important source of risk is when firms encounter national champions in the marketplace. The selection of national champions is sometimes based on ideological or geopolitical objectives rather than purely economic criteria; and governmental support for those champions can greatly distort markets. Firms not receiving equivalent support will therefore find it difficult to compete on a level playing field with national champions. In this environment, private firms need to understand the channels of state support to those champions—either through development banks or other funds— and monitor trends in the extent and type of governmental interference. For instance, it will be extremely risky to pursue an aggressive expansion strategy when massive governmental support leads champions to overinvest in their sectors. Alternatively, some private firms may try to create their own connections to receive support. However, this move can be equally risky, given that, as we saw in Chapter 9, governments may use their minority investments to meddle with the firm's strategy and management.

Choosing the right partner in a context of state intervention can also be challenging. Since the transformation of state capitalism in the 1980s and 1990s, Western multinational enterprises doing business in emerging markets have had to be careful about whom they partner with in their host countries. This is particularly important in terms of how they secure contracts with domestic firms that may have the government as a minority shareholder. For instance, as part of the Foreign Corrupt Practices Act (U.S.), the

Anti-Bribery Act (UK), and other OECD laws, companies cannot bribe officers of a company to get a contract, even if that company has only minority government ownership. In 2010, the U.S. Department of Justice fined the French company Alcatel-Lucent for irregular payments to Telekom Malaysia, a telecommunications firm in which the Malaysian government held 43 percent of equity.

As multinationals commonly use intermediaries and agents to get contracts, the complication for these firms will be how to find out who the ultimate owner of a corporation is. Remember from Chapters 1 and 2 that governments sometimes have holding companies that in turn own corporations that then hold shares in private companies. Because there is no financial regulation forcing the disclosure of a company's ultimate government ownership, determining whether or not the government is an owner can be problematic. A careful examination of the nature and motivations of the ultimate shareholders becomes critical.

A New Agenda

Our proposed taxonomy of varieties of state capitalism and the empirical findings we present suggest that future research should examine alternative models of state capitalism in a more nuanced way, identifying the conditions under which each model is most likely to be profitable, productive, and contribute to a nation's welfare. There are plenty of opportunities to examine in more detail the effects of SOE governance reforms and the performance implications of minority state investments in various countries.

There is also an opportunity to better explore channels of state capital not covered in detail here. For instance, although in Chapter 2 we documented the rise of SWFs and other state-related institutional investors (such as pension funds), we did not pursue a deeper discussion of their benefits and risks for state investment and the implications of such investment for receiving firms. We expect the results to be similar to what we found for BNDES's investments in Brazil, also because SWFs and pension funds tend to be active investors.

Additionally interesting questions can arise from examining the effects of investments by national funds and development banks when they allocate their investments beyond their home countries. By 2011, Norway's sovereign wealth fund had equity investments in around 8,400 firms throughout the world (Chambers et al. 2011), and cross-border investments can bring diplomatic tension. In 2006, the partial acquisition of Thailand's Shin Corporation by Singapore's Temasek fund stirred protests against foreign ownership and even contributed to a local coup (Goldstein and Pananond 2008). Do these funds bring advantages to host countries? Do they provide more benefits in less developed countries? We did not touch upon these issues, especially on how state-backed organizations can affect foreign investment and foreign relations.

Also, given that most of our chapters use data from Brazil, some of our results may be idiosyncratic to that country and to its particular mechanisms of minority or majority state participation. Thus, future work can replicate or adapt our analyses to other developing and emerging economies, examining the effects of other vehicles of state capitalism and other types of outcomes. In particular, we believe that we need much more work examining why minority state equity remains generally widespread. In Chapter 8, we hypothesized that those minority stakes can help firms subject to scarce external financing. But then how can we explain the presence of minority stakes by the state in more developed economies with active and liquid capital markets (e.g., OECD 2005)? A possible explanation, discussed earlier, is that such stakes exist because of political pressure against total privatization. If this is the case, then we can hypothesize that a change in the ideology of the dominant political coalition may influence the extent and reach of minority stakes. Testing alternative explanations for the presence of majority and minority government investments can be another possible avenue of future research.

In addition, we need more studies of the potential risk of misallocation associated with state capital. For instance, our analysis of BNDES's loans in Chapter 11 shows that large firms in Brazil are not using BNDES loans to invest in projects that would otherwise go unfunded. In fact, it seems as if BNDES is lending to high-performing firms that will repay the loans (and make executives at BNDES look like diligent managers). If this is the case, then governments need to more carefully choose their target firms. On the one hand, funding such state-owned banks can generate a series of distortions, such as an increase in payroll taxes. In particular, if the government borrows to fund the bank or uses savings that could be deployed elsewhere, it may be crowding out private investment. This problem is likely aggravated if, by lending to large firms, the government inhibits the development of a private market for long-term credit. Under such a scenario, private banks may become reluctant to cater to smaller, higher-risk firms that should be the natural targets of development banks. Yet we need more studies to examine alternative channels of misallocation associated with subsidized capital (e.g., Antunes et al. 2012; Cull et al. 2013).

Last but not least, we did not address a key outcome potentially affected by state capital: *innovation* (Mahmood and Rufin 2005). Some authors have forcefully proposed that the state was instrumental in fostering basic research in various sectors such as computing, health, and agriculture (Graham 2010; Mazzucato 2011; Mowery 1984). Aghion et al. (2013) found that the presence of "institutional" investors can positively affect innovation, perhaps because those investors can increase managerial incentives to execute riskier, long-term innovation projects. As we discussed in Chapter 3, the state itself is supposed to be a long-term, "patient" investor. Therefore, it would be important to study if different levels of state ownership yield higher levels of innovation, or if the pressures of politicians to pursue political goals or other short-term objectives tame such efforts.

Along these lines, one could also examine the effect of state ownership on R&D expenditures, patents, and knowledge spillovers across firms (or within firms before and after they receive government investments). Such an examination may help governments elucidate how to spend their funds to support innovation. For instance, should governments invest in firms directly, or should they just promote the infrastructure for private firms to pursue such research? Should governments use loans or equity to fund new entrepreneurs? Which conditions will favor the adoption of each model?

In sum, future research should delve into the various models of state capitalism, as well as its various potential outcomes, instead of seeing state capitalism as a monolithic model opposed to free markets. The debate on whether Leviathan should or should not participate in the economy is irrelevant, because in many countries the state is an important player and will not be going away anytime soon. A more interesting and useful agenda will be to examine the conditions under which Leviathan can work well—how to make the "grabbing hand" of the state a collection of "helping hands" conducive to industrial and economic development.

Notes

1. Introduction

1. For further details of JBS's acquisitions see Bell and Ross (2008). For a discussion of BNDES's support for JBS see Almeida (2009).

2. We conceptualize SOEs as *enterprises;* that is, they produce and sell goods and services. Such companies should be distinguished from government entities in charge of providing public services (such as courts, the police, social security, and national health services), which often do not have a corporate form and depend directly on orders from government officials.

3. Our work thus contributes to the evolving literature on the varieties of capitalism (Hall and Soskice 2001; Schneider and Soskice 2009) by introducing a taxonomy of the ways in which states intervene in the management of firms. Yet, we are concerned with variation in ownership and corporate governance at the firm level, while the literature on varieties of capitalism examines the coordination of economies as a whole—the connections between governments, firms, and labor. This literature has paid little attention to state ownership, despite the fact that some of the largest firms in OECD countries still have the government as a shareholder. One exception is Gourevitch and Shinn (2005), who explicitly link the active role of governments as investors in publicly traded firms to greater coordination among economic actors.

4. "China Buys Up the World," *Economist,* November 13, 2010. See also the discussion in the *Economist's* special issue on state capitalism (A. Wooldridge 2012)

5. We made these calculations using Capital IQ data on market capitalization and ownership and then tracing ultimate ownership. That is, for each firm, we trace who is the controlling shareholder, and, if it is a company, we then track the ultimate ownership of that company. In China, SASAC and other state holding companies are the ultimate owners and controllers of much of the stock market; in India, the government and Life Insurance Corporation own equity in hundreds of firms; in Brazil, the government has direct stakes in some companies and

uses its development bank, BNDES, to control others; in Russia, the government uses its flagship SOEs to own other firms. See Chapter 2 for some examples.

6. Among the largest transactions were the IPOs of Agricultural Bank of China, which raised $22.1 billion, and Industrial and Commercial Bank of China, which raised $21.9 billion, and the secondary issue of shares of Petrobras, which on paper raised $70 billion. For the IPO list see "State Capitalism's Global Reach: New Masters of the Universe; How State Enterprise Is Spreading," *Economist*, January 21, 2012. For details of the Petrobras offer see Dwyer (2011).

7. Morgan Stanley, "EEMEA & Latam Equity Strategy: State Controlled Companies—Where to Invest Now," Morgan Stanley Research Europe, May 24, 2012, p. 1.

8. All lists taken from the *Fortune* "Global 500" web page, at http://money.cnn .com/magazines/fortune/global500/ (accessed March 3, 2012).

9. Note that we emphasize that comparisons are *on average*. Under certain conditions, firms with state ownership or control perform as well as private firms or even better, for example when firms face competitive environments (Bartel and Harrison 2005). Also, SOEs seem to perform as well as private firms do when they follow the management and corporate governance practices of private firms (Kole and Mulherin 1997).

10. The term "grabbing hand" comes from Shleifer and Vishny (1998) and represents the idea that governments or bureaucrats run state-owned enterprises for political objectives rather than to solve market failures or to make profits.

11. In that sense we contribute to an existing literature on both the determinants of private participation in former state-owned enterprises and the possible implications of partial privatizations (Ramamurti 2000; Doh 2000; Doh et al. 2004; Dharwadkar et al. 2000; Gupta 2005).

12. In fact, the process of learning and experimentation with SOE reform does not seem that long when compared to the slow process of transformation of the corporate governance regime of the largest corporations in the United States. At the turn of the twenty-first century, investors were still surprised by corporate scandals, by generous executive compensation packages, by boards of directors that were not monitoring managers effectively, and so on. For a discussion of this process of transformation in private firms see chapter 3 of Khurana (2002).

13. Some papers comparing the performance of SOEs and private firms acknowledge that there are different forms of state ownership. They usually divide SOEs into (fully) state-owned, SOEs with private ownership, and private firms, and they usually find that private firms consistently perform best of all (Boardman and Vining 1989; Gupta 2005; Dewenter and Malatesta 2001). These works, however, do not look at the variation in the corporate governance arrangements of privatized firms. They also ignore the implications of minority ownership.

14. A good example of the shades of gray in between full state ownership and private ownership is in the analysis of privatization of telecommunications com-

panies by Doh et al. (2004). There they explain why private investors will prefer to invest more or less to partner with the government.

15. For examples of state-controlled pyramids in Europe see Bortolotti and Faccio (2009).

16. This hybrid model of state capitalism should also be distinguished from hybrid *public-private partnerships* crafted to execute specific infrastructure projects or to provide public services such as water, transport, and prisons (Bennett and Iossa 2006; Cabral et al. 2010).

17. For instance, a series of papers studies how lending in state-owned commercial banks is correlated with political cycles (Cole 2009; Sapienza 2004; Dinç 2005) and how entrepreneurs with political connections are more likely to obtain loans from state-owned banks than the average entrepreneur (Bailey et al. 2011; Khwaja and Mian 2005). The literature on state-owned commercial banks in Brazil is particularly extensive (Baer and Nazmi 2000; Makler 2000; Ness 2000; Beck et al. 2005) but focuses largely on explaining why they were privatized and how well they performed before and after privatization.

18. Millward (2000) is one of the exceptions in the literature. He shows that, before the 1980s, productivity in SOEs in the United Kingdom was in fact higher than productivity in comparable American private firms.

2. The Rise and Fall of Leviathan as an Entrepreneur

1. The relationship between crises and state ownership in Latin America is explored in Marichal (2011).

2. The literature on IRI is too long to summarize here. For further reference see the two-volume history of IRI (Castronovo 2012; Amatori 2012) or the recent summary of the history of IRI (Conte and Piluso 2011).

3. Sharp (1946, 4) notes that SOEs dominated Poland's economic system even before the war. In 1938, the Polish government owned 100 percent of the "production of potassium salts, alcohol, tobacco, aircraft, automobiles, air transportation, post, telegraph, and radio," as well as over 90 percent of maritime transportation, railways, dyestuff production, and fire insurance. The Polish government also had majority control of the salt company and of telephony, smelting, insurance, spas, and health resorts. Additionally, the government had minority ownership in companies producing gas, coal, chemicals, lumber, and tools.

4. See tables 14.7 and 14.8 in Millward (2005, 277–279).

5. Although we do not have detailed data on nationalizations in Europe after World War II, they also played an important role in the rise of state capitalism. While in developing countries, nationalization was a way to limit foreign ownership of firms, especially ownership by firms of former colonial powers, nationalization in Europe had a protectionist tone and was also a consequence of poor performance by companies that governments had championed.

6. All of these figures come from R. P. Short's excellent survey of the size of state-owned enterprises in mixed economies. See Short (1984).

7. The Japanese government also tried to export its model of economic planning. According to Mary Shirley, who served as public enterprise adviser and senior adviser at the World Bank during the 1980s, officials at Japan's Ministry of International Trade and Industry were trying to export their model and were disbursing foreign aid to support SOE reforms in developing countries (interview with Mary Shirley, Bethesda, MD, January 2012).

8. For an example of how those weighted averages worked in India see Trivedi (1989).

9. Interview with Mary Shirley, public enterprise adviser and senior adviser at the World Bank, Bethesda, MD, January 2012.

10. We explain the causes and consequences of the 1982 Latin American debt crisis in more detail in Chapter 6.

11. Interview with John Nellis, Bethesda, MD, January 11, 2013.

12. Ibid.

13. For a discussion of the reasons why the IMF introduced these new measures see "A Manual on Government Financial Statistics (GFSM 1986)," at http://www.imf.org/external/pubs/ft/gfs/manual/1986/eng/index.htm. The World Bank also asked countries that received support for SOE reform to follow a similar way of reporting SOE financials. See the guide in Shirley (1989).

14. The structure of Brady bonds varied according to the type of instrument each bank chose. U.S. treasury secretary Nicholas Brady made such bonds palatable for foreign investors by offering, in exchange for the original claim, "full collateralization of principal using U.S. Treasury zero-coupon bonds, which countries bought using reserves and financing from international financial institutions . . . in addition, reserves [from developing countries] were placed in escrow to cover any possible interruption of interest payments for up to one year" (Sturzenegger and Zettelmeyer 2006, 18).

15. For detailed data on privatizations by country during the 1980s see Berg and Shirley (1987).

16. We think the figures reported by the OECD (2005, Table 2.3) seriously underreport the number of SOEs. In Germany, for instance, a report on privatization showed that, in 2003, there were still 192 state-owned companies, with about 159,000 employees. See Jens Hermann Treuner, "Privatisation: The German Example," PowerPoint presentation for the INTOSAI Working Group on the Audit of Privatization, at www.nao.org.uk/nao/intosai/wgap/10thmeeting/10thgermany.ppt (accessed June 6, 2012).

17. OECD (2005, 34). It is difficult to know how much control these governments have with their minority positions, because in some cases they have "golden shares" that give them veto power over certain decisions. For further discussion

of the complexity of trying to ascertain a government's share of equity see Bortolotti and Faccio (2009).

18. In Brazil, a notable exception is Trebat (1983).

19. This is based on an analysis of LIC's investments in the privatizations (divestments) of NPC, NMDC, SJVN, Engineers India, Power Grid Corporation, the Shipping Corporation of India, PTC India Financial Services, and ONGC. LIC had a cumulative loss of 24 percent in these investments by April 2012. For data on the government of India's and LIC's ownership, as well as on the performance of LIC's investments, see Vaidyanathan and Musacchio (2012).

20. See http://1-million-dollar-blog.com/top-300-worlds-largest-pension-funds -2012/ (accessed April 8, 2013).

21. On the evolution and professionalization of SWFs see Abdelal et al. (2008) and Truman (2010).

22. Information from Mubadala's web site, http://mubadala.ae/portfolio/ (accessed May 17, 2012).

23. Data from http://www.temasekreview.com.sg/portfolio/major_companies .html (accessed May 17, 2012). There is controversy regarding the role of Temasek; Goldstein and Pananond (2008), for instance, suggest that it acts more like an SOHC than an SWF.

3. Views on State Capitalism

1. See Yeyati et al. (2004) for a discussion focused on state-owned banks.

2. For an English-language history of the Brazilian government's intervention in the ethanol market see Cordonnier (2008). (In Portuguese see Bray et al. 2000; Santos 1993.) For the development of cellulosic ethanol by Petrobras see "Cellulosic Ethanol in Brazil by 2013: Petrobras, KL Energy Partner" in *BioBasedDigest*, http://www.biofuelsdigest.com/bdigest/2010/08/24/cellulosic-ethanol-in-brazil -by-2013-petrobras-kl-energy-partner/ (accessed July 3, 2012).

3. Focusing on China, Nee and Opper (2007) describe what they call "politicized capitalism," characterized by complex interactions between governments and private actors. However, while the authors see politicized capitalism as a situation of "disequilibrium" (p. 96), we submit that political exchanges have been at the helm of hybrid state capitalism, which has been a more or less stable form in several countries.

4. It is not clear that this result holds for developing countries, where nondemocratic governments carried out some of the most thorough privatization programs. Moreover, recent evidence from India shows that the government delayed privatization in regions where the governing party faced more competition from the opposition (Dinç and Gupta 2011).

5. This is obviously a contentious issue because there are plenty of agency problems in private firms that even in the most sophisticated markets in the world have not been eliminated (Djankov et al. 2008).

6. We heard this opinion in interviews with Banco do Brasil officials. This also happens in other countries; see, for example, Khanna et al. (2009) and Musacchio et al. (2011).

4. The Evolution of State Capitalism in Brazil

1. For the history of railway subsidies in Brazil see Summerhill (2003), Duncan (1932), and Saes (1981). For a history of the gradual increase in state ownership of railways in Brazil see Musacchio (2009, 250–251).

2. In 1965, President Castelo Branco opened the refining sector to private competition. Evans (1979) describes how the private sector participated, sometimes in partnership with Petrobras, in different refinery projects in the 1970s (see esp. chap. 5).

3. Firms were so independent that when it came to the selection of CEOs for some of the largest SOEs, Motta (1980) argues that "the ministry [in charge of regulating it]—the majority of times—does not have the power to name the president or directors [of the SOE]," because the top executives of the firm were "politically more important than the minister himself" (p. 75).

4. We thank Elio Gaspari for calling our attention to this memorandum and providing us with a copy.

5. For the difficulties SOEs faced after 1982 and for the changes in regulation see Werneck (1987), Trebat (1983), SEST reports, and Decree no. 92,005, November 28, 1985, which orders the reduction in payroll outlays by 10 percent between 1985 and 1986. In theory, CEOs and members of the board could lose their jobs if they did not meet their targets; in practice, the decree was rarely enforced.

6. Since 1976, the Brazilian government has required companies to "correct" the value of their fixed assets according to inflation, using an official index that often underestimated inflation. Companies have to revalue their fixed assets using an official inflation index, and the amounts that those adjustments represent have to be increased to the value of shareholders' capital. See Law 6,404, December 15, 1976.

7. Interview with Delfim Netto, former minister of finance and minister of planning, São Paulo, Brazil, August 2012.

8. Ibid.

9. For a more detailed discussion of the change of beliefs and in entitlements and how that led to deficits and economic instability see Alston et al. (2013).

10. For an excellent summary of how each plan was implemented and how it worked or ultimately failed see Fishlow (2011, chap. 3).

11. This section is based largely on Pinheiro (2002).

12. For more detail on the privatization program and the "currencies" used for the initial stage of the PND see BNDES (2002b).

13. See Fishlow (2011) for slightly different estimates of the privatization receipts, esp. chap. 3.

14. For more detail see the new Joint Stock Company Law no. 10,303 of 2001. In particular, Section IV on controlling shareholders and Section XIX on "Mixed Enterprises" or SOEs.

15. See Bovespa's decision at http://cvmweb.cvm.gov.br/SWB/Sistemas/SPW /FRelevantes/Arq/68EC0BBFF2944A4E8D6B71D812B5E244.pdf.

16. See "Sabesp entrará no Novo Mercado," *Estado de São Paulo,* January 26, 2001.

5. Leviathan as a Manager

1. We know that the CEOs of many publicly traded SOEs are selected by either the board of directors or the shareholders. But even in those companies, as we argue in the next chapter, it is very common to see the government appointing members of the board and thus indirectly selecting the CEO.

2. In fact, the reasons to fire CEOs in SOEs are not that different from what the literature finds for private companies (Virany et al. 1992; Pfeffer and Salancik 1978).

3. Total factor productivity (TFP) is the contribution to output that comes from improvements in the efficiency with which factors of production are used.

4. The CEOs we include in this sample differ only slightly from the other CEOs in our database. For instance, CEOs who switched firms were more likely to be educated abroad or to have a graduate degree. Yet only 22 percent of them attended an elite university.

5. Additionally, military academies in Brazil have a long tradition of being progressive institutions teaching officers leadership skills that can be applied both on the battlefield and in politics. The two first presidents of Brazil (in the 1890s) were military officers. Getúlio Vargas, president of Brazil from 1930 to 1945 and from 1950 to 1955, was also a graduate of a military academy.

6. Few CEOs in our sample studied abroad, and those who did usually also had a bachelor's degree from a Brazilian university. CEOs of SOEs who studied abroad *did not* attend top-tier universities.

7. Data from Schneider (1991), p. 53.

8. Companies had to revalue their fixed assets using an official inflation index, and the amounts that those adjustments represented had to be increased to the value of shareholders' capital. See Law 6,404, December 15, 1976.

9. The IGP-DI is a price index calculated by the Fundação Getúlio Vargas using the arithmetic mean of the wholesale price index (IPA), the consumer price index (IPC), and the construction price index (INCC). The "DI" means it only

looks at internal prices and does not take into account the prices of exports. Our logic in choosing this index was that we wanted to use a deflator that would over-estimate inflation. Yet, even with this index, our data in the late 1980s—the period of hyperinflation—have large jumps.

6. The Fall of Leviathan as an Entrepreneur in Brazil

1. Unfortunately, given the historical nature of our data, we were unable to obtain precise information on the exact moment when the government replaced the CEO of an SOE or when the board of a private company replaced its CEO; neither do we have the reasons for the change. We only compute this variable when we have information on the name of the CEO in two subsequent years; otherwise, we treat the information as missing. We also exclude a few cases in which SOEs reported two CEOs. For a description of our CEO database see Chapter 5.

2. A drawback of this approach is that without interactions, the effect of the political change variables can be confounded with year effects. Therefore, in split-sample regressions we omit the year dummies because they are collinear with events of presidential change.

3. The coefficients of the reported interactive variables represent the reactions of SOEs relative to private companies.

4. Interview with Delfim Netto, São Paulo, Brazil, August 2012.

7. Taming Leviathan?

1. The strategy of privatizing minority equity positions in large SOEs was first suggested as a strategy governments should follow to signal to voters their commitment to privatization and markets by Perotti and Biais (2002). The idea was that the median voter would turn into a shareholder, and politicians would gain political support the more they committed to the new regime of partial privatization.

2. "Ministros e diretor da ANP vão prestar esclarecimentos no Senado," *Revista Época*, August 4, 2011.

3. The details of the transaction are publicly known in Brazil. We base our analysis on the detailed work of Dwyer (2011).

4. Some of these arguments came out in the press, but we also heard some of them from one of the most influential minority investors, who preferred to remain anonymous.

5. "Graça defende correção do preço dos combustíveis," *Agência Estado*, February 27, 2012.

6. "O longo e pedregoso caminho que Graça Foster começou a trilhar," *Valor Econômico*, July 20, 2012.

8. Leviathan as a Minority Shareholder

1. For a note on GM's purchase of equity in Peugeot, see Jonathan Karl, "An American Auto Bailout—for France?" at http://abcnews.go.com/blogs/politics/2012 /03/an-american-auto-bailout-for-france/ (accessed July 10, 2012).

2. In this chapter we present a very simple approach to think about government minority equity positions. We pursue more complex empirical tests in Inoue et al. (2013).

3. Still another possibility is that the government, despite being a minority shareholder, will have an ability to influence the firms with minority state equity. This problem of *residual* state interference in the Leviathan as a minority investor model is discussed at length in Chapter 9.

4. The literature on the institutional conditions that inhibit or promote financial market development is extremely large (among the most relevant papers see Beck and Levine 2005; Haber et al. 2008; La Porta et al. 1998; Lamoreaux 1994; Engerman and Davis 2003; Haber 2012; Hoffman et al. 2000).

5. Dyck and Zingales (2004) called this abuse of minority shareholders "private benefits of corporate control" and calculated it using the difference in price between voting and nonvoting shares at the time of a corporate takeover.

6. Other institutional contingencies may also affect the benefits of state versus private ownership. Assessing infrastructure projects in the telecommunication sector, Doh et al. (2004) find that private ownership increases with the extent of local economic development and market liberalization. In a different vein, Vaaler and Schrage (2009) argue that minority state ownership may be beneficial because it will signal a willingness of the state to support private owners of the privatized firms. They also argue and find that this positive effect will be reduced when there is political stability in the country.

7. We compiled the financial and ownership data from the databases Economática, Interinvest, and Valor Grandes Grupos. Further financials and most of our ownership information were compiled from the reports companies have to file with the Brazilian Securities and Exchange Commission (Comissão de Valores Mobiliários, or CVM).

8. Thus, cases with $q = 1$ indicate that a unit increase in total assets is expected to yield an increase in firm market value by more than one monetary unit. In other words, the firm can create market value by expanding its assets (David et al. 2006). Tobin's q is proxied by the market value of stocks plus the book value of debt, divided by the book value of total assets.

9. Interview in the *Veja* magazine, July 27, 2011.

10. In our analyses, we used lagged values of *ROA, Leverage,* and *Fixed* because BNDES will likely take past performance into account in its allocation decisions. Also, given that *BNDES* is a discrete variable, and we want to control for unobservable firm-specific characteristics that may affect BNDES's choice of companies in

which to participate, we used the so-called conditional Logit model (Chamberlain 1980), which is a fixed-effect specification for discrete data. To check whether effects change when we consider the percentage of direct stakes held by BNDES, we ran additional OLS regressions with fixed effects using our continuous measure, *BNDESDir,* as a dependent variable. See Inoue et al. (2013).

11. There would obviously be a problem if there was a universe of firms in which BNDESPAR invests that are not in our sample. Our sample of equity investments, however, covers almost 70 percent of the total equity held by BNDES in 2009. Therefore, we have to assume that the investments that are not in our sample performed in the same way as those in our sample in order to generalize our results. Unfortunately there are private equity investments in non-listed firms that we cannot capture in our database.

12. See "Continua financiamento da Globo iniciado em 1997," *Gazeta Mercantil,* July 11, 1999; "Mídia nacional acumula dívida de R\$ 10 bilhões," *Folha de São Paulo,* February 15, 2004.

13. Interview in the newspaper article "Para BNDES, ajuda à Globo não é garantida," *O Estado de São Paulo,* March 17, 2002.

14. See "Securitization of Eletrobras Debt Will Benefit Energy Sector," *Gazeta Mercantil Invest News,* November 10, 1997; "Agora, Eletrobrás quer pagar à vista dívida de Furnas com geradoras," *Folha de São Paulo,* December 28, 2000; "Eletrobras Wants to Measure 'True Amount of Excess Costs,' " *Gazeta Mercantil Invest News,* January 29, 1997; and "Dez anos de Petrobras e Eletrobrás," *O Estado de São Paulo,* September 16, 2007.

15. "Brazil's Eletrobras Transfers Shares of Light to BNDESpar," *Bloomberg,* August 1999.

16. From Aracruz's Annual Report and Form 20-F, submitted to the U.S. Securities Exchange Commission.

17. From Spers (1997).

18. "BNDES Explains Director's Position in Aracruz," *Gazeta Mercantil Invest News,* April 24, 1997.

9. Leviathan's Temptation

1. In the organizational economics literature, this bargaining problem is commonly referred to as the "holdup" problem.

2. For a detailed description of how the obsolescing bargain can play out in utilities see Wells and Ahmed (2007).

3. Iron ore is a mineral substance from which metallic iron can be extracted. It is the raw material to make pig iron, the main input—together with coke, a derivative of coal, and limestone—to make steel. Even though iron can be sold in fines (finely crushed iron ore), lumps, or pellets (spheres of iron ore), the latter two

are preferred for the production of steel since they can be processed more effectively by steel mills.

4. "Evolução do desempenho da Vale," Vale, DEFB/DIRI , September 2009, p. 2.

5. Eliezer Batista was the CEO of Vale from 1961 to 1964 and from 1979 to 1986.

6. Guilherme Evelin and Raquel Ulhôa, "Senado estuda restrições à venda da Vale do Rio Doce," *Folha de São Paulo,* August 29, 1995, at http://www1.folha.uol .com.br/fsp/1995/8/29/brasil/4.html (accessed November 4, 2009).

7. Ibid.

8. Heródoto Barbeiro, "Transcript of Fernando Henrique Cardoso's Interview to CBN Radio," *Folha de São Paulo,* April 19, 1997, at http://www1.folha.uol.com .br/fsp/brasil/fc190416.htm (accessed November 8, 2009).

9. "Evolução do desempenho da Vale," Vale Company Report, September 2009.

10. Data from the Ministry of Social Security, at http://www.mpas.gov.br/con-teudoDinamico.php?id=501 (accessed February 15, 2010).

11. Estimated by Lazzarini et al. (2013) using data from IBGE, Pesquisa Industrial Annual.

12. "Lula afirma que empresários 'exageraram' nas demissões," *Folha de São Paulo,* February 14, 2009, at http://www1.folha.uol.com.br/fsp/dinheiro/fi1402200926.htm (accessed September 21, 2012).

13. "Eike Batista negocia fatia da Vale e critica Agnelli," *Estado de São Paulo,* October 11, 2009.

14. "Agnelli deixa Vale com lucro de R$ 11,3 bi," *Folha de São Paulo,* May 6, 2011.

10. Leviathan as a Lender: Development Banks

1. In January 2011, the U.S. Congress introduced a bill calling for the creation of a National Infrastructure Development Bank. See http://www.opencongress. org/bill/112-h402/show (accessed July 12, 2012).

2. Stock market capitalization, which had been at 17 percent of GDP in 1914, fell to close to 9 percent in the 1940s. The total stock of corporate bonds, which reached 15 percent of GDP in 1914, fell to close to 5 percent in the 1940s. See Musacchio (2009, 64–220).

3. For a detailed political economy of BNDES see also Pinto (1969).

4. The National Development Plan II of 1974 (known in Brazil as PNDII) stated that the government and BNDE had to give special attention to the support of the following industries: steel, nonferrous metals, petrochemical products, fertilizers, paper and cellulose, cement and construction materials, and the raw materials for these industries (Brazil 1974).

5. Vinicius Neder, "Perdas com estatais e 'campeãs nacionais' derrubam lucro do BNDES," in *O Estado de São Paulo,* February 25, 2013, at http://economia.estadao.com.br/noticias/economia-geral,perdas-com-estatais-e-campeas-nacionais-derrubam-lucro-do-bndes,145063,0.htm.

6. See Lei Complementar no. 26, September 11, 1975, for details.

7. See Law no. 8,019 of April 11 and Law 7,998 of January 11, 1990.

8. There are two of these workers funds, the unemployment insurance fund, known as Fundo de Amparo ao Trabalhador (FAT), and the Constitutional FAT. The latter takes 40 percent of individual worker accounts known as PIS and PASEP. For more information see Prochnik and Machado (2008) and the Ministry of Labor web site, http://www.mte.gov.br/fat/historico.asp (accessed November 26, 2011).

9. It is important to note that, for workers accounts deposited at BNDES (ironically called FAT in Portuguese), the bank pays the TJLP, up to a maximum of 6 percent per year. If TJLP is larger than 6 percent, the additional interest payments are accrued to the FAT account, which in practice is a perpetual debt BNDES has with the Ministry of Labor's workers accounts. The only circumstance under which BNDES would amortize part of the FAT debt is if the unemployment insurance funds held at the Ministry of Labor were not enough to cover payments (e.g., during a deep recession). See Porchnik and Machado (2008), especially p. 15.

10. Data from *Doing Business Report 2010,* at www.doingbusiness.org (accessed October 2010).

11. We calculate the raw beta using the daily trading prices of Banco do Brasil and the Ibovespa in a simple regression. We used the stock prices for Banco do Brasil available at Bloomberg.

11. Leviathan as a Lender: Industrial Policy versus Politics

1. To protect the identity of the executives we interviewed, we do not disclose their names.

2. Results not reported here, but available upon request.

3. Studies performed by governmental research agencies using larger data sets (which are not disclosed to the public for confidentiality reasons) also have failed to find consistent productivity-enhancing effects of BNDES loans. For instance, Ottaviano and Sousa (2007) find that although some BNDES credit lines positively affect productivity, other lines have a negative effect. In another study, Sousa (2010) reports an overall null effect of those loans on productivity. Coelho and De Negri (2010) find that loans have a larger effect on more productive firms. De Negri et al. (2011) find an effect of loans on employment and exports, but not on productivity.

12. Conclusions and Lessons

1. One could argue, alternatively, that having the government as an entrepreneur may stifle the development of capital markets and private industries. But in economies with many market failures and weak rule of law, private entrepreneurs will not undertake major infrastructure investments. Governments may have to first develop such sectors, then privatize them once the basic infrastructure is in place. Concessions or private-public partnerships may be an alternative to this model; but if private entrepreneurs are still extremely risk-averse, Leviathan as an entrepreneur may be the only option.

2. The delegation of management to skilled technical professionals may be accompanied either by the introduction of salaries with bonuses or prizes based on meeting specific goals or by merit-based promotions within the government. In China, for instance, performance-contingent contracts for SOE managers are common (Bai and Xu 2005; Mengistae and Xu 2004). Furthermore, skilled technical professionals may develop distinctive competencies in their industry or activity (Klein et al. 2013); autonomy will thus beget further learning and specialization.

Bibliography

Abdelal, Rawi. 2007. *Capital Rules: The Construction of Global Finance*. Cambridge, MA: Harvard University Press.

Abdelal, Rawi, Ayesha Khan, and Tarun Khanna. 2008. "Where Oil-Rich Nations Are Placing Their Bets." *Harvard Business Review* 86 (9): 119–128.

Acemoglu, D., and J. A. Robinson. 2006. *Economic Origins of Dictatorship and Democracy*. Cambridge: Cambridge University Press.

Adams, Renee, Heitor Almeida, and Daniel Ferreira. 2005. "Powerful CEOs and Their Impact on Corporate Performance." *Review of Financial Studies* 18 (4): 1403–1432.

Ades, Alberto, and Rafael Di Tella. 1997. "National Champions and Corruption: Some Unpleasant Interventionist Arithmetic." *Economic Journal* 107 (443): 1023–1042.

Aghion, P., O. Blanchard, and R. Burgess. 1994. "The Behavior of State Firms in Eastern Europe Pre-privatization." *European Economic Review* 38:1327–1349.

Aghion, Philippe, John Van Reenen, and Luigi Zingales. 2013. "Innovation and Institutional Ownership." *American Economic Review* 103 (1): 277–304.

Ahroni, Yair. 1986. *The Evolution and Management of State-Owned Enterprises*. Cambridge, MA: Ballinger Publishing.

Aivazian, Varouj A., Ying Ge, and Jiaping Qiu. 2005. "Can Corporatization Improve the Performance of State-Owned Enterprises Even without Privatization?" *Journal of Corporate Finance* 11:791–808.

Alchian, Armen A. 1965. "Some Economics of Property Rights." *Il Politico* 30:816–829.

Almeida, Mansueto. 2009. "Desafios da real política industrial brasileira no século XXI," Texto para discussão 1452, IPEA.

Alston, Lee J., Marcus Melo, Bernardo Mueller, and Carlos Pereira. 2013. *Beliefs, Leadership and Critical Transitions: Brazil, 1964–2014*. Unpublished book manuscript.

Amatori, Franco. 2012. *Storia dell'IRI. 2. Il "miracolo" economico e eil ruolo dell'IRI*. 2 vols. Vol. 2, *Storia e Societa*. Roma, Italy: Laterza.

Amatori, Franco, and Andrea Colli. 2000. "Corporate Governance: The Italian Story." Working paper available at ftp://ns1.ystp.ac.ir/YSTP/1/1/ROOT/DATA/PDF/unclassified/CGITALY.PDF.

Amatori, Franco, Robert Millward, and Pierangelo Maria Toninelli. 2011. *Reappraising State-Owned Enterprise: A Comparison of the UK and Italy.* Routledge International Studies in Business History. New York: Routledge.

Amsden, Alice H. 1989. *Asia's Next Giant: South Korea and Late Industrialization.* New York: Oxford University Press.

———. 2001. *The Rise of "The Rest": Challenges to the West from Late-Industrializing Economies.* Oxford: Oxford University Press.

Antunes, António, Tiago Cavalcanti, and Anne Villamil. 2012. "The Effects of Credit Subsidies on Development." Working paper.

Anuatti-Neto, Francisco, Milton Barossi-Filho, Antonio Gledson de Carvalho, and Roberto Macedo. 2005. "Costs and Benefits of Privatization: Evidence from Brazil." In *Privatization in Latin America: Myths and Reality,* edited by A. Chong and F. López-de-Silanes, 145–196. Washington, DC: World Bank and Stanford University Press.

Araújo, Caetano Ernesto Pereira de. 2004. "Financiamento de campanhas eleitorais." *Revista de Informação Legislativa* 41:59–66.

Armendáriz de Aghion, Beatriz. 1999. "Development Banking." *Journal of Development Economics* 58:83–100.

Aronovich, Selmo, and Andréa G. Fernandes. 2006. "A atuação do governo no mercado de capitais: Experiências de IFDs em países desenvolvidos." *Revista do BNDES* 13 (25): 3–34.

Bae, Kee-Hong, Jun-Koo Kang, and Jin-Mo Kim. 2002. "Tunneling or Value Added? Evidence from Mergers by Korean Business Groups." *Journal of Finance* 57 (6): 2695–2740.

Baer, Werner. 1969. *The Development of the Brazilian Steel Industry.* Nashville, TN: Vanderbilt University Press.

———. 2008. *The Brazilian Economy: Growth and Development.* 6th ed. Boulder, CO: Lynne Rienner Publishers.

Baer, Werner, Isaac Kerstenetzky, and Annibal Villela. 1973. "The Changing Role of the State in the Brazilian Economy." *World Development* 11 (1): 23–34.

Baer, Werner, and Nader Nazmi. 2000. "Privatization and Restructuring of Banks in Brazil." *Quarterly Review of Economics and Finance* 40:3–24.

Bai, Chong-En, and Lixin Colin Xu. 2005. "Incentives for CEOs with Multitasks: Evidence from Chinese State-Owned Enterprises." *Journal of Comparative Economics* 33:517–539.

Bailey, Warren, Wei Huang, and Zhishu Yang. 2011. "Bank Loans with Chinese Characteristics: Some Evidence on Inside Debt in a State-Controlled Banking System." *Journal of Financial and Quantitative Analysis* 46 (6): 1795–1830.

Bandeira-de-Mello, Rodrigo, and Rosilene Marcon. 2005. "Unpacking Firm Effects: Modeling Political Alliances in Variance Decomposition of Firm Performance in Turbulent Environments." *Brazilian Administration Review* 2 (1): 21–37.

Bartel, Ann P., and Ann E. Harrison. 2005. "Ownership versus Environment: Disentangling the Sources of Public-Sector Inefficiency."*Review of Economics and Statistics* 87 (1): 135–147.

Baumol, W. J., Robert E. Litan, and Carl J. Schramm. 2007. *Good Capitalism, Bad Capitalism, and the Economics of Growth and Prosperity.* New Haven, CT: Yale University Press.

Beatty, Randolph P., and Edward J. Zajac. 1987. "CEO Change and Firm Performance in Large Corporations: Succession Effects and Manager Effects." *Strategic Management Journal* 8:305–317.

Bebchuk, Lucian A., and Mark J. Roe. 1999. "A Theory of Path Dependence in Corporate Ownership and Governance." *Stanford Law Review* 52 (1): 127–170.

Beck, Thorsten, Juan Miguel Crivelli, and William Roderick Summerhill. 2005. "State Bank Transformation in Brazil—Choices and Consequences." *Journal of Banking and Finance* 29 (8–9): 2223–2257.

Beck, Thorsten, and Ross Levine. 2005. "Legal Iinstitutions and Financial Development." In *Handbook of New Institutional Economics,* edited by C. Menard and M. M. Shirley, 251–280. Amsterdam: Springer.

Becker, G. S. 1962. "Investment in Human Capital: A Theoretical Analysis." *Journal of Political Economy* 70 (5): 9–49.

Behr, Patrick, Lars Norden, and Felix North. 2012. "Financial Contraints of Private Firms and Bank Lending Behavior." Working paper, EBAPE (Brazilian School of Public and Business Adminstration).

Bell, David E., and Catherine Ross. 2008. "JBS Swift & Co." Harvard Business School Case No. 9-509-021.

Benmelech, Efraim, and Carola Frydman. 2010. "Military CEOs." Working paper.

Bennedsen, Morten. 2000. "Political Ownership." *Journal of Public Economics* 76:559–581.

Bennett, John, and Elisabetta Iossa. 2006. "Building and Managing Facilities for Public Services." *Journal of Public Economics* 90:2143–2160.

Berg, Elliot, and Mary M. Shirley. 1987. "Divestiture in Developing Countries." World Bank Discusion Paper WDP 11, Washington, DC.

Bertrand, Marianne, Francis Kramarz, Antoinette Schoar, and David Thesmar. 2007. "Politicians, Firms and the Political Business Cycle: Evidence from France." Unpublished working paper.

Bertrand, Marianne, Paras Mehta, and Sendhil Mullainathan. 2002. "Ferreting Out Tunneling: An Application to Indian Business Groups." *Quarterly Journal of Economics* 117 (1): 121–48.

Bertrand, Marianne, and Schoar Schoar. 2003. "Managing with Style: The Eeffect of Managers on Firm Policies." *Quarterly Journal of Economics* 118 (4): 1169–1208.

Bertrand, Marianne, Simeon Djankov, Rema Hanna, and Sendhil Mullainathan. 2007. "Obtaining a Driver's License in India: An Experimental Approach to Studying Corruption." *Quarterly Journal of Economics* 122 (4): 1639–1676.

BNDES. 1953–2010. *Annual Reports, 1953–2010.* Rio de Janeiro: BNDES.

———. 1987. *Informações Básicas.* Rio de Janeiro: BNDES.

———. 2002a. *50 Anos: Histórias Setoriais.* São Paulo: DBA Artes Gráficas.

———. 2002b. *Privatização no Brasil.* Ministério do Desenvolvimento, Indústria e Comércio Exterior, Rio de Janeiro.

———. 2003. *A promoção do desenvolvimento: Os 50 anos do BNDES e do Banco do Nordeste.* Rio de Janeiro: BNDES and José Olympio Editora.

Boardman, A. E., and A. R. Vining. 1989. "Ownership and Performance in Competitive Environments: A Comparison of the Performance of Private, Mixed, and State-Owned Enterprise." *Journal of Law and Economics* 32:1–33.

Boas, Taylor, F. Daniel Hidalgo, and Neal Richardson. 2011. "The Spoils of Victory: Campaign Donations and Government Contracts in Brazil." Working paper, Boston University.

Bodenhorn, Howard. 2003. *State Banking in Early America: A New Economic History.* New York: Oxford University Press.

Bogart, Dan. 2009. "Nationalizations and the Development of Transport Systems: Cross Country Evidence from Railroad Networks, 1860–1912." *Journal of Economic History* 69 (1): 202–237.

Bogart, Dan, and Latika Chaudhary. 2012. "Regulation, Ownership, and Costs: A Historical Perspective from Indian Railways." *American Economic Journal: Economic Policy* 4 (1): 28–57.

Bortolotti, Bernardo, Carlo Cambini, and Laura Rondi. Forthcoming. "Reluctant Regulation." *Journal of Comparative Economics.*

Bortolotti, Bernardo, and Enrico Perotti. 2007. "From Government to Regulatory Governance: Privatization and the Residual Role of the State." *World Bank Research Observer* 22 (1): 53–66.

Bortolotti, Bernardo, and Mara Faccio. 2009. "Government Control of Privatized Firms." *Review of Financial Studies* 22 (8): 2907–2939.

Bortolotti, Bernardo, Marcella Fantini, and Domenico Siniscalco. 2004. "Privatisation around the World: Evidence from Panel Data." *Journal of Public Economics* 88 (1–2): 305–332.

Bower, Joseph L., Herman B. Leonard, and Lynn S. Paine. 2011. *Capitalism at Risk: Rethinking the Role of Business.* Boston: Harvard Business Review Press.

Boycko, Maxim, Andrei Shleifer, and Robert Vishny. 1996. "A Theory of Privatization." *Economic Journal* 106 (435): 309–319.

Brahm, Richard. 1995. "National Targeting Policies, High-Technology Industries, and Excessive Competition." *Strategic Management Journal* 16:71–91.

Bray, Sílvio Carlos, Enéas Rente Ferreira, and Davi Guilherme Gaspar Ruas. 2000. *As políticas da agroindústria canavieira e o PROALCOOL no Brasil.* Marília, SP: Unesp-Marília Publicações.

Brazil. 1974. *II Plano Nacional de Desenvolvimento (1975–1979).* Rio de Janeiro: IBGE.

Bremmer, Ian. 2010. *The End of the Free Market: Who Wins the War between States and Corporations?* New York: Portfolio/Penguin.

Bresser Pereira, Luiz Carlos. 2008. "The Dutch Disease and Its Neutralization: A Ricardian Approach." *Revista de Economia Política* 28 (1): 47–71.

Bruck, Nicholas. 1998. "The Role of Development Banks in the Twenty-First Century." *Journal of Emerging Markets* 3:39–67.

Bureau of Railway Economics. 1935. "A Brief Survey of Public Ownership and Operation of Railways in Fifteen Foreign Countries." In Bureau of Railway Economics. Washington, DC: Bureau of Railway Economics.

Cabral, Sandro, and Sergio G. Lazzarini. 2010. "The 'Guarding the Guardians' Problem: An Empirical Analysis of Investigations in the Internal Affairs Division of a Police Organization." Working paper.

Cabral, Sandro, Sergio G. Lazzarini, and Paulo Furquim Azevedo. 2010. "Private Operation with Public Supervision: Evidence of Hybrid Modes of Governance in Prisons." *Public Choice* 145 (1–2): 281–293.

Calomiris, Charles, Raymond Fisman, and Youngxiang Wang. 2010. "Profiting from Government Stakes in a Command Economy: Evidence from Chinese Asset Sales." *Journal of Financial Economics* 96 (3): 399–412.

Cameron, Rondo E. 1961. *France and the Economic Development of Europe.* Princeton, NJ: Princeton University Press.

Campos, Roberto de Oliveira. 1969. "A Retrospect over Brazilian Development Plans." In *The Economy of Brazil,* edited by H. S. Ellis, 317–344. Berkeley: University of California Press.

Caprio, Gerard, Jonathan L. Fiechter, Robert E. Litan, and Michael Pomerlano. 2004. *The Future of State-Owned Financial Institutions.* Washington, DC: Brookings Institution Press.

Card, D., and A. Krueger. 1994. "Minimum Wages and Employment: A Case Study of the Fast-Food Industry in New Jersey and Pennsylvania." *American Economic Review* 84 (4): 772–793.

Cardoso, E. 1989. "The Macroeconomics of the Brazilian External Debt." In *Developing Country Debt and the World Economy,* edited by J. D. Sachs, 81–100. Chicago: University of Chicago Press.

Cardoso, F. H., and R. A. Setti. 2006. *A arte da política: A história que vivi.* Rio de Janeiro: Civilização Brasileira.

Cardoso, Fernando Henrique, and Enzo Faletto. 2004. *Dependência e desenvolvimento na América Latina: Ensaio de interpretação sociológica.* Rio de Janeiro: Civilização Brasileira.

Carreras, Albert, Xavier Tafunell, and Eugenio Torres. 2000. "The Rise and Decline of Spanish State-Owned Enterprises." In *The Rise and Fall of State-Owned Enterprise in the Western World,* edited by P. A. Toninelli, 208–236. Cambridge: Cambridge University Press.

Carvalho, Daniel. 2010. "The Real Effects of Government-Owned Banks: Evidence from an Emerging Market." Working paper, USC Marshall School of Business.

Castronovo, Valerio. 2012. *Storia dell'IRI. 1. Dalle origini al dopoguerra.* 2 vols. Vol. 1, *Storia e società.* Roma: Italy: Laterza.

Caves, Douglas W., and Laurits R. Christensen. 1980. "The Relative Efficiency of Public and Private Firms in a Competitive Environment: The Case of Canadian Railroads." *Journal of Politica Economy* 88 (5): 958–976.

Centro de Estudos Fiscais. 1973. "Atividade empresarial dos governos federal e estaduais." *Conjuntura Econômica,* June 1973, 80.

Centro de Memória da Eletricidade. 2000. *Energia Elétrica no Brasil: 500 Anos.* Rio de Janeiro: Centro de Memória da Eletricidade.

Chadeau, Emmanuel. 2000. "The Rise and Decline of State-Owned Industry in Twentieth-Century France." In *The Rise and Fall of Public Enterprise in the Western World,* edited by P. A. Toninelli, 185–207. Cambridge: Cambridge University Press.

Chamberlain, Gary. 1980. "Analysis of Covariance with Qualitative Data." *Review of Economic Studies* 47:225–238.

Chambers, David, Elroy Dimson, and Antti Ilmanen. 2011. "The Norway Model." Available at ssrn.com/abstract=1936806.

Chong, Alberto, and Florencio López-de-Silanes, eds. 2005. *Privatization in Latin America: Myths and Reality.* Washington, DC: World Bank and Stanford University Press.

Christiansen, Hans. 2011. "The Size and Composition of the SOE Sector in OECD Countries." In *OECD Corporate Governance Working Papers No 6.* Paris.

Claessens, Stijin, Erik Feijen, and Luc Laeven. 2008. "Political Connections and Preferential Access to Finance: The Role of Campaign Contributions." *Journal of Financial Economics* 88:554–580.

Coe, Neil M., Peter Dicken, and Martin Hess. 2008. "Global Production Networks: Realizing the Potential." *Journal of Economic Geography* 8 (3): 271–295.

Coelho, Danilo, and João Alberto De Negri. 2010. "Impacto do financiamento do BNDES sobre a produtividade das empresas: Uma aplicação do efeito quantílico de tratamento." Working paper, IPEA.

Cole, Shawn. 2009. "Fixing Market Failure or Fixing Elections? Agricultural Credit in India." *American Economic Journal: Applied Economics* 1 (1): 219–250.

Colli, Andrea. 2013. "Coping with the Leviathan: Minority Shareholders in State-Owned Enterprises: Evidence from Italy." *Business History* 55 (2): 190–214.

Conte, Leandro, and Giandomenico Piluso. 2011. "Finance and Structure of the State-Owned Enterprise in Italy: IRI from the Golden Age to the Fall." In *Reappraising State-Owned Enterprise: A Comparison of the UK and Italy*, edited by F. Amatori, R. Millward, and P. M. Toninelli, 119–144. New York: Routledge.

Cordonnier, Vanessa M. 2008. "Ethanol's Roots: How Brazilian Legislation Created the International Ethanol Boom." *William and Mary Environmental Law and Policy Review* 33 (1): 287–317.

Cull, Robert J., Wei Li, Bo Sun, and Lixin Colin Xu. 2013. "Government Connections and Financial Constraints: Evidence from a Large Representative Sample of Chinese Firms." Washington, DC: World Bank Working Paper 6352.

Curralero, Cláudia Regina Baddini. 1998. "A atuação do sistema BNDES como instituição financeira de fomento no periodo 1952–1996." Instituto de Economi, Universidade Estadual de Campinas, Campinas.

David, Parthiban, Toru Yoshikawa, Murali D. Chari, and Abdul A. Rasheed. 2006. "Strategic Investments in Japanese Corporations: Do Foreign Portfolio Owners Foster Underinvestment or Appropriate Investment?" *Strategic Management Journal* 27:591–600.

De Alessi, L. 1980. "The Economics of Property Rights: A Review of the Evidence." *Research in Law and Economics* 2:1–47.

Dean, W. 1969. *The Industrialization of São Paulo, 1880–1945*. Austin: For the Institute of Latin American Studies by the University of Texas Press.

De Negri, Joao Alberto, Alessandro Maffioli, Cesar M. Rodriguez, and Gonzalo Vázquez. 2011. "The Impact of Public Credit Programs on Brazilian Firms." IDB Working Papers, IDB-WP-293.

De Paula, Germano Mendes, João Carlos Ferraz, and Mariana Iootty. 2002. "Economic Liberalization and Changes in Corporate Control in Latin America." *Developing Economies* 40 (4): 467–496.

Dewenter, Kathryn L., and Paul H. Malatesta. 2001. "State-Owned and Privately Owned Firms: An Empirical Analysis of Profitability, Leverage, and Labor Intensity." *American Economic Review* 91 (1): 320–334.

Dharwadkar, Ravi, Gerard George, and Pamela Brandes. 2000. "Privatization in Emerging Economies: An Agency Theory Perspective." *Academy of Management Review* 25 (3): 650–669.

Díaz-Alejandro, Carlos F. 1984. "Latin American Debt: I Don't Think We Are in Kansas Anymore." *Brookings Papers on Economic Activity* 1984 (2): 335–403.

Dieguez, Consuelo. 2010. "O desenvolvimentista." *Revista PIAUI*.

Di John, Jonathan. 2009. *From Windfall to Curse? Oil and Industrialization in Venezuela, 1920 to the Present*. University Park: Penn State University Press.

Dinç, I. Serdar. 2005. "Politicians and Banks: Political Influences on Government-Owned Banks in Emerging Markets." *Journal of Financial Economics* 77:453–479.

Dinç, I. Serdar, and Nandini Gupta. 2011. "The Decision to Privatize: Finance and Politics." *Journal of Finance* 66 (1): 241–269.

Dixit, Avinash. 2002. "Incentives and Organizations in the Public Sector: An Interpretative Review." *Journal of Human Resources* 37 (4): 696–727.

Djankov, Simeon, Rafael La Porta, Florencio López-de-Silanes, and Andrei Shleifer. 2008. "The Law and Economics of Self-Dealing." *Journal of Financial Economics* 88 (3): 430–465.

Doh, Jonathan P. 2000. "Entrepreneurial Privatization Strategies: Order of Entry and Local Partner Collaboration as Sources of Competitive Advantage." *Academy of Management Review* 25 (3): 552–571.

Doh, Jonathan P., Hildy Teegen, and Ram Mudambi. 2004. "Balancing Private and State Ownership in Emerging Markets' Telecommunications Infrastructure: Country, Industry, and Firm Influences." *Journal of International Business Studies* 35:233–250.

Draibe, Sônia. 1985. *Rumos e Metamorfoses: Um estudo sobre a constituição do Estado e as alternativas da industrialização no Brasil, 1930–1960.* Rio de Janeiro: Paz e Terra.

Duncan, Julian Smith. 1932. *Public and Private Operation of Railways in Brazil.* New York: Columbia University Press.

Durant, Robert F., and Jerome S. Legge Jr. 2002. "Politics, Public Opinion, and Privatization in France: Assessing the Calculus of Consent for Market Reforms." *Public Administration Review* 62 (3): 307–323.

Dwyer, Rob. 2011. "How Petrobras Struck $70 Billion." *Euromoney.*

Dyck, Alexander, and Luigi Zingales. 2004. "Private Benefits of Control: An International Comparison." *Journal of Finance* 59 (2): 537–600.

Edwards, Sebastian. 2007. *Capital Controls and Capital Flows in Emerging Economies: Policies, Practices, and Consequences.* National Bureau of Economic Research Conference Report. Chicago: University of Chicago Press.

Ehrlich, Isaac, Georges Gallais-Hamonno, Zhiqiang Liu Liu, and Randall Lutter. 1994. "Productivity Growth and Firm Ownership: An Analytical and Empirical Investigation." *Journal of Political Economy* 102 (5): 1006–1038.

Einaudi, Mario. 1950. "Nationalization of Industry in Western Europe: Recent Literature and Debates." *American Political Science Review* 44 (1): 177–191.

Engerman, Stanley L., and Lance Edwin Davis. 2003. *Finance, Intermediaries, and Economic Development.* Cambridge: Cambridge University Press.

Escobar, Janet Kelly. 1982. "Comparing State Enterprises across International Boundaries: The Corporacion Venezolana de Guayana and the Companhia Vale do Rio Doce." In *Public Enterprise in Less-Developed Countries,* edited by L. P. Jones, 103–127. Cambridge: Cambridge University Press.

Evans, Peter. 1979. *Dependent Development: The Alliance of Multinational, State, and Local Capital in Brazil.* Princeton, NJ: Princeton University Press.

———. 1995. *Embedded Autonomy: States and Industrial Transformation.* Princeton, NJ: Princeton University Press.

Faccio, Mara. 2006. "Politically Connected Firms." *American Economic Review* 96 (1): 369–386.

Falck, Oliver, Christian Gollier, and Ludger Woessmann. 2011. "Arguments for and against Policies to Promote National Champions." In *Industrial Policy for National Champions,* edited by O. Falck, C. Gollier, and L. Woessmann, 3–9. Cambridge, MA: MIT Press.

Fazzari, Steven M., R. Glenn Hubbard, and Bruce C. Petersen. 1988. "Financing Constraints and Corporate Investment." *Brookings Papers on Economic Activity* 1:141–195.

Fishlow, Albert. 2011. *Starting Over: Brazil since 1985.* A Brookings Latin America Initiative Book. Washington, DC: Brookings Institution Press.

Frieden, Jeffry A. 1991. *Debt, Development, and Democracy: Modern Political Economy and Latin America, 1965–1985.* Princeton, NJ: Princeton University Press.

Furtado, Celso. 1959. *Formação econômica do Brasil.* Rio de Janeiro: Fundo de Cultura.

Gaspari, Elio. 2000. "A privataria quer mais dinheiro." *Folha de São Paulo,* August 20.

———. 2002a. *A ditadura envergonhada.* São Paulo: Companhia das Letras.

———. 2002b. *A ditadura escancarada.* São Paulo: Companhia das Letras.

———. 2003a. *A ditadura derrotada.* São Paulo: Companhia das Letras.

———. 2003b. *A ditadura encurralada.* São Paulo: Companhia das Letras.

George, Gerard, and Ganesh N. Prabhu. 2000. "Developmental Financial Institutions as Catalysts of Entrepreneurship in Emerging Economies." *Academy of Management Review* 25 (3): 620–629.

Gerschenkron, Alexander. 1962. *Economic Backwardness in Historical Perspective.* Cambridge, MA: Harvard University Press.

Giannetti, Mariassunta, and Luc Laeven. 2009. "Pension Reform, Ownership Structure, and Corporate Governance: Evidence from a Natural Experiment." *The Review of Financial Studies* 22 (10): 4091–4127

Goldsmith, Raymond William. 1986. *Brasil 1850–1984: Desenvolvimento financeiro sob um século de inflação.* Curitiba São Paulo, SP: Banco Bamerindus do Brasil; Editora Harper & Row do Brasil.

Goldstein, Andrea, and Pavida Pananond. 2008. "Singapore Inc. Goes Shopping Abroad: Profits and Pitfalls." *Journal of Contemporary Asia* 38 (3): 417–438.

Gómez-Ibañez, José Antonio. 2007. "Alternatives to Infrastructure Privatization Revisited: Public Enterprise Reform from the 1960s to the 1980s." Policy Research Working Paper. Washington, DC: World Bank.

Gourevitch, Peter Alexis, and James Shinn. 2005. *Political Power and Corporate Control: The New Global Politics of Corporate Governance*. Princeton, NJ: Princeton University Press.

Graham, Margaret B. W. 2010. "Entrepreneurship in the United States, 1920–2000." In *The Invention of the Enterprise: Entrepreneurship from Ancient Mesopotamia to Modern Times*, edited by D. S. Landes, J. Mokyr and W. J. Baumol, 401–442. Princeton: Princeton University Press.

Gregory, Paul. 1990. "The Stalinist Command Economy." *Annals of the American Academy of Political and Social Sciences* 507:18–25.

Grier, Kevin, and Robin Grier. 2000. "Political Cycles in Non-traditional Settings: Theory and Evidence from Mexico." *Journal of Law and Economics* 43 (1): 239–263.

Griesedieck, Joe. 2006. "Military Experience and CEOs: Is There a Link?" Los Angeles: Korn/Ferry International.

Groysberg, Boris, Andrew Hill Hill, and Toby Johnson. 2010. "Which of These People Is Your Future CEO?" *Harvard Business Review*, November, 80–85.

Guajardo Soto, Guillermo. 2013. "La empresa pública en América Latina: el pasado de un Leviatán que no muere." In *El Estado resurgente: Empresas públicas y desarrollo en América Latina y el mundo*, edited by D. Chávez, 105–116. Montevideo: Transnational Institute.

———. Forthcoming. "Empresas públicas en América Latina: Historia, conceptos, casos y perspectivas futuras." *Revista de Gestión Pública*.

Guillén, Mauro F. 2005. *The Rise of Spanish Multinationals: European Business in the Global Economy*. Cambridge: Cambridge University Press.

Gupta, Nandini. 2005. "Partial Privatization and Firm Performance." *Journal of Finance* 60:987–1015.

Haber, Stephen. 2002. "Introduction: The Political Economy of Crony Capitalism." In *Crony Capitalism and Economic Growth in Latin America: Theory and Evidence*, edited by Stephen Haber, xi–xxi. Stanford, CA: Hoover Institution Press.

———. 2012. "Politics and Banking Systems." In *Economic Development in the Americas since 1500: Endowments and Institutions*, edited by S. L. Engerman and K. L. Sokoloff, Cambridge: Cambridge University Press, 31–56.

Haber, Stephen H., Douglass Cecil North, and Barry R. Weingast. 2008. *Political Institutions and Financial Development*. Social Science History. Stanford, CA: Stanford University Press.

Haggard, S. 1990. *Pathways from the Periphery: The Politics of Growth in the Newly Industrializing Countries*. Ithaca, NY: Cornell University Press.

Hainz, Christa, and Hendrik Hakenes. 2008. "The Politician and the Banker." Working paper, Max Planck Institute for Research on Collective Goods.

Hall, Peter A., and David Soskice. 2001. "An Introduction to Varieties of Capitalism." In *Varieties of Capitalism: The Institutional Foundations of Comparative Advantage*, edited by P. A. Hall and D. Soskice, 1–70. Oxford: Oxford University Press.

Hannah, L. 2004. "A Failed Experiment: The State Ownership of Industry." In *The Cambridge Economic History of Modern Britain*. Vol. 3, *Structural Change and Growth, 1939–2000*, edited by R. Floud and P. Johnson, 84–111. Cambridge: Cambridge University Press.

Hansmann, Henry, and Reinier Kraakman. 2004. "The End of History for Corporate Law." In *Convergence and Persistence in Corporate Governance*, edited by J. N. Gordon and M. J. Roe, 33–68. Cambridge: Cambridge University Press.

Haque, Chowdhury Emdadul. 1987. *Bangladesh: Politics, Economy, and Society.* Winnipeg: Bangladesh Studies Assemblage, University of Manitoba.

Hart, Oliver D., Andrei Shleifer, and Robert W. Vishny. 1997. "The Proper Scope of Government: Theory and an Application to Prisons." *Quarterly Journal of Economics* 112 (4): 1127–1161.

Hausmann, Ricardo, and Dani Rodrik. 2003. "Economic Development as Self-Discovery." *Journal of Development Economics* 72:603–633.

Heckman, James J., Hidehiko Ichimura, and Petra E. Todd. 1997. "Matching as an Econometric Evaluation Estimator: Evidence from Evaluating a Job Training Programme." *Review of Economic Studies* 64 (4): 605–654.

Hermann, Jennifer. 2005. "Auge e declínio do modelo de crescimento com endividamento: O II PND e a crise da dívida externa." In.*Economia brasileira contemporânea*, edited by F. Giambiagi and A. A. Villela, 94–115. Rio de Janeiro: Elsevier, Editora Campus.

Hirschman, Albert O. 1958. *The Strategy of Economic Development.* New Haven, CT: Yale Economic Press.

———. 1982. *Shifting Involvements: Private Interest and Public Action.* Princeton, NJ: Princeton University Press.

Hoffman, Philip T., Gilles Postel-Vinay, and Jean-Laurent Rosenthal. 2000. *Priceless Markets: The Political Economy of Credit in Paris, 1660–1870.* Chicago: University of Chicago Press.

Holmstrom, Bengt, and Paul Milgrom. 1991. "Multitask Principal-Agent Analyses: Incentive Contracts, Asset Ownership, and Job Design." *Journal of Law, Economics and Organization* 7:24–52.

Hults, David R., Mark C. Thurber, and David G. Victor. 2012. *Oil and Governance: State-owned Enterprises and the World Energy Supply.* Cambridge, UK; New York: Cambridge University Press.

Hurwicz, Leonid. 2008. "But Who Will Guard the Guardians?" *American Economic Review* 98 (3): 577–585.

Inoue, Carlos F. K. V., Sergio G. Lazzarini, and Aldo Musacchio. 2013. "Leviathan as a Minority Shareholder: Firm-Level Performance Implications of Equity Purchases by the Government." *Academy of Management Journal* 56 (6): 1775–1801.

Iyer, Lakshmi, and Anandi Mani. Forthcoming. "Traveling Agents: Political Change and Bureaucratic Turnover in India." *Review of Economics and Statistics*.

Jensen, Michael C., and William H. Meckling. 1976. "Theory of the Firm: Managerial Behavior, Agency Costs and Ownership Structure." *Journal of Financial Economics* 3:305–360.

Johnson, Simon, Rafael La Porta, Florencio López-de-Silanes, and Andrei Shleifer. 2000. "Tunnelling." *American Economic Review* 90 (2): 22–27.

Jones, Geoffrey. 1981. *The State and the Emergence of the British Oil Industry.* Studies in Business History. London: Macmillan in association with Business History Unit, University of London.

———. 2005. *Multinationals and Global Capitalism: From the Nineteenth to the Twenty-First Century.* Oxford: Oxford University Press.

Jones, Leroy, and Il Sakong. 1980. *Government, Business, and Entrepreneurship in Economic Development: The Korean Case.* Cambridge, MA: Harvard University Press.

Kaldor, Nicholas. 1980. "Public or Private Enterprise—the Issue to Be Considered." In *Public and Private Enterprises in a Mixed Economy,* edited by W. J. Baumol, 1–12. New York: St. Martin's.

Kalyvas, Stathis, N. 1994. "Hegemony Breakdown: The Collapse of Nationalization in Britain and France." *Politics & Society* 22 (3): 316–348.

Kane, Joseph A. 1975. *Development Banking: An Economic Appraisal.* Lexington, MA: Lexington Books.

Kang, David. 2002. *Crony Capitalism: Corruption and Development in South Korea and the Philippines.* Cambridge: Cambridge University Press.

Karpoff, Jonathan M. 2001. "Public versus Private Initiative in Arctic Exploration: The Effects of Incentives and Organizational Structure." *Journal of Political Economy* 109 (1): 38–78.

Kato, Takao, and Cheryl Long. 2006. "Executive Turnover and Firm Performance in China." *American Economic Review* 96 (2): 363–367.

Kaufmann, Daniel, and Paul Siegelbaum. 1996. "Privatization and Corruption in Transition Economies." *Journal of International Affairs* 50 (2): 419–458.

Kenyon, Thomas. 2006. "Socializing Policy Risk: Capital Markets as Political Insurance." Available at SSRN: http://ssrn.com/abstract=896562 or http://dx .doi.org/10.2139/ssrn.896562.

Khanna, Tarun, Aldo Musacchio, and Rachna Tahilyani. 2009. "Indian Railways: Building a Permanent Legacy?" Harvard Business School Case 710-008.

Khanna, Tarun, Aldo Musacchio, and Ricardo Reisen de Pinho. 2010. "Vale: Global Expansion in the Challenging World of Mining." Harvard Business School Case 710-054.

Khanna, Tarun, and Krishna Palepu. 2000. "The Future of Business Groups in Emerging Markets: Long-Run Evidence from Chile." *Academy of Management Journal* 43 (3): 268–285.

Khanna, Tarun, Krishna Palepu, and Jayant Sinha. 2005. "Strategies That Fit Emerging Markets." *Harvard Business Review,* June, 63–76.

Khanna, Tarun, and Yishay Yafeh. 2007. "Business Groups in Emerging Markets: Paragons or Parasites?" *Journal of Economic Literature* 45:331–372.

Khurana, Rakesh. 2002. *Searching for a Corporate Savior: The Irrational Quest for Charismatic CEOs.* Princeton, NJ: Princeton University Press.

Khwaja, Asim Ijaz, and Atif Mian. 2005. "Do Lenders Favor Politically Connected Firms? Rent Provision in an Emerging Financial Market." *Quarterly Journal of Economics* 120 (4): 1371–1411.

Kikeri, Sunita, John Nellis, and Mary M. Shirley. 1992. *Privatization: The Lessons of Experience.* Washington, DC: World Bank.

Klein, Benjamin, Robert A. Crawford, and Armen Alchian. 1978. "Vertical Integration, Appropriable Rents, and the Competitive Contracting Process." *Journal of Law and Economics* 21:297–326.

Klein, Peter G., Joseph T. Mahoney, Anita M. McGahan, and Christos N. Pitelis. 2013. "Capabilities and Strategic Enterpreneurship in Public Organizations." *Strategic Entrepreneurship Journal* 7:70–91.

Kobrin, Stephen J. 1984. "Expropriation as an Attempt to Control Foreign Firms in LDCs: Trends from 1960 to 1979." *International Studies Quarterly* 28 (3): 329–348.

Kohli, Atul. 2004. *State-Directed Development: Political Power and Industrialization in the Global Periphery.* Cambridge: Cambridge University Press.

Kole, Stacey R., and J. Harold Mulherin. 1997. "The Government as a Shareholder: A Case from the United States." *Journal of Law and Economics* 40 (1): 1–22.

Kornai, Janos. 1979. "Resource-Constrained versus Demand-Constrained Systems." *Econometrica* 47 (4): 801–819.

Krueger, Anne O. 1990. "Government Failures in Development." *Journal of Economic Perspectives* 4 (3): 9–23.

Krugman, Paul. 1993. "The Current Case for Industrial Policy." In *Protectionism and World Welfare,* edited by D. Salvatores, 160–179. Cambridge: Cambridge University Press.

Kuczynski, Pedro-Pablo. 1999. "Privatization and the Private Sector." *World Development* 27 (1): 215–224.

Lamenza, Guilherme, Felipe Pinheiro Pinheiro, and Fabio Giambiagi. 2011. "A Capacidade de Desembolso do BNDES Durante a Década de 2010." *Revista do BNDES* 36: 43–88.

Lamoreaux, Naomi R. 1994. *Insider Lending: Banks, Personal Connections, and Economic Development in Industrial New England.* NBER Series on Long-Term Factors in Economic Development. Cambridge: Cambridge University Press.

———. 2009. "Scylla or Charybdis? Historical Reflections on Two Basic Problems of Corporate Governance." *Business History Review* 83: 9–34.

La Porta, Rafael, and Florencio López-de-Silanes. 1999. "The Benefits of Privatization: Evidence from Mexico." *Quarterly Journal of Economics* 114:1193–1242.

La Porta, Rafael, Florencio López-de-Silanes, and Andrei Shleifer. 2002. "Ownership of Banks." *Journal of Finance* 57 (1): 265–302.

———. 2006. "What Works in Securities Laws?" *Journal of Finance* 61 (1): 1–32.

La Porta, Rafael, Florencio López-de-Silanes, Andrei Shleifer, and Robert W. Vishny. 1998. "Law and Finance." *Journal of Political Economy* 106 (6): 1113–1155.

Lazzarini, Sergio G. 2011. *Capitalismo de laços: Os donos do Brasil e suas conexões.* Rio de Janeiro: Campus/Elsevier.

Lazzarini, Sergio G., Aldo Musacchio, Rodrigo Bandeira-de-Mello, and Rosilene Marcon. 2012. "What Do Development Banks Do? Evidence from Brazil, 2002–2009." Working paper, Insper, available at SSRN: http://ssrn.com/abstract=1969843.

Lazzarini, Sergio G., Marcos S. Jank, and Carlos F. V. Inoue. 2013. "Commodities no Brasil: Maldição ou bênção?" In *O Futuro da Indústria no Brasil*, edited by E. Bacha and M. B. de Bolle, 201–226. Rio de Janeiro: Civilização Brasileira.

Leff, Nathaniel H. 1968a. *The Brazilian Capital Goods Industry, 1929–1964.* Cambridge, MA: Harvard University Press.

———. 1968b. *Economic Policy-Making and Development in Brazil, 1947–1964.* New York: John Wiley & Sons.

———. 1978. "Industrial Organization and Entrepreneurship in the Developing Countries: The Economic Groups." *Economic Development and Cultural Change* 26 (4): 661–675.

Levine, Ross. 2005. "Finance and Growth: Theory and Evidence." In *Handbook of Economic Growth*, edited by P. Aghion and S. Durlauf, 865–934. Amsterdam: Elsevier.

Lieberson, Stanley, and James F. O'Connor. 1972. "Leadership and Organizational Performance: A Study of Large Corporations." *American Sociological Review* 37 (2): 117–130.

Lin, Justin, and Ha-Joon Chang. 2009. "Should Industrial Policy in Developing Countries Conform to Comparative Advantage or Defy It? A Debate between Justin Lin and Ha-Joon Chang." *Development Policy Review* 27 (5): 483–502.

Lin, Justin Y., and Guofu Tan. 1999. "Policy Burdens, Accountability, and the Soft Budget Constraint." *American Economic Review* 89 (2): 426–431.

Lin, Li-Wen, and Curtis J. Milhaupt. 2011. "We Are the (National) Champions: Understanding the Mechanisms of State Capitalism in China." Working paper, Columbia University. Lioukas, S., D. Bourantas, and V. Papadakis. 1993. "Managerial Autonomy of State-Owned Enterprises: Determining Factors." *Organization Science* 4 (4): 645–666.

Mahmood, Ishtiaq, and Carlos Rufin. 2005. "Government's Dilemma: The Role of Government in Imitation and Innovation." *Academy of Management Review* 30 (2): 338–360.

Majumdar, Sumit K. 1998. "Assessing Comparative Efficiency of the State-Owned Mixed and Private Sectors in Indian Industry." *Public Choice* 96 (1/2): 1–24.

Makler, Harry M. 2000. "Bank Transformation and Privatization in Brazil: Financial Federalism and Some Lessons about Privatization." *Quarterly Review of Economics and Finance* 40:45–69.

Malmendier, Ulrike, Geoffrey Tate Tate, and Jonathan Yan. 2010. "Overconfidence and Early-Life Experiences: The Impact of Managerial Traits on Corporate Financial Policies." NBER Working Paper 15659.

Manzano, Osmel, and Francisco Monaldi. 2008. "The Political Economy of Oil Production in Latin America." *Economia* 9 (1): 59–98.

Marichal, Carlos. 2011. "El estado empresarial en America Latina: Pasado y presente." *H-industri@. Revista de historia de industria, los servicios y las empresas en América Latina* 5 (9): 1–9.

Marshall, Alfred. 1920. *Principles of Economics*. London: Macmillan.

Martins, Carlos Estevam. 1974. *Tecnocracia e capitalismo: A política dos técnicos no Brasil*. São Paulo: Brasiliense.

Mauro, Paolo, Nathan Sussman, and Yishay Yafeh. 2006. *Emerging Markets and Financial Globalization: Sovereign Bond Spreads in 1870–1913 and Today*. Oxford: Oxford University Press.

Mazzucato, Mariana. 2011. *The Entrepreneurial State*. London: Demos.

McDermott, Gerald A. 2003. *Embedded Politics: Industrial Networks and Institutional Change in Postcommunism*. Ann Arbor: University of Michigan Press.

McGuire, Martin C., and Mancus Olson Jr. 1996. "The Economics of Autocracy and Majority Rule: The Invisible Hand and the Use of Force." *Journal of Economic Literature* 34 (1): 72–96.

Megginson, William L. 2005. *The Financial Economics of Privatization*. New York: Oxford University Press.

Megginson, William L., and Jeffry M. Netter. 2001. "From State to Market: A Survey of Empircal Studies of Privatization." *Journal of Economic Literature* 39:321–389.

Meller, Patricio. 1996. *Un siglo de economía política chilena (1890–1990)*. Santiago, Chile: Editorial Andrés Bello.

Mello, Magno. 2003. *A face oculta da reforma previdenciária*. Brasília: Letrativa Editora.

Mengistae, Taye, and Lixin Colin Xu. 2004. "Agency Theory and Compensation of CEOs of Chinese State Enterprises." *Journal of Labor Economics*
  22:615–637.
Messick, Richard E. 1996. *World Survey of Economic Freedom, 1995–1996.* A Freedom House Study. New Brunswick, NJ: Transaction Publishers.
Millward, Robert. 2000. "State Enterprise in Britain in the Twentieth Century." In
  The Rise and Fall of State-Owned Enterprise in the Western World, edited by
  P. A. Toninelli, 157–184. Cambridge: Cambridge University Press.
———. 2005. *Private and Public Enterprise in Europe: Energy, Telecommunica-
  tions and Transport, 1830–1990.* Cambridge: Cambridge University Press.
Minor, Michael S. 1994. "The Demise of Expropriation as an Instrument of LDC
  Policy, 1980–1992." *Journal of International Business Studies* 25 (1): 177–188.
Moe, Terry M. 1984. "The New Economics of Organization." *American Journal of
  Political Science* 28 (4): 739–777.
Monsen, R. J., and K. D. Walters. 1983. *Nationalized Companies: A Threat to Amer-
  ican Business.* New York: McGraw-Hill Co.
Morck, Randall. 2000. *Concentrated Corporate Ownership.* A National Bureau
  of Economic Research Conference Report. Chicago: University of Chicago
  Press.
Morck, Randall, Daniel Wolfenzon, and Bernard Yeung. 2005. "Corporate Gover-
  nance, Economic Entrenchment, and Growth." *Journal of Economic Litera-
  ture* 43 (3): 655–720.
Motta, Paulo Roberto. 1980. "O Controle de Empresas Estatais no Brasil." *Revista
  de Administração Pública* 14 (2): 69–82.
Mowery, David C. 1984. "Firm Structure, Government Policy, and the Organiza-
  tion of Industrial Research: Great Britan and the United States, 1900–1950."
  The Business History Review 58 (4): 504–531.
Murphy, Kevin M., Andrei Shleifer, and Robert W. Vishny. 1989. "Industrializa-
  tion and the Big Push." *The Journal of Political Economy* 97 (5): 1003–1026.
Musacchio, Aldo. 2009. *Experiments in Financial Democracy: Corporate Gover-
  nance and Financial Development in Brazil, 1882–1950.* Cambridge: Cambridge
  University Press.
Musacchio, Aldo, and Emil Staykov. 2011. "Sovereign Wealth Funds: Barbarians
  at the Gate or White Knights of Globalization?" Harvard Business School
  Case Study 712-022.
Musacchio, Aldo, Eric Werker, and Jonathan Schlefer. 2009. "Angola and the Re-
  source Curse." Harvard Business School Case Study 711-016.
Musacchio, Aldo, Gustavo Herrero, and Cintra Scott. 2011. "Banco Ciudad (A):
  Who Is the Owner?" Harvard Business School Case 712-029.
Musacchio, Aldo, Lena G. Goldberg, and Ricardo Reisen De Pinho. 2009. "Petro-
  bras in Ecuador (A)." Harvard Business School Case Study 309-107.

Najberg, Sheila. 1989. "Privatização de recursos públicos: Os empréstimos do sistema BNDES ao setor privado nacional com correção monetária parcial," Economics Department, PUC-RIO, Rio de Janeiro.

Nee, Victor, and Sonja Opper. 2007. "On Policized Capitalism." In *On Capitalism*, edited by V. Nee and R. Swedberg, 93–127. Stanford, CA: Stanford University Press.

Nellis, John R. 1991. "Contract Plans: A Review of the International Experience." In *Privatization and Control of State-Owned Enterprises*, edited by R. Ramamurti and R. Vernon, 279–323. Washington, DC: World Bank.

———. 2006. "Back to the Future for African Infrastructure? Why State-Ownership Is No More Promising the Second Time Around." Center for Global Development Working Paper no. 84.

Nenova, T. 2005. "Control Values and Changes in Corporate Law in Brazil." *Latin American Business Review* 6 (3): 1–37.

Ness, Walter L. 2000. "Reducing Government Bank Presence in the Brazilian Financial System: Why and How." *Quarterly Review of Economics and Finance* 40:71–84.

Nichols, Austin. 2007. "Causal Inference with Observational Data." *Stata Journal* 7:507–541.

North, Douglass C. 1990. *Institutions, Institutional Change and Economic Performance, Political Economy of Institutions and Decisions*. Cambridge: Cambridge University Press.

Norton, Edward C., Hua Wang, and Chunrong Ai. 2004. "Computing Interaction Effects and Standard Errors in Logit and Probit Models." *Stata Journal* 4 (2): 154–167.

Nunes, Edson de Oliveira. 1997. *A grámatica política do Brasil: Clientelismo e insulamento burocrático*. São Paulo: J. Zahar Editor.

OECD. 2005. "Corporate Governance of State-Owned Enterprises: A Survey of OECD Countries." Organisation for Economic Co-operation and Development. Paris.

Ottaviano, Gianmarco I. P., and Filipe Lage Sousa. 2007. "The Effect of BNDES Loans on the Productivity of Brazilian Manufacturing Firms." Working paper.

Overy, R. J. 1994. *War and Economy in the Third Reich*. Oxford: Oxford University Press.

Pack, Howard, and Kamal Saggi. 2006. "Is There a Case for Industrial Policy? A Critical Survey." *World Bank Research Observer* 21 (2): 267–297.

Pargendler, Mariana. 2012a. "State Ownership and Corporate Governance." *Fordham Law Review* 80 (6): 2917–2973.

———. 2012b. "The Unintended Consequences of State Ownership: The Brazilian Experience." *Theoretical Inquiries in Law* 13:503–523.

Pargendler, Mariana, Aldo Musacchio, and Sergio G. Lazzarini. 2013. "In Strange Company: The Puzzle of Private Investment in State-Controlled Firms." *Cornell International Law Journal* 46 (3).

Perkins, Susan, and Ed Zajac. 2012. "Signal or Symbol? Interpreting Firms' Strategic Response to Institutional Change in the Brazilian Stock Market." Mimeo MIT.

Perotti, Enrico Camillo, and Bruno Biais. 2002. "Machiavellian Privatization." *American Economic Review* 92 (1): 240–258.

Perotti, Enrico Camillo, and Ernst-Ludwig von Thadden. 2006. "The Political Economy of Corporate Control and Labor Rents." *Journal of Political Economy* 114 (1): 145–175.

Pfeffer, Jeffrey, and Gerald R. Salancik. 1978. *The External Control of Organizations*. New York: Harper & Row.

Pinheiro, Armando Castelar. 2002. "The Brazilian Privatization Experience: What's Next?" University of Oxford Centre for Brazilian Studies, Working Paper CBS-30-02.

Pinheiro, Armando Castellar, and Fabio Giambiagi. 1994. "Lucratividade, dividendos e investimentos das empresas estatais: Uma contribuição para o debate sobre a privatização no Brasil." *Revista Brasileira de Economia* 51:93–131.

Pinto, Rogerio Feital S. 1969. "The Political Ecology of the Brazilian National Bank for Development (BNDE)." Organization of American States. Washington DC: OAS.

Pistor, Katharina, and Joel Turkewitz. 1996. "Coping with Hydra—State Ownership after Privatization." In *Corporate Governance in Central Europe and Russia*, edited by R. Frydman, C. W. Gray and A. Rapaczynski, 192–246. Budapest: Central European University Press.

PIW. 2011. "*PIW* Ranks the World's Top 50 Oil Companies." *Petroleum Intelligence Weekly* Special Supplement Issue.

Polito, Rodrigo, Claudia Shuffner, and Marta Nogueira. 2012. "Medidas podem restringir os investimentos." *Valor Econômico*, September 12.

Porter, Michael E. 1990. "The Competitive Advantage of Nations." *Harvard Business Review* (March–April): 73–93.

Prebisch, Raúl. 1950. *The Economic Development of Latin America and Its Principal Problems*. New York: United Nations.

Prochnik, Marta. 1995. "Fondes de recursos do BNDES." *Revista do BNDES* 2 (4): 143–180.

Prochnik, Marta, and Vivian Machado. 2008. "Fontes de recursos do BNDES 1995–2007." *Revista do BNDES* 14 (29): 3–34.

Przeworski, A. 1991. *Democracy and the Market: Political and Economic Reforms in Eastern Europe and Latin America*. Cambridge: Cambridge University Press.

Rajan, Raghuram G., and Luigi Zingales. 1996. "Financial Dependence and Growth." *American Economic Review* 88 (3): 559–586.

———. 2004. *Saving Capitalism from Capitalists: Unleashing the Power of Financial Markets to Create Wealth and Spread Opportunity.* Princeton, NJ: Princeton University Press.

Ramamurti, Ravi. 1987. *State-Owned Enterprises in High Technology Industries: Studies in India and Brazil.* London: Praeger.

———. 2000. "A Multilevel Model of Privatization in Emerging Economies." *Academy of Management Review* 25 (3): 525–550.

Rodrik, Dani. 1995. "Getting Interventions Right: How South Korea and Taiwan Grew Rich." *Economic Policy* 20:55–107.

———. 2004. "Industrial Policy for the Twenty-First Century." CEPR Discussion Paper.

———. 2007. *One Economics, Many Recipes: Globalization, Institutions, and Economic Growth.* Princeton, NJ: Princeton University Press.

Roe, Mark J., and Jordan Siegel. 2006. "Legal Origin and Modern Stock Markets." *Harvard Law Review* 120:460–527.

Romero, Cristiano. 2012. "Crise econômica mundial mudou convicções de Dilma." *Valor Econômico,* August 17, A14.

Rosenstein-Rodan, Paul N. 1943. "Problems of Industrialisation of Eastern and South-eastern Europe." *Economic Journal* 53: 202–211.

Ross, Michael. 2012. *The Oil Curse: How Petroleum Wealth Shapes the Development of Nations.* Princeton, NJ: Princeton University Press.

Rostás, Renato. 2012. "Estrangeiros criticam eleição de conselho e plano da Petrobras." *Valor Econômico,* May 9.

Rotemberg, Julio J., and Garth Saloner. 1993. "Leadership Style and Incentives." *Management Science* 39 (11): 1299–1318.

———. 2000. "Visionaries, Managers, and Strategic Direction." *RAND Journal of Economics* 31 (4): 693–716.

Sachs, Jeffrey, and Andrew Warner. 2001. "The Curse of Natural Resources." *European Economic Review* 45 (4–6): 827–838.

Saes, Flávio Azevedo Marques de. 1981. *As ferrovias de São Paulo, 1870–1940, Coleção Estudos históricos.* São Paulo: Editora Hucitec em convênio com o Instituto Nacional do Livro, Ministério da Educação e Cultura.

Saiani, Carlos C. S. 2012. "Competição política faz bem à saúde? Evidências dos determinantes e dos efeitos da privatização dos serviços de saneamento básico no Brasil." Unpublished doctoral disseration, Fundação Getúlio Vargas.

Salancik, Gerald R., and Jeffrey Pfeffer. 1977. "Constraints on Administrator Discretion: The Limited Influence of Mayors on City Budgets." *Urban Affairs Quarterly* 12:475–498.

Samuels, David. 2002. "Pork Barreling Is Not Credit Claiming or Advertising: Campaign Finance and the Sources of Personal Vote in Brazil." *Journal of Politics* 64 (3): 846–863.

Santos, Maria Helena de Castro. 1993. *Política e políticas de uma energia alternativa: O caso do Proálcool.* Rio de Janeiro, RJ: ANPOCS: Notrya Editora.

Sapienza, Paola. 2004. "The Effects of Government Ownership on Bank Lending." *Journal of Financial Economics* 72 (2): 357–384.

Saraceno, Pasquale. 1955. "Iri: Its Origin and Its Position in the Italian Industrial Economy (1933–1953)." *Journal of Industrial Economics* 3 (3): 197–221.

Sarkar, J., S. Sarkar, and S. K. Bhaumik. 1998. "Does Ownership Always Matter? Evidence from the Indian Bank Industry." *Journal of Comparative Economics* 26:262–281.

Schapiro, Mario G. 2013. "Ativismo Estatal e Industrialismo Defensivo: Instrumentos e Capacidades na Política Industrial Brasileira." *Texto para Discussão, IPEA, Brasília.*

Schneider, Ben Ross. 1991. *Politics within the State: Elite Bureaucrats and Industrial Policy in Authoritarian Brazil.* Pittsburgh: University of Pittsburgh Press.

———. 2004. *Business Politics and the State in Twentieth-Century Latin America.* Cambridge: Cambridge University Press.

Schneider, Ben Ross, and David Soskice. 2009. "Inequality in Developed Countries and Latin America: Coordinated, Liberal and Hierarchical Systems." *Economy and Society* 38 (1): 17–52.

SEST, Brazil. 1981–1985. *Relatório SEST.* v. Brasília: Secretaria de Controle de Empresas Estatais.

———. 1985–1994. *Relatório anual SEST.* v. Brasília: Secretaria de Controle de Empresas Estatais.

Shapiro, Carl, and Robert D. Willig. 1990. "Economic Rationales for the Scope of Privatization." In *The Political Economy of Public Sector Reform and Privatization,* edited by E. N. Suleiman and J. Waterbury, 55–87. London: Westview Press.

Sharp, Samuel L. 1946. *Nationalization of Key Industries in Eastern Europe.* Washington, DC: Foundation for Foreign Affairs.

Sheshinski, Eytan, and Luis F. López-Calva. 2003. "Privatization and Its Benefits: Theory and Evidence." *CESifo Economic Studies* 49 (3): 429–459.

Shirley, Mary M. 1989. *The Reform of State-Owned Enterprises: Lessons from World Bank Lending.* Edited by T. W. Bank. Policy & Research Series. Washington DC: World Bank.

———. 1996. "Enterprise Contracts: A Route to Reform." *Finance and Development* 33 (3): 6–9.

———. 1999. "Bureaucrats in Business: The Roles of Privatization versus Corporatization in State-Owned Enterprise Reform." *World Development* 27 (1): 115–136.

———. 2005. "Why is Sector Reform so Unpopular in Latin America?" *The Independent Review* 10 (2): 195–207.

Shirley, Mary, and John Nellis. 1991. *Public Enterprise Reform: The Lessons of Experience*. Washington, DC: Economic Development Institute of the World Bank.

Shirley, Mary M., and Lixin Colin Xu. 1998. "The Empirical Effects of Performance Contracts: Evidence from China." Policy research working paper. Washington, DC: World Bank, Development Research Group.

Shleifer, Andrei. 1998. "State versus Private Ownership." *Journal of Economic Perspectives* 12 (4): 133–150.

Shleifer, Andrei, and Robert W. Vishny. 1994. "Politicians and Firms." *Quarterly Journal of Economics* 109:995–1025.

———. 1998. *The Grabbing Hand: Government Pathologies and Their Cures*. Cambridge, MA: Harvard University Press.

Shonfield, Andrew. 1965. *Modern Capitalism: The Changing Balance of Public and Private Power*. London: Oxford University Press.

Short, R. P. 1984. "The Role of Public Enterprises: An International Statistical Comparison." In *Public Enterprise in Mixed Economies: Some Macroeconomic Aspects*, edited by R. H. Floyd, C. S. Gray, and R. P. Short, 110–181. Washington DC: International Monetary Fund.

Simonsen, Mário Henrique. 1969. "Inflation and the Money and Capital Markets of Brazil." In *The Economy of Brazil*, edited by H. S. Ellis, 133–161. Berkeley: University of California Press.

Skidmore, Thomas E. 1988. *The Politics of Military Rule in Brazil, 1964–85*. New York: Oxford University Press.

Sousa, Filipe Lage. 2010. "Custos, BNDES e produtividade." Textos para discussão, Universidade Federal Fluminense.

Spers, Eduardo E. 1997. "Aracruz Celulose S.A.: Uma estratégia financeira de emissão de ADRs." PENSA case study, University of São Paulo.

Stark, David. 1994. "Path Dependence and Privatization Strategies in East-Central Europe." In *Transition to Capitalism? The Communist Legacy in Eastern Europe*, 63–99. New Brunswick, NJ: Transaction Publishers.

———. 1996. "Recombinant Property in East European Capitalism." *American Journal of Sociology* 101 (4): 993–1027.

Stevens, Paul. 2012a. "Kuwait Petroleum Corporation (KPC): An Enterprise in Gridlock." In *Oil and Governance: State-Owned Enterprises and the World Energy Supply*, edited by D. R. Hults, M. C. Thurber, and D. G. Victor, 334–378. Cambridge: Cambridge University Press.

———. 2012b. "Saudi Aramco: The Jewel in the Crown." In *Oil and Governance: State-Owned Enterprises and the World Energy Supply*, edited by D. R. Hults, M. C. Thurber, and D. G. Victor, 173–233. Cambridge: Cambridge University Press.

Stiefel, Dieter. 2000. "Fifty Years of State-Owned Industry in Austria, 1946–1996." In *The Rise and Fall of Public Enterprise in the Western World*, edited by P. A. Toninelli, 237–252. Cambridge: Cambridge University Press.

Sturzenegger, Federico, and Jeromin Zettelmeyer. 2006. *Debt Defaults and Lessons from a Decade of Crises*. Cambridge, MA: MIT Press.

Summerhill, William Roderick. 2003. *Order against Progress: Government, Foreign Investment, and Railroads in Brazil, 1854–1913*. Social science history. Stanford, CA: Stanford University Press.

Sylla, Richard, John B. Legler, and John Joseph Wallis. 1987. "Banks and State Public Finance in the New Republic: The United States, 1790–1860." *Journal of Economic History* 47 (2): 391–403.

Tendler, Judith. 1968. *Electric Power in Brazil*. Cambridge, MA: Harvard University Press.

Thomas, A. 1988. "Does Leadership Make a Difference to Organizational Performance?" *Administrative Science Quarterly* 33:388–400.

Thurber, Mark C., and Benedicte T. Istad. 2010. "Norway's Evolving Champion: Statoil and the Politics of State Enterprise." Program on Energy and Sustainable Development, Stanford University, working paper 92.

Timpson, William M. 2006. *147 Practical Tips for Teaching Sustainability: Connecting the Environment, the Economy, and Society*. Madison, WI: Atwood.

Toninelli, Pier Angelo. 2000. "The Rise and Fall of Public Enterprise: The Framework." In *The Rise and Fall of Public Enterprise in the Western World*, edited by P. A. Toninelli, 3–24. Cambridge: Cambridge University Press.

Topik, Steven. 1987. *The Political Economy of the Brazilian State, 1889–1930*. 1st ed. Latin American monographs / Institute of Latin American Studies, the University of Texas at Austin. Austin: University of Texas Press.

Tordo, Silvana, Brandon S. Tracy, and Noora Arfaa. 2011. "National Oil Companies and Value Creation." World Bank Group. Washington, DC.

Torres Filho, Ernani Teixeira. 2009. "Mecanismos de direcionamento do crédito, bancos de desenvolvimento e a experiência recente do BNDES." In *Ensaios sobre Economia Financeira*, edited by F. M. R. Ferreira and B. B. Meirelles, 11–56. Rio de Janeiro: BNDES.

Trebat, Thomas J. 1983. *Brazil's State-Owned Enterprises: A Case Study of the State as Entrepreneur*. Cambridge: Cambridge University Press.

Triner, Gail D. 2011. *Mining and the State in Brazilian Development*. Perspectives in Economic and Social History. London: Pickering & Chatto.

Trivedi, Prajapati. 1989. "Performance Evaluation System for Memoranda of Understanding." *Economic and Political Weekly* 24 (21): M55–M59.

Truman, Edwin M. 2010. *Sovereign Wealth Funds: Threat or Salvation?* Washington, DC: Peterson Institute for International Economics.

Vaaler, Paul M., and Burkhard N. Schrage. 2009. "Residual State Ownership: Policy Stability and Financial Performance following Strategic Decisions by Privatizing Telecoms." *Journal of International Business Studies* 40:621–641.

Vaidyanathan, Sanjeev, and Aldo Musacchio. 2012. "State Capitalism in India and Its Implications for Investors." Harvard Business School, mimeo.

Vernon, Raymond. 1971. *Sovereignty at Bay: The Multinational Spread of U.S. Enterprises*. London: Longman.

Vianna, Marcos P. 1976. "Estatização da Economia Brasileira. Nota confidencial para o Min. Reis Veloso." In P. d. R. S. N. d. Informações. Brasilia.

Vickers, John, and George Yarrow. 1988. *Privatization: An Economic Analysis*. Cambridge, MA: MIT Press.

Villela, Andre. 1995. "Taxa de investimento e desempenho do BNDES: 1985/94." *Revista do BNDES* 2 (4): 129–142.

Virany, Beverly, Michael L. Tushman, and Elaine Romanelli. 1992. "Executive Succession and Organization Outcomes in Turbulent Environments: An Organization Learning Approach." *Organization Science* 3 (1): 72–91.

Visão. 1976. "A filogénese das estatais." *Visão. Quem é Quem*, August 31, 88–111.

Waclawik-Wejman, Agata. 2005. "Corporate Governance of State-Owned Enterprises in Poland." World Bank.

Wade, James. 1995. "Dynamics of Organizational Communities and Technological Bandwagons: An Empirical Investigation of Community Evolution in the Microprocessor Market." *Strategic Management Journal* 16:111–133.

Wade, Robert. 1990. *Governing the Market: Economic Theory and the Role of Government in East Asian Capitalism*. Princeton, NJ: Princeton University Press.

Wallsten, Scott J. 2001. "An Econometric Analysis of Telecom Competition, Privatization, and Regulation in Africa and Latin America." *Journal of Industrial Economics* 49 (1): 1–19.

Wahrlich, Beatriz. 1980. "Controle Político das Empresas Estatais Federais no Brasil—Uma Contribuição ao seu Estudo." *Revista de Administração Pública* 14 (2): 69–82.

Wan, William P., and Robert E. Hoskisson. 2003. "Home Country Environments, Corporate Diversification Strategies, and Firm Performance." *Academy of Management Journal* 46 (1): 27–45.

Wang, Xiaozu, Lixin Colin Xu, and Tian Zhu. 2004. "State-Owned Enterprises Going Public: The Case of China." *Economics of Transition* 12 (3): 467–487.

Warshaw, Christopher. 2012. "The Political Economy of Expropriation and Privatization in the Oil Sector." In *Oil and Governance: State-Owned Enterprises and the World Energy Supply*, edited by D. R. Hults, M. C. Thurber, and D. G. Victor, 35–61. Cambridge: Cambridge University Press.

Wasserman, Noam, Bharat Anand, and Nitin Nohria. 2010. "When Does Leadership Matter?" In *Handbook of Leadership Theory and Practice: A Harvard Business School Centennial Colloquium*, edited by N. Nohria and R. Khurana, 27–63. Cambridge, MA: Harvard University Press.

Weber, Max. 1968. *Economy and Society: An Outline of Interpretive Sociology.* 3 vols. New York: Bedminster Press.

Weiner, N. 1978. "Situational and Leadership Influence on Organization Performance." *Proceedings of the Academy of Management,* 230–234.

Weiner, N., and T. A. Mahoney. 1981. "A Model of Corporate Performance as a Function of Environmental, Organizational, and Leadership Influences." *Academy of Management Journal* 24:453–470.

Wells, Louis T., and Rafiq Ahmed. 2007. *Making Foreign Investment Safe: Property Rights and National Sovereignty.* Oxford: Oxford University Press.

Wengenroth, Ulrich. 2000. "The Rise and Fall of State-Owned Enterprise in Germany." In *The Rise and Fall of Public Enterprise in the Western World,* edited by P. A. Toninelli, 103–127. Cambridge: Cambridge University Press.

Werneck, Rogerio. 1987. *Empresas estatais e política macroeconômica.* Rio de Janeiro: Editora Campus.

Williamson, Oliver E. 1988. "Corporate Finance and Corporate Governance." *Journal of Finance* 43:567–591.

———. 1999. "Public and Private Bureaucracies: A Transaction Cost Economics Perspective." *Journal of Law, Economics and Organization* 15 (1): 306–342.

Wilson, James O. 1989. *Bureaucracy: What Government Agencies Do and Why They Do It.* New York: Basic Books.

Wirth, John D. 1970. *The Politics of Brazilian Development, 1930–1954.* Stanford, CA: Stanford University Press.

Wooldridge, Adrian. 2012. "The Visible Hand." *Economist,* January 21.

Wooldridge, Jeffrey M. 2002. *Econometric Analysis of Cross-Section and Panel Data.* Cambridge, MA: MIT Press.

World Bank. 1996. *Bureaucrats in Business: The Economics and Politics of Government Ownership.* Oxford: Oxford University Press.

Yeyati, Eduardo Levy, Alejandro Micco, and Ugo Panizza. 2004. "Should the Government Be in the Banking Business? The Role of State-Owned and Development Banks." RES Working Papers 4379, Inter-American Development Bank, Research Department.

Yiu, Daphne, Garry D. Bruton, and Yuan Lu. 2005. "Understanding Business Group Performance in an Emerging Economy: Acquiring Resources and Capabilities in Order to Prosper." *Journal of Management Studies* 42 (1): 183–206.

Zhu, Tian. 1999. "China's Corporatization Drive: An Evaluation and Policy Implications." *Contemporary Economic Policy* 17 (4): 530–539.

Acknowledgments

This book was the product of very fruitful conversations and cooperation with colleagues in Brazil, Mexico, the United States, and Europe. A large number of colleagues were extremely generous with their time and commented extensively on our working papers and book drafts. In particular we wish to thank Rawi Abdelal, the late Alice Amsden, Werner Baer, Dirk Boehe, Rafael Di Tella, Stanley Engerman, Paulo Furquim, Elio Gaspari, Andrea Goldstein, Claudio Haddad, Geoff Jones, Joe Love, Carlos Melo, Tom Nicholas, Mariana Pargendler, Julio Rotenberg, Ben Ross Schneider, Alberto Simpser, Judy Tendler, Gunnar Trumbull, and Richard Vietor.

Some of the chapters were discussed as papers in seminars in Brazil and the United States. From those seminars we want to express our thanks for the comments of Patrick Behr, Effi Benmelech, Ricardo Brito, Vinicius Carrasco, Carlos Cinelli, Mariano Cortes, Rohit Despande, Elizabeth Farina, Erik Feijen, Cláudio Ferraz, Carola Frydman, Marcio Garcia, Martin Goetz, Tarun Khanna, Catiana Garcia-Kilroy, Eric Hilt, Emanuel Kohlscheen, Lakshmi Iyer, Alain Ize, Gabriel Madeira, Ricardo Madeira, Rosilene Marcon, João Manoel P. de Mello, Luiz Mesquita, Steven Nafziger, Walter Novaes, Marcos Rangel, Carlos Saiani, Marcelo Santos, Jordan Siegel, Rodrigo Soares, Augusto de la Torre, Lou Wells, and Eric Werker. We also wish to thank other seminar participants at the Harvard Business School, Harvard, PUC-Rio, FEA/USP, Insper, Universidad de Desarollo, University of Illinois at Urbana-Champaign, the World Bank, the Central Bank of Brazil, and the 2011 Strategic Management Society Special Conference in Rio. John Nellis and Mary Shirley shared their views on the efforts of the World Bank to reform state-owned enterprises. Delfim Netto and Shigeaki Ueki provided us with important information on the management of Brazilian state-owned firms during the military dictatorship (1964–1985). Additionally, Aldo Musacchio wants to express his thanks for the helpful comments on previous versions of the book by his colleagues from the Business, Government, and the International Economy Unit and the Business History Initiative, both at Harvard Business School.

Part of the research for the book was conducted during two cold winters in Boston when Sergio Lazzarini was a visiting scholar at the Weatherhead Center for International Affairs at Harvard University, with financial support from Insper and CAPES (process BEX 3835/09–0), and at the Harvard Business School (HBS). Aldo Musacchio thanks the financial support from HBS, Insper, and the University of São Paulo for trips to Brazil in 2009, 2011, and 2012. Sergio Lazzarini acknowledges the financial support from CNPq (Brazilian National Council for Scientific and Technological Development) and Insper. The majority of this project, though, was financed by the Harvard Business School Dean for Research and Faculty Development.

Some of the chapters are based on research we did with our colleagues. Chapter 4 is based on the work we did with Claudia Bruschi for a working paper entitled "Do the CEOs of State-Owned Enterprises Matter? Evidence from Brazil, 1973–1993." Chapter 7 was based on the work we did with Mariana Pargendler for the paper "In Strange Company: The Puzzle of Private Investment in State-Controlled Firms," *Cornell International Law Journal* 46, no. 3 (2013). Chapter 8 summarizes some of the findings of our paper with Carlos Inoue, "Leviathan as a Minority Shareholder: Firm-Level Implications of Equity Purchases by the State," *Academy of Management Journal* 56, no. 6 (2013). Finally, Chapter 11 uses some of the findings of our paper with Rodrigo Bandeira-de-Mello and Rosilene Marcon, "What Do Development Banks Do? Evidence from Brazil, 2002–2009," Harvard Business School Working Paper, no. 12-047, December 2011.

We would not have been able to put together all of the databases for this book if it were not for the incredible job Claudia Bruschi did coordinating research assistants, and doing original research using archival materials, magazines, and the site of the Brazilian Securities and Exchange Commission. Also, Carlos Inoue, Jenna Berhardson, Daniel Miranda, and Rodolfo Diniz helped us to design and put together some of the most important databases of the book. Lastly, we are grateful to a large number of students who, over the years, assisted us in collecting data, among them Guilherme de Moraes Attuy, Fernando Graciano Bignotto, Rodolfo Diniz, Diego Ferrante, Rafael de Oliveira Ferraz, Fabio Renato Fukuda, Carlos Laercio de Goes, Lucille Assad Goloni, Luciana Shawyuin Liu, Marcelo de Biazi Goldberg, Carlos Inoue, Gustavo Joaquim, Darcio Lazzarini, Diego Ten de Campos Maia, and William Nejo Filho.

Behind every academic book there is a copy editor and a group of librarians that deserve credit. First, we want to thank John Elder, who diligently copyedited different drafts of the manuscript, and G. Novak who did the final copyediting for Harvard University Press. Additionally, we have to thank the librarians in Brazil and the United States who helped us to get reports, documents, and books from all over the Western Hemisphere. In Brazil we want to thank Suzana Monteiro Huguenin de Carvalho and Shirlene Silva at the library of BNDES in Rio de Janeiro for their help. The staff at the libraries of FGV Rio de Janeiro, FGV São

Paulo, University of Campinas, Harvard Widener Library, Insper, and FEA-USP helped us to put together the most comprehensive collection of photocopies and scans of reports of Brazilian state-owned enterprises and of documents on the history of BNDES. At Harvard Business School's Baker Library, Leslie Burmeister and Julie Savsovitz made sure we had relevant books from all over the United States for as long as we could. Deb Wallace, the director of Baker Library, was also a big supporter of our research. Kathleen Ryan, Kristine Rivera, and James Zeitler helped us to navigate the complexities of the databases of S&P Capital IQ and Bloomberg.

Above all we have to thank the support and love of our families. They were supportive throughout the process of writing this book and were particularly loving and tolerant during the long periods of time we had to spend away from them.

Index